Project Management

Harvey Maylor

third edition

FINANCIAL TIMES
Prentice Hall

An imprint of **Pearson Education**

London · New York · Toronto · Sydney · Tokyo · Singapore · Hong Kong · Cape Town
New Delhi · Madrid · Paris · Amsterdam · Munich · Milan · Stockholm

Pearson Education Limited
Edinburgh Gate
Harlow
Essex CM20 2JE
England

and Associated Companies throughout the world

Visit us on the World Wide Web at:
www.pearsoneduc.com

First published in Great Britain in 1996
Second edition 1999
Third edition 2003

ISBN 0 273 65541 8

British Library Cataloguing-in-Publication Data
A catalogue record for this book is available from the British Library

Library of Congress Cataloging-in-Publication Data
Maylor, Harvey.
    Project management / Harvey Maylor.—3rd ed.
        p. cm.
    Includes bibliographical references and index.
    ISBN 0-273-65541-8 (pbk.)
    1. Project management.   I. Title.
HD69.P75 M3796 2002
658.4′04—dc21   2002070945

10 9 8 7 6 5 4 3 2
06 05 04 03 02

Typeset in 10/12.5pt Sabon by 35
Printed by Ashford Colour Press Ltd., Gosport

Dedication

To those who said it could be done again, especially my wife Kara, with love.

Contents

Preface

Since writing the second edition the profile of project management in the business world has increased unbelievably. Organisations and individuals that had previously considered project management as something of interest to construction or engineering managers only suddenly realised that there was potential here. Reflecting this, project management is developing in business and management education at a significant rate, alongside its traditional habitat of engineering, construction and IT. Its acceptance as a core business process has had ramifications for all concerned and the subject has to meet the challenge of this change.

In the interests of 'beginning with the end in mind', and just in case you were in any doubt, this is a textbook. This positions it somewhere between the practitioner guide (the short how-to book) and the handbook – monumental tomes that try to cover everything. Its predominant role is therefore to accompany a programme of study, and to provide an overview of areas of management knowledge relevant to the field. I have also attempted to provide some insight into the usage and applicability of the ideas discussed, as well as signposts to further sources of information. It is therefore not intended to be comprehensive on every particular aspect, current and emerging, of project management. Whether you are studying project management as part of a course or for personal development, I wish you well with it. If you are looking for a subject with scope for change, take the challenge – get involved and help make the changes. If you are looking for a career, again take the challenge. It is likely to be the most rewarding path you could choose.

Acknowledgements

If you are reading this to check that I have acknowledged your input, I hope you are not disappointed!

Thanks to many students and managers who have been on my courses and taken the time to provide feedback on their learning experiences. Socrates used the principle that if you want to really find out whether your knowledge base is sound, you should teach it. I can honestly say that writing a book takes that testing to another level – it is far more difficult to do a U-turn from what you have said in a book!

Other deserveds are Professor Tony Davies of EEDS – the EU project was fun; Professor Nigel Slack of Warwick Business School for inspiration; my colleagues at Kasetsart University for reminding me to include more diagrams; Neil Butterill of I&J Munn Ltd; colleagues at Bath for their contributions of ideas, including all the operations management group (Professor Steve Brown, Professor Richard Lamming, Dr Paul Cousins, Dr Kate Blackmon) and Dr Jerry Busby from the Department of Mechanical Engineering; former colleagues at Cardiff Business School, especially Professor Mick Silver (top PhD supervisor) and Dr Nick Rich (great discussions) and Professor Dan Jones (thanks again for the foreword); Trevor Rose for helping me to understand what old people think of project management; members of the Project Management Development Group for starting what could be a great driver in the development of project management knowledge, especially Margaret Greenwood and Professor Ralph Levene; many people who have bothered to keep me in the loop as to what is happening in project management teaching in their part of the world.

Three reviewers have given phenomenal input to each batch of chapters as they were completed: Dr Paul Walley of Warwick Business School, Prof. J.M. Robertson of Cranfield University, and Bob Saunders of Open University. Their comments were challenging and always supported by positive suggestions. For these, I am incredibly grateful as I am for all comments on the book. The development team, for as long as it stayed in place, were great. Penelope Woolf and Stuart Hay for backing the development, Patrick, Claire etc, for their chivvying and chasing and insightful comments.

Lastly, I want to acknowledge the input of my family. We thank God for our two completely wonderful children, new additions since the last edition. Having to say 'not at the moment' to the request of 'Daddy, come and look' taxes their patience, and such a substantial rewrite has taken me away from them for more time than I care to remember. Kara has been my project manager through this, as well as my in-house communications expert, counsellor, and coach. Her knowledge, love and red pen have been incredible.

All mistakes are of course mine.

Dr Harvey Maylor
Bath, UK
December 2001

Foreword

Project Management is no longer about managing the sequence of steps required to complete the project on time. It is about systematically incorporating the voice of the customer, creating a disciplined way of prioritising effort and resolving trade-offs, working concurrently on all aspects of the project in multi-functional teams, and much more. It involves much closer links between project teams and downstream activities, e.g. in new product development, integration with manufacturing, logistics and after-sales support – in this case 80% of the costs are determined before they take over!

There are huge opportunities for eliminating wasted time and effort in almost every project. In manufacturing, Toyota estimate that only 5% of activities actually add value, 35% are necessary but do not add value, whilst the remaining 60% is pure waste – 'muda' in Japanese! By halving the effort in designing a new car, they show this *muda* can be reduced by good project management. Every project manager in the future has not only to manage their own project but to seek ways of eliminating the *muda* in their systems so they can do more for less, and more quickly next time! Perhaps the biggest opportunities, however, can be found in thinking beyond the management of individual projects to standardising and streamlining the project management process itself. Although each project presents its own challenges, the ability to launch new products quickly, on time and with no errors, is what leads to sustained business growth. Getting the project management process right should be a key strategic priority for every firm.

This book takes a fresh look at the new techniques used by best-practice companies to improve their project management performance. It shows how the disciplines used by Toyota and the Deming approach to management can be applied to any kind of project in any industry. Students will find the mixture of academic debate and practical case-studies helpful and teachers will welcome the discussion questions after each chapter.

Professor D.T. Jones,
Director,
Lean Enterprise Research Centre,
Cardiff Business School,
University of Wales, Cardiff.

1 Introduction

In 1993, the London Ambulance service launched its computer-aided despatch system. It failed. People died and a £1.5 million project was written off. A 1996 survey by the University of Sheffield showed that of the projects that they had polled, 80 per cent had run late. The total cost of IT project overruns alone is put at several billion US dollars in the USA alone. This performance is not limited to the IS/IT sector. Recent evidence suggests that the vast majority of projects, from the simplest to the most complex, in all sorts of organisations run late, overbudget or both. The Channel Tunnel – 31 miles of tunnel linking the UK and mainland Europe – was several years late and £5 billion over budget.

Is there a problem with projects and their management? There is significant evidence to suggest that there is. Even the British Standards Institute acknowledges that:

> Research suggests that the overall track record of British organisations in managing projects, including take-overs, leaves much to be desired. The delivery of results on time, within predetermined cost and of the requisite standard within set safety and quality criteria is less frequent than it should be. (BS 6079: 2000)

This is not just a British problem. Also, is it less frequent than it should be? A conservative estimate of the problem puts the magnitude at in excess of 80 per cent of projects not delivering what was required of them in one or more substantive way.

Projects are important for individuals, organisations and economies. For the individual, project management can provide one of the most challenging career paths. For organisations, there is the opportunity to derive competitive advantage from their projects. For nations, the performance of projects will have an impact on their economies.

With this level of importance and the level of problems being faced comes the opportunity for a rethink of the way that we run projects. The issue for the modern project manager, which is reflected in this text, is the need for a holistic approach to project management. That is, we must consider the project to be more than the product of a technical activity. Our consideration must include human issues and recognise that projects often have a sizable creative element. This creative element requires a different approach. It is described as the product of order and chaos. Managing the chaos without stifling the creative nature of the process is a major challenge for the project manager.

The subject of project management is changing fast and the economic importance of the area is finally being recognised. This has led to many changes in the methods and scope of the subject. There is also increasing recognition of the excitement and challenges associated with the profession of project manager in many different contexts. The challenge for students of the subject is to grow with the body of knowledge and recognise the potential that exists for individuals and organisations in this area.

Contents

Learning Objectives

By the time you have completed this chapter, you should be able to:
- Define a project, the role of project managers;
- Recognise the new opportunities and constraints that exist for the subject of project management;
- Describe the evolution of the subject of project management;
- Identify the current issues faced by project management practitioners and researchers;
- Start to incorporate the existing bodies of knowledge into your studies and projects.

1.1 Introduction and Objectives of this Book

An increasing number of organisations are recognising that they are 'project-based', that is, the majority of their value-adding work is carried out through projects.

These organisations are not limited to the traditional project-based organisations of the heavy engineering, construction, IT and consultancy sectors. They are a whole host of blue-chip firms (including Xerox, Hewlett-Packard, Intel, Motorola), smaller firms as well as local and national government agencies all over the world. Suddenly individuals and organisations who had previously taken little interest in the subject are clamouring to know more. This is a significant change and one that has many repercussions for the subject of project management. In addition, as a result of the influence that many world-class firms are having on this subject we are in a period of rapid evolution of the practices and processes of project management. Organisations are devoting significant effort to improving their project performance, which does have a major economic benefit for the organisation.

As projects in most sectors become more important to those organisations, so too do the project managers. We have seen the development of parallel career paths for managers – allowing them to be promoted either through their line activity (sales, marketing, finance, human resources) or through their excellence in managing projects. This provides a real incentive for individuals to take this route seriously and change their own methods and views of the subject. For many years, project management has been referred to as the *accidental profession* – where people have not selected it, but ended up doing it anyway. Today, we may have the choice – to accept the challenge of being an excellent project manager and become a true 'project management professional'. Therefore, project management is important for both organisations and individuals, and this importance is increasingly being recognised.

To further this, the objectives of this book are:

- to demonstrate the importance of project management as a management specialism in its own right, and the potential positive contribution that it can make to organisations;
- to provide a source of ideas and a guide to new approaches that can be used by individuals and organisations in the execution of their work;
- to demonstrate the progression from strategy formulation to execution of the project and subsequent activities;
- to provide a set of tools and techniques applicable by the project manager at different stages in the life of the project;
- to consider the role of the project manager in the organisation and management of people;
- to highlight examples of world-class performance in project management and to take lessons from these;
- to provide a path for the individual to seek self-improvement in their project management expertise, through the study of both good and poor performance (through recognising where mistakes were made and avoiding these in future) from case studies.

The final objective of the book is to recognise project management as one of the most challenging and creative tasks that a person can undertake. In this respect, it can even be, yes, fun. The opportunity for an individual to make their mark on the project is immense. For many project managers the following quotation is typical:

The great thing about being the project manager is that I get leverage on all my ideas. I think of one way that a problem can be overcome, and the team add to it in ways that I never could have imagined on my own.

Before we can discuss the area further, it is important that some definitions are established, as these are by no means universal, and time after time we see that one person's project is another's ongoing activity!

1.2 Definition of a Project

When is a project not a project? When it doesn't meet the following criteria. Definitions include:

- any non-repetitive activity;
- a low-volume, high-variety activity;
- 'a temporary endeavour undertaken to create a unique product or service' (PMI, 2000);
- any activity with a start and a finish;
- 'A unique set of co-ordinated activities, with definite starting and finishing points, undertaken by an individual or organisation to meet specific performance objectives within defined schedule, cost and performance parameters' (BS 6079: 2000).

The first of these is a very constrained view (see below) and does not describe well the true nature of projects. The idea of assessing volume and variety of activities comes from the study of operations management (see Brown *et al.*, 2001). This definition is worth exploring further as it concentrates on the activity rather than the outcome. This is a process view of projects and will be a recurrent theme throughout this book. Furthermore, it will be shown that the definition of what constitutes 'a project' has changed in the recent past.

The relationship between volume and variety is shown in Fig. 1.1. As you can see in the figure, there is generally an inverse relationship between volume and variety.

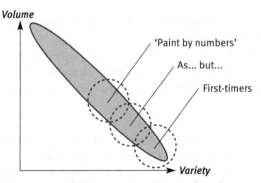

Figure 1.1 Volume versus variety and projects

For example, McDonald's is a high-volume, low-variety business – they provide a high volume of products that are (depressingly) the same wherever in the world you go (very low variety). A management consultant, on the other hand, operates at the other end of the scale – providing a low volume of services, carried out according to the needs of each client, having a high variety.

The traditional project management area is low-volume, high-variety processes, where the notion of *uniqueness* prevailed. These are indicated on the figure as *first-timers*. Examples of these are the first moon landing and the development of the first computer. It is noticeable with the wider adoption of project management that individuals and organisations are running projects, often over time periods as short as a few weeks or months, and that these are being carried out on a regular basis as part of ordinary business activity. Here, the end product may be different, but the process by which it is delivered is often repeated over time. Two scenarios are identified here. The first is where there is some similarity to previous work, in terms of either the process followed or the product being delivered. These are referred to in Fig. 1.1 as '*as . . . but . . . s*', that is, *as* the job we did last time, *but* with the following differences. The second of these is where there is a high degree of commonality in both process and outcome. These are termed *painting by numbers* projects[1] because the process and the outcome are well known. The project team has the task of following the path to the required outcome. Projects such as carrying out a financial audit of a company will be project-based, but the processes and the outcomes (a set of reports and accounts) are well known in advance. Marketing research projects are similarly painting by numbers projects in many instances.

While it is a characteristic of projects that there will be a degree of uniqueness, the removal of focus from the product and onto the process means that there is considerable scope for ongoing improvement – particularly if the organisation adopts the 4-D model of projects shown later in this chapter. It is for this reason that the PMI definition is also rather limited, as again it focuses on the uniqueness rather than the consistent elements of process. There is an ongoing discussion as to what actually constitutes a project. For the purpose of this book, the widest view of what constitutes a project will be taken – encompassing all three of the categories of projects from Figure 1.1.

Having a defined start and finish is undoubtedly a characteristic of projects, though it is insufficient to define them on its own. It is a useful discipline though, as it is often seen that projects do not have a defined start point, they just emerge from other activities. Organisations also often appear reluctant to put a finish date on projects, resulting in activities that continue to consume time and resources. For individuals, this is also vital – personal projects are often started with no notion of when they will be completed. They then add to an already full to-do list, causing stress and frustration. Not starting further projects without some sort of selection process (see Chapter 3) and then putting deadlines on these is a good discipline, therefore, for both individuals and organisations.

The last definition is more of a wish-list for many project managers than a *de-facto* definition. As shown in Fig. 1.1, there is a significant group of projects that do not have these characteristics, at least at the outset. While they may develop them over time, it would be wrong to exclude them from our consideration of projects.

The above definitions have provided a range of characteristics of projects and these will be developed in section 1.5 when the characteristics of project management are compared with general management. It can also be seen that there is no completely consistent agreement as to what is a project and what is not. Some characteristics about which there is agreement include:

- there are constraints (usually centred around time and resources, but also including all aspects of the process and the outcome);
- projects are a process – in many cases a core business process for organisations;
- the particular goal in mind shows that it is a focused activity and often this is *change*. Organisations carry out many different types of change through projects, and are a major area for application of the principles and practices of project management.

Having defined a project, we can now consider the evolution of the subject area, leading to the current issues for project management, in both practitioner and academic environments.

1.3 An Historical Perspective on Project Management

In theory, we should be able to learn from how humans have managed projects since the start of civilisation. This should be an enlightening area for study, but is one that appears to have yielded little of practical use for project managers today. For one, the constraints are hardly the same today as they were. One very successful civilisation – the Roman Empire – did not have the same resource constraints that project managers face today. As one historian pointed out, if they wanted any more resources to complete their projects, they simply had to go and conquer the region that had those resources and take them. Maybe this is more reminiscent of industrial practice today than we credit . . . In addition, timescales and expectations were much less. Construction of some of Europe's great churches was accomplished over periods of many decades, or often over hundreds of years. Today, the expectation is that it will be ready tomorrow. In addition, we do have a 'survivor bias' for projects carried out by them – we do not find so much evidence of their failures as of their successes.

Recently, the nature of project management has changed. It has ceased to be dominated by the construction industry, where much of the case material under this heading is based, and is now applicable in all organisations. Project management is now an advanced and specialised branch of management in its own right. As a result, the nature of project management has had to change. It is no longer simply an extension of a technical specialism (e.g. engineering or marketing), but requires a full structure to take a project from strategy to action. In addition, the hard systems approach, which treated the project as a mechanical activity, has been shown to be flawed. A further elaboration of the development of the subject is shown in Table 1.1.

Table 1.1 Historical development of project management

Stage	Era	Characteristics
1	Pre-1950s	No generally accepted or defined methods
2	1950s	'One best way' approach, based on numerical methods established in the USA for managing large-scale projects
3	1990s	A contingent approach based on strategy

Obviously, small- and large-scale projects were undertaken before the 1950s. Individuals managed events and other situations. For example, the Pyramids were constructed, wars were fought, and products were developed. However, project management in the way that we would understand it today did not exist until the 1950s.

During the 1950s, formal tools and techniques were developed to help manage large, complex projects that were uncertain or risky. The chemical manufacturer Du Pont developed Critical Path Analysis (CPA – see Chapter 5) for scheduling maintenance shutdowns at the company's production facilities. At the same time, the defence contractor RAND Corp. created Programme Evaluation and Review Technique (PERT) for planning missile development. These tools focused almost exclusively on the project planning phase, and there were no close rivals for their use. The methods have survived and became 'the way it is done', despite never apparently having been the subject of any trial that questioned their usefulness. The principles of these will be the subject of the discussion in Chapter 6.

As well as project planning and control, the role of projects is today being reconsidered. A strategic approach is taken to the design of the project process, rather than the highly reactive approach that has been prevalent until recently. Conventional methods developed to manage large-scale direct-value-adding projects with timescales of years such as heavy engineering are too cumbersome when projects require short timescales to exploit market openings quickly, in particular in an information-based economy.

The third stage of project management emphasises the strategic role of projects, especially those processes that the project manager must put in place to deliver the end objective of the project and satisfy the needs of all the project's customers. In this new approach, project managers become project *integrators*, responsible for integrating the required resources, knowledge, and processes from the project's beginning to end. This third stage has also been greatly influenced by the changes that have occurred in the context in which modern projects operate. In particular, the ready availability of technology (especially communications technology) has led to the emergence of *virtual teams* as a means of running projects. Similarly, there has been considerable development of powerful project planning and software and the computer processing power to support it. Both of these have the potential to change the way that we work in projects.

This consideration of the evolution of the subject brings us to the issues that practitioners and academics are facing today.

1.4 Current Issues in Project Management

There is only one consistent feature of modern business and that is change.

Organisations are constantly required to change what they do and how they do it. The most successful commercial organisations are those that have become best at changing. World-class performance is seen to be possible through the development of excellent management, one significant part of which is the management of projects. However, working against this is a number of issues, which are exemplified by the following quotations:

1 'Ready, fire, aim.'
2 'It's all in my head.'
3 'We work in a nanosecond environment, we don't have time to do this stuff.'
4 'Project management – we have a procedure for that.'
5 'It's all just common sense, isn't it?'
6 'We've done this lots of times before. It never worked then, why should it this time?'
7 'It won't work here!'

'Ready, fire, aim'

'Ready, fire, aim' is the fate of many projects. Here the project is started with no clear objectives. The motto is *shoot first – whatever you hit, call it the target*. There are still some corners of the commercial world that tolerate this approach to managing projects, but in general, this is not associated with any great success. As will be seen in subsequent chapters, this approach may work fine for the early stages of a project or where the benefit is in carrying out the process of the project, rather than in achieving any particular outcome. In most organisations today, this is being replaced with a highly structured system of justifications that any project must go through. However, if you do work in this environment, setting your own targets at the end of the project is the easiest method for the project manager, without a doubt!

'It's all in my head'

The second represents the approach that is taken to many projects. The project manager will set out with all the information in his or her head. This may work well where the project is very small, but the lack of any system will soon start to tell on the individual and the results if there are any problems or if the scale of the project escalates. Here, the application of the structures and systems will greatly help, enabling better-grounded decisions to be made and avoiding many problems to which this approach will inevitably lead. It remains a challenge for many individuals and organisations to move away from this usually random approach to managing projects. This links to the next point.

'We work in a nanosecond environment, we don't have time to do this stuff'

This was a regular quotation from managers in fast-moving e-commerce firms. Given the demise of so many of these, one can only speculate on the impact that the unwillingness to deal with anything as messy and un-hip as good project management had on those businesses. There may be changes to the basic practices of project managers that are required under such circumstances, but this is more of adaptation rather than radical re-invention. This scenario is in sharp contrast to the next one.

'Project management – we have a procedure for that'

Having a procedure or a documented set of processes for projects provides a highly structured approach that is favoured in some industries. Indeed, there are many where the slavish dedication to highly restrictive methods is necessary as part of the requirements of customers (military procurement and areas where safety considerations are paramount are two such areas). The result is high levels of documentation (the procedures manual for projects at one international bank ran to several thousand pages) and considerable bureaucracy associated with it. Decision-making can be very slow and the overhead costs associated with such systems significant. This represents the other end of the formalisation scale from the previous scenarios; it is a challenge for project managers to deal with this high degree of formalisation, and yet try to engender creativity into the project and the people working on it. It is a constant theme among project management professionals just how much formalisation is required in systems. While some will have the levels specified by the requirements of the project, the vast majority, particularly for smaller projects, require an approach that is more appropriate to the particular situation.

'It's all just common sense, isn't it?'

Well yes, but that depends on what you mean by common sense. If you mean 'the obvious after it has been explained',[2] then possibly. However, this statement usually just shows that things about which little or nothing is known appear obvious as exemplified by the bar-room philosopher with easy answers to life, the universe and everything, if only they would listen . . . This is a great challenge for project management today. The past 50 years of the subject will be shown to have provided a substantial knowledge base for project managers to use. The art is in knowing the relevant parts of that base and tailoring that knowledge to the particular environment.

'We've done this lots of times before. It never worked then, why should it this time?'

Here we see the experienced project worker showing the exasperation that comes with the application of many different approaches, only to be regularly confronted with the same results – projects running late, overbudget or delivering less than was required of them. This is not at all uncommon, because the real causes of failure are rarely addressed by organisations. The failures deserve more careful study – they are a significant opportunity for learning and are generally very costly – to individuals, the organisation or both.

'It won't work here!'

Lastly, the challenge is for new methods that have been developed in other areas of business to find how they might be applied with benefit to the project environment. These must overcome this often-heard rejection of anything new as it was 'not invented here, therefore it cannot be of any relevance to us'. The pressure for change in most organisations is such that ideas need to be brought in from wherever possible and adapted for projects and then the particular application. Examples of changes that are having an impact on the project environment include taking operations initiatives (including *Lean* and *Agile*) and applying the principles to the project environment (see Chapter 15). As was commented in the previous section, there is no longer just one best way to run a project. Now there are many possible options, and it is this choice of processes that will be discussed in subsequent chapters.

One final issue should be shelved very quickly. Many managers have not recognised that they are project managers, despite the statistic from those who study such things that the average manager now spends upwards of 50 per cent of their time on projects or project-related issues. Their line responsibilities (finance, marketing, design) involve them in a variety of day-to-day activities plus longer-term projects. The skills and techniques used in the line-management function will differ from those required in projects, as we shall see. The more enlightened organisations will provide a basic skills grounding in the best ways to run projects, and help, coach and mentor individuals in recognising and developing their project roles.

The subject of project management needs to move on. The incorporation of a substantial strategy element in this text reflects the need for the subject to change its reactive nature and move to the situation where it aspires to be a source of competitive advantage. This advantage has been amply demonstrated in the operations management area, and the contribution of operations to the success of major businesses such as Toyota has become legendary. Unless the strategy is right, even the best management practice in the execution of projects is wasted. It has become evident that project managers have been woefully ill equipped to take this strategic role. This text takes a much wider view of project management to prepare for a discussion, much of which can rightly be placed at the highest levels of organisations.

A further issue that was raised in the opening of this chapter is that of the ongoing extent of project failure. This presents a significant opportunity to organisations to improve their performance, through improving the way that both operational projects (those that directly earn revenue) and change projects (those that change the way that the organisation or an individual works) are managed.

One issue that has already been raised in this section is that many project managers fail to recognise that this is indeed a major part of their role. In order to help recognise this element and where the differences exist between project and general management, the following section will develop this theme.

1.5 The Relationship between Project Management and General Management

Figure 1.2 shows a conventional management hierarchy with the lines on the diagram representing lines of reporting or responsibility. At the head of each of the major functions within an organisation there will be functional or line managers. These managers have the responsibility for the people who work under them in their departments.

The project manager may have a line management role as well, but is responsible for projects that may run across several functions. The figure shows the project manager being responsible for people drawn from every function in their activities in relation to that project.

The project manager's role differs from that of the line manager in the nature of the task being carried out. Table 1.2 gives the major differences.

As Fig. 1.3 shows, the split between tasks that can be considered as maintenance (maintaining the status quo) and innovation is changing. In the figure, the trend is for the line AB to move downwards – increasing the degree of innovation activities required

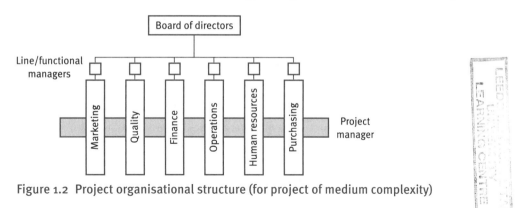

Figure 1.2 Project organisational structure (for project of medium complexity)

Table 1.2 Project versus general management

General management	Project management
• responsible for managing the status quo	• responsible for overseeing change
• authority defined by management structure	• lines of authority 'fuzzy'
• consistent set of tasks	• ever-changing set of tasks
• responsibility limited to their own function	• responsibility for cross-functional activities
• works in 'permanent' organisational structures	• operates within structures which exist for the life of the project
• tasks described as 'maintenance'	• predominantly concerned with innovation
• main task is optimisation	• main task is the resolution of conflict
• success determined by achievement of interim targets	• success determined by achievement of stated end-goals
• limited set of variables	• contains intrinsic uncertainties

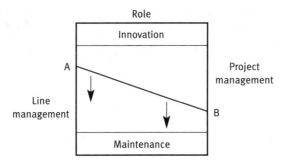

Figure 1.3 Innovation/maintenance activities in line and project management

from line managers. The result of this is a change in the role of line managers and a reduction in the difference in the roles of line and project managers. Indeed, as already stated, this blurring of project management into general management provides for considerable confusion. Reference back to the definitions of projects will show those activities that are and are not project-based. The box below illustrates this.

Environmental health manager

The role of the environmental health office includes visiting food premises (restaurants, cafés, school canteens and mobile catering outlets) to determine whether the practices that they are following in the preparation, storage and serving of food constitute any danger to public health. They have considerable powers (including closure of the premises) where deficiencies are identified. The manager of the area was convinced that he was a project manager – each of these visits lasted for several hours and was, therefore, an activity with a start and a finish. QED, it was a project. Except that these are not projects. The process that was followed each time (arrange visit, visit, report and follow-up) was the same (low-variety process), and each inspector was visiting one or two premises a day (medium volume). This was *operations* rather than *project management*.

It was, however, only one part of his role. Where there was a public health issue raised (such as an outbreak of a particular disease), this was indeed a project. These were fortunately rare events and each one had its own characteristics. They also had to be preplanned, so that no time was wasted when they did occur. Other projects included regular initiatives to highlight particular aspects of public health – such as an autumn campaign of promoting influenza vaccination.

The role of this manager was therefore split between the general management associated with the ongoing activities and the project management of both initiatives and reactions to 'crises'. He was advised to look to operations management as a subject to help with the management of the day-to-day tasks, but to build a relevant knowledge-base and set of practices for the project that he ran.

The above case is not unique and there are many managers who face this multiple role – part general management and part project management. Others are full-time project managers. Further discussion of these roles is contained in the Project Management in Practice section at the end of this chapter. For now, a consideration of 'what we know' about project management follows – vital if we are to avoid reinventing the wheel each time a project is undertaken.

1.6 The Project Management Knowledge Base

There is a vast amount written about project management. There is also a great deal of knowledge about 'what works where' in any particular scenario. As we will see in Chapter 14, however, this is not always readily accessible just when you need it. Even the so-called handbooks of project management cannot be this comprehensive – there are too many scenarios and too many potential variables.

The books on project management range from the short pocketbook approach to project management (see Further Information at the end of this chapter) to the generalist text (such as this one), to collections of academic work that form the handbooks. Alongside all these are myriad special-interest books and articles.

While the handbooks try to be comprehensive, there are many short self-help books that will claim to 'make you an expert in a week'. It is interesting that we insist that other management professions (e.g. accountants and lawyers) spend years training for their profession, but when it comes to project management, people will often be put in the position of managing a project with little or no training or education in the subject. The pocketbooks do provide a first level of awareness-raising of some of the issues for the aspirant project manager, and are often useful checklists for the first-time manager. Indeed, it often surprising how far people go with little more than the rough guidelines contained in such books.

Project management as a profession is almost unique in having institutions concerned with its development who promote what they term their *Body of Knowledge*. This is certainly not the case in other management areas, finance, marketing, purchasing, human resources and operations. Project management has no less than three relevant bodies of knowledge, all very different in their purpose and content.[3] For the purpose of this book, we will be referring throughout to the APM and PMI bodies of knowledge, showing the areas that are pertinent to each of the major topics covered here. This provides a further point of reference for those studying the area, whether this is for personal study as part of a course or in preparation for the relevant professional examinations (see Web addresses in the Further Information section at the end of this chapter). These will be expanded as part of the discussion on structures in the following chapter.

A further development of this knowledge base comes through specific standards for processes. Standards may be particular to the organisation as discussed above, or follow a generic standard, such as PRINCE2. Further discussion of PRINCE2 is included in the Appendix at the end of this book.

1.7 Introduction to the Following Chapters

This chapter has provided an overview of the nature of projects and their importance. They are important to individuals as a means of carrying out their work and with an increasingly recognised career path as project management professionals. Organisations can benefit too from having the capability to deliver excellence in this area. There does appear to be a problem, however, with projects and their management, with evidence of widespread failure to achieve project objectives, regardless of size, scope or sector in which the project is being run. Some of this must be down to the history of the subject, with a reliance on 'one best way,' regardless of its reliability or applicability. Other aspects include the failure of many individuals and organisations to recognise that they are involved with project management, and to take the subject, and all it has to offer, seriously. The subject is moving on from this at a significant pace, with the bodies of knowledge that were outlined here providing a grounding from which organisations and individuals can develop their own knowledge bases.

The above discussion provides the rationale as to why this subject is worth studying and books like this are needed. The following maps out the following chapters and outlines the contents of each.

The chapters broadly fit into the 4-D model shown in Fig. 1.4. The starting point for any consideration of project management is the structures and frameworks that can be applied to the process to assist in forming our thinking on the subject. This is vital, as even moderately complex projects will swamp you unless you have a system to deal with them. From the frameworks described in Chapter 2, the first of the major inputs to the project – through the strategy process – will be unpacked in Chapter 3. Having set the strategy, the next step is to develop the ideas for both project outcome and process. This is done in Chapter 4. This concludes the definition stage of the project life-cycle.

Having determined to continue with the project, the next stage in the life-cycle is designing of project process in some detail. Time planning is considered in Chapter 5, cost and quality in Chapter 7. This shows the benefits of the 'project management approach' and includes some of the techniques for describing both the technical (the hard elements) and human (the soft elements) of projects. Chapter 6 presents a

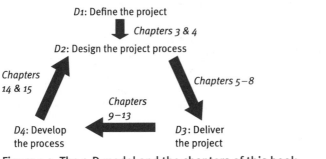

Figure 1.4 The 4-D model and the chapters of this book

relatively novel approach – that of the *theory of constraints* approach to planning – the *critical chain*. The chapter will argue that this is one way that tackles some of the fundamental problems with current approaches to projects.

Having constructed plans or models of the activities to be undertaken, many projects then start. This misses one of the key opportunities that project managers have for reflection on their plans and to avoid problems in the future. Chapter 8 therefore presents strategies and techniques for analysing the plans and models that have been generated – in particular with respect to **risk analysis**. This includes the subject of justification of project budgets. While a full discussion of financial justification process and practice is outside the scope of this text, some appreciation is required of the issues to be considered. Financial discussions should not be the domain solely of accountants. Following the theme of analysing plans, the high level of failure of projects has led to a re-evaluation of the tools and techniques of project management.

The third element of the project model is the delivery phase, or *'Do it!'* and this is the subject of the next batch of chapters. In bringing together the resources to execute the plans, the project manager has to be in a position to make objective decisions about structure, i.e. the arrangement of people and groups, relative to lines of authority and responsibility. This is the subject of Chapter 9, which includes a discussion of how teams work on projects and an introduction to the contribution that individual personalities will make. Chapter 10 continues the theme of the management of people, with a discussion of management and leadership in the project environment.

Chapter 11 considers the information that will be needed in medium- to large-scale projects in order to maintain a degree of control over the ongoing activities. It is, after all, of little practical use to find at the end of the project that all tasks have run late, that the budget was overspent and the 'customer' or other influential parties were dissatisfied with the outcome. The delicate balance of ensuring that the project stays on track without overburdening it with bureaucratic controls will be discussed, with the objective of maximising the visibility of project progress.

Chapter 12 looks at the increasing role of supply chains in our projects. As more projects are run as joint ventures, and the trend to outsource major parts of projects becomes a facet of organisational life, it is vital for the modern project manager to have a grasp of the impact such ventures will have on the practices that will need to be adopted for the project.

Decisions should be made on the basis of good information. What constitutes 'good information'? In addition, what should a project manager do with that information? Approaches to problem-solving and decision-making are discussed in Chapter 13. This issue concludes the management of the execution phase of the project. If the objective of continuous improvement is to be met, however, this is not where the activities of the project manager end. The continual improvement of the process through two cycles – 'learning by doing' and 'learning before doing' – are considered in Chapter 14 on project close-out and review. Some of the main influences on the project management process are then discussed and a future agenda proposed in Chapter 15. These include the quality revolution, the desire to make project processes leaner, business process re-engineering and benchmarking. In addition, the means by which these are applied are discussed. Finally, the question 'What next?' is debated in the context of developing the subject of project management.

The Appendix covers issues that are relevant to many project managers across all phases of the project – those related to standards. This is a major constraint for many, and some knowledge of these and their purpose is useful. The key standards that are considered include those related to general processes (including ISO 9000 and BS 6079) and one that is very specific about how projects and the supporting organisation should be structured – PRINCE2.

1.8   Summary

Projects are important issues to both individuals and organisations. There are some key questions to be answered if we are to understand the meaning and potential of the subject and profession of project management and the activity of managing projects today. The first is: what is it? For some people, the image that is conjured up is of large-scale construction projects – the many buildings for the millennium or major events such as the Sydney Olympics. The second is: what is the role of management in this? For many, project management is often associated with its basic tools and techniques or a particular software package. These views are limiting and do not do justice to the range or scope of project management today. To counter the first point, project management is a live subject – going on around us all the time, and not just in organisations that undertake large-scale projects. On the second point, rather than just being a limited set of tools and techniques, it is also a true profession, with a growing recognition of its contribution to all walks of working life. The role of project management covers the entire spectrum of management knowledge, making it a broad-based study, not confined to tools and techniques or technical issues.

On a business level, there are projects ongoing in every organisation. These are vital as they are the execution of all the visions, missions and strategies of that organisation. There are many books and distinguished articles written on strategy, but relatively little on how to deliver it. On a personal level, we all have a number of projects ongoing – pursuing a course of study, buying a house or organising a holiday. The level of complexity differs, the underlying principle of delivering the result at a given point in time is the same. At a commercial level, the effectiveness of the project management process will determine whether or not those projects play a role in providing a source of competitive advantage (or even continued existence) for an organisation. But this is not usually the case, as the opening of the chapter showed. There is a problem with projects and their management, as demonstrated by the large percentage of projects that run late, cost more than was expected, or fail to deliver what was required of them.

The first step on the way to understanding projects was their definition. This showed that there was a considerable diversity in the characteristics of projects, and that these require different approaches to their management. After we identified the nature of projects, the next discussion was to see how we arrived at the current state of the subject. Having emerged from the 'one best way' era of project management, we are faced with a large number of challenges, not least in terms of where the subject is going now. This is both helped and constrained by the current knowledge base, with high-profile bodies of knowledge being at the core of the professional discipline.

The arrangement of this book is based around the four stages of the project life-cycle, with the first part of this being the structures that project managers can apply to their projects. As already discussed, these ideas are often very simple in principle, their application requires considerable creativity to adapt them to the particular circumstance in which you find yourself. That is the challenge of project management.

Project Management in Practice

Three project managers with distinctly different roles

1 The site manager of a housing development

'I am in charge of the construction of the buildings you see around you [he gestured with his hand to the mixture of partially and fully completed properties] and of making sure they go from this stage [he indicates a pile of drawings and building schedules] to the point where we can hand them over to the sales people to sell. Most of the work is supervisory, ensuring that orders are placed and materials arrive on time, people turn up, do the job properly and get paid for it at the end of the week. There are always arguments between the various tradespeople to resolve and problems just get dumped on the desk. Some of the toughest problems come with the people you have to work with. Some of them will do anything to try to get one over on you – they'll tell you a job is finished when you can see it is only half done. Unless you go and check it yourself you're in trouble. Also, they don't give a damn for my schedule. How do you get a roofer, at four o'clock in the afternoon when it is raining rather heavily [not the words actually used] when you know he has a long drive home, to get back on the roof and finish the job he is doing so that other jobs which rely on this being completed can start at eight o'clock the following morning? It wouldn't be the first time we had to block his car in with a pallet of bricks to stop him leaving.'

2 Implementing Total Quality Management – the quality director

'The quality director was appointed with the brief to introduce Total Quality Management (TQM) to the company. It was his responsibility to put the proposal as to how it could be done, and then to carry it out. As he described at the outset of the project "[this] is one of the most complex projects that we could undertake at this time". The complexity came because the project would hopefully change the way that everyone in the company thought and worked [i.e. both attitude and procedures]. This would have to be done through consultation, training and the demonstration through piloting small-scale improvement activities, that the move towards TQ was worthwhile. The initial phase as part of the proposal process was to carry out a company-wide quality audit to determine attitudes, knowledge and current practice. The results paved the way for the carrying out of targeted efforts where needed most. The first phase of execution was to take the board of directors of the company on awareness training – showing them how working under a TQ environment would benefit them, and what changes would be needed. The next level of management were then trained and so on down the hierarchy until the middle management level. These managers then trained their own people – a process known as "cascading". The project to introduce the new philosophy to the company took several years, and has now moved on to become an accepted way of working. The quality director was initially involved in the management of the introduction process, where the employees and suppliers needed to be convinced that this was a good route for the company to take. His role then became one of project sponsor of a variety of improvement projects, which may be considered as sub-projects of the main one.'

3 Project manager in financial management system implementation

'The main roles of the job include:

- organisation – from the design of the system to determining support issues and providing training;
- anticipation of future requirements of the system;
- monitoring of progress of the implementation;
- communication and information – providing progress reports to local team members and national common-interest groups;
- audit – ensuring the housekeeping, procedures and system security are in order.

The initial system design work involved coordinating with external system designers, the providers of the software and the in-house IT group. Our local area network (LAN) needed upgrading to run the new system. Other organisational issues were the role that consultants would play in the system design and training of users and the allocation of the budget between activities.

Anticipation was required as the requirements of the system would change over its life. For example, higher-level monthly indicators of financial performance would need to be provided where they had not been needed before. In addition, a management accounting system would be required to provide budgetary controls.

The monitoring system we used for the project was PRINCE. This provided a basic set of planning tools, and we filled in the blanks on the planning sheets. A team was set up to monitor progress against the plan.

Training was one area where I was personally involved with the users, showing them how to use the system. People are very frightened of technology and do not always grasp immediately ideas you think are very simple. This is where the greatest attribute of the project manager was needed in plenty – patience.'

Case discussion

1 Identify the title which might be given to the project management role in each case.
2 Describe the role of the project manager in each of the cases.
3 Describe the desirable characteristics of each project manager using the set of skills and attributes as a starting point.

The Big Dig

Any project that involves tunnelling is risky. Any project that involved tunnelling under a city whilst trying to keep that city fully operational, is very risky. When that city is Boston in the USA, it is in a risk category all of its own. This does not, however, excuse the financial performance of this project, the results of which are exceptional and even make the performance of previous 'stars of disaster' such as the Channel Tunnel, look good.

During the 1950s, the Commonwealth of Massachusetts commissioned new roads as part of a national road-building frenzy that took place at that time. The result was a partly elevated freeway that cut the city off from its old harbour and over time coped increasingly less well with the volumes of traffic that were trying to use it. For many years, the project had been the subject of much politicking and had been rejected by a number of national administrations. In 1993, it was given the go-ahead.

At this time the budget was $US2.6 billion, an enormous sum of money for an 8-mile tunnel, but given the technical complexity of the task, this was considered acceptable. Gradually the costs rose, until in 1998, the estimated final cost was $10.4 billion. By mid-2000 this had risen to $13 billion and by mid-2001 to over $15 billion. It was still considered a technical success, but both politically and economically, it was a disaster. In project management terms it is also a disaster – a 500 per cent-plus overrun on budget can only be described as 'talented'.

How did such a financial disaster occur? The first is a feature of many large 'political' projects – that the 'real cost' would not be politically acceptable. The original budget was deliberately deflated to make the project happen. The second is technical risk – that of the tunnelling process. The ground through which the tunnelling is being carried out is reclaimed land that was originally under the sea. The tunnelling process being used was also new, presenting a degree of technical novelty.

Case discussion

1 How might the project be considered a technical success but an economic, political and project management disaster?
2 Suggest how the 500 per cent-plus overrun might have come about.

project	4-D
change	management maintenance
general management	innovation and creativity
first-timers	as . . . but . . .
painting by numbers	volume and variety
failure	body of knowledge
life-cycle model	

Review Questions and Further Exercises

1 Carry out a search using a library or a good Internet search engine to find more examples of project failure. From your search, are there any common themes in the failures? What are the costs of these in each case? How widespread would you say that the problem of failure was?

2 The Sydney 2000 Olympics were considered to be a great success by most people. Carry out a search of the news of the time and the relevant websites to identify the characteristics of the project management that led to the success. Compare with the example of 'The Big Dig' given above and the results of your own researches in the answer to 1.

3 Explain the differences between project and general management. In what you are doing at the moment which parts are project and which are ongoing?

4 What are the benefits and problems with the 'one best way' approach to project management?

5 Select a sector of interest. For this sector, identify the likely pressures on project managers and the implications for them as a result of these.

6 Find examples of projects that fit into each of the categories of project – first-timers, as . . . but . . . s, and painting by numbers. Briefly discuss how the category would influence how you would expect to manage the particular project.

7 'A project manager should not have other managerial responsibilities.' Discuss.

References

APM (2000) *Project Management Body of Knowledge*, Dixon, M. (ed.), Association for Project Management, High Wycombe.

BS 6079 Part 1: 2000, *Guide to Project Management*, British Standards Institute, Milton Keynes (www.bsonline.org).

Brown, S., Blackmon, K., Cousins, P. and Maylor, H. (2001) *Operations Management: Policy, Practice and Performance Improvement*, Butterworth-Heinemann, Oxford.

Deming, W.E. (1986) *Out of the Crisis – Quality Productivity and Competitive Position*, MIT Center for Advanced Engineering Study, Cambridge, MA.

Maylor, H. (2001) 'Beyond the Gantt Chart: Project Management Moving On', *European Management Journal*, Vol. 19, No. 1, pp. 92–100.

Obeng, E. (1994) *All Change! The Project Leader's Secret Handbook*, Financial Times Management, London.

PMI (2000) *A Guide to the Project Management Body of Knowledge*, PMI, Upper Darby, PA.

Turner, J.R. (1994) 'Project Management: Future Developments for the Short and Medium Term', *International Journal of Project Management*, Vol. 12, No. 1, pp. 3–4.

Turner, J.R. (2000) 'Editorial: The Global Body of Knowledge . . . ', *International Journal of Project Management*, Vol. 18, No. 1, pp. 1–5.

Womack, J., Jones, D. and Roos, J. (1990) *The Machine That Changed The World*, Rawson Associates, New York.

Further Information

Badiru, A.B. (1993), *Managing Industrial Development Projects*, Van Nostrand Reinhold, New York.

Bradley, K. (1993) *PRINCE: A Practical Handbook*, Computer Weekly/Butterworth-Heinemann, Oxford.

Brown, M. (1998) *Successful Project Management in a Week*, 2nd edition, Institute of Management/Hodder & Stoughton, Abingdon.

Brown, S., Blackmon, K., Cousins, P. and Maylor, H. (2001) *Operations Management: Policy, Practice and Performance Improvement*, Butterworth-Heinemann, Oxford.

Buttrick, R. (2000) *The Project Workout*, 2nd edition, Financial Times Management, London.

Collins, A. and Bicknell, D. (1998) *Crash: Ten Easy Ways to Avoid Computer Disaster*, Simon & Schuster, New York.

Frame, J.D. (1995), *Managing Projects in Organizations: How to make the best use of time, techniques and people*, Jossey-Bass, San Francisco, CA.

Gido, J. and Clements, J.P. (1999) *Successful Project Management*, ITP, Ohio.

Gray, C.F. and Larson, E.W. (2000) *Project Management: The Managerial Process*, McGraw-Hill, Singapore.

Field, L. and Keller, L. (1998) *Project Management*, Open University Press, Milton Keynes.

Holmes, A. (2001) *Failsafe IS Project Delivery*, Gower, Aldershot.

Kerzner, H. (1992) *Project Management*, 4th edition, Van Nostrand Reinhold, New York.

Kleim, R.L. and Rudlin, I.S. (1993) *The Noah Project: The Secrets of Practical Project Management*, Gower, Aldershot.

Lock, D. (2000) *Project Management*, 7th edition, Gower, Aldershot.

Meredith, J.R. and Mantel, S.J. (2000) *Project Management: A Managerial Approach*, 4th edition, Wiley, New York.

Peters, T. (1999) *The Project 50*, Alfred Knopf, New York.

PMI (1996, 2000) *A Guide to the Project Management Body of Knowledge*, PMI, Upper Darby, PA (parts are downloadable free from www.pmi.org).

Turner, J.R. (1999) 'Editorial: Project Management: A Profession Based on Knowledge or Faith?' *International Journal of Project Management*, Vol. 17, No. 6, pp. 329–330.

Verzuh, E. (1999) *The Fast Forward MBA in Project Management*, Wiley, Chichester.

Young, T.L. (1998) *The Handbook of Project Management: A practical guide to effective policies and procedures*, Kogan Page, London.

www.pmi.org – for information about the Project Management Institute in the USA and referral to national sites of interest (including UK).

For information about the Association for Project Management (UK) see www.apm.org.uk or contact
The Association of Project Management
150, West Wycombe Road,

High Wycombe,
HP12 3AE,
UK

PRINCE2 – www.prince2.com – some description of the processes associated with PRINCE2.

Journals
Project Management Journal (published four times a year by PMI)
International Journal of Project Management (published by Elsevier)
PM Network – monthly publication of PMI
Project – monthly publication of APM
Project Management Today – professional journal

Notes

1 Eddie Obeng (1994) coined this term for use in project management.

2 I am indebted to Keith Sutton of Chelmsford Technical College for this definition.

3 Turner (2000) provides a comparison of these three.

2

Structures and frameworks

So, where do we start? The answer is that before we can undertake any activities on a project the thinking behind it must be right. This involves placing the project and its consideration in the right structures. The purpose of structures and frameworks is to provide a means to think about projects and structures to help with their delivery. This is the first stage in gaining understanding of what can be highly complex undertakings and vitally prevent the inevitable reinventing of various wheels that takes place, particularly during the early stages of a project.

The chapter starts with a basic model of a project as a whole. This is then broken into the four main phases of the project life-cycle. The issues that a project manager will have to deal with in each phase are then considered using the 7-S framework. How each of these issues is developed is determined by the project environment (one aspect of which is the project complexity) and these are the next two issues considered. It will be shown that the nature of the project management task is determined by this complexity. Important developments in recent years include the provision of documented 'bodies of knowledge' by professional institutes. These are outlined and points of reference with this book are identified.

Contents

By the time you have completed this chapter, you should be able to:
- Apply basic models to help understand the project process;
- Determine the inputs, constraints, outputs and mechanisms for a project;
- Recognise the phases of a project and the different activities carried out in each phase;
- Identify the major issues facing project managers;
- Provide a basic measure of the complexity of a project and show its implications for the management task;
- Recognise the PMI and APM bodies of knowledge and their implications for project managers.

2.1 The Project Model

Having a model to base our thinking around is the first step in gaining an understanding of the processes of projects and the accompanying managing that we will suggest should be taking place. For many years, the most basic model of any operating system has been the input–output model.[1] This applies well here as the basic unit of analysis of project activities.

The project is viewed as a conversion or transformation of some form of input into an output, under a set of constraints and utilising a set of mechanisms to make the project happen. As Fig. 2.1 shows, the inputs are some form of want or need which is satisfied through the process. The project will take place under a set of controls or constraints – those elements generally from outside the project which either provide the basis for any assumptions or limit the project. The mechanisms are those resources that make the transformation process possible.

Inputs

The desire to develop a new bagless vacuum cleaner was the starting point for James Dyson's massively successful product range. The project did not start with any formalisation, just a want or need to develop a product that would not suffer from the drawbacks associated with a paper bag being the filter for particles passing through a vacuum cleaner.[2]

For many organisations, this need will be encapsulated into a *brief* – a document describing the nature of the work to be undertaken, before the resources will be released to do even the most preliminary work. For the project manager, there will be both explicitly stated requirements (original needs) and those that emerge during the course of the project due to the customer's changing needs or perceptions (emergent needs). Such emergent needs cause considerable angst to the project manager, and need to be managed (see the discussion on *scope management* in Chapter 4 and *change control / configuration management* in Chapter 11).

Constraints

The brief will also set out the constraints, which principally focus on time, cost and quality, but will also have a wider range of issues for the project manager to reconcile with the wants or needs. The main constraints are:

- time – all projects by definition have a time constraint. In practice, it is often found to be the most challenging to meet;
- cost – the value and timing of financial resources required to carry out the project work;
- quality – the standards by which both the product (the output of the process) and the process itself will be judged.

In addition to these three, the following constraints can prove limiting on the project:

- legal – this may not be explicitly stated but there will be legal constraints, e.g. a building may not be constructed unless the planning permission for it has been obtained;
- ethical – a major area for many organisations today, particularly those where the ethics of their organisational policies has been questioned in the past (e.g. Shell and Nike);
- environmental – the deluge of environmental legislation that has been generated by governments has changed the role of environmental control from a subsidiary issue to one which is at the forefront of management thinking in many sectors;
- logic – the need for certain activities to have been completed before a project can start;
- activation – actions to show when a project or activity can begin;
- indirect effects – it is practically impossible for any change to take place in isolation. There will be ripple effects, which will need to be taken into account at the outset.

Outputs

Figure 2.1 describes the output as a 'satisfied need'. This will usually be in the form of:

- converted information, e.g. a set of specifications for a new product;
- a tangible product, e.g. a building;
- changed people, e.g. through a training project, the participants have received new knowledge and so are part of the transformation process as well as being a product of it.

The outputs may be tangible or intangible and this affects the criteria by which they are judged.

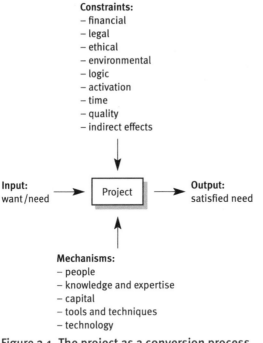

Constraints:
- financial
- legal
- ethical
- environmental
- logic
- activation
- time
- quality
- indirect effects

Input: want /need → Project → **Output:** satisfied need

Mechanisms:
- people
- knowledge and expertise
- capital
- tools and techniques
- technology

Figure 2.1 The project as a conversion process

Mechanisms

The means or mechanisms by which the output is achieved are as follows:

- people – those involved both directly and indirectly in the project;
- knowledge and expertise – brought to the project by the participants and outside recruited help (e.g. consultants) of both technical specialisms and management processes;
- financial resources;
- tools and techniques – the methods for organising the potential work with the available resources;
- technology – the available physical assets that will be performing part or all of the conversion process.

From this Inputs, Outputs, Constraints and Mechanisms (ICOM) model one of the major roles of project managers becomes apparent. They are required to be the *integrator* of the elements of the project – the need or want with the available mechanisms or resources under the conditions imposed by the constraints. This is a key skill of the project manager. The nature of this task will change during the life of a project, and this will be described in the following section.

2.2 The Four Phases of Project Management

Improve constantly and forever every activity in the company, to improve quality and productivity and thus constantly decrease costs. (Deming, 1986)

Figure 2.2 Hedgehog syndrome

Two parties to a contract, a county council and a construction contractor, ended up taking their claims[3] and counter-claims to court following the construction of a new leisure centre. Seven years later, the same two parties were in court again, to settle their claims and counter-claims, following the construction of an almost identical facility and very similar claims being made. How did this happen? Why had the parties not learned from their earlier, expensive mistakes? The only people with an interest in this kind of process are the lawyers.

This is depressingly common in many organisations, particularly those that use a large proportion of contract staff (who leave once the project is completed) and will be termed the *hedgehog syndrome*, as shown in Fig. 2.2.

We see this problem regularly on our roads, where the unsuspecting hedgehog encounters a car and the result is fairly predictable. Worse, as long as there are hedgehogs, roads and cars, we will continue to find our little flat friends. Why then, don't hedgehogs learn from this? The reason is that there is no feedback to hedgehog-kind of the knowledge that the road is a dangerous place for them to be, so that they can amend their behaviour accordingly. All too often the same applies to projects – the same mistakes are repeated over and over again. Unless there is an opportunity to develop the project processes and provide the feedback to the organisation, the knowledge is lost.

Organisations such as Hewlett-Packard, on the other hand, use previous projects and their reviews as the starting point for new projects. Their focus on the lessons from both good and bad experiences means that there is some path for continuous improvement in projects. The process that is followed in carrying out projects has four identifiable phases. The last of these is the point where we ensure that the learning points from a project are carried forward to future projects. The four phases were shown in Chapter 1, and are repeated here in Fig. 2.3:

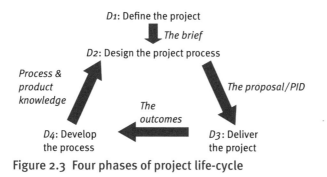

Figure 2.3 Four phases of project life-cycle

Table 2.1 The four phases of project management

Phase	Key issues	Fundamental questions
Define the project	Project and organisational strategy, goal definition	What is to be done? Why is it to be done?
Design the project process	Modelling and planning, estimating, resource analysis, conflict resolution and justification	How will it be done? Who will be involved in each part? When can it start and finish?
Deliver the project (do it!)	Organisation, control, leadership, decision-making and problem-solving	How should the project be managed on a day-to-day basis?
Develop the process	Assessment of process and outcomes of the project, evaluation, changes for the future	How can the process be continually improved?

The four phases are described in more detail in Table 2.1, but before continuing there are two points worth noting. The first is that projects are terminated prior to completion for all sorts of reasons. For instance, a project to move a bank to a new premises was scrapped as a result of an economic downturn. The project was going well but the additional costs and facilities were suddenly deemed unnecessary. The second is that there are often many stages in each of these main phases. Indeed for large projects, the project life-cycle can be replicated within each phase, as each of them becomes a mini-project in its own right. This cycles-within-cycles is common to many other project processes. Such an approach does represent the reality of many projects well, as they are more akin to cycles of activities rather than the linear progression indicated by Fig. 2.3. The real world is rarely so well defined!

The 4-D can be described as follows:

- *Define the project* – this is the time when it is determined what the project is about , its reasons for existence and the intentions that it intends to progress. It is a time to explore the possibilities, find alternatives to the problems presented;
- *Design the process* – construct models to show how the needs will be developed, evaluate these to determine the optimum process for the task and minimise risk;
- *Do It! or Deliver the project* – carry out the project in line with the models or plans generated above;
- *Develop the project process* – improve the products and processes in the light of the experience gained from the project.

There is no 'most important phase' – they represent a chain of activities. Like a chain, ongoing project performance will only be as good as the weakest part of

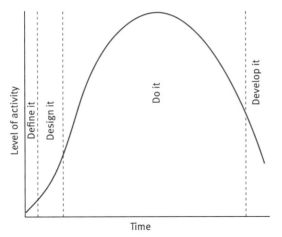

Figure 2.4 Graph showing how level of activity varies with time

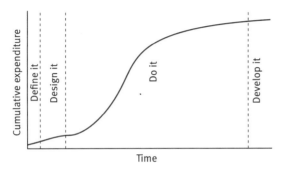

Figure 2.5 Graph of cumulative expenditure against time

the process. The last phase has a significant input to the performance of subsequent projects, in addition to elements of it determining the performance of the current project.

There are a number of tasks and issues to be addressed in each phase. This provides a degree of complexity for the project manager and is one reason that there are few truly excellent examples of project management available. Taking the analogy of the project as a *chain*, it is important that there is general competence across the phases. This is preferable to there being excellence in one area, with other areas falling down.[4]

The generic life-cycle for a project involves consideration of how the level of activity varies with time. This is illustrated in Fig. 2.4 and shows how the level of activity is relatively low during the early phases, increases through the doing phase when the major volume of work is done, and decreases through the development phase.

This pattern is reflected in the graph of cumulative expenditure against time (Fig. 2.5). Outgoings are generally low in the early stages but grow rapidly during the execution phase. The graph also demonstrates why the develop it phase is so vital – by the time the majority of the doing phase is completed, the probability is that in excess of 98 per cent of the total project expenditure will have been incurred.

Table 2.2 Development of the project life-cycle

Stage in project life-cycle	Activity	Description
Define the project	Conceptualisation	Generate explicit statement of needs
	Analysis	Identify what has to be provided to meet those needs – is it likely to be feasible?
Design the project process	Proposal	Show how those needs will be met through the project activities
	Justification	Prepare and evaluate financial costs and benefits from the project
	Agreement	Point at which go-ahead is agreed by project sponsor
Deliver the project (do it!)	Start-up	Gather resources, assemble project teams
	Execution	Carry out defined activities
	Completion	Time/money constraint reached or activity series completed
	Handover	Output of project passed to client/user
Develop the process	Review	Identify the outcomes for all stakeholders
	Feedback	Put in place improvements to procedures, fill gaps in knowledge, document lessons for the future

The last phase is the time when the project team themselves can benefit from the process and ensure that lessons (good and bad) are applied in the future. The excuse is often used that organisations cannot review projects because there is no budget for the review work. Given that mistakes are observed to occur repeatedly (hedgehog syndrome), organisations seem perfectly prepared to pay when things inevitably go wrong. This last phase is therefore an investment in future performance, just as spending money on a new piece of equipment would be. It is discussed further in Chapter 14.

The life-cycle may be further broken down as shown in Table 2.2. Key additional features include some explicit analysis of the idea during the definition stage, and the focus on a business case being prepared for the project right from the outset. This is expanded during the justification activities of the second-stage processes.

This is still generic, however, and the practice of phasing the project is best illustrated by an application. Table 2.3 shows how a new management information system was supplied to a hospital through a software company with the description of how the project was broken down and the activities that were undertaken in each phase.

Table 2.3 illustrates the early structuring that took place within the project. This had a number of plus-points for both the hospital and the IT firm, not least in the clarity that the phasing presented to each side. At a high level, the activities could be tracked to see progress (or lack of it).

Table 2.3 Supply of a management information system to a hospital project

Sub-phase of project	Activities
D1 – Conceptualisation	Software house receives an outline from the MIS department of the hospital; various pieces of information and points of clarification are requested.
D1 – Analysis	The concept is converted into the terminology of the software house (every organisation has its own set of jargon). An initial feasibility check is carried out to see what could be achieved at what cost. Objectives are set for the system to be developed and the interfaces with other systems studied. The analysis phase was completed by an appraisal of the capability of the company to provide what was being asked for by the client.
D2 – Proposal	The proposal document is submitted for approval by the client's MIS department in terms of whether or not it would meet the requirements set out in the initial request. The client organisation is offered the opportunity to visit the software house's premises and existing clients to view their systems.
D2 – Justification	There are two parts to this process. First, the software house carries out an financial analysis to show whether or not it is feasible for them to undertake the project. Second, the MIS people at the hospital need to provide evidence that the new system will provide a return. This has to be agreed by the financial managers.
D2 – Agreement	After the justification has been prepared by both sides, the formal act of preparation and signing of contracts can take place. This is the basis of the agreement between supplier and customer. The terms and conditions will have to go through each of the party's legal advisers (see Chapter 12).
D3 – Start-up	The software house starts to gather resources as soon as the contract looks likely to go ahead. Formal commitments are not made until the deal is formally signed. A project manager within the company is allocated to provide a single point of contact for the customer. The project team is gathered, external programmers hired and resources (development computers, pre-written software) procured. The project elements are allocated to individuals and specifications written for what each of the elements must achieve.
D3 – Execution	The project team starts work on the system – this is a mixture of importing existing code, modifying other parts and writing totally new elements. At the completion of each section of the work the modules are tested to ensure integration. Gradually the system is pieced together, and debugged. The client is involved in the process, with modules being demonstrated as they are completed, so that amendments are made at the time rather than at the end of the entire process.

Table 2.3 (cont'd)

Sub-phase of project	Activities
D3 – Completion	Towards the end of the development the units being tested are getting larger and more complex. The in-house specialist staff are kept on and the programmers who were hired in continue to other jobs. The major task to be completed at this stage is the documentation of the system.
D3 – Handover	The software is transported to the user's site and installed on the machines. The software specialists are on hand to see that any problems can be resolved quickly. Staff are trained in the usage of the system and the MIS staff on its maintenance and support. Ongoing support is to be provided by the software house.
D4 – Review	The way in which each of the modules was developed is documented to provide a rich picture of the process. Mistakes and good practice are identified and customer perceptions of the system canvassed. The results to the company in financial terms are compared with the proposal.
D4 – Feedback	Where deficiencies were highlighted, e.g. in the documentation of the system, the company put in place new procedures and practices that would ensure (a) that the problem for the customer was resolved in this case and (b) that it did not occur in subsequent projects.

The four phases each have different characteristics and different management requirements. Some points are of note here. The first is that many project managers will not be involved in the early stages and will be handed a brief for the project after the initial definition work has been done by another party. There are many reasons why this causes problems, not least because the project manager cannot be involved in problem avoidance measures at the early stage (see *Fast-track Projects* in section 5.9).

Before we are ready to give the project any detailed consideration a further structure is needed. This prevents the project manager becoming lost in the morass of issues to be considered in each phase – particularly in more complex projects. The following 7-S framework allows segregation of the issues.

2.3 The 7-S of Project Management

The 7-S framework provides a comprehensive set of issues that need to be considered. It also allows classification of tasks within the remit of the project manager, which reduces the complexity of the role. In addition, classifying issues in this manner ensures that the project manager will know where to look to find sources of

Table 2.4 The 7-S of project management

Element	Description
Strategy	The high-level requirements of the project and the means to achieve them
Structure	The organisational arrangement that will be used to carry out the project
Systems	The methods for work to be designed, monitored and controlled
Staff	The selection, recruitment, management and leadership of those working on the project
Skills	The managerial and technical tools available to the project manager and the staff
Style/culture	The underlying way of working and inter-relating within the work team or organisation
Stakeholders	Individuals and groups who have an interest in the project process or outcome

help if novel situations arise. Knowing that interpersonal problems in a team are aggravated by the style/culture that a project manager promotes provides a means for finding solutions to the problems.

The 7-S framework of management issues was promoted by McKinsey and Co., management consultants. Their original 7-S is amended for the project environment, with a description of each of the elements, as shown in Table 2.4.

Rather than being simply an outcome or a statement, *strategy* is a process. It involves a high-level consideration of objectives, which can be seen as points of principle rather than activity-level details. Success starts with a rational strategy process, which then guides and informs the decisions made in all areas of the project. The element of strategy will be discussed further in Chapter 3, along with the means by which organisational strategy is pursued through activities, including projects.

Structure is the arrangement of human resources relative to lines of command and control. A key question for the project manager concerns the nature of this structure. For example, should the project team be a dedicated, full-time team, or one where staff are 'borrowed' from other parts of the organisation or other organisations, only as and when needed? This is elaborated in Chapter 9.

Systems are 'the way we work'. Both formal and informal systems will need to be designed or at least recognised for key tasks, including communication and quality assurance. Formal systems can be demonstrated through statements of procedure – simply put, 'under these conditions, we carry out this action'. Informal systems, particularly for information transfer, are far less easy to describe and control. It is normal, however, for these to be the main mode of communication within groups. A theme within the systems element is the focus of the systems on 'process'. That is, ensuring that all activities carried out are contributing to the end objective of the project in a constructive manner. Systems are a recurring theme throughout this text.

Staff need to be selected, recruited and then managed. How they respond to their treatment will have a large impact on the success or otherwise of the project. Yet this element has traditionally been neglected by texts on project management. The role of the manager in the element of staffing is discussed in Chapter 10, in addition to a consideration of the *skills* they require.

Style/culture is part of the 'soft' side of management. Indeed, it cannot be managed in the short term in the same way that the finances of a project, for example, can be managed. This element will also be discussed in Chapter 10, in particular with reference to the cross-cultural nature of many projects.

Stakeholders are an important consideration for project managers. Their importance has only recently been realised and methods for the management of expectations and perceptions developed. Issues concerned with stakeholders are considered further in Chapters 4 and 7.

Having considered the framework for consideration of issues by managers, some current issues for project managers are now discussed.

2.4 The Project Environment

There is the view that 'work can be done almost anywhere'. The Mazda MX5 (Miata) car, for example, was designed in California, financed in Tokyo and New York, tested in the UK, assembled in Michigan and Mexico using components designed in America and made in Japan. Shipbuilding – a predominantly project-based environment – has faced competition coming from parts of the world that 20 years ago had little or no capability in this area. Traditional not-for-profit organisations (including many health services) are now required to meet performance targets and individual activities are being subjected to previously unthinkable commercial constraints.

Within the expanding European Union and World Trade Organization, trade barriers have fallen and the number of international collaborative ventures has increased. Projects have become more complex as:

- generally the simplest ideas have been exploited first – it is becoming more difficult but more vital to be innovative;
- businesses are becoming more complex – it is less likely for a company to provide a commodity, product or service but to provide a 'package' which meets an entire need rather than just part of that need;
- projects are moving towards turnkey contracts – where the end-user does none of the interfacing between the different parts of the system but deals with a single supplier in the provision of an entire system.

In addition:

- effective quality management has been shown to be the basis of many organisations obtaining a competitive advantage. Your quality system carrying a recognised certification (such as BS–EN–ISO 9000) is a requirement for supplying goods or services into many markets – not just aerospace and defence where the standards originated.

The change in the competitive environment in which the majority of organisations operate has necessitated a major rethink of the way in which projects are managed. The effects of the changes on projects and their managers include the following:

- Time has become a major source of competitive advantage, whether it be in the construction of a road or the development of a new product.
- Human resource management has moved from considering that members of a project team should be treated as anonymous cogs in the machine to the idea that individual creativity can be harnessed. The concept is often heard expressed in the form 'with every pair of hands you get a free brain'.
- Rates of change in technology and methods have increased – not only is the change continuing, but the speed at which changes are occurring is increasing.
- Organisations are having to become customer focused and exceed rather than just meet customer requirements. Customer expectations of the way products and services are delivered are increasing all the time.
- There is a trend towards integration and openness between customers and suppliers. Company information that would previously have been closely guarded secrets is often shared in a move towards partnership rather than adversarial relationships.
- The most fundamental change in management has occurred through the investigation of the Toyota production system. Toyota was seen to have achieved significant competitive advantage in the automotive market through its management philosophy and the application of associated tools and techniques. The principles have been taken and applied in many unrelated business areas with considerable benefits.
- The service sector has been the biggest growth area in the past ten years. The economy of the majority of European Union countries has had to cease its dependence on manufacturing and rely on the growth of the service sector to provide employment and economic growth.

A further pressure on the project environment is the search for competitiveness. Many firms have gone a long way in improving their repetitive operations. As a result, the opportunities for improvement in performance that are available in these systems without significant investment are declining. Projects are therefore a major source of competitiveness that many organisations have yet to realise.

The project environment may be summarised by the four Cs. These are:

- complexity;
- completeness;
- competitiveness;
- customer focus.

These are shown in Fig. 2.6. The first, complexity, is elaborated in the following section.

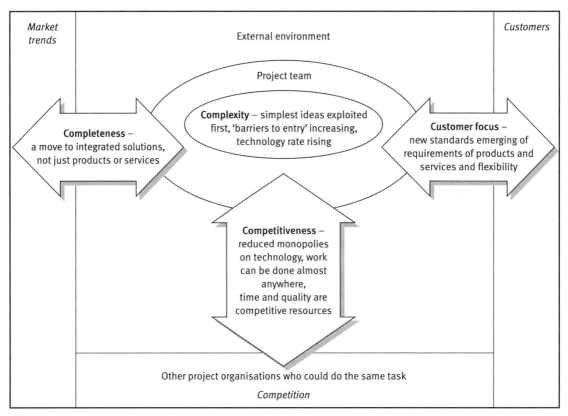

Figure 2.6 The external environment

2.5 The Complexity of Projects

Not all tools, techniques and management ideas are universally applicable – the project that takes one person a week to complete clearly has very different managerial requirements from the multi-site, high-budget project. In order to provide meaningful consideration of the function of management in such a variety of settings, a classification of the complexity will be applied. In general, there will be a high correlation between the level of complexity of a project and the amount of resources required to manage it.

The level of complexity of an activity is a function of three features:

- *organisational complexity* – the number of people, departments, organisations, countries, languages, cultures and time zones involved;
- *resource complexity* – the volume of resources involved often assessed through the budget of the project;
- *technical complexity* – the level of innovation involved in the product or the project process, or novelty of interfaces between different parts of that process or product.

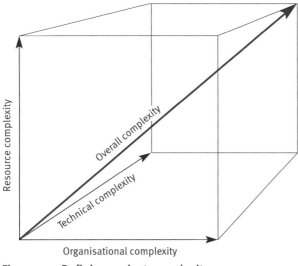

Organisational complexity

Figure 2.7 Defining project complexity

This complexity model is shown in Fig. 2.7. As the overall complexity increases, so will the difficulty of the management task to ensure that the goals of the project are reached. Therefore the degree of systematisation of the project will have to increase to enable people to deal with the complexity. Project plans will need to be explicitly stated in writing and formal procedures for evaluation and justification of the project derived. This bureaucracy is neither appropriate nor necessary for the less complex projects, where the additional resources required to formalise matters would more than outweigh any benefits from the additional activities.

Many firms have complex systems for handling projects and the question is often put – how do you decide the level of formalisation that is appropriate to the project? A highly formalised system for a very simple project is likely to cause unnecessary work and, most importantly, becomes discredited by the people who have to use it. The alternative is to use some overall complexity measure and determine the system from there. Whilst some organisations use the project value as the main measure of scale, this has been shown to be only one aspect of the complexity for managers – the resource complexity. Using the three factors defined above can be highly effective in discerning the scale of the management task. Ranking each of them out of ten with the overall complexity being the product of these three provides a measure that, with calibration over time, can provide a useful 'rule of thumb.' The measure is expressed as:

Overall complexity =
[organisational complexity] × [resource complexity] × [technical complexity]

Table 2.5 describes three projects, each of very different complexities, and the ratings that were applied to each by the project teams.

The complexity of project 1 is clearly very low. For 2, although the scale of the project is larger than 3, it is a simpler project. There are certain to be challenges faced, but the management task is greatest in project 3 (reflecting the 180 complexity

Table 2.5 Complexity calculations

Factor	Project 1 Review of company operations	Project 2 Engineering design project	Project 3 Closing down site and relocating personnel and equipment
Organisational complexity	There is a little organisational complexity, but as the review is being carried out by one function, this is limited – say 3/10	This is very limited in organisational complexity. It is being carried out almost exclusively by one function within the company – the engineering designers. Whilst they will have to work with the client on limited aspects of the design the complexity is comparable to project 1 – say 3/10	The parties involved in this project include all the technical specialists that are being moved. They work for different departments. The equipment must be moved by specialists. The move is being staggered and there has to be extensive preparation of a new facility, involving coordination with other firms – say 6/10
Resource complexity	There is no formal budget for this project – the people working on it are doing so in addition to their normal work. This is low – say 2/10	The value to the organisation of the contract is over £500 000. Resource complexity on this measure is therefore reasonably high – say 7/10	The total budget for the relocation is £250 000. Resource complexity is therefore moderate – say 5/10
Technical complexity	There is little new about this review, the people have done it before and the process is well established – say 2/10	This is standard design work with no new interfaces and standards well established. The complexity is low – say 4/10	There are many novel aspects of the move, not least for the organisation. The interfaces between the human aspects (such as ensuring that the new working conditions were greatly improved from the old ones), and the technical aspects (moving equipment that was never intended to be moved) mean that this has some complexity – say 6/10
Overall complexity	$3 \times 2 \times 2 = 12$	$3 \times 7 \times 4 = 84$	$6 \times 5 \times 6 = 180$

measure compared with 84 for project 2). This result gives us an indication that the management resource requirement will be highest in project 3, and that this should be included in the consideration of the workload of the project manager at the start of the project.

The method is not intended to be scientific, but it has been shown to be very effective at the outset of a project to determine the nature of the management task and the workload that the project would place on the project manager. As stated above, individuals can calibrate these measures over time and with experience of their usage will develop means appropriate to that organisation of determining the systems and the management that should accompany any particular project. They may also add or change the rating system. For instance, one organisation wanted to be able to take into account the additional management effort that would be expended on high-visibility projects (for instance those with a new client) or those that had particular strategic importance. For these, points were added to the organisational complexity scale to reflect the additional effort that would be required.

Having provided a model for the project, broken that into phases, looked at the issues in each phase, how these are affected by the environment and finally considered how to determine the nature of the management task, the following section shows the relevant areas of the two main bodies of knowledge to this subject of structuring.

2.6 The Structures of the Bodies of Knowledge

The two bodies of knowledge are included as they are used by many organisations as the basis for their own project management systems and thereby, the skills base of their people. They do not intend to be totally comprehensive about everything that is known about project management; rather they provide some guidance to some of the common ground between projects. For the PMI version, the guide is relatively extensive compared with the APM version, but neither is intended to be a text or a standard for operation. Another aspect as a result of their derivation is that they tend to be focused on aspects of first-time projects (see Chapter 1) rather than the vast majority of project management activity that takes place in as . . . but . . . s and painting-by-numbers projects. They also assume that the relationship between the party carrying out the project and the 'customer' is contractual. For some sectors this is still the case. In others, such arrangements have been replaced. Many projects are also not 'direct revenue earners' instead being change projects (reorganising a firm, a merger or acquisition, or an individual undertaking a course of study, for instance). As a result of these factors, the application of the bodies of knowledge is not universal, and large areas are discounted by organisations as being too cumbersome or simply inappropriate. Such a decision should be regularly reviewed, however, in the light of the knowledge that individuals and organisations acquire from their experiences with projects, and this is not to dismiss the utility of either. Given that both are associated with professional qualifications, the contribution of these to the subject area is significant. Yet it is still not as significant as it could be given the extent of project-based activities. Whilst the membership of both APM and PMI has soared in recent years, the vast majority of firms are ignorant of this knowledge base. Again, this is not to discredit what is here, but instead this represents an opportunity for those organisations and their project managers. Wider application of the principles included in the bodies of knowledge, if linked to the 4-D cycle and a promotion of learning from projects, presents the possibility that the principles can be developed to cover a wider array of projects in the future.

This section presents two tables (2.6 and 2.7), each containing an overview of the bodies of knowledge. These provide points of reference to the approach and identify some of the areas of overlap with the content of this text.

Table 2.6 The APM body of knowledge

Section	Title	Issues
1	General	The definition referred to is BS 6079, and the basic model of projects is the same as described earlier in this chapter – the ICOMs model. Programmes and portfolios of projects are introduced and differentiated.
2	Strategic	The definition of strategic is totally different from the consideration that we will use in this text. Strategic in the APM sense is the integrating framework, rather than matters of strategy. The topics covered include the project success criteria (and linkage with Key Performance Indicators – KPIs), the discussion of what constitutes a plan, value, risk and quality control, heath, safety and environmental considerations. These are important issues, but hardly strategic.
3	Control	'Planning, measuring, monitoring and taking corrective action are all usually included in the control cycle . . . The heart of a planning and monitoring system is prediction and trend analysis, based on reliable performance information.' The areas included are work content, scope and scope change management, time and cost control, resource management, earned value and information management.
4	Technical	This area is unusual in providing the interface between project management and the technical aspects of the project. It does assume that there is a significant technical aspect to the project and the terminology is that of the engineering sector. There are overlaps with other areas of the body of knowledge, including *configuration management*. This refers to product changes, as opposed to process changes, that are referred to elsewhere in terms of change management.
5	Commercial	This provides a useful reminder of the *raison d'être* of a large proportion of projects – that of generating a financial return. It considers the interfaces with other commercial functions, including marketing and sales, finance, procurement (see comments above on PMI) and legal.
6	Organisational	This organisational applies to the organisational structures that people work in as well as to the organisation of project activities. The structures include the definition of the basic organisational roles with respect to a project, including the sponsor, programme and project managers and the role of the support office. The phasing of activities suggested is consistent with the work covered in Chapter 4 of this text.
7	People	This claims to cover the 'soft issues' issues surrounding projects – including communications, teamwork, leadership, conflict management, negotiation and personnel management. This is rather limited a view of the 'people' aspects of project management, and the term 'personnel' was replaced by 'human resources management,' along with a broadening of its role several years ago.

Table 2.7 The PMI body of knowledge

Chapter	Title	Summary
1	The Project Management Framework	This sets out the purpose of the guide and the definitions of projects and project management. Like Chapter 1 of this book it also considers the relationship with other management disciplines.
2	The Project Management Context	This outlines a project life-cycle that broadly maps to the 4-D model. The context of projects and the key skills required of projects managers are also considered.
3	Project Management Processes	The guide identifies 39 processes within the five groups of initiating, planning, executing, controlling and closing activities. These are mapped to nine key areas of the body of knowledge – the subjects of the next nine chapters.
4	Project Integration Management	Integration management refers to bringing together the different aspects of a project in a coordinated way. This key project management skill of integration was discussed earlier in this book, but PMI define it very specifically as involving planning, executing the plan, and change control.
5	Project Scope Management	The scope of the project is defined in terms of a written statement of what is to be included in the project and what is specifically excluded. The main scoping work is carried out in the first two phases of the project, and PMI include a specific element of *scope verification* as a check on what is being agreed. *Scope change control* is also identified as a specific item, separate but linked to other aspects of change control.
6	Project Time Management	As the guide states, 'Project Time Management includes the processes required to ensure timely completion of the project.' Activities identified during scope management processes are compiled into an activity list, sequenced and times assigned to each activity. This then leads to the schedule for these activities – the times at which each must be completed to ensure the project as a whole finishes on time. As will be discussed in Chapter 6 of this text, such processes are subject to some interesting human behaviour that results in these processes having questionable value if left as defined here.
7	Project Cost Management	Similar to the process for time management, each of the activities is associated with a cost. This becomes the budget for each activity and there will need to be control measures to ensure that deviations from 'the plan' as a result of project problems and customer changes are 'managed.' Measures including earned value (see Chapter 11 in this book) are suggested.
8	Project Quality Management	The focus on the carrying out of planning, assurance and control is comparable in many ways to the intention of ISO 9000 – that of providing *conformance*. As for the other two key measures – time and cost – in this text it is considered that conformance is only the minimum requirement of a project, and that the current commercial environment for many organisations requires *performance* above and beyond these minimum standards.

Table 2.7 *(cont'd)*

Chapter	Title	Summary
9	Project Human Resource Management	The main areas here are planning the organisational structure in which people will work, documenting their roles and reporting relationships, identifying the necessary individuals and developing the team. This is a highly formalised approach but contains many aspects of current good practice, identifying such challenges for the project manager as performance appraisal of teams and individuals, and managing health and safety.
10	Project Communications Management	There are four aspects to this area: communications planning, information distribution, performance reporting and administrative closure. The guide provides a set of practices that are applicable to most projects, but are often neglected.
11	Project Risk Management	Having this as a separate chapter in its own right shows the early roots of this highly specialist area of project management. The six stages PMI identify to the risk management process are summarised in Chapter 8 of this book, as *identification*, *quantification* and *ongoing response control*. While most projects would undoubtedly benefit from the application of basic risk management practices, the PMI approach suggested here would be inappropriate for most projects.
12	Project Procurement Management	This area looks least at home in the current management environment. Many organisations do not even have procurement departments any more – having replaced these with more strategically aligned sourcing or supply chain management activities (see Chapter 12 in this text).

For other publications related to this body of knowledge, see www.pmi.org

As the tables show, the format of the APM document is rather different from that of the PMI, with the themes arranged into sections, and specific sub-sections within each covering particular topics. The guide does far less by way of description or definition, instead acting as a point of referral with many sections simply containing lists of references to other texts on the area. The references are dominated by the construction and engineering industries, which limits the application of this work significantly. There is also little indication of how to determine 'what works where' from this document.

2.7 Summary

Where do we start? First – get the thinking right. Most projects will benefit significantly from a full consideration of the issues. Many will appear obvious on the surface, even where they have been undertaken before. It is only through the application of the models and structures discussed that the process will start out in the right way. The first part of this consideration is that a project can be modelled through analysing the inputs, constraints, outputs and mechanisms (ICOMs). This provides the overall statement of need that will be met through the application of resources within the identified constraints. The next part of this opening activity is to break down the project into the four phases. As the Project Management in Practice at the end of this chapter will show, this is applicable for the smallest to the largest projects. This will also provide the highest level of the breakdown of the project that will be pursued in Chapter 4 and ensure that the repetition of problems (*hedgehog syndrome*) is avoided in the future.

There are many issues for the project manager to consider, and for ease these are summarised in the 7-S. This again provides a semi-comprehensive list to assist in the development of the project process. The project environment was explored and again a checklist of issues presented in the 4-Cs. This led us to consider the scale of the management task for each project. This is defined by the project complexity. Reinventing the wheel was a feature of thinking associated with failure – as described at the start of this chapter. The recognition of the significant content of the bodies of knowledge is a step to finding the best practices for your projects.

Project Management in Practice

Structures for an improvement project – the Permanent Way Company

The Permanent Way Company is a global player in the construction and maintenance of railway infrastructure – lines, signalling and communications systems. The work relies on the formation of teams to carry out projects and these are drawn from different divisions of the company. The divisions of the firm are based around the different relevant specialisms, mechanical, electrical, electronics and signalling, construction and surveying. Within each of the different divisions of the firm there are different specialisms – for instance, designers, cost engineers, marketing engineers and IT specialists. Most projects involve working across several divisions, often drawn from geographically diverse locations.

As a result of major worldwide growth in the market for their services, the firm undertook a review of their processes. Key weaknesses identified included their ability to deliver projects on time. This was consistently the main complaint of their clients (usually national rail operators) who were becoming increasingly concerned with the ability of their suppliers to deliver. A new 'project system' had been put in place that stated the documentation requirements for large projects, but this had not been well implemented, and its use was very inconsistent within the firm.

A Project Management improvement team was convened and tasked with improving the processes of the firm, with a nominal 12 months to see some results. The question that they faced at the first meeting was: where do we start? Everybody had their own ideas – we should start training people straightaway, we should employ a firm of consultants to find our needs, we should write a report to the board, we should adopt one of the bodies of knowledge and base our work around that. The meeting broke up with no agreement of the way forward, other than that another meeting should be held.

1 What are the inputs, outputs, constraints and mechanisms for the project?
2 Using the 4-D model of the project, identify the work that the team should be undertaking in each phase within the indicated timescale. Suggest an appropriate period for each phase of work.
3 Show how the 7-S would help identify the issues that needed to be tackled in each phase.
4 What is the complexity of this project? Try to estimate it on the scales suggested in this chapter.
5 How might the application of one of the bodies of knowledge help in this scenario. Use the web addresses provided to find out more about the bodies of knowledge to help you answer this question.

Project Management in Practice

Structuring a personal project

At various times during a course of study or during working life a project has to be undertaken. Consider the following scenario, then answer the questions below.

You have been asked to prepare a report on the potential for the Internet in helping to manage projects. The report should be of no more than 3000 words.

1 Using the 4-D structure, describe the activities that you would undertake at each stage in the process. How might this help you to structure your work?
2 Evaluate the complexity of the project. What are the implications for project management of your assessment of the complexity?

Key Terms

structures	frameworks
inputs, outputs, constraints and mechanisms	project life-cycle
continuous improvement	systems approach
hedgehog syndrome	phases
4-D	7-S
4-C	technical complexity
resource complexity	organisational complexity
overall complexity	scale of management task
bodies of knowledge	

Review Questions and Further Exercises

1 Identify a personal project that you have completed in the recent past – this may be a piece of coursework, a DIY project, etc. Consider the way in which the

project was planned, carried out, the results analysed and then acted upon. What would you do differently if you were doing it all over again?

2 Taking the example of a personal project that you have recently completed (as for question 1), identify the inputs, outputs, constraints and mechanisms for the project. What is the importance of defining the nature of constraints on a project prior to starting work on it?

3 How would you describe the competitive environment of the following organisations?

- automotive industry;
- construction industry;
- banking;
- further/higher education?

What constraints does this place on projects being carried out in such an environment?

4 Why is it necessary to define the complexity of a project?

5 Identify the likely complexity of the following projects:

- the development of a new office block;
- the development of a new office complex where a radical new design is proposed;
- a project to put a new telescope in space by the European Space Agency;
- implementing a robotised assembly line in a manufacturing company.

6 Why is it necessary to consider the continuous improvement of the processes by which projects are carried out?

7 Identify the criteria for success or failure of the projects that you discussed in question 1 and question 2.

8 Show how developing a new product, for example a new range of vehicle engines, could benefit through the analysis of previous development projects.

9 Write a commentary on the bodies of knowledge, and how they could relate to your own work environment both now and in the future.

10 Explore the possibilities for gaining professional qualification and recognition in project management, through both APM and PMI. How well would these fit with your own intentions regarding your profession?

References

APM (2000) *Project Management Body of Knowledge*, Dixon, M. (ed.), Association for Project Management, High Wycombe.

Clark, K.B. and Fujimoto, T. (1991) *Product Development Performance: Strategy, Organisation and Management in the World Automotive Industry*, Harvard Business School Press, Boston, MA.

Deming, W.E. (1986) *Out of the Crisis – Quality Productivity and Competitive Position*, MIT Center for Advanced Engineering Study, Cambridge, MA.

Dyson, J. (2000) *Against the Odds*, Taxere Publishing, London.

PMI (2000) *A Guide to the Project Management Body of Knowledge*, PMI, Upper Darby, PA.

Slack, N., Chambers, S. and Johnston, R. (2001) *Operations Management*, 3rd edition, Financial Times Prentice Hall, Harlow.

Womack, J., Jones, D. and Roos, J. (1990) *The Machine That Changed The World*, Rawson Associates, New York.

Further Information

Caupin, G., Knöpfel, H., Morris, P.G.W., Motzel, E., Pannebäcker, O. (eds) (1999) *IPMA Competence Baseline*, IPMA.

Lidow, D. (1999) 'Duck Alignment Theory: Going Beyond Classic Project Management to Maximise Project Success', *Project Management Journal*, Vol. 30, Issue 4, pp. 8–14.

Stewart, T.A. (1995) 'The Corporate Jungle Spawns a New Species', *Fortune*, 10 July, pp. 121–122.

Notes

1 A further discussion of the use of such models in operations management can be found in Slack *et al.* (2001).

2 For a further description of this development see Dyson (2000).

3 It is the usual practice in some industries to have a period of claims following a contract completion. In the case of a building, there may be additional work as a result of clients changing specifications during the project or where there were unknowns (for instance, ground conditions) that were the risk of the client, not the contractor. Where these cannot be resolved amicably, a regular occurrence is the trip to court at the end of the project.

4 This is supported by, among others, the findings of Clark and Fujimoto's study of excellence in the world automotive industry – see Clark and Fujimoto (1991).

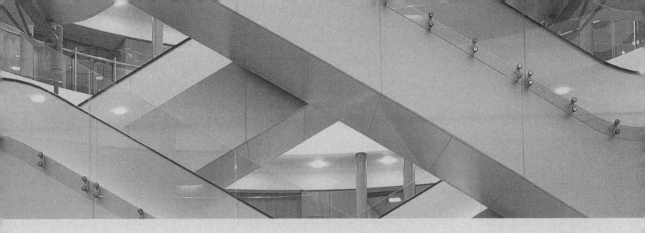

Phase One
Define the Project

3

Strategy and project management

The project is a vehicle for the execution of strategy – both organisational and personal. This implies that a high-level consideration of the role of projects is appropriate, particularly to demonstrate how they should fit with other activities being undertaken simultaneously. Within the projects themselves, there is also a requirement for the consideration of strategy, as priorities will need to be managed as part of the ongoing decision-making processes of management.

This strategic consideration has been missing from the subject of project management in the past, leaving the focus of attention on detail issues. While these do need to be addressed they should follow the priorities and issues raised by the process of strategy. Although increasing the number of issues to be considered by the manager at the outset of the project, this has been found to be consistent with high levels of performance both organisationally and personally.

Contents

By the time you have completed this chapter, you should be able to:
- define the role of strategy in projects;
- recognise a process for the deployment of strategy;
- demonstrate the role of programmes of projects and the possible roles of a project office;
- identify the objectives and accompanying success measures for a project.

3.1 Why Strategy?

Over 90 per cent of defects belong to the system, not the individual. (Dr W. Edwards Deming)

Projects routinely fail and appear to be likely to continue doing so, unless something fundamental is changed about the way that we manage them. Deming's quote above states that the system is at fault for what he termed defects or, as applicable here, project failures. Surely then, this simply means project managers throwing up their hands and saying that this justifies what they have always known – that the failures were not their fault? In many cases they would be right, but this does not remove responsibility for doing something constructive about the situation. As will be discussed, the first issue that must be addressed is to gain recognition of the problems caused by the decisions or lack of decisions made at a high level in our organisations. The alternative to gaining this recognition of the problems, is to pursue one of the 'strategies' demonstrated by the following quotations:

'Our projects never fail. They regularly come out the wrong side of the win line, but they never fail.' (Senior manager, large consulting firm)

'Our projects never run late. Whenever it looks like we might run late, we adjust the baseline.'[1] (Projects manager, construction industry)

Discussion of project failures is not easy for the organisations concerned, but does provide substantial material for analysis. The first stage, however, beautifully avoided by the two individuals quoted above, is recognition that there is a problem with projects. The failure can then be the subject of analysis.

So, with projects in general, what are the strategic issues that contribute to the failure of a project? An analysis is shown in Fig. 3.1.

Figure 3.1 shows the end-effect at the top of the diagram – that 'projects will continue to routinely fail' in the longer term as long as the two causes leading to failure still exist. These are that 'projects routinely fail now' (well discussed already) and there is 'no project capability development route', that is, there is no means to make the necessary changes. Looking further into these issues generates the causes behind each of the effects given here.[2]

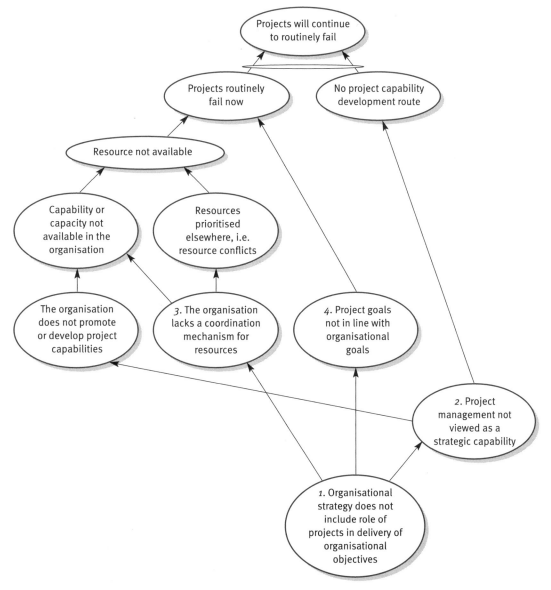

Figure 3.1 Partial analysis of project failure

Working down the diagram, we come to causes numbered 1–4. These are the main themes that will be addressed through this chapter. They appear diverse in nature, but are all linked through the causes of failure analysis given above.

1 '*Organisational strategy does not include role of projects in delivery of organisational objectives.*' As stated in Chapter 1, projects are increasingly recognised by organisations as the means by which a significant proportion of their activities are carried out. This recognition is important, but with it comes the need to move to a more coordinated approach to working with projects. It has been

demonstrated by many world-class organisations that considering organisational strategy as a **linked** series of projects is most effective and there is now significant evidence to support this. This linkage between the projects and the organisational goals, and between the projects themselves, requires a significant coordination effort on the part of management – particularly for large organisations. This will be demonstrated in the following section.

2 *'Project management not viewed as a strategic capability.'* As for the next two items, this is partially a consequence of point 1. There are many levels at which the project manager can influence an organisation. For too long, the subject of project management has focused on the tactical/operational level, ignoring its role in the development and deployment of strategy. This has resulted in projects being carried out in a reactive mode with many of the problems that the project will face being already built into the work. In addition, project managers are being brought into the process too late to have any input to the strategy process and so prevent problems or to use their knowledge of operational capability to maximise effectiveness of the project. This is a two-way problem. The first part of this is that project managers did not possess the necessary frameworks to discuss these issues. With many project managers constrained to only having Gantt charts (see Chapter 5) and schedules, there is little reason for this issue to be taken seriously at a senior level. Second and related to this, it was not seen that project management had the potential to deliver strategic capability. More on these issues in section 3.3.

3 *'The organisation lacks a coordination mechanism for resources.'* Many organisations are unable to provide a list of all the projects that are being undertaken and their resource requirements. The result is that there is a fundamental over-optimism about what can be achieved, and no rational basis for dealing with decisions such as 'should we undertake this project?' A secondary result of this is resource conflicts – where limited resources are the subject of contention between project managers. These can be resolved through the application of the structures shown in section 3.4.

4 *'Project goals not in line with organisational goals.'* Here the requirement is for coherence between the goals of the organisation and those of the project. The project manager will need a rational basis for making decisions about priorities and trade-offs. These will be covered in section 3.5.

This list provides some of the explanation of the recurrent failure of projects to deliver what is expected of them, despite this being within the control of the organisations that run these projects. The nature of project management has changed and having project managers who understand the strategy process and who can make an input to it is a major step towards improvement of project performance.

3.2 Organisational Strategy and Projects

After more than 30 years of evolution, from a planning methodology associated with PERT and CPM, Project Management has finally come of age. No longer simply a middle management tool for planning, organising and controlling human and other resources, project management can now be regarded as an essential means of turning strategic objectives into operational ventures. (Lord, 1993)

This is a change from the previous traditional approach (as described in Chapter 2), and requires different characteristics of the project managers. One of these characteristics is an understanding of strategy and the potential of the strategy process.

The role and definition of organisational strategy

Before we get to strategy, there are other terms that need to be understood. The first is the *vision* of where an organisation is going. This has been well described as:

'We're standing on this hill here. The vision is that we want to be on that hill over there.'

This implies that there is knowledge of our current position and a notion of where we want to be at a point in the future. Many organisations pay lip-service to this principle, but few manage to achieve this becoming the point of focus for all the resources of the organisation. Often the vision degenerates into generalities, with bland *mission statements* attempting to encompass the vision, such as the one seen proudly displayed in the reception office of a small firm:

'Our mission is to be the best producer in the world of high-technology solutions which delight our customers.'

The firm was a small player in a large market, who survived by their ability to supply quickly to local markets. They did not need to be the 'best in the world' at *everything* – their market was well defined. The mission statement impressed no one – neither employees nor customers – and certainly did not provide a focus for the activities of the company. Other firms have provided the vision in highly quantitative terms, stating clear objectives of improving performance in terms of:

- quality – e.g. we will improve customer satisfaction ratings by 20 per cent and customer retention rates by 40 per cent this year;
- cost – e.g. we will reduce our unit costs by 3 per cent this year;
- delivery – e.g. we will reduce the time from customer contact to fulfillment of orders by 2 weeks this year.

These are clear targets, set within a predetermined time period, though not necessarily providing a motivating vision! This also does not provide any notion of what it is that the business is going to be doing differently in the future. One trucking firm, who were needing to go through a period of change as their customers reduced their numbers of suppliers, expressed this vision as:

'We will become the preferred suppliers of transport solutions to our three major existing customers and be capable of credibly bidding for further large accounts.'

This indicated that instead of just 'trucking' they would have to become providers of 'transport solutions' which incorporated greater logistics and inventory management capabilities. This presented the firm with a clear notion of 'where they were going'.

The role of senior management in providing this vision includes setting objectives for the organisation. The strategy is concerned with providing a path for it to progress towards those objectives. Using the 'hill over there' analogy, the *strategy* is the route that needs to be taken to reach that place. Good strategy is considered as central to success in any organisation, providing the means to achieve the vision.

The strategy process

Strategy is the outcome of a *strategy process*. Traditionally, strategy was considered to be a one-way process. Figure 3.2 shows the differences between this and the strategy processes of world-class organisations today.[3] The *traditional approach* has been described above, with little guidance given to project managers. The alternative is the *strategic approach* where projects contribute in two ways to the organisational strategy. The first is through deployment of the strategy and the second is through contribution to that strategy. This is discussed further later in the chapter.

Using a traditional approach, it is often found that rather than aiming to create competitive advantage through projects, project managers are forced into the mode of trying to 'minimise the negative potential'[4] of projects. In this mode the focus is on *conformance* regardless of the real needs of performance of the organisation (this is discussed further below), and an attitude of 'just don't mess up'. Strategy is the concern of senior management only and is implemented in a top-down manner, often regardless of the realities of what is possible at a project level.

The strategic approach has a number of important differentiating features. These include the strong link between strategy and activities at the project level. Strategy formulation is still carried out by senior management in the organisation, but importantly, there are inputs from the project level. These concern:

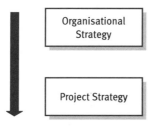

Traditional Approach – weak link between project and organisational strategy, lack of coordination between projects, inevitable resource conflicts, project managers 'minimise negative potential of projects'.

Strategic Approach – coherent, coordinated, focused, strategy-driven, contributing to strategy-forming and strategy deployment, strategic competence in project management provides source of competitive advantage.

Figure 3.2 Traditional versus strategic approaches

- progress on existing work;
- current workloads and capacities;
- limitations of existing capabilities and potential new capabilities;
- ideas as to how new opportunities that have emerged from project activities can be developed.

The notion here is simple – by creating an involving process of two-way communication throughout the organisation, the strategy process becomes more consensual and people are aware of the realities of capabilities and limitations 'on the ground'. Projects become, as Lord described, the '. . . essential means of turning strategic objectives into organisational ventures'. More than this, they will also contribute to developing future strategic objectives. Now we have the outline of the process that is needed to deal with problem 1, we return to the problems identified, and consider the second of these – *'project management not viewed as a strategic capability'*.

3.3 Project Management as a Strategic Capability

During a recent study of new product development practices in a wide range of firms, one of the issues addressed was 'Tell me how you manage projects'. Many responses were to the effect of 'If you mean "do we have a Gantt chart for every project?" The answer is no.' (Gantt charts will be described in Chapter 5.) It wasn't what was meant, but the fact that so many people during this study and in other discussions viewed the Gantt chart as representing 'project management' is indicative of a very limited approach to the subject. The Gantt chart alone is a blunt instrument and, as noted above, is likely to be of little interest to the board of a company. Indeed, for many it was the only tool that they had to carry out discussions about project management and as a result, it often appeared to show that 'if the only tool you have is a hammer, everything starts to look like a nail'.

As other professions have made their way to the boardrooms of our organisations, so it is with project management. The development of the subjects of operations management and purchasing and supply management are good models here. Twenty years ago, there was little senior representation of either of these. Today, those organisations that do not have such representation are in the minority.

Among the problems resulting from not viewing project management as a strategic capability are the two identified in Fig. 3.1. The first was *'the organisation does not promote or develop or promote project capabilities'*. For many years, organisations have promoted people only through functional routes. Be a good accountant, you will be promoted within the finance function. Where does project management fit into this? In some project-based sectors such as construction there is often a well-defined route to board level for aspirant project managers. In other sectors, this is not in place and the skill set of working across functions goes unrecognised. This was identified in Chapter 1. This is not just poor for the individuals concerned it also results in a dearth of this vital resource. This is related to the second effect – *'no project capability development route'*.

So, what would it mean to have a strategic capability in project management? There are two aspects to this for organisations. The first is the ability to deliver excellent results through projects – vital if this is your main means of earning revenue (see section 3.5). The second is that competitive advantage can be gained through it. It might be as a direct result of the capability, or indirectly, through being able to change the organisation to meet an emerging need.

This issue of capability cannot be tackled alone, however. It needs to be done in the context of the following processes – those of coordination of resources and strategy deployment.

3.4 Resource Coordination

'The first time we assessed our total project load, we found that we had scheduled three times as much work in one year as we could reasonably handle. The results weren't very pleasant or productive.' (Programme manager – automotive supply firm)

The above scenario is very typical of many organisations that have no mechanism for determining their total workload. The alternative is to move to *programme* or *portfolio management*. A programme is a number of projects being undertaken with a particular element in common – sometimes a strategic objective (e.g. an environmental management programme), other times a particular client or group of clients (e.g. one IT firm has a programme developing solutions for the water industry) and others a particular technology (e.g. all the mobile communications firms have programmes for the development of products associated with the third generation of mobile communications devices). Portfolio management is very similar, except that there is less of a common theme to the projects, other than the resource set being used.

Programme management is facilitated by two major devices:

- an aggregate project plan;
- a project office.

The aggregate project plan

The aggregate project plan is essential to keep control of the projects that the organisation is undertaking. Firms often have a good picture of their repetitive operations – they have a high level of visibility and it is generally easy to see what is happening with them. Projects, on the other hand, with the exception of major construction projects, are less visible and require some overall picture to be maintained of precisely what is going on in the organisation. Aggregating or providing a concise statement of all project activities is the objective of the aggregate project plan.

An aggregate project plan does the following:

- assesses the contribution of each project to the organisational strategy;
- determines using objective criteria what projects are to be undertaken;

- ranks the relative importance of the projects being carried out;
- sets the timing of those projects;
- assesses the capability, resource and logic requirements of each project.

Without this step, it can be observed that firms:

- take on too many projects, resulting in overstretched resources and diluting the attention paid to the really important projects;
- fail to limit the scope of projects, allowing non-benefit-generating activities to carry on unchecked (see Chapter 4 for more on scope management);
- tend to expend resources on what Drucker (1955) referred to as 'investments in managerial ego' – projects that will yield little benefit but have an emotional attachment for the manager or director promoting them;
- have project goals that are out of line with organisational objectives;
- ignore key issues concerning projects until it is too late;
- lack balance between short-term (reactive) goals and long-term (strategic/ proactive) ones.

Having assessed the workload of project staff (which in many cases will include ongoing work in addition to project tasks), many firms are surprised to find just how overloaded their personnel are. Keeping track of the workload is an important contribution that programme management can make. The means for this is to keep a log of the available person-hours (number of people multiplied by the hours they are available in a time period) and to allocate these by project. There is frequently a tendency to underestimate the amount of time required for activities (particularly where there is some uncertainty regarding the outcome), resulting in an over-commitment of resources. Furthermore, there is no scope for any flexibility, which, as we will see both later in this chapter and in section 4.1 on innovation, is a key component of success for many projects.

The capabilities or competencies required for the project portfolio should also be considered at this level. There may be key resources or people that are critical to the processes. In addition, many firms do not consider their key competencies, trying instead to do everything themselves. This is rarely a successful strategy – particularly where technology is concerned. Where a requirement is outside the firm's set of core competencies, the requirements of external partners or contractors should be discussed.

There is an additional consideration for the aggregate project plan. People rarely know the relative importance of the projects on which they are working or their contribution to organisational strategy. Furthermore, taking on too many projects causes stress for the people carrying them out. This is compounded by confusion about what is urgent and what is important. There should be only a restricted set of activities that any individuals undertake that are both urgent and important. It is the responsibility of the senior management team to ensure this.

The above raises the fundamental question of just how many projects a firm can undertake at any one time. There is, of course, no universal answer. However, one firm, visited as part of a research project, had 72 development projects ongoing at the time, with one manager and eight staff. The result was an obvious confusion about the relative priorities of the projects, and a highly stressful work environment. Furthermore, the task for the manager was enormous. For instance, which projects should each person be working on at any one time? Inevitably, the projects worked on were those where the customers were screaming the loudest. The knock-on effect was that staff would start work on one project, and then be moved onto another as the priorities changed, to appease the latest angry customer. The effects of this are very stressful for the individual and highly unproductive for the organisation. They will be discussed further in Chapter 6.

For the development organisation, a move away from the old system of 'whoever shouts loudest' to a clear system of priorities reduced the workload from 72 projects to 12. This sounds draconian, as many projects had to be put on-hold or abandoned completely. The positive effect was incredible – the firm successfully completed twice as many projects that year as it had ever done in the past with the same resources. In addition, the working conditions improved immeasurably and the workload and flow through the department became not only faster, but more predictable.[5]

Having established the programme or portfolio of projects that the organisation will undertake in any given time period, the issue then comes of how to support these projects in their execution and ensure their continued contribution to organisational objectives. One increasingly popular means of achieving this is through the application of a *project office*.

The project office

Many organisations, particularly from sectors that regularly run large-scale projects, use project offices to assist in all aspects of the management of project work. This is constituted as a function alongside other functions within the organisation. At one time, it was limited to large-scale engineering firms, but now the project office is a regular feature in companies including Vodafone, Computacenter and most of the high-street banks (though we are still more likely to find a project office in a large organisation than a small one). These firms have added this function, to run alongside other functions in the business where much of their activity becomes project-focused. This additional function provides recognition of the importance of project activities, and in particular, the need for project management professionals to run projects. The relationship between the project and the project office is shown in Fig. 3.3.

The office provides a central facility with the skills and knowledge of how to run project processes. This can be drawn on by the project manager to help ensure that the project is given the best chance of success. The office can provide key project staff, often including the project manager, but also including project planners, accountants, staff to carry out review activities and consultants. Resources that may be under the control of the project office include any project planning software system that is used. The support role includes one of personal support to individuals, including training and mentoring (personal counselling and assistance), and sharing of experience where problems are encountered that have occurred elsewhere. The project office can also provide checks and controls on the project processes,

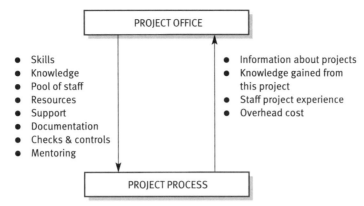

Figure 3.3 Relationship between the project and the project office

assisting in the establishment of checkpoints (see Chapter 4) and control measures (see Chapter 11).

All this additional support to the project process does not come free and, it must be stated, is contrary to the current business pressures to de-layer and remove people not directly concerned with working on the project outcome. It is maintained by those organisations that do use this way of working that any downside element, including the increased overhead cost, is more that compensated for by the increased project success. Experience also showed that there was considerable benefit from having a consistent approach to running projects and the advice provided prevented problems such as teams overpromising on project deliverables or failing to properly analyse the risks associated with their work.

The projects must, however, bear the overhead cost of running the office. Other contributions from the project to the office include the stream of knowledge and experience that the projects generate. The role of the office in this respect is marshalling and managing this knowledge. People who have been working on projects and show an interest in a project management career can use the project office as a way of moving to take a greater role in future projects. For example, a marketing person may enjoy the project environment more than the day-to-day activities of the marketing function and wish to become more involved with projects. The professionalisation of the role through the project office provides a route for such an individual to progress within the organisation.

The following quotation summarises the discussion of the resource co-ordination function.

'Managing projects is, it is said, like juggling three balls – cost, quality and time. Programme Management (portfolio management, multi-project management) is like a organising a troupe of jugglers all juggling their three balls and swapping balls from time to time.' (Reiss, 1996)

The issue of 'juggling' cost, quality and time (and other objectives), is the subject of the next section.

3.5 Project and Organisational Goals

There are many facets of the issue of relating project strategy to organisational strategy. The issues are shown in Fig. 3.4.

The figure shows that projects can be broadly classified as either *'direct revenue-earning'* or *'organisational change'*. The first category would include completing a consultancy assignment, a construction project or generally any work usually carried out for a third party for which you or your organisation is paid. The second category would include changes to an organisation's IT system, a merger or a new business start-up. These projects do not directly earn anything, though the intention is that there will be some benefit from them in the long run. Their cases do have some overlap, but the strategic aspects of each are essentially different. These will be considered in turn.

Strategy and direct revenue-earning projects

The strategic input here is the organisational objectives, as shown in Fig. 3.4. This would be of the form – we are in business to be the fastest **OR** the best **OR** the cheapest providers of these projects. This can then be reflected into the project objectives – as conformance and performance objectives for key criteria – usually starting with time, cost and quality. These form the so-called *'iron triangle'*. However, such an approach is limited. We will consider whether there is a need to consider the further element of *flexibility* and whether a wider range of measures would, in fact, be beneficial.

The first consideration is to determine the nature of the three key objectives. These have been at the heart of consideration in project management for many years, and while limited on their own, are still the basis for any consideration of project objectives. As a minimum, the project manager must define these and then put in place a project process to ensure that these objectives are met. This approach stresses *conformance* to the stated objectives as being the most important

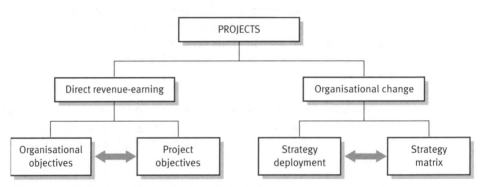

Figure 3.4 Projects and organisational strategy

Table 3.1 Conformance versus performance attributes of time, cost and quality

	Time	*Cost*	*Quality*
Performance	Shortest possible	Cheapest possible	Highest level
Conformance	As planned	As budgeted	As specified

for measuring project success. This is a measure of the reliability required of the project system, expressed as:

- Can the project be guaranteed to deliver on time?
- Will the project finish within budget?
- Will the project meet the specified level of quality?

Taking this further, the emphasis in many business projects today has shifted to excellence being defined in terms of real *performance*, expressed as:

- What is the shortest possible project duration?
- What is the lowest cost?
- What is the highest level of quality that can be achieved?

The mechanisms by which the project manager assures conformance are different from those that ensure performance. For example, by selecting low-cost suppliers, the project manager may attempt to ensure that the project is delivered at minimum cost (performance). Whether it is in fact deliverable is determined by the actions of that manager to secure guarantees that the price (in addition to delivery and quality) will be achieved in practice (conformance). Table 3.1 summarises these characteristics.

Time and cost criteria are relatively straightforward concepts. In practice, determining whether key objectives have been achieved can be a matter of some argument and commercial significance. However, one of the least understood concepts is *quality*. There are a number of manufacturing and service definitions which we will explore later in this text, including the relationship between expectations and perceptions of customers (and other stakeholders) of both the project process and its outcomes.

Time, cost and quality are incomplete as a statement of requirements for a project, as they assume that such objectives are fixed and known in advance of the project starting. In an ideal world and many project managers' dreams, this would indeed be the case. The process of developing strategy for projects would be easier if customers always knew exactly what they wanted at the outset and were able to communicate this. As will be discussed later, it is the responsibility of the project manager to ensure that customer input is obtained by the project, and there are a number of methods available for doing this. There are, however, many occasions when the requirements of the customer are likely to change as the project progresses. The ability of the project system to address this change is expressed by its flexibility. Such flexibility needs to be accounted for at the outset, as there are penalties in relation to the other objectives – flexibility costs. For example, a firm that makes custom-engineered components is contracted to supply parts to an automotive assembler. It is asked to provide a quotation for new parts, but the specification requires some flexibility, as it will not be determined exactly until the last minute. With this required flexibility, the firm will need to hold back the making up of tooling, requiring this to be made by an express service rather than its normal supplier. This design flexibility therefore has potential cost implications, which, unless built into the estimates, will cause the firm to perform poorly on the cost conformance aspect.

How do we decide which are the most important objectives and thereby come up with the project objectives? First, we need to understand the nature of the trade-offs that exist in the project. Then, with knowledge of our organisational strategy, we can decide which of the objectives are required to conform and which must be pursued as performance.

Trade-off decisions

Consider the following scenario. You have been set a task, whether an academic assignment or one at work. You are required to produce a particular result in a given time. At the outset of the task you are able to plan your activities towards achieving the goal in the time required. The quality of the outcome is dependent on the time that you have – the longer you have, the more research you would be able to do and the more effort you could possibly put into the presentation of the end result. If you only have a very short time, this clearly limits what you can do, though you could hire somebody to help you. This shows clearly the relationship between three elements of project strategy: time, cost and quality. We say that there is a *trade-off* between these three – that you can have the task completed very quickly, but unless you are prepared to compromise on the quality, you may have to pay more.

A trade-off is, therefore, the prioritisation of the objectives of a project. It is important at this stage, as there are two major occasions where it will affect the decisions made. The first is during planning. If a customer indicates that a specification for a set of project activities is non-negotiable, the resources of time and cost will need to be manipulated around this central objective. Furthermore, it focuses the project on what is really important, as many projects start with unnecessary assumptions regarding what needs to be achieved.

Second, it will affect the decisions made during execution. For example, if the most important objective for a project is to achieve a particular level of cost performance, where problems exist and decisions need to be made, time and quality could be compromised to ensure that the cost objective is met. This does look like a poor compromise but it is the reality, particularly where there are inherent uncertainties in the project. Resources cannot be increasingly stretched to obtain goals that are passing out of sight due to unforeseen problems. It is vital to know in advance what

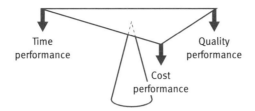

Figure 3.5 Trade-offs in project management

can and cannot be moved should this scenario arise, no matter how undesirable this is in principle. Figure 3.5 illustrates this.

Some authors have claimed that the necessity to consider trade-offs has been removed by modern management practices. The evidence for this is not as convincing as suggested and the pragmatic project manager is still faced with making these decisions. Before committing to a course of action, the manager should, however, consider the assumptions that underlie each of the criteria. For example, if a project is running up against time constraints, it may be worth considering the sequence of activities to see if their rearrangement will yield the necessary time savings. This is before any compromise is made on the cost element (reducing time by other means could incur additional costs).

Having determined the nature of the trade-offs in the project, the most important ones are determined by our organisational strategy. As stated earlier, this provides the guidance that we compete in a market or market segment by offering projects as the fastest or best or cheapest supplier. If the organisational objective is to be the fastest, then this is a *performance objective*, while the cost and quality criteria are *conformance objectives*. As a minimum, we must hit our conformance objectives. We will focus on improving in our performance objectives. The Permanent Way Company, identified in Project Management in Practice at the end of Chapter 2, started their improvement project by considering their conformance and performance objectives. Their customers were telling them that their technical quality and costs were acceptable but their major complaint was that projects took too long and were often late. This set the scene for determining both organisational objectives, and in turn feeding into an organisational change programme. Their conformance objectives were therefore to be quality and cost, and their performance objective was time.

Other objectives can form part of the conformance requirements of the project – not just time, cost and quality. These may be environmental, ethical, legal, health and safety – indeed any of the constraints identified at the start of Chapter 2 can become objectives. For the majority of projects though, the iron triangle is a good starting point for consideration.

Having set the framework for determining the conformance and performance objectives of revenue-earning projects, we can now look at an area that has become a significant user of project management practices in recent years – that of organisational change.

Strategy in organisational change projects

Chaos Inc.

> A major bank was in the middle of a drive to cut cash-handling costs at the same time as it was trying to recruit business customers to make more use of ATMs. For the business users, the incentive being offered was that corporate credit card holders would be able to draw cash from ATMs – something they had not been previously allowed to do. Great publicity was generated by this move. The bank's other functions were not so happy about it and this is where the project ran into trouble. The ATMs were operated by one division of the bank, were filled with money by another, connected into the IT system by another and maintained by an outside contractor. All these parties had strong views on who should use the machines, and in particular there was the drive to cut cash-handling costs. Lack of strong leadership meant that the project was stalled for years trying to gain agreement of all the parties concerned. This should have been agreed and sorted at a senior level in the firm before project staff were engaged to operationalise it. The same organisation later found that they had over 500 IT projects running at any one time. No one individual could or was overseeing these and you can imagine the clashes that such a number produced.

The challenge for organisations here is twofold. The first is to determine a programme of projects that will meet key organisational change requirements. This is *strategy deployment*. The subject of strategy is well developed, as are the methods for delivering projects. The process of strategy deployment comes between these two, and is less well developed. Having determined the projects that will be carried out as part of the desired organisational change, the task is then to ensure that the downside elements of each are resolved. This is achieved through a *strategy matrix*.

Strategy deployment

The task of strategy deployment[6] is well established in a few world-class organisations, but less so both in general practice and academic writings. It was a central feature of the Total Quality Management movement and more recently in business excellence models – such as that of the European Foundation for Quality Management. The principle is that the strategies and projects of an organisation should show a high level of '*coherence*'. This is where, as a minimum, all projects are part of some overall plan for the organisation and forming a recognisable contribution to that plan. Chaos Inc. above clearly needed some help here!

Masters of this particular art include the Toyota Motor Company and further examples of the tools of policy deployment are included in Chapter 15. Particular features of this process of deployment are:

Table 3.2 **Strategy deployment table**

Objectives Level 1	Activities Level 1	Objectives Level 2	Activities Level 2	Objectives Level 3	Activities Level 3
Reduce new product lead-time by 20%	1 Establish managed portfolio of projects	Achieve balanced work allocations	Determine workload due to current projects		
		Close down 80% of projects that are over 2 years old	Examine potential of all projects over 2 years old		
	2 Re-engineer project processes	Understand current processes	Map current processes	Identify strengths and weaknesses in processes	Conduct review of all major projects over the past 3 years
		Increase level of concurrency in processes	Co-locate staff for major projects		
			Train project facilitators		
	3 Implement new design technology	Reduce prototyping time by 80%	Install rapid-prototyping equipment		
		Reduce product engineering time by 38%	Install new version of design software		

- Objectives aligned throughout the organisation by making strategy highly visible and well understood. Conflicts between functional and project objectives are resolved at a high level;
- All members of the organisation are responsible for the process – strategy is no longer the domain of senior management alone and individuals can show the impact of their contribution to organisational objectives through their contribution to change projects;
- Progress towards objectives monitored through highly visible measures (see Chapter 11);
- Objectives are based on customer needs – retaining the customer-focused nature of the organisation – as illustrated by the Permanent Way Company example in the previous chapter.

The strategy deployment table (Table 3.2) provides a means for project managers to agree objectives for their projects and illustrate how these relate to organisational objectives. These are ideal where an organisation has a large number of projects ongoing and a manager is responsible for more than one project. They can be used both between and within organisations to ensure consistency of objectives.

Table 3.2 shows the deployment of a strategy by a firm to reduce its new product lead-time (how long it takes to bring a new product through from the initial idea to

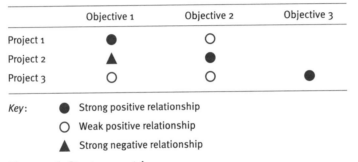

	Objective 1	Objective 2	Objective 3
Project 1	●	○	
Project 2	▲	●	
Project 3	○	○	●

Key: ● Strong positive relationship

○ Weak positive relationship

▲ Strong negative relationship

Figure 3.6 Strategy matrix

when it is launched into a market) by 20 per cent. It is important that the objective set is quantifiable wherever possible – particularly a higher-level objective. This is then deployed into a series of second-level objectives. These include achieving balanced workloads, that is, a balance between the amount of time available and the amount of work that is required to be carried out. As is the case for 'increase level of concurrency in processes', objectives may have more than one activity associated with them.

Having ascertained the portfolio of projects and obtained objectives for each of them, these will need to be amplified into a full strategy for each project. This moves us to the next stage of the strategy process – that of using the strategy matrix to balance the objectives.

An example of a *strategy matrix* is shown in Fig. 3.6. This will be used further in the consideration of the issue of *policy deployment*. The map shows the relationship between three projects and three key strategic objectives. Each of the projects addresses one of the key strategic objectives. However, Project 2 will have a negative effect on Objective 1. This indicates that the project should be reconsidered to see precisely the nature of this impact, and whether the negative effect can be removed. Having determined the project objectives, these are then implemented through the measurement system that is put in place.

3.6 Project Performance Measurement

Tell me how you measure me, and I'll tell you how I'll behave. (Goldratt, 1990)

Consider the following (unlikely) scenario. A new call management system is installed in an call-centre on time and on budget. It meets all its requirements in terms of the specification provided for it. Surely this must be considered to be a success? With the conventional time, cost and quality measures, it certainly would be.

However, further investigation shows that regardless of the specification, the users of the system are very unhappy with it and are threatening to stop using it. Their needs were not considered and the system has made their task far more lengthy than it used to be, making it far more difficult for the operators to earn their bonuses. The adverse reaction has meant that the payback time for the system is going to be far longer than planned, causing problems with the client firm's plans

Table 3.3 NPD metrics

Type of measure	Characteristic measured
Process measures	Product development cost, time and conformance to quality procedures
Short-term outcome measures	Product performance level, desirability to market, flexibility of design to be changed to meet emergent customer needs
Longer-term outcome measures	Payback period, customer satisfaction, percentage of business being generated by the new product, market share, customisability for high-margin markets

for expansion. The firm decide not to do further business with the system supplier. Now how much of a success was the project?

If we purely consider the short-term conformance measures, we are limiting what project managers will aim for. A wider, more appropriate set is required. In the area of new product development, for instance, a selection of a set of metrics is frequently used as shown in Table 3.3.

So not only what do we measure, but how and when do we measure it? There are clearly a range of measures, even within the basic time, cost and quality criteria. Measurement will be discussed further in Chapters 11 and 14, but these are vital as the means of checking whether strategy is in fact being implemented.

3.7 Relevant Areas of the Bodies of Knowledge

There is little in either of the bodies of knowledge concerning the strategic context or aspects of projects. Given the importance of this area and the impact that it has on projects in general, this is a significant omission. There are some points of relevance in the APM version for programme management, and these are given in Table 3.4.

Table 3.4 Relevant area of the APM body of knowledge

Relevant section	Title	Summary
11	Programme management	Defines programme management and some of the tasks that are done under this heading.
20	Project success criteria	Defines some of the terms used here, including requirements, critical success factors and key performance indicators.

3.8 Summary

Many of the problems faced by project managers are caused by decisions or lack of decisions at a high level in their organisations. If project performance is to be reformed, changes must be made to the way that projects are managed, right through the organisation. A summary of this process is shown in Fig. 3.7.

Figure 3.7 shows how the vision created for an organisation is reflected through to the project activities. The input from competitive analysis might include, for example, an analysis of the organisation's strengths, weaknesses, opportunities and threats (SWOT). It may also consider the impact of changes in technology, new entrants to the market (if a commercial organisation) and other market force changes (e.g. currency movements, legal changes) that will affect the organisation. The other input to this process comes from the organisation itself – demonstrating that strategy is a two-way process.

The vision is to be realised through the organisational strategy in the first instance. This provides a focus for all the activities of the organisation, including all projects. Focus is an important concept here, which we define as those aspects of our product or service offering into which we are going to invest time, money and effort, with the objective of securing improved/superior performance.

Having determined the theoretical focus, it has been observed that many senior management teams make the mistake of assuming that this will automatically be followed through by those who make decisions within the organisation. This does

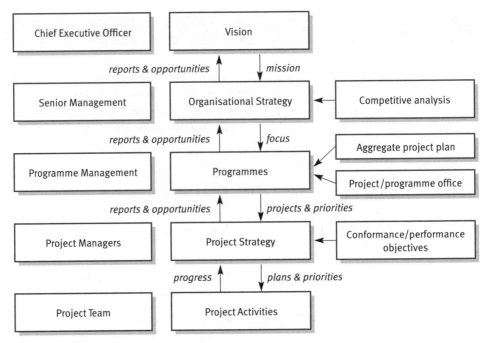

Figure 3.7 The total process

not always happen and results in problems for project managers trying to operate in the middle of interdepartmental conflicts, where different views of the mission and focus prevail. The alternative is to instigate programme or portfolio management. Two of the devices that assist programme management are the aggregate project plan and the project office. These ensure that the capacity and capability exist to do the work required by the strategy, and to keep an overview of the many projects going on in an organisation at any one time.

Programmes consist of a number of projects. These may be externally generated – as direct revenue earners which will require their own set of strategies. This must be in line with corporate objectives regarding the basis on which the organisation will compete in order to meet customer needs. The project strategy in this case would include both conformance and performance objectives. In addition, organisational change projects should be part of the strategy deployment of the organisation and their objectives should be put through a strategy matrix to remove conflicts before the project starts.

The objective of this process is to clear the way for project activities to be undertaken in a coherent manner with the organisational objectives, focused and with minimal conflict. This process is simple in concept, but very challenging in application. It is notable that in organisations where this does happen, there is an almost palpable feeling of everybody working in the one direction, with many of the stresses and failures that are caused by 'the system' avoided. This is surely a worthwhile objective for our organisations!

Project Management in Practice

A new campus for the University of Rummidge (with apologies to David Lodge)

In May 1999 a chance meeting between the leader of the town council of Splot and the Vice-chancellor of the University of Rummidge started a project that would lead to the opening of a new campus in Splot.

This appeared to be an ideal opportunity for both parties – the university was unable to expand further on its existing site due to local planning restrictions. This was despite having a well-known brand-name in the market, particularly for management education. The town was in the process of applying to become a city – a status that would confer additional prestige on the area, and almost certain political success for whoever could make it happen. It had been the recipient of around €4 billion of investment in recent years from leading-edge companies in the automotive and electronics sectors. These new firms were providing a major demand for a wide variety of higher education services that the existing institutions were incapable of providing. Local unemployment was virtually zero and firms were having problems recruiting for all types of work.

A number of opportunities presented themselves to the Splot council (see below for organisational structure). These included setting up their own university, in conjunction with local businesses, and accessing a remote provider through a virtual campus. The first was rejected on the grounds that they did not have the expertise to do this, and the second on the basis that despite the low unemployment and prevalance of high-technology industries, the majority of the people of Splot did not have Internet access. The availability of school premises in the middle of the town, which could be readily converted into a campus and which was in an area prioritised for redevelopment, sealed the decision. Shutting down the school was a decision eased by the falling numbers of pupils.

For the University of Rummidge, there were likewise other options. Expansion into areas that would relieve the dependence on government funding was always a priority, and operations beyond the physical limitations of the campus were increasingly attractive. Internet-based activities were an option for investment, but there were other initiatives in place to promote these. In addition, forming direct relationships with one or more of the large companies in the area for provision of integrated higher education services was considered. The university's management team favourably viewed the opening of a new campus.

In order to progress the work, a joint venture organisation entitled 'The University of Rummidge in Splot' was established with the brief to '. . . *explore all the various options that will permit the establishment of a permanent and physical presence by the University of Rummidge in Splot*'.

The joint venture organisation reported in September 1999, recommending to both the university and the council that the school premises be converted ready for courses to be run in September 2000. A budget for the conversion of the premises and establishment of the campus (including provision of library and IT facilities) of €15 million was suggested and funding was underwritten by both organisations, subject to grants being approved from central government and sponsorship being obtained from local companies.

It is September 1999 and the main part of the project is now about to start. Academic staff at Rummidge are not impressed by this move as much of the negotiation has taken place without their input. Moreover, Splot is around a one-hour drive from Rummidge, traffic permitting. There are also significant reservations about the location of the campus in a relatively run-down district of the town, and whether there will be sufficient buy-in from local people to make it worthwhile. In addition, there was debate as to whether courses (both undergraduate and postgraduate) would be run at both sites, and whether there would be resources available to assist with the workloads of the departments (both academic and administrative) caused by the new courses. Some of the administrative departments were also unclear as to how the new campus would affect their workloads.

The organisational structures are shown in outline in Figures 3.8 and 3.9.

Case questions

1 What are the strategic objectives for each of the organisations involved? Are there any conflicts in these objectives?
2 There are many projects that will be taking place in the process of opening the new campus. How might running them as a programme help the chances of success?
3 How might a project office be of use in this case?
4 What would appropriate success measures be for the project?

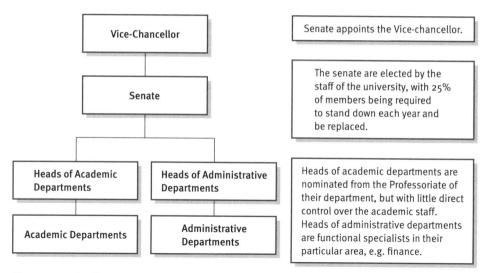

Figure 3.8 Outline structure – University of Rummidge

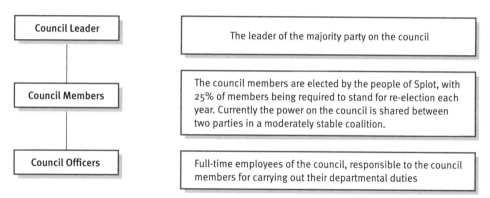

Figure 3.9 Outline structure – Splot Town Council

Selecting a personal project

A group of students, as part of their coursework, have to carry out a group project where they run an event or perform a particular task to demonstrate their ability to plan, execute and review a project. They are assessed on the basis of originality of their idea, the quality of the planning process and the content of a report following the project that reflects on their experiences of the project. They have a meeting and come up with a number of ideas. These are:

	Originality	Demonstrate skills	Produce good report	Stretching	Independent of others	Avoids financial risk	FUN
Yearbook	✗	✓	✓	–	–	✗	✗
Video	✓	✓	✓	✓	✓	–	✓
Ball	–	✓	✓	✓	✗	✗✗✗	✓
Treasure hunt	✗	–	–	✗	–	✓	–
Accident awareness day	✓	✓	–	–	✗	✓	–

Figure 3.10 Decision matrix

- Produce a yearbook for their class group;
- Develop a short video promoting the course that they are studying;
- Run a formal ball for the entire department;
- Organise a treasure hunt one Sunday;
- Organise an 'accident awareness' day for schoolchildren.

The meeting then had to consider which one of these was the first choice. The next activity was then to decide on the decision criteria by which each of the proposals would be judged. The first three were given by the requirements of the assessment – that of originality of idea, whether the idea would allow demonstration of project management skills and whether it would enable them to produce a good report. The group added some further characteristics that they felt that they wanted their project to have. These were:

- It should be sufficiently stretching of the group;
- It should not depend too heavily on other people for its success;
- It must not require them to undertake any large financial risk;
- It must be fun for the group to do.

They then put this together as shown in Fig. 3.10.

You may disagree with the rating that the group gave some of the items, but this is how the group saw the options. They also saw very clearly as a group that there was one clear choice for them – the video. It also told them that the financial risk element (cost of hiring editing facilities and production of the finished product) needed to be minimised.

Case questions/exercises

1 Under what circumstances might this approach to selection be beneficial?
2 Use the iron triangle to produce a prioritised set of objectives for the project.
3 How might the measures of success change over time?

Key Terms

vision

mission

strategy process

performance

programme / portfolio management

project office

revenue-earning

objectives

strategy deployment

trade-offs

performance measurement

coherence

strategy

conformance

strategic capability

aggregate project plan

multi-tasking

organisational change

focus

strategy matrix

iron triangle

Review Questions and Further Exercises

1 Is there more to project management than a Gantt chart?

2 What does 'the system' mean in the context of project management?

3 What are the impacts at a project level of poor strategy processes?

4 What is coherence and why is it worth pursuing?

5 What is the role of strategy in project management?

6 At the project level, what is the strategy process?

7 Why is an aggregate project plan beneficial for an organisation that pursues a number of projects at the same time?

8 What is the difference between conformance and performance objectives?

9 What is a trade-off in the context of a project that you are involved with? How did you resolve the problem of choosing which aspect you would compromise on? Was this the right choice?

10 Why is it so important for project activities to be in line with organisational strategy?

References

Buttrick, R. (2000) *The Project Workout*, 2nd edition, Financial Times Management, London.

Deming, W.E. (1986) *Out of the Crisis – Quality Productivity and Competitive Position*, MIT Center for Advanced Engineering Study, Cambridge, MA.

Drucker, P. (1955) *Management*, Butterworth-Heinemann, Oxford.

Goldratt, E.M. (1990) *The Haystack Syndrome*, North River Press, New York.

Hayes, R.H. and Wheelwright, S.C. (1984) *Restoring Our Competitive Edge: Competing Through Manufacturing*, Wiley, New York.

Johnson, G. and Scholes, K. (1999) *Exploring Corporate Strategy*, 5th edition, Financial Times Prentice Hall, Harlow.

Lord, M.A. (1993) 'Implementing Strategy Through Project Management', *Long Range Planning*, Vol. 26, No. 1, pp. 76–85.

Reiss, G. (1996) *Programme Management Demystified*, E & FN Spon, London.

Further Information

Akao, Y. (ed.) (1991) *Hoshin Kanri – Policy Deployment for Successful TQM*, Productivity Press, New York.

Atkinson, R. (1999) 'Project Management: Cost, Time and Quality, Two Best Guesses and a Phenomenon, its [sic] Time to Accept Other Success Criteria', *International Journal of Project Management*, Vol. 17, No. 6, pp. 337–342.

Baccarini, D. (1999) 'The Logical Framework Method for Defining Project Success', *Project Management Journal*, Vol. 30, No. 4, pp. 25–32.

Bernstein, S. (2000) 'Project Office in Practice', *Project Management Journal*, Vol. 31, No. 4, pp. 4–6.

Block, T.R. and Frame, J.D. (1998) *The Project Office*, Crisp Learning, Menlo Park, CA.

Fowler, A. and Walsh, M. (1999) 'Conflicting Perceptions of Success in an Information Systems Project', *International Journal of Project Management*, Vol. 17, pp. 1–10.

Grundy, A. and Brown, L. (2001) *Strategic Project Management: Creating organisational breakthroughs*, Thomson Learning, London.

Obeng, E. (1995) 'The Role of Project Management in Implementing Strategy' in Crainer, S. (ed.) *The Financial Times Handbook of Management*, Financial Times Pitman Publishing, London, pp. 178–93.

Mintzberg, H. (2000) *The Rise and Fall of Strategic Planning*, Financial Times Prentice Hall, Harlow.

Newbold, R. (1999) *Project Management in the Fast Lane*, St Lucie Press, Boca Raton, FL.

Wheelwright, S.C. and Clark, K.B. (1992) 'Creating Project Plans to Focus Product Development', *Harvard Business Review*, March–April, pp. 70–82.

www.efqm.org for more information on the European Foundation for Quality Management Business Excellence Model.

Notes

1 The project baseline is the original schedule of activities for the project. By changing the baseline you are 'moving the goalposts', as described in 'Ready, fire, aim' in Chapter 1.

2 For explanation of this technique and further examples, see Chapter 13.

3 It is not intended to provide a detailed consideration of the many and varied views of strategy here. For this, you should refer to dedicated texts, such as Johnson and Scholes (1999).

4 This follows the terminology of Hayes and Wheelwright, (1984) in describing the relationship between operations strategy and organisational strategy.

5 For further examples of this type of change, see Newbold (1999).

6 Another term that is used to describe this process is *Hoshin Kanri* or Policy Deployment.

4 Project definition

Even the longest journey begins with a single step.

A project may begin in many ways: a blinding flash of inspiration on the part of an individual or group, one that responds to a stated need on the part of a particular client, or one that is the inevitable poisoned chalice – handed to you and already set up for disaster. Whatever the root of the project, the study of excellence in projects has shown that they are characterised by a combination of order and chaos. Indeed, the chaos usually comes first, followed by the order or system that a well-developed process can bring. This order and chaos do not always exist comfortably together, but are vital components of projects.

The purpose of this chapter is to outline the process that a project will follow. This understanding of the process will facilitate the detailed planning (see Chapter 5). Moreover, we will need to determine whether any further work on the project should be carried out or the project terminated.

Before we start with detailed planning, which will itself consume time and resources, it is necessary to take an overview of the project. This provides a notion of whether the project is in fact feasible and, if so, then we can proceed with the detailed planning. This overview step is vital if we are to retain the focus of the project on the key objectives. It further provides a framework for what follows.

This chapter focuses on developing the content of the project through to the first stage of designing the process by which it will be delivered. These provide the basis for the detailed planning that follows. Running through this is the need to gain support for the work to be carried out from all stakeholders.

Contents

Learning Objectives

By the time you have completed this chapter, you will be able to:
- Demonstrate the role and importance of creativity in projects;
- Identify the need for and the features of a scope control system;
- Provide an outline of a project process;
- Construct basic stage-gate models;
- Recognise the benefits of constructing a process map at this stage and identify a process mapping technique;
- Demonstrate the importance of stakeholder management and the features of a basic communications plan.

4.1 Developing the Concept

Chapter 2 identified that there are many different types of activities, all taking place under the heading of 'projects'. Depending on their degree of novelty these were first-timers, as . . . but . . . s and painting by numbers. In Chapter 3 we identified two further groups of projects – direct revenue earning and organisational change projects. All these have need for creative input to the product (the outcome of the project) or the process (the means by which the project is carried out), but especially where there is a high degree of novelty. Projects start by a huge range of means – some are presented as well-worked and highly documented, through to the individual who wants to pursue a particular idea.

A common format in industries where projects are undertaken for external clients involves the customer or client providing a *brief* or *terms of reference* and the project manager replying with a *proposal* or *Project Initiation Document* (PID). For many personal and corporate projects (including new product development), the first stage of any project is *conceptualisation* (see Chapter 2). During this part of the work, there is great opportunity for creativity, as the options open to the emerging project team (which may be nothing more than an informal group at this point) are identified, discussed and evaluated. This creative maelstrom is so important to modern projects, but so often is squeezed out of the process by tight deadlines and an ever-present need for quick results. Indeed, read many project management books and the topic of creativity is rarely given a mention. Yet some of the most successful firms in the world have this at the centre of their processes, and create space within their people's time for innovation. What we need now is to enshrine this into the process so that it becomes part of the 'way we work' rather than an optional extra. There are situations where leaving the brief as wide open as possible is essential. While this is an example of a large corporation and their efforts to bring creativity to the organisation, the opening phase of the project is an opportunity to envision the future – to see what the project might do. As discussed in the Project Management in Practice example at the end of Chapter 2, the early stage of a personal project or dissertation should be one of exploration, where there are more questions than answers, and the objective is to create as many options for the project as possible. As the boxed example below shows, this is vital in many areas, including new product development projects.

Concept development in new product development

New product development is rarely a linear activity – with the outcome logically following the intention at the start. Particularly in the early stages of the work, there will be an increase in the number of possibilities available, as new ideas emerge. This is highly desirable, provided that the scope of the project is maintained (see following section). At some point however, the ideas will have to be narrowed down, as they are unlikely to all be feasible. This is done by *screening* – where the ideas are gradually filtered by, for example:

- Marketing assessment of the ideas – which ones are most attractive to the market;
- Financial appraisal, such as potential to develop a good rate of return on the investment required of it;
- Strategic – does this product fit with our current mission?

This process is illustrated in Fig. 4.1.

Figure 4.1 shows the inputs to the process, including R&D (research & development), suppliers (see Chapter 12), customers and competitors. Staff also have a big input to the process, and this is not just applicable to physical products. The Disney Corporation, for example, employs a number of 'imaginers' who have the job of creating new ideas in entertainment – they are there to '*blue-sky*' – a term which infers that they spend the day gazing skyward waiting for inspiration as to what the next *Lion King* will be.

At the output side, it is intended that there will a successful new product, but as the 3M example below will show, there are other routes for exploitation of ideas. These include licensing (another organisation paying for the use of your idea), selling the idea, or, as used by many firms today when a new idea comes along, starting a new business to exploit it. Some ideas will also be rejected and some will need to be recycled – possibly into development projects of their own at a later date.

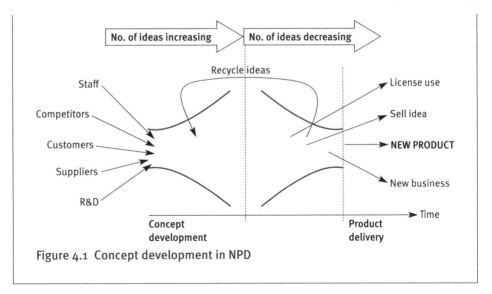

Figure 4.1 Concept development in NPD

So what are the characteristics of highly creative processes? There have been many attempts to develop sets of rules, but they can be summarised in the following list:

- Allow time and space for individuals to carry out the exploration. 3M famously allow their development staff up to 15 per cent of their working time to pursue 'personal projects' – work that is not necessarily directly related to their normal role. The result is a stream of new products, which include the eponymous Post-It note, and a turnover in the sale of these ideas that is predicted to exceed their sales of their own products. There is clearly a financial case therefore for such innovation;
- Protect ownership of ideas. If people feel that the organisation is simply trying to take their ideas from them, they are unlikely to contribute much;
- Encourage *rapid prototyping* to try ideas right at the start and see how they work. This approach to rapidly test ideas and rehearse them – walk through the process and see how they work in practice – should become a cornerstone of modern project management practices;
- Have people at a senior level in the organisation prepared to act as *project champions* who will promote particular ideas and attempt to obtain the necessary resources from the organisation to progress projects with good potential;
- Have a rapid development process ready to take on such ideas and see them through to fruition. This must include clear criteria as to what will be supported by the organisation and what will not.

Instead, we too often kill the innovation to products and processes through over-restrictive processes or, just as badly, through believing that no process at all is required leave the idea with no path for development. Either of these is a considerable loss.

3M and other world-class organisations are notable by not only having this creativity present but also by the effectiveness of the process that follows from that. This is well-planned and directed (not at all as chaotic and unstructured as many would think) and includes the elements of process planning that are described in the rest of this chapter. For the present, the issue of the content of the project rather than the process will continue to be the focus, with the consideration of the role that the project scope plays.

4.2 Scope Management

What is the big issue concerning scope management? Why is it that both the bodies of knowledge considered here and PRINCE2 dedicate significant quantities of effort to ensuring that this is managed not just at the outset but throughout the project? One of the reasons may be seen in the box below.

The Sinclair C5

Initially conceived in the mid-1970s as a four-seater, electrically powered vehicle for under £1000, the concept grabbed a lot of attention. Because it came from such a renowned inventor – Sir Clive Sinclair, famous for one of the first calculators and personal computers – it was a highly popular idea and had no shortage of backers, including Hoover, who kitted out part of their factory for its manufacture. The result at the end of the process was rather different, as shown in Fig. 4.2.

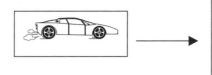 

Figure 4.2 Scope creep
(*Source*: Reproduced courtesy of Austin Area Electric Automobile Association and Mark Polglaze)

The figure shows the results of the phenomenon known as *scope creep*. The original purpose was subtly changed until it no longer represented the original concept. The result was disastrous – the product was a flop and all the firms involved lost substantial sums of money.

Other reasons for the need for explicit management of scope includes making sure that all the parties to the project are agreed what it is that the project is going to do. In many cases, it is appropriate to leave the scope loose early on to enable the creativity described in the previous section. At the end of the definition phase, however, a statement of scope should be agreed as the basis for planning and managing the work that follows. Scope management involves the elements shown in Fig. 4.3.

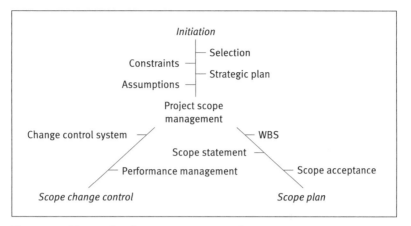

Figure 4.3 Elements of scope management

As can be seen, there are three parts to this – the initiation, which we have already covered. The next part is the generation of a scope plan – including the work breakdown structure (see section 4.4) and generation of a scope statement. This specifies very clearly what is included in the project and, just as importantly, what is excluded. This means that certain related but excluded activities will be performed by others or left for further work. For example, a project to produce a marketing plan for a new product a company was launching had to specifically scope out (exclude) the carrying out of direct market research as part of the process. This would have made the process too long and costly for the organisation concerned. This did, however, provide a limitation to the project.

The last part of the scope generation is to obtain acceptance. This may be via a formal sign-off process where a paying client is involved or simply that a meeting is called where everyone agrees to the scope statement as written. It is useful at least to start with agreement on where the project is going and what it is going to do!

The scope management and control aspects will be discussed further in Chapter 11 on project control. Having outlined the content and the purpose of the product through the concept and scope development activities, the next consideration will be the process by which the project will be delivered.

4.3 The Project Process

So, how will we deliver the project that we have outlined above? The level of formalisation required here, as mentioned above, differs between organisations. Some systemisation here is good, too much is bad – but that is rarely helpful to the project manager. We have two issues to consider here. The first is the level of complexity, as described in Chapter 2. The higher the level of complexity, the higher the level of systemisation that is required. The second factor is custom and practice in the industry or organisation in which you are working. That does not legitimise where inappropriate practices are used in an industry but does recognise the reality of the constraints under which many project managers have to work.

Where a formal proposal is required it should be considered in the following light:

- Who is the proposal for – the investment decision maker or a third party?
- Why is the proposal being requested?

The first part of the analysis in the proposal development should consider the potential customers for the work – are they internal to the organisation or external? In addition, are the customers end-users, investment decision makers or a third party acting on the behalf of one of these? The degree of formalisation will need to be tailored – a bid to an external organisation usually requiring a much higher degree of formality.

In addition, if the project is:

- for an internal customer, there needs to be consistency with the organisation's stated goals or aims;
- for an external customer, the most basic requirement is that they will be able to pay for the work to be carried out. It is pointless generating detailed proposals only to find that the 'customer' is insolvent or the transaction cannot be completed for other reasons. Where the customer is from overseas, it is worth investigating at a very early stage whether or not they are eligible for export credit guarantees, for example;
- going to be appraised by a set of people, it is useful to know their backgrounds. For example, where a client has a detailed knowledge of the subject area, more detail of the nature of the work to be carried out should be included, or, for an investment decision maker, details of the cost–benefit analysis.

The reason for the proposal being requested should also be examined to ensure that the result is appropriate:

- if it is to be part of a full competitive bid for funding, then it is probably worth investing the time to prepare a detailed proposal;
- if it is to be a first examination of the possibilities of such a project, with the customer deciding to find out what would be involved if the project were to be undertaken, then an overview proposal should be submitted;
- if the proposal has been requested as part of organisational policy to consider more than one supplier for any product or service, it is worth finding out whether or not an existing supplier already has the contract before investing your time. Providing a very rough proposal can be dangerous as the impression that is left with the customer may not favour you in the future. It may be worth in such a case declining to put in a proposal – though this again should be determined by the aims of the organisation.

Other scenarios where the supplier may decide not to submit a proposal (also called a 'bid') include when the capability (organisational capability), resource (e.g. if capital is already tied up in other projects) or desirability (e.g. moving into direct competition with an existing customer) is questionable.

The process of preparing and submitting the proposal is the organisation's opportunity to sell itself to the potential customer. 'You only have one chance to make a good first impression', so basics like ensuring that the proposal document reaches the customer on time, is presented in a way that demands attention and is free from stupid mistakes (particularly spelling and grammatical errors) is essential. This is only part of the process. The pre-sell to the client can involve visits, informal discussions and general information gathering by both parties. The intention, as set out in describing the project environment, is to foster partnership relationships between the two parties. The focus is on long-term mutual benefit rather than short-term gain at the expense of the longer term.

The proposal itself should contain:

- an executive summary – provides the basic information in a few words, ideally one that can be read in one minute;
- the main body of the report – diagrams and pictures convey information much better than reams of text. In order to ensure that the presentation is consistent, a standard set of forms is often used which also makes it far more difficult to leave items out (see PMI, 1998). Checklists are also of great value in compiling documents;
- appendices – any information that is summarised in the main report can be included in longer form here, along with supporting evidence for any major points made.

The plan is the first step in providing the means of satisfying the requirements of the project owner (the person wanting the outcome) or sponsor (the person in charge of the funding for the outcome). It is the beginning of the project manager's input to ensuring that, wherever possible, potential problems are identified and solved in advance. The plan is an explicit statement of the intended timing of project activities and the basis for estimating the resource requirements. Problem and error prevention, rather than rectification, is one of the main drivers of the planning process.

The objective of this part of the process is to provide an overview of what the project, should it go ahead, would look like. With the plethora of modern tools available through the medium of the computer, it is easy to forget the objectives of the plan, which are discussed here. Some of the basic techniques for establishing the logic and timing of activities are presented.

A first look at planning

To call project planning a 'process' implies that there is a well-defined route for the planner to take. This is not always clear, and a generic model of planning is difficult to construct. Planning as a process involves the consumption of resources – it has costs associated with it. The project manager has to decide on the balance between the costs incurred in the process and the benefits that will be reaped from it, as illustrated by Fig. 4.4. Costs associated with the planning process include:

- planned labour and associated expenses (travel, subsistence, etc.);
- planner's tools – may include computer assistance;

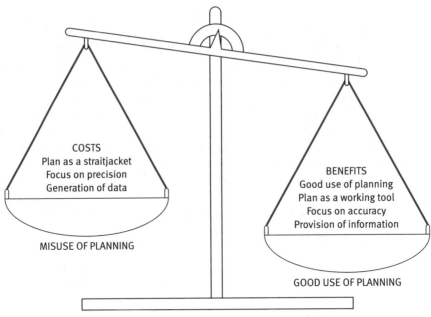

Figure 4.4 Balancing costs and benefits

- cost of preparing the written plan – typing, binding, etc.;
- opportunity cost – what the planner and others drawn into the planning process could have been doing otherwise (e.g. working on an existing project).

In order for the planning process to be value adding and not just cost adding, the benefits of the activity have to be shown. These may be identified as:

- avoiding the costs of the chaos that would otherwise take place with an unplanned activity;
- providing a basis for a formalised evaluation process – filtering out projects that will provide a negative return;
- identifying problems in advance and being able to resolve them on paper.

The time that a planner spends preparing the plan should reflect the potential benefits of the activity. Figure 4.4 shows the positive and negative effects that the plan can have on project activities.

The plan as a working tool or organisational straitjacket

One of the paradoxes that the project manager has to address is whether the output of the planning process remains a working tool or becomes a form of organisational 'straitjacket'. As a working tool, plans are used to help decision-making and guide future activities. A well-balanced plan will guide the actions of the project team, without the need to define to the absolute detail level what each person will do for every minute of every day. Project plans should change as circumstances change. People can get so involved in the plan that the project objectives are forgotten, with the planning becoming an end in itself rather than a means to an end. If the techniques that follow are applied intelligently, changed circumstances can be matched by a new course of action. The phrase 'because it says so in the plan' is the defence of a person who, wrongly, does not use the plan as a working tool.

Planning accuracy or precision?

A further argument which should be vocalised is the conflict between precision and accuracy – would you rather be roughly right or precisely wrong? The conflict is illustrated in the box below.

'The Sniper's Tale' (Price, 1984)

You are a sniper. You have a rifle with five rounds in the magazine. You spot your target; he is sitting under a tree leaning against its bole, his rifle resting across his knees. (He is a sniper as well, and he has got five rounds in his magazine.) You aim and fire five rapid shots. There are five thuds as each round bores into the tree trunk nine inches above your target's head. The holes they make are so tightly clustered you could cover them with a cigarette packet.

That is precision.

He jerks the muzzle of his gun and quickly fires his five bullets. The first hums past your ear, the second smacks into your thigh, the third clips your hair, the fourth smashes into your chest and the last drills into your head.

That is accuracy.

Often, what is termed a 'quick and dirty' approach (with the objective of being as accurate as possible) may be far more beneficial than months of painstaking planning (with the objective of being as precise as possible). Precision, as Frank Price describes it, is pretty; accuracy is deadly.

There is clearly a role for detailed planning, but not before an overview plan has been worked through. Evaluating the overview reveals fundamental flaws in assumptions. Until this level of plan satisfies basic criteria such as financial or technical feasibility, detailed plans are inappropriate.

Do plans provide information or just data?

One of the benefits of modern business systems is the ease and speed with which vast quantities of data can be generated. However, there is a tendency for managers to become overrun with data. Data are the numbers on the page. Information is the part or summary of that which can be usefully applied. The rest is just noise and clutters the thought and analysis process. One of the major roles of the project manager in projects, other than the smallest, will be to gather data from the relevant

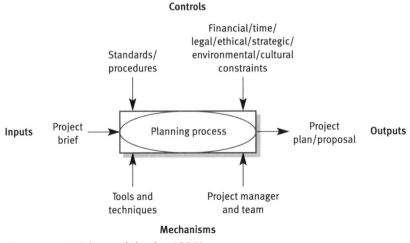

Figure 4.5 Activity model using ICOMs

sources. Simply passing the data on is unlikely to be a value-adding activity. The project manager therefore needs to be not just a collector of data but also a provider of information, usually in the form of management reports. The one-page executive summary is one of the most beneficial of these in terms of information gleaned per time committed.

The process of project planning – inputs, outputs and the process itself

The process of project planning takes place at two levels. At one level, it has to be decided 'what' happens. This, the tactical-level plan then needs to be converted into a statement of 'how' it is going to be carried out (or operationalised) at the operational level. Figure 4.5 shows an activity model as would be used to analyse systems of activity by considering the inputs, controls, outputs and mechanisms (ICOMs) for the activity. The inputs are the basis for what is going to be converted by the activity – in this case the project brief. The output is the project plan, or more specifically the project proposal. The controls provide the activation, the constraints and the quality standards for the planning process in addition to its outputs, and the mechanisms provide the means by which the process can happen.

At the operational level, the way in which the proposal is generated should not be viewed as a one-off activity but should go through many cycles of suggestion and review before the 'final' document is produced. As Fig. 4.5 shows, the first cycles are to provide the major revisions, where significant changes are made. Once these have been done and the project team is happy with the basic format, the last stages are those of refinement, where small adjustments are made.

It is important for the overview to be verified first, before further effort is committed to planning at a detailed level – as discussed above. The life-cycle of planning in Fig. 4.6 shows the stages that the plan should go through. Cases such as the one given below are examples where the detail was considered before the major issues. As the example shows below, this is very wasteful of management time.

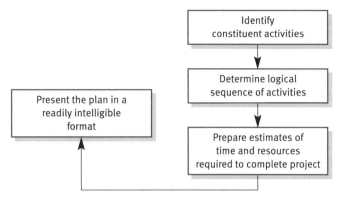

Figure 4.6 The project planning process

The upside-down business plan

Business plan meetings were serious affairs – they always were. The concept was quite attractive – to set up an exclusive nursery school with an appealing teaching method in a smart area of the city. So far so good. This was, however, where the rough planning stopped and the group succumbed to the virus that plagues so many projects at this point – detailitus. The discussions were then waylaid by the need to have safety tyres on the school minibus and by the detailed wording of the liability insurance. No matter that the lag between the money being spent on the buildings and equipment and any income from fees received would create interest payments that the company could never hope to meet . . .

The revision/refinement process considers the necessary sub-projects (if any), the results of any numerical analysis (may be financial, resource, risk analysis or some form of mathematical simulation), the element of 'gut feel' (also referred to as the subconscious or back-of-the-mind element) as well as experience. The sponsor and other stakeholders will usually have some input to be considered in this process.

Managing the planning process

Most projects of low complexity will bias the ratio of planning:action heavily towards the action. As complexity increases, so does the necessity for a formalised plan. This is both a systematic analysis of the project (which provides its own set of benefits) and an opportunity to show that the project manager has been systematic in the planning process (by showing the level of consideration that the project manager has given to issues). 'Traceability' has become a major issue in many companies – allowing products to be traced back to records of their constituent parts. The same is required of a project plan. In the event of an unsatisfactory result, for whatever reason, a good plan can show that the planner took every possible precaution to ensure that the result was positive. Conversely, should the project go particularly well, you will have an assignable cause for this – namely your planning!

The benefits of using a systematic methodology in planning include:

- breaking down complex activites into manageable chunks (see section 4.4);
- determining logical sequences of activities;
- providing an input to subsequent project management processes, including estimating the time and resources required for the project;
- providing a logical basis for making decisions;
- showing effects on other systems;
- filtering frivolous ideas and activities;
- providing a framework for the assessment of programmes (the post-project review process relies on comparing the achieved result with the original plan, particularly for the purpose of improving the planning process);
- being essential for the revision/refinement process;
- allowing lessons to be learned from practice;
- facilitating communication of ideas in a logical form to others.

What follows shows how these benefits can be achieved through the application of tried and tested methods within a systematic framework. The first stage is to break down the activities associated with the project into manageable chunks of work, through the work breakdown structure.

4.4 Work Breakdown Structure (WBS)

'So how do you eat an elephant (or vegetarian equivalent)?'
'Just one slice at a time.'

The breaking down of large activities into comprehensible or manageable units is a fundamental part of project management. Figure 4.7 shows how a systems project – the installation of a new computer system – was broken down into elements that one person or one department could tackle as an activity in its own right at the lowest level in the project.

WBS is also known as 'chunking' or 'unbundling'. This is attractive as it gives people responsibility for a manageable part of the project. WBS also facilitates financial control activities, as individual parts can have their consumption of resources tracked. The sensitivity of such control is preferable to keeping track of a single large activity.

Projects can be broken down in a number of ways. The example given above is an activity breakdown – the first level of breakdown is into the major groups of activities that will be undertaken. Other forms of breakdown include a functional breakdown, where the project is divided into its functional areas (in this case IT, purchasing and operations) and the activities for each area identified. A further type of breakdown is by physical grouping – in this case it could be split up into hardware issues and software issues. These alternatives and the accompanying breakdowns are shown in Figs 4.8 and 4.9.

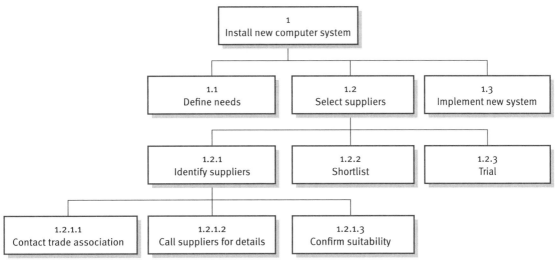

Figure 4.7 Example of a work breakdown structure (WBS)

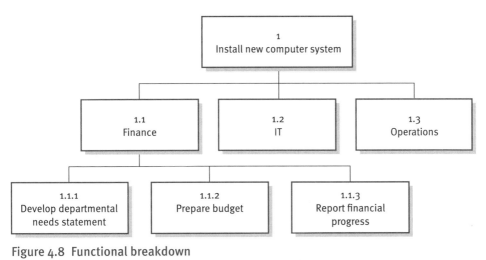

Figure 4.8 Functional breakdown

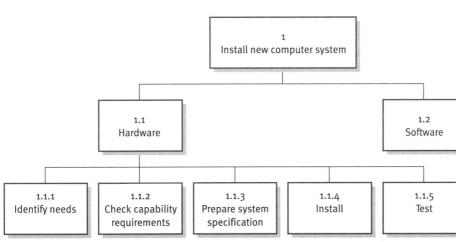

Figure 4.9 Physical breakdown

The role of WBS is to create a linked, hierarchical series of activities, which are independent units, but at the same time still part of the whole, and here lies the major problem with WBS. Whatever type of structure you choose, there are inevitable conflicts, as demonstrated by a London Underground refurbishment project.

During a line refurbishment the project was broken down into track/tunnel units and train/rolling stock units. Communication between the two was problematic, and when the refurbished (French) trains were delivered they did not fit into the tunnels. Nobody had been assigned to manage the interfaces between the teams during the project, as a result of which everybody relentlessly pursued their own part of the work – regardless of the consequences that it would have elsewhere.

The issues centre around the need for coordination between the different parts of the breakdown. Often this may be achieved through having a liason person or exchanging staff. Practically, one of the ways of achieving this has been through changing the scheduling of activities to run more of them in parallel, but with much greater interfacing and team-working – as will be discussed in the next chapter. This looks like such a simple set of activities, yet it is one of the fundamental steps in achieving success. Trying out different types of breakdown is often beneficial, as is the conscious management of the interfaces. Some organisations have interface managers to ensure that issues do not fall between different parts of the breakdown.

The work breakdown structure provides the first attempt at modelling the project process. Whichever type of breakdown is used, at the bottom level will be a list of activities that are passed on to the detailed planning stage.

Once completed to the satisfaction of those involved, the next stage is to consider more detail of the elements of the process and their interaction. Constructing process maps is one method that can be used.

4.5 Process Mapping

How do we describe a process? Many organisations have procedure manuals that run to thousands of pages, and are only dusted off for annual quality audits (see Chapter 7 and the Appendix). Process mapping techniques, such as those discussed throughout this book, work far better and greatly reduce the amount of documentation required, while improving the usefulness of the end result.

One graphical technique is four fields mapping or deployment flow charting (FFM/DFC). As shown in Fig. 4.10, it is a way of relating four information fields:

- the team members;
- the logical phases of an activity;
- tasks to be performed including decisions made;
- the standards that apply for each task.

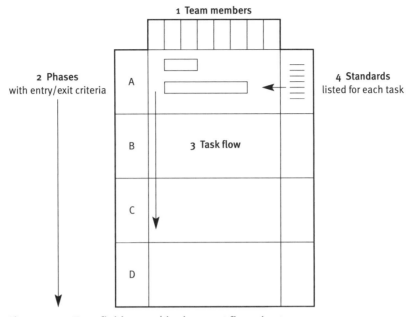

Figure 4.10 Four fields map/deployment flow chart
(*Source*: Dimancescu, 1995)

By incorporating the standards element into the plan not only are the time and activity planned in detail but the controls also specified so that the sharing of information across an organisation needed to make the project work can take place.

Figure 4.11 shows the use of the technique in the selection of a replacement coating product used in the manufacture of computer disks. The entry and exit criteria at each phase ensure that the project does not move on without the team having met certain criteria at that point. For example, at the end of the first phase the outcome must be that the specifications meet the criteria set. No phase can be completed until all errors have been corrected and the causes identified. This, as can be seen, does not sit very comfortably with the conventional ideas of project planning, where activities just proceed at some stated point in time, regardless.

The following section considers further the nature of the check-points between the phases of a project.

4.6 Establishing Check-points

In the above mapping it was suggested that the project be broken into phases. This is part of the role of the planner – to determine the nature and objectives of each phase in a project that will lead to successful completion of the overall project. The use of check-points or gates between the phases provides an additional check for the manager of progress (or otherwise). More importantly, you do not

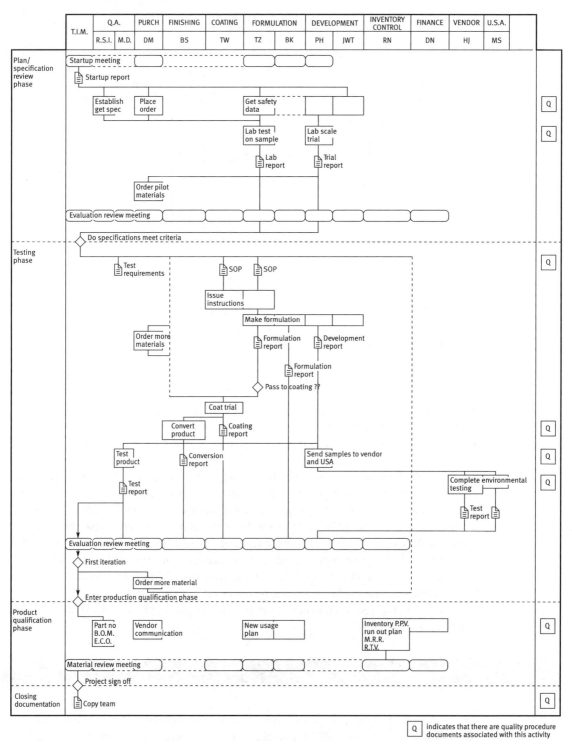

Figure 4.11 The use of FFM/DFC in planning the introduction of a new coating material

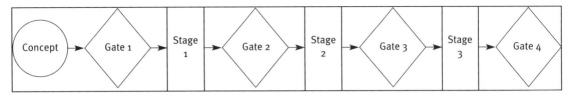

Figure 4.12 Stage-gate model of projects
(*Source*: after Cooper, 1988)

have to wait until the project budget or time allowance expires to find out that there is a fundamental problem. Figure 4.12 shows the basic arrangement of the check-points.

The criteria for passing to the next stage must be laid down in advance – as was done using the four fields mapping planning tool, where *exit criteria* (that determine a project has completed the work in a phase) rather than time determined when a project should pass between phases. Calling a halt to activities can save future expenditure, and must never be discounted as an option, particularly where:

- the majority of the benefits from the activities have already been achieved by the organisation;
- the initial plans and estimates have turned out to be wildly inaccurate;
- a new alternative that is more attractive has materialised;
- organisational strategy changes and the project outcome cease to be in line with the new strategy;
- key personnel leave the organisation;
- the project requires a higher level of capability than the organisation possesses;
- to continue would endanger the organisation financially.

All projects require check-points as a fundamental discipline. Some – such as where the project is delivering to a contract – are unlikely to be stopped where problems arise. Others can and should be. The nature of a 'failure' at a gate therefore differs between projects. The options include the winding-up of the activities (which often causes bad feeling among the project team and can lead to future disenchantment) or finding ways of maximising the potential benefit while minimising the risk or expenditure. Many development projects have got to the point where they were about to be commercialised and the large amount of finance required (which can be hundreds of millions of pounds, particularly in industries such as pharmaceuticals) could not be provided by the originators. Taking on joint partners and licensing are possible remedies in such a case.

The stage-gate system derives from NASA's Phases Review Process (PRP). This favoured the use of gates between activities of different functions within an organisation. As will be discussed in the following section, this caused problems to be passed on rather than resolved. The systems used by many organisations (as described by Cooper, 1988) consider logical elements of the output product. Each stage in this model involves cross-functional activity. This is an important difference.

Not all organisations approve of having gated processes. For some, the possibility that a project may be stopped does cause instability and a sense of a lack of commitment to the project from the organisation. Also, the downside of a project that is stopped at a gate may be loss of morale by the project team.

An example of the stage-gate method in practice is described in the Project Management in Practice at the end of this chapter. All this preparation and planning is, however, futile if there is no support for your project. This might be from inside your organisation in the case of an organisational change project, or from a client in the case of a direct revenue earner. Support will only be achieved if stakeholders and associated communications are 'managed'.

4.7 Stakeholder Management

Jersey Airport

The construction of a new airport terminal building at Jersey Airport started well. The design was approved by all the necessary authorities, and contractors were appointed to carry out the work.

The main concern was the deadline for completion – it had to be in the spring, in time for the island's main tourist influx in the summer. This was achieved and everyone was, for a time, very happy with the new facility. That was until a few problems arose.

These all concerned the impact that the new building was having on the operation of the airport. First, the air traffic controllers (ATCs) complained that they were being dazzled by sunlight reflected from the roof of the new terminal building. No problem, said the Chief Executive of the Jersey Airport Authority – well, at least not during the winter.

A further complaint was that the new building affected the accuracy of the airport's wind speed indicator when the wind was in a certain direction. While a new site for the indicator was being sought, the air traffic controllers were having to advise pilots to use their own judgement regarding the wind speed when it was blowing in that direction. Furthermore, the new building obscured the view of parts of the taxiway to the ATCs (they are responsible for aircraft movements on the ground as well as in the air). The solution – install closed-circuit cameras which would relay the obscured area to the control tower.

When questioned about these problems, the Chief Executive reminded his interviewer that safety was still a top priority. In the light of these problems, the *Financial Times* reminded potential visitors to Jersey that '. . . they can easily go by boat!'

(*Source*: Adapted from *Financial Times*, 15 October 1996)

This is an often neglected part of the task of the project manager – as highlighted by the above example. Stakeholders have been defined in Chapter 2 and it is essential that their needs be considered. External customers, for example, will need to know that you have considered their requirements carefully and are being explicit as to how you have met them. Customer satisfaction is essential if you are to obtain repeat business from this group. Customers are, however, notoriously fickle. Unless they receive a high level of satisfaction (delight) from the transactions with your organisation they will be liable to go to someone else. While many project organisations would consider the length of a commercial relationship to be the duration of the contract, many have ongoing relationships through a series of projects. The nature of the benefit of an ongoing customer relationship needs to determine the importance given to stakeholder marketing activities. In addition, though, it is a perpetual challenge to balance their often-conflicting requirements.

However, during project definition it is often vital that the right support is being developed for your project to ensure that it has a chance of progressing. It is highly frustrating to see good project ideas fail to get support simply because the people involved were not prepared to go and seek it. There are a number of aspects of this:

1 gaining early adopters
2 gaining a project champion
3 obtaining trials and testimonials of your ideas
4 selling.

Early adopters

The idea of *rapid prototyping* has been discussed in section 4.1. Early adopters are people or organisations who see and like the idea, and are prepared to try it out – even before it has been fully developed. 3M use this to great effect in their medical products division (see Von Hippel *et al.*, 1999) with surgeons ready to be involved in trials of new products from a very early stage. These customer developers are essential to the process. Microsoft gains a large customer base for new releases of products by carrying out massive-scale beta tests – where products are put out with users to trial as part of the process of development. This is also very effective in small-scale projects.

Gaining a project champion

The summer ball that gained a local radio presenter to be its champion was enormously successful. The promotion that just one celebrity gave to an idea meant that the rest of the project snowballed for the organisers – with people ready to be involved because that person was acting as the project champion. There are many other cases where this works well, and many organisations that actively encourage their directors to champion projects. The champion role is not to take anything away from the project manager, more to assist with increasing the profile of the project.

Gaining trials and testimonials of your ideas

If you read the brochures of many consulting firms they are usually very keen to promote the list of blue-chip firms for whom they have worked. These provide implicit testimonials and do give some assurance of the quality of the products. So how good is your project? Gaining trials for the ideas and then people's comments will certainly help in developing the concept, and can greatly increase the likelihood that a project will be continued.

Selling

In many countries this is a highly unfashionable term, associated with dishonest second-hand car dealers. The phases of a selling process are of considerable importance, however, if you want key stakeholders to buy-in to your ideas. The phases are:

- Consult – are you talking with the right people? If not, who are the right people to talk to? Who are the decision-makers?
- Understand their need – ask lots of questions, find out what they are really after – not just what they say they are after.
- Develop the need – build on those elements of their need that you can deliver.
- Show how your solution can meet their real needs.
- Close the deal – gain sign-off for that PID!

This brings together the other three aspects of this phase of the stakeholder management process. It will be further discussed in Chapter 7 as part of the consideration of quality planning. (For more ideas on this see Peters, 1999.)

4.8 Relevant Areas of the Bodies of Knowledge

Tables 4.1 and 4.2 summarise the relevant sections. Both of these approaches to this phase of the project suggest that proceduralisation is more important than creativity

Table 4.1 Relevant area of the APM body of knowledge

Relevant section	Title	Summary
30	Work content and scope management	This suggests that not only is the project broken down into manageable units, but that the same should happen to the product, and that this comes from a formalisation of the scope definition. The WBS defines the organisational breakdown structure and the cost breakdown structure.
36	Information management	This section covers the formal documentation requirements for large-scale projects, and their storage retrieval and distribution. Mention is also made of the communications plan (see Chapter 7 in this text).
51	Marketing and sales	The interactions with marketing and sales are identified through the three primary processes of customer requirements identification, order winning, and customer perceptions management.

Table 4.2 Relevant area of the PMI body of knowledge

Relevant section	Title	Summary
2.2	Project stakeholders	Covers the identification of different stakeholder groups and the often-seen conflict in their requirements.
5.1	Project scope management – initiation	The variety of initiation routes for projects is described, tools and techniques for project selection (see Chapter 6 in this book) and the outcome of the initiation phase should be summarised in a *project charter*. This provides one of the inputs to scope planning – the next section.
5.2	Project scope management – scope planning	This activity carries out some appraisal of the project in terms of cost–benefit analysis and the identification of alternatives. The output from this process is in the form of a scope statement that can be signed-off before continuing, and a scope management plan – specifically how changes will, in principle, be accommodated in the project.
5.3	Project scope management – scope definition	This covers the development of product and the work breakdown structures and organisational breakdown structures – the allocation of activities to work units.
10.1	Communications planning	The generation of a communications management plan is demonstrated through the analysis of stakeholder requirements and the preparation of a plan as described in section 4.7 of this book. Additional points made include the need for regular review of the communications plan, and establishment of the means by which information can be obtained by relevant parties between the scheduled communications.

in projects. They also assume that customers know what they want from a project, and that this is enshrined in a written document of commitment – such as a contract. This environment is alien to many project managers. The disciplines suggested by both of these can be beneficial, however, even in relatively small projects, as they formalise the process of gaining 'buy-in' from key stakeholders.

4.9 Summary

Projects are started through an enormous variety of means and their manner of progression is no less diverse. However, there are some principal structures that are generic and of benefit to most projects. These include the formal definition of phases, including a time and process to allow creativity into the development of the concept. This is then enshrined into a scope statement, which allows the start of the development of the process by which the project will be delivered. Key elements of this process are its deconstruction into phases and then manageable work units (through the WBS). These can be modelled through the application of techniques

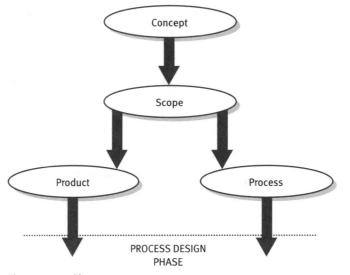

Figure 4.13 Chapter summary

such as Four Field Mapping to produce a highly visible process. Gates at each stage allow for review and in some cases will prevent failing projects continuing to consume time, energy and resource.

Finally, a theme that needs to be addressed at this early stage, and which runs throughout the life of the project, is that of stakeholder management. Expectations and perceptions need to be the subject of active management, partly achieved through the development of a communications plan. A simplified version of the process that this chapter has followed is shown in Fig. 4.13.

Project Management in Practice

Use of gated processes at a major telecommunications manufacturer

To assist in the development of new products the managers responsible for the process (there would be several processes ongoing at any one time) had devised a series of gates in the process. Table 4.3 shows these and gives examples of the criteria by which a project would be judged at each stage.

The last gate is a check on the success of the project as a whole. Other checks provide an opportunity for the project managers to reassess their goals and objectives in the light of progress and changes in conditions such as markets or technology.

Case discussion

1 Who should be in the group that would determine whether the project should continue?

Table 4.3 Gate criteria

Gate	Key question	Example of deliverables
0	Should we launch this project?	Market analysis report, preliminary funding requirements, manufacturing assessment
1	Should we proceed with the design strategy?	Approved product specification, field introduction requirements, project plan, technical support plan
1A	Are we making appropriate progress?	Project cost update, test specifications, prototype manufacturability assessment
2	Is the product ready to ship to the first end-user?	Updated sales and marketing plan, type approval complete, first piece evaluation report
2A	Are we ready to ship to end-users?	Project cost update, final customer documentation, preliminary field introduction report
3	Is the product ready for volume shipment?	Market readiness report, field return rate, final ordering procedures in place, manufacturing readiness
4	Following a period of standard production, has the product met its long-term objectives?	Assessment of key metrics from marketing, quality, manufacturing, training and technical support

2 Using the classification of time, cost or quality objectives, which category would each of the deliverables fall into?

3 What other checks could be included in such a process to ensure that there are adequate controls?

Key Terms

concept development	early adopters
terms of reference	brief
proposal	PID
creativity	screening
rapid prototyping	planning process
scope creep	data versus information
precision versus accuracy	mapping
work breakdown structure	check-points
FFM/DFC	exit criteria
stage-gate	satisfaction
stakeholder management	project charter
communications plan	project champion
organisational breakdown structure	selling

Review Questions and Further Exercises

1 Why would creativity be essential in a personal project, such as an assignment or dissertation? How might this be incorporated into your plan of work?

2 Why should the plan be viewed as a value-adding activity?

3 Identify the costs and potential negative effects of the misuse of plans.

4 Why is the use of a work breakdown structure important to the project manager?

5 To whom does the project manager have to 'sell' a proposal?

6 When is it important for the brief to be highly precise and when should it be left as loose as possible?

7 Why is it important to know the customer for a proposal document?

8 What is the benefit to be gained from mapping a process before proceeding with the detailed planning?

9 From a project with which you are familiar, how might providing gates and gate criteria have helped in its management?

10 Using the University of Rummidge in Splot as a case, identify the key stakeholders and their requirements. What are the conflicts likely to be here, and how might they be resolved?

References

Cooper, R.G. (1988) 'The New Product Process: A Decision Guide for Management', *Journal of Marketing Management*, Vol. 3, No. 3, pp. 238–55.

Dimancescu, D. (1995) *The Seamless Enterprise, Making Cross Functional Management Work*, Wiley, New York.

Peters, T. (1999) *The Project 50*, Alfred Knopf, New York.

PMI (1998) *The PMI Book of Project Management Forms*, PMI, Upper Darby, PA.

Price, F. (1984) *Right First Time*, Gower, Aldershot.

Schrage, M. (2000) *Serious Play*, HBS Press, Boston, MA.

Von Hippel, E. *et al.* (1999) 'Creating Breakthroughs at 3M', *Harvard Business Review*, September–October, pp. 47–57.

Further Information

PMI (2001) *Practice standard for work breakdown structures*, PMI, Upper Darby, PA.

Sobek, D.K. II, Liker, J.K. and Ward, A.C. (1998) 'Another look at How Toyota Integrates Product Development', *Harvard Business Review*, July–August, pp. 36–49.

Drucker, P.F. (1998) 'The Discipline of Innovation', *Harvard Business Review*, Nov.–Dec., pp. 149–157.

www.prince2.com – downloads available of PID documents
www.teamflow.com – FFM/DFC software

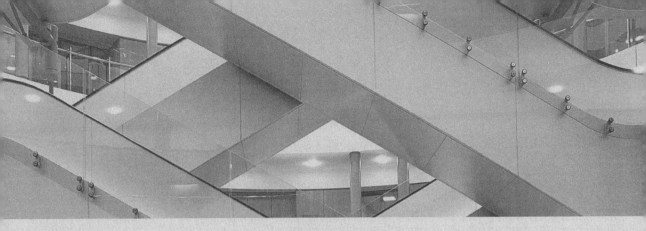

Phase Two
Design the Project Process

5

Time planning

'If you fail to plan, you plan to fail!' (old adage)

The production of plans is often treated as an end in itself. This misses the point and the value that such an activity can add. Its objectives are twofold. First, it must provide an opportunity for the planner to optimise the project system. Second, it must present an opportunity for problem avoidance. These two objectives create the rationale for what follows.

Having prepared the overview models, it is now the task of the planner to put in place the detail. High-level consideration of the objectives and resolution of potential conflicts of the project provide a strong foundation on which to build. This chapter presents the means by which these details can be put in place, to provide the information required to all the stakeholders. Graphical techniques are preferred, as these create the greatest potential for involving others to gain their insight and commitment. However, the objective of such detail must remain at the forefront of the planner's mind. In itself it has little merit. The strength that it offers is in the ability to probe the plans to identify potential improvements to the methods, which may present opportunities for either better performance or risk avoidance. These will be examined in Chapter 8.

For the project manager, this is one of the most developed parts of the subject – the methods have been in use for over 50 years. They must, however, be considered in the light of experience, and this is discussed in the following chapter.

Contents

Learning Objectives

By the time you have completed this chapter, you should be able to:
- Demonstrate basic tools for the modelling of time, cost and quality requirements of projects;
- Carry out basic calculations on a project plan;
- Make these plans amenable to optimisation (improvement and risk avoidance);
- Undertake a first attempt at resource allocation;
- Identify the benefits and pitfalls of fast-track projects.

5.1 Time Planning – the Process

In Chapter 2 one of the issues that proponents of good project management will face is that of people who keep it all in their head. This may work well where projects are very short-term or have little complexity. For the other 98 per cent of projects, some planning is essential.

The project planning process was described in the previous chapter as having four main stages – identify the constituent activities, determine their logical sequence, prepare estimates of time and resource, and present the plan in a readily intelligible format. This last step allows the plan to be communicated to all parties involved with the project and analysis (the subject of the next chapter). The general approach to planning involves starting with a rough overview and conducting revisions of this through the process shown below. This is known as *iterative* – it involves going through the cycle several times to test the effects of the changes you make on the outcomes. The objective is to make the major revisions early in the planning cycle and then make minor refinements to the plan. Following these, though, there should be a period of stability otherwise the plans lose credibility. The revision–refinement cycle is shown in Fig. 5.1.

This section is concerned with developing detailed time plans and the techniques that follow are of increasing complexity. However, despite the diversity of projects being considered, one area of commonality between project managers is the use of various graphical techniques to:

- allow the construction of a comprehensive but comprehensible picture of the project activities;
- communicate this with others.

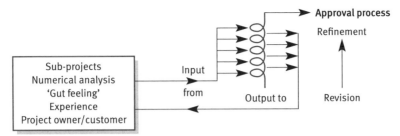

Figure 5.1 Planning sequence

The preference for graphical techniques is more than 'a picture telling a thousand words'. The whole revision–refinement process is built around people being able to understand what is going on. This is known as *visibility*, and is an essential feature of both the plan and the process. One of the most commonly used techniques is the bar or Gantt chart.

5.2 Gantt Charts

The purpose of the graphical techniques is to illustrate the relationships between the activities and time. The simplest form is a horizontal bar chart, as in Fig. 5.2. This shows activity A represented by the shaded bar starting at time 1 and finishing at time 3. Multiple activities can be built up on the same chart, using the same timescale.

The following example involves a dissertation planning exercise. The student has a number of options as to how to present the information. The supervisor, being a busy person, has asked for the information to be presented in graphical form.

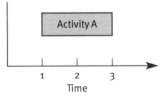

Figure 5.2 Horizontal bar chart: activity A starts at time 1 and finishes at time 3

Planning a dissertation

The basic planning steps need to be followed here, namely:

- identify the constituent activities;
- determine their sequence;
- estimate the time and resources required;
- present the plan.

The time constraints are the start and end dates. The original statement looked as follows:

```
Project start date              |
1. carry out literature review  ******
2. arrange visits                     **
3. prepare questionnaire                ***
4. review questionnaire                    **
5. deliver questionnaire                     *******
6. analyse results                                 ******
7. write up                                             *****
Hand-in date                                                |
                              2/5    20/6   8/8   26/9   2/11   9/12
```

Figure 5.3 Project plan in graphical form

Activity	Time
Project start date	2/5
1 carry out literature review	2/5–20/6
2 arrange visits	20/6–4/7
3 prepare questionnaire	4/7–25/7
4 review questionnaire	25/7–8/8
5 deliver questionnaire	8/8–26/9
6 analyse results	26/9–2/11
7 write up	2/11–9/12
Hand-in date	9/12

The requirement to present the plan graphically is the next step. In this case, simply showing a week by a star is possible and requires nothing more than pen and paper or a wordprocessor, as shown in Fig. 5.3. In this example, there was:

- a level of logic established; and
- conventions used (time goes from left to right, activities are arranged top to bottom in order of their occurrence).

In addition, the student has had to undertake two critical activities:

- forward schedule – started the activities at a given date and followed them forwards in time to determine the end date;
- backward schedule – looked at the time by which the project needed to be completed and worked the logic of activities backwards.

The tasks have had rough times allocated to see whether they meet the two constraints of start- and end-times. Where there was insufficient time, activities have been shortened. Any excess time (or slack) is used to lengthen activities.

Figure 5.4 shows an alternative presentation to the above. Logical links are indicated by the use of arrows. The head of the arrow points to an activity that cannot proceed until the activity at the tail of the arrow is completed. The diamond

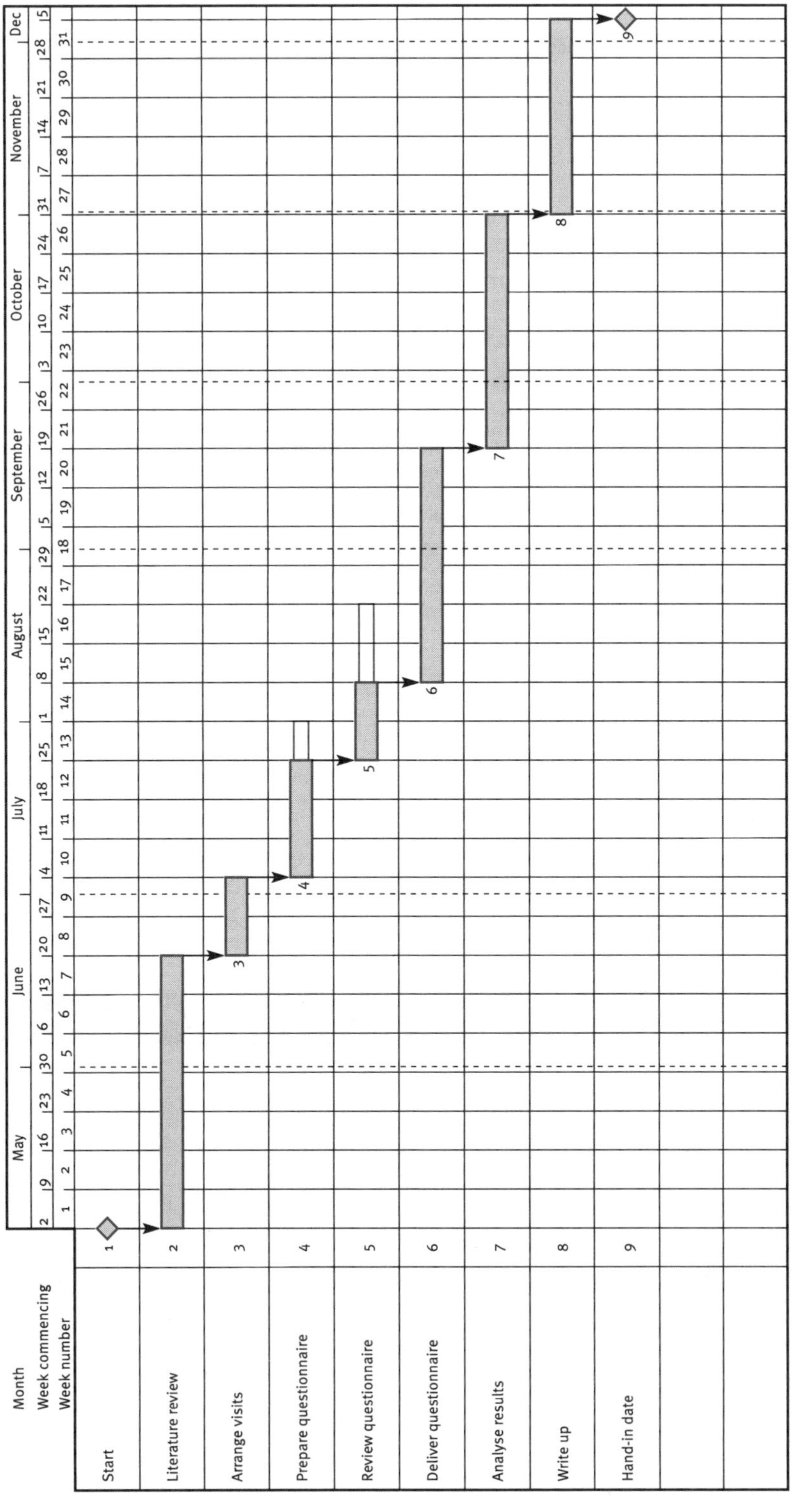

Figure 5.4 Logical links indicated by arrows

shapes on the chart are used to indicate 'milestones', i.e. important points in the life of the project – in this case the start and the hand-in dates.

Such a chart is often referred to as a Gantt or linked-bar chart, as it is part of a family of techniques developed at the turn of the last century by Henry Gantt. They were originally used in industrial planning.

Gantt charts, drawn by hand, are best suited to relatively simple projects, i.e.:

- the number of activities and resources is low;
- the environment is fairly static;
- the time periods are relatively long – days and weeks rather than hours.

They do not make the link between time and cost and therefore do not provide a method for determining how resources should optimally be allocated, e.g. there are two activities, X and Y, for which the times have been estimated and which use the same resource. If the resource could be shifted from activity X to activity Y, Y could be completed in a shorter time; X would obviously take longer, but how would this affect the project overall? This kind of analysis with projects of any complexity is assisted by software – see Further Information at the end of this chapter.

Gantt charts – summary

Good points
- simple to draw and read
- good for static environments
- useful for providing overview of project activities
- very widely used
- the basis of the graphical interface for most PC software

Limitations
- difficult to update manually where there are many changes – charts can quickly become obsolete and therefore discredited
- does not equate time with cost
- does not help in optimising resource allocation

5.3 Estimating

So, how long will it take you to complete a major report for your boss or a 3000-word assignment for a course of study? Many questions then arise, including:

- How precise do you need to be – is a rough/ballpark figure required or are we using this for detailed planning?
- Do we have any previous experience of doing this? If so, how long did it take last time?
- What are the likely pitfalls that may arise that would cause significant delay?
- What other tasks are going to get in the way of doing this (see multi-tasking in Chapter 6).

Estimating is a key part of project planning, though, as we shall see, it is one that is subject to more games-playing and delusion that almost any other field of human

Table 5.1 The nature, role and accuracy of estimate types

Name	Nature	Role	Accuracy
Rough/finger-in-the-air/ballpark	Much uncertainty as to what is involved	Early check on feasibility of brief	Very low
As-buts	As was carried out previously, but with the following amendments – some quantitative data exists	With an appropriate contingency factor – can be used for proposals	Moderate
Detailed estimates	Some initial work is carried out to determine what the likely problems are going to be	Proposals	Moderate
. . . to finish	Much of the project is completed and additional funding is needed to complete the tasks	Additional funds request	High

activity. The basics of estimating are discussed here, but it should be remembered that estimates are otherwise called '*guesses*'. We should therefore be careful how scientifically we treat the numbers that come from this process, and in particular, not be committed in a hurry to making rough estimates that we later get held to. The impacts of this activity are examined in Chapter 6.

The project manager's role in the estimation process will vary from the collection of estimates from other people in the preparation of the proposal to the provision of detailed financial cost–benefit analysis. It is imperative that this function does not operate in a vacuum – that the feedback from previous plans and estimates is used to guide the process. Estimation is an activity which continues during the project life-cycle. As the project nears completion, the manager will have more certainty of the final times, resources, and therefore costs. The accuracy of the estimates is therefore going to get better. The types of estimates, their nature, role and accuracies are shown in Table 5.1.

Having the estimates of times and resources required are one part of compiling the plans. In modelling time, these then need to be built into models of the likely project system that will enable key variables such as project duration and then schedules to be established. As already discussed, Gantt charts are limited in this respect, and the used of network diagrams is appropriate for most projects beyond the simplest.

Dealing with increased complexity through network diagrams

Gantt charts are very useful at low levels of complexity. Many projects, however, require a higher degree of sophistication and a method, which better lends itself to analysis. Rather than representing an activity as a bar on a bar chart, it can be represented as either:

- an arrow – known as activity-on-arrow (A-o-A);
- a node – known as activity-on-node (A-o-N).

These will be discussed in some detail to illustrate the basics of planning. The type of analysis that can be applied is then demonstrated before the use of A-o-N is covered. Finally, there is a summary of the debate as to which method should be used.

5.4 Activity-on-arrow (A-o-A) Diagrams and Critical Path Analysis (CPA)

Under this convention the following 'rules' apply:

- the arrow runs from left to right indicating time running from left to right;
- the arrow starts and ends at an event (for the present this can simply be defined as a 'point in time');
- the events and activities should be given unique identifiers or labels;

e.g. activity A on its own would be represented as running from event 1 to event 2, as in Fig. 5.5.

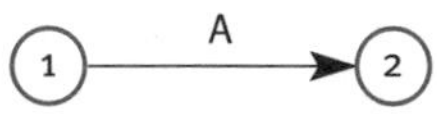

Figure 5.5 Activity-on-arrow diagram

The planning sequence identified above of:

- identify constituent activities;
- determine their sequence;
- estimate the times for each;

gives a verbal statement of the activities. This will now be converted into the A-o-A format for presentation, e.g. Fig. 5.6 shows two activities, A and B; B cannot start until A has finished and the times for A and B are five and seven days respectively. This logic is known as dependency (e.g. don't drive into the car wash before shutting the windows and removing the aerial) and can be expanded as shown in Figs 5.7 and 5.8. Here, more than one activity is dependent on another, in this case B, C and D cannot start until A has been completed. Likewise, H cannot start until all of E, F and G are finished.

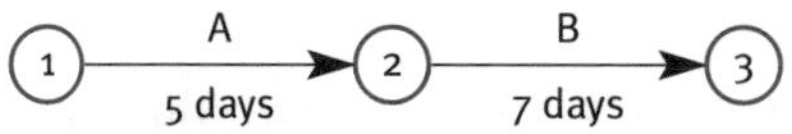

Figure 5.6

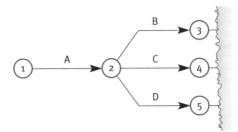

Figure 5.7

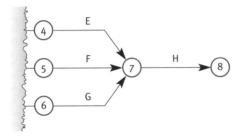

Figure 5.8

Essential to this convention, where all but the simplest projects are being described, is the addition of 'dummy' activities where:

- the logic of the activities' sequence needs to be preserved;
- the dummy will clarify the diagram;

e.g. taking the verbal statement that 'activity L is dependent on activity J but activity M is dependent on both activities J and K' would lead to Fig. 5.9. Simply writing it like this would add an extra logic dependency, however – namely that of activity L on K. In this case a dummy is added to preserve the logic. It is written as a dotted arrow and in essence is an activity with zero duration, as in Fig. 5.10.

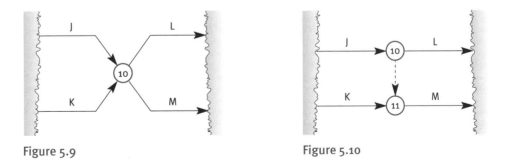

Figure 5.9

Figure 5.10

Clarification should be added where two activities have the same start and end events. Figure 5.11 should be expressed as Fig. 5.12.

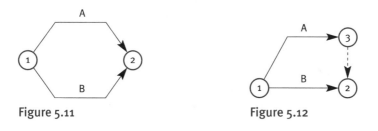

Figure 5.11   Figure 5.12

Analysing the network – critical path analysis (CPA)

In order to provide a consistent format for the analytical phase the convention for the symbols being used is as shown in Fig. 5.13. In order to facilitate the revision of diagrams, the event labels will now go up in tens or fives – allowing interim events to be added without modifying the labels to all subsequent events.

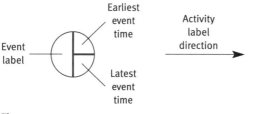

Figure 5.13

There are two new terms to be introduced to the diagrams:

- earliest event time (EET) – determined by the activities preceding the event and is the earliest time at which any subsequent activities can start;
- latest event time (LET) – is the same or later than the EET and is the latest time at which all the previous activities need to have been completed to prevent the whole network being held up.

Figure 5.14 shows the simplest case with a single activity.

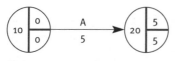

Figure 5.14

Figure 5.15 will be used as the basis for the calculation of the EETs and LETs – please complete these on the page. The calculation of the two times is split into two processes.

(a)

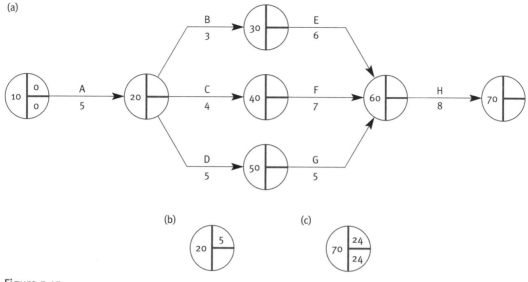

Figure 5.15

1 Forward pass to determine the EET

The first event is assumed to start at time 0 for the purposes of this exercise. The forward pass starts at the first event (10) – the EET in this case is 0. Moving left to right, the subsequent activity time is added to this EET to give the EET for event 20, i.e.:

EET at 20 = [EET at 10] + [activity A duration]
= 0 + 5
= 5

This can now be added to the diagram. Event 20 should now look as in Fig. 5.15(b). The same process can be repeated for events 30, 40 and 50. At event 30:

EET = [EET at 20] + [duration of connecting event (activity B)]
= 5 + 3
= 8

Add this to the diagram as before and do the EETs for 40 and 50.

The first logic snag occurs at event 60. As a reminder, the event cannot happen until all the preceding activities have been completed. In this case there are three possible EETs as shown:

[EET at 30] + [activity E duration] = 8 + 6 = 14
[EET at 40] + [activity F duration] = 9 + 7 = 16
[EET at 50] + [activity G duration] = 10 + 5 = 15

In this case the earliest that all the preceding activities will have been completed is 16 (i.e. the *latest* of the EETs) and therefore this is the EET at 60. Enter this on the diagram and calculate the EET for event 70.

The EET for the last event is the earliest time that the project can be completed, with the times and precedence given. Assuming that the project is required to be completed in the shortest possible time, this figure provides the basis for the next step.

2 Reverse pass to determine the LET

As the name suggests, the analysis begins on the right-hand side of the diagram at the last event. If the assumption that the project is required to be completed in the shortest possible time is correct, the LET of the final event is the same as its EET. Enter the LET for event 70 so that it looks like Fig. 5.15(c).

Working backwards from the end, the next activity is 60, and the LET for 60 is calculated by:

$$
\begin{aligned}
\text{LET at } 60 &= [\text{LET at } 70] - [\text{activity H duration}] \\
&= 24 - 8 \\
&= 16
\end{aligned}
$$

Do the same calculations for events 30, 40 and 50 and note that in two cases the EETs and LETs of those events are different. Enter these on the diagram. A logic challenge now occurs when trying to calculate the LET for event 20 similar to that in the forward pass. There are three possible LETs as shown:

$$
\begin{aligned}
[\text{LET at } 30] - [\text{activity B duration}] &= 10 - 3 = 7 \\
[\text{LET at } 40] - [\text{activity C duration}] &= 9 - 4 = 5 \\
[\text{LET at } 50] - [\text{activity D duration}] &= 11 - 5 = 6
\end{aligned}
$$

In making the choice we again check the logic definition of the LET as the time at which all previous activities (in this case, activity A) will have to be completed to prevent the whole network being held up. Here the LET is 5 – if it occurs any later than this, the whole project will be set back and is therefore the *earliest* of the LETs. Fill in the diagram and satisfy yourself that the original LET for event 10 still holds.

Having completed the network diagram, it is now possible to identify the critical path, which we define as:

that sequence of activities which begin and end in events where the EET = LET

You should now be able to identify this from the diagram. Marking the critical path activities should be done using one of the methods shown in Fig. 5.16.

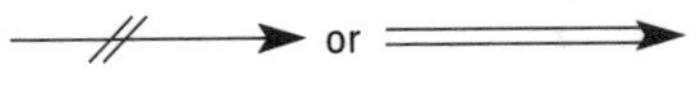

Figure 5.16 Marks used for critical path activities

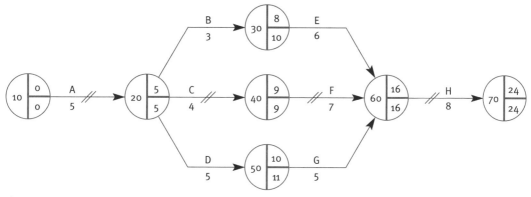

Figure 5.17 Completed network

We define *float* or *slack* as follows:

Float or slack = LET – EET

The critical path is that sequence of activities which have no float or slack. In the example, the path B–E has some slack which is evident at event 30. The slack is 10 – 8 = 2. Either of these events could:

- start late;
- take longer than expected;

or

- there could be a gap between E finishing and H starting;

and provided that the total of these deviations does not add up to more than two, the project will not be held up due to these activities.

The completed network is shown in Fig. 5.17.

Origin of CPA

The 'invention' of the techniques that have been described here as CPA are variously attributed, depending on the particular book you read. The time of first use, 1957/8, is less debated. The first users/developers are credited as being:

- the Catalytic Construction Company for the planning and control of a construction project for Du Pont Corporation;
- Du Pont Consulting;
- J. Kelly of Remington-Rand and M. Walker of Du Pont.

Whoever instigated its usage, the applications are now far and wide – it is only a shame that unlike products such as the ring-pull on cans, such methods cannot be patented. If they were given just 0.1p every time a company had produced a CPA diagram. . . .

5.5 Activity-on-node (A-o-N) Diagrams

This technique is included here because some project managers and their customers prefer it as a convention of project planning. The relative advantages and disadvantages of each method are included later in the chapter.

The most common way of representing the activity-on-node is as Fig. 5.18. Rather than talking about EETs and LETs, the method considers the activities directly and records the earliest start times and latest start times directly on the diagram as shown. The activities are linked in a similar way, but there are four ways in which activities can link (see Fig. 5.19). Precedence is indicated by arrows going from:

- the start of an activity (top left-hand or bottom left-hand corner of the box);
- the finish of an activity (middle of right-hand edge of box);

to:

- the start of an activity (middle of left-hand edge of box);
- the finish of an activity (top right-hand or bottom right-hand corner of the box).

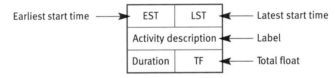

Figure 5.18 Activity-on-node diagram

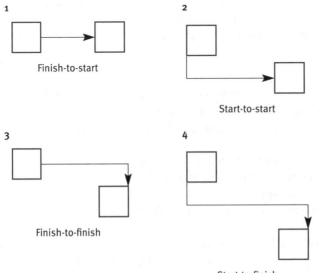

Figure 5.19 Four ways to link A-o-N activities

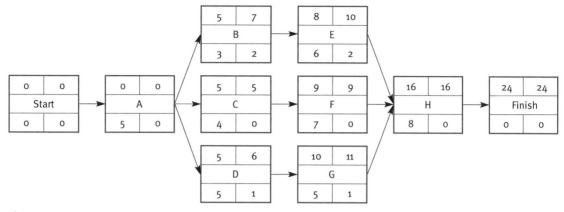

Figure 5.20

The four ways in which activities can link are:

- finish-to-start – the second activity cannot start until the first has finished;
- start-to-start – the second activity cannot start until the first has started;
- finish-to-finish – the second activity cannot finish until the first has finished;
- start-to-finish – the second activity cannot finish until the first has started.

The arrows represent a potential time lag in the logic, e.g. if there was a figure, say 2 on the arrow in the start-to-finish case, the second activity could not finish until 2 time units after the first had started.

The way in which activities are built up into projects is very similar to that already discussed for A-o-A diagrams – with the exception that dummies are not required for clarification or maintaining logic flow.

The same example will be used to illustrate the process of carrying out a critical path analysis with this technique. The logic diagram that was demonstrated in Fig. 5.15 now looks like Fig. 5.20.

Starting from the left of the diagram, the first activity is labelled 'Start'. The EST and the LST are zero as if the project starts late, it will finish late. The duration of the activity is set at zero – it is merely a point in time. The total slack is the difference between the earliest and the latest start times for the activity – in this case zero. The first real activity is activity A – the second box from the left. In the same way as was carried out with the A-o-A diagrams, we will carry out a *forward pass* to determine the project duration and a *reverse pass* to determine the critical path through the activities.

The forward pass

The forward pass determines the ESTs and starts at the left-hand side of the diagram with the EST for the first activity. This is zero. The next activity, activity A, cannot start until this has finished, and so the EST for A is the EST for the start plus the start duration (0) – zero, as you would expect. Activity A has a duration of 5 and so the ESTs for B,C and D are all:

$$0 + 5 = 5$$

Continuing with the ESTs, the EST for the E, F and G are as follows:

EST (E) = EST (B) + duration of B = 5 + 3 = 8
EST (F) = EST (C) + duration of C = 5 + 4 = 9
EST (G) = EST (D) + duration of D = 5 + 5 = 10.

These are now entered onto the diagram. Activity H presents a small challenge in that there are three possible ESTs. These are:

EST (E) + duration of E = 8 + 6 = 14
EST (F) + duration of F = 9 + 7 = 16
EST (G) + duration of G = 10 + 5 = 15.

As for the A-o-A case, activity H cannot start until all three preceding activities have been completed – in this case at time 16 (the *latest* of the ESTs).

Following this through to the end of the network gives the EST (FINISH) as 16 + 8 = 24. This is the project duration.

The reverse pass

The reverse pass starts from the end of the network and assigns the LSTs for each activity. The LST at the finish is assumed to be the same as the LST for that activity – with the meaning that we want the project to be completed as soon as possible. Working backwards, the LST for H is the LST for the finish minus the duration of H. That is, it is the latest time that H could start without delaying the entire project. This is 24 – 8 = 16, the same as the EST.

Continuing with the analysis, the LSTs for each of the activities E, F and G can now be calculated.

LST (E) = LST (H) – duration of E = 16 – 6 = 10
LST (F) = LST (H) – duration of F = 16 – 7 = 9
LST (G) = LST (H) – duration of G = 16 – 5 = 11

and similarly for B, C and D:

LST (B) = LST (E) – duration of B = 10 – 3 = 7
LST (C) = LST (F) – duration of C = 9 – 4 = 5
LST (D) = LST (G) – duration of D = 11 – 5 = 6

The LST for A is another case where there is more than one possibility. The three possible LSTs are:

$$LST(B) - \text{duration of } A = 7 - 5 = 2$$
$$LST(C) - \text{duration of } A = 5 - 5 = 0$$
$$LST(D) - \text{duration of } A = 6 - 5 = 1$$

The choice is the *earliest* of the LSTs – zero. Checking back to the start activity, confirm that this is correct.

The additional task with A-o-N is to calculate the *float* in each activity. This is:

$$\text{Float} = LST - EST$$

This is then inserted in the bottom right-hand side of the activity box.

Where there is no float, that means that the activity is *critical*, and any delay in this activity will delay the project as a whole. The critical path through the network is therefore:

$$A - C - F - H$$

The most used package for project planning, Microsoft Project, uses a different format for its A-o-N diagrams. An example of the format is shown in Fig. 5.21.

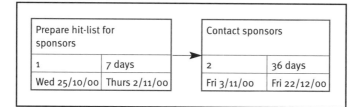

Figure 5.21 Microsoft Project output

In Fig. 5.21 the activity description is given in the top of the box. The next row down contains the activity number (simply a label) and the activity duration. The bottom row of the box contains the start and the finish times of that activity. In the example, the duration of 7 days does not include weekend working – hence the start on the Wednesday and not finishing until the Thursday of the following week. The calculation is done for you with this package – hence the apparent lack of detail. This presentation does not allow you to see whether there is any float in the activity, though there are other means of doing this, including showing it in the Gantt chart for the project.

5.6 Activity-on-arrow versus Activity-on-node Method

The preference for A-o-A is determined by whether you are going to attempt the planning process manually or use a software package. A-o-A is arguably easier to

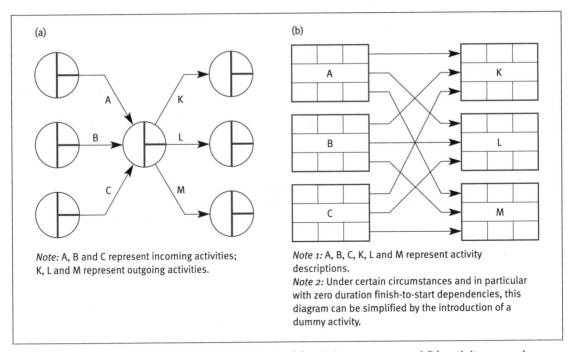

(a)

Note: A, B and C represent incoming activities; K, L and M represent outgoing activities.

(b)

Note 1: A, B, C, K, L and M represent activity descriptions.
Note 2: Under certain circumstances and in particular with zero duration finish-to-start dependencies, this diagram can be simplified by the introduction of a dummy activity.

Figure 5.22 Comparison of network drawing modes (a) activity-on-arrow and (b) activity-on-node

construct manually, while A-o-N is the basis of the majority of software packages, including Microsoft Project. Other issues are contained in the table below:

A-o-A	A-o-N
• easier to prepare and modify • non-experts have a better chance of understanding the network • milestone events are easily marked • where there are multiple precedence relationships (see Fig. 5.22), this is much more clearly illustrated	• easier to show complex relationships, e.g. start-to-finish precedence with time lag (complex with A-o-A) • no dummy activities – keeps the number of activities the same as in the verbal statement (except when showing milestones) • all the information about the activities is contained within the box – easier to ensure the right numbers are associated with the right activity

Example – planning the marketing of a new product

In Fig. 5.23 all the principles so far discussed are used to plan the launch of a new food product. It is possible through examining the EETs and LETs to determine which activities are on the critical path. The diamonds are included to show milestones in the project, i.e. go-ahead and product. Trying to convey this volume of

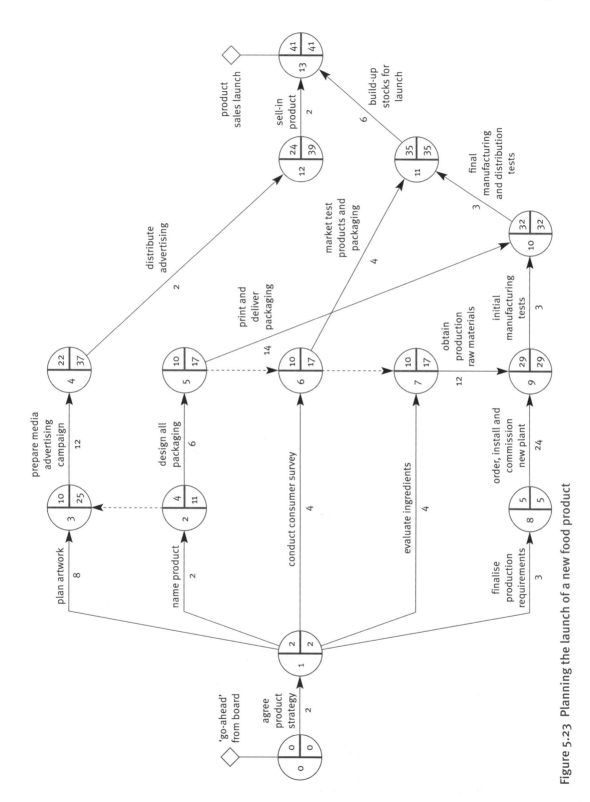

Figure 5.23 Planning the launch of a new food product

information through a verbal statement would clearly be a nightmare for both the planner and the reader, and would not lend itself to the kind of analysis that could be done with this diagram.

5.7 Scheduling

Knowing the sequence and duration of activities is a major step. This does not, however, answer the question of 'When will activities need to be carried out?' The schedule provides this. As already shown by the critical path analysis, critical activities have to take place at a particular time or the entire plan will be disrupted. In order for this to happen, the necessary resources need to be in place in time for the critical activity. In an ideal world, this would allow a very simple schedule to be used for critical activities and everything else arranged around these. The reality is far less appealing – people are not available when you need them, resources have a long lead-time and there are likely to be clashes with other project schedules in a multi-project environment. This provides a constraint on the scheduling process, and as a result of trying this, the activities and sequence will often have to be changed. This is where an additional element of complexity enters and makes a mess of your nice plans!

For example, a plan to refurbish a number of retail units at London Heathrow was thrown into problems by a contractor. All personnel working on the airport need security clearance, a process that takes 6 weeks. One firm did not get their people pre-approved, resulting in considerable delay to the project – the resource was not going to be available when needed to do the job.

Similarly, what happens when a resource – for instance, a key individual – is overloaded and becomes a constraint? This problem is discussed further in the following chapter. This provides another cycle of iteration to the development of plans.

The inputs to the process of developing the schedule are shown in Fig. 5.24.

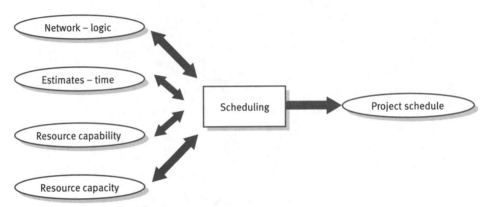

Figure 5.24 Schedule development process

The arrows for the inputs to the scheduling process are two-way. The network provides the logic for the order in which activities need to be carried out. Having completed this, the input of the time estimates may show that the time that the project requires for completion is longer than is available. This may necessitate a reconsideration of both the network and the time estimates.

The *resource capability* is the set of tasks that the resources available to the project manager can reasonably undertake. These resources are often referred to as the *resource pool*. For example, where a project is being undertaken by a particular project team, these are the resource pool. If additional staff can be brought in as needed, they should also be considered as part of that pool. This part of the allocation process requires that the project manager have some knowledge of the capabilities and limitations of the resources concerned.

The *resource capacity* depends on the volume of resources available and issues such as the *resource calendar*. For instance, whilst a machine may be scheduled for utilisation 24 hours a day, 7 days a week (with time allowed for maintenance), the same cannot be said of humans. The calendar is those times that the resource is available, allowing for all the usual times when no work takes place (e.g. weekends, public holidays, personal holidays, sick leave). This does significantly limit when work can be carried out. Again the process of scheduling is iterative, with the schedule being developed, the resource availability checked and subsequently rescheduled. Where resources are over- or under-loaded, corrections may be made at this point.

This iterative process is often supported for medium and large-scale projects by the use of software – allowing rapid calculation of key project times and evaluation of the impact of difference scenarios. The role of such software is discussed in the following section.

5.8 Computer-assisted Project Planning

Ask for a training programme on project management, and many organisations would send you on a course for one of the major software packages. The key ones are listed at the end of this chapter under Further Information. The Gantt chart is probably the most widely used tool for presenting time information, and one of the reasons is that it is the graphical interface for most planning software. This does encourage a one-step approach to planning. As a result of the presentation capabilities of modern planning packages, the visual quality of colour charts means that they gain an implicit credibility. This can result in staff being unwilling to challenge the charts, and so they gain a momentum all of their own. In addition, they encourage the project manager to overcontrol the project rather than devolve the responsibility for the time-plan to team members. With the increasing power and availability of the PC, and increased functionality and interfaceability of the software, there is the tendency for the project manager to become not just 'keeper of the charts' but also computer operator. This will often occur in a vain attempt to keep the computer version of the project plan up to date. Many consider the predominance of planning software not to be as helpful to the profession as the vendors of such systems would have us believe. Indeed as the projects director of a large construction company recently commented, 'I believe that computer-based project management software has set the subject back 20 years.'

Many truly excellent organisations do not use the CPA approach to planning projects. One of Hewlett-Packard's UK plants uses whiteboards and Post-It notes for project planning at the top level with individual sub-project managers free to use computerised planning software at the task level. This approach is an adaptation of the principle so well demonstrated by Japanese manufacturers in planning and scheduling – that of ensuring *visibility*. To assist in moving towards more visual methods of planning, there are many tools and techniques available to the project manager. Deployment flow charts are just one such example, which allow whole processes to be mapped simply. That said, there is significant power in modern planning packages that can be used to some benefit. With very large projects, many consider them vital.

5.9 Fast-track Projects

This issue does provide an input to the practicalities of how to arrange a schedule. For instance, the dissertation plan shown at the start of this chapter (Fig. 5.3) does show all the activities running sequentially, i.e. one after the other. This is by far the simplest way to look at it from a scheduling point of view, but it is unlikely to be good representation of reality or the best way to finish the project in a given time. In particular, where different groups are involved in different stages of a project, the effect is often seen that people focus on their part of the project only, with no consideration of the outcome as a whole. This is illustrated by the conventional life-cycle for a new product development (NPD) project, as shown in Fig. 5.25. This suffers from two major drawbacks.

- The message or customer specification is interpreted by different people at each stage of the process. The information that reaches the manufacturing people

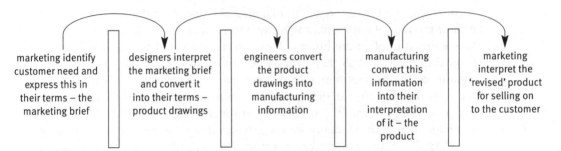

Figure 5.25 Conventional approach to new product development

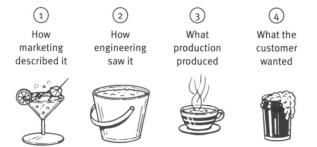

Figure 5.26 Effect of 'Chinese-whispers' syndrome on new product development

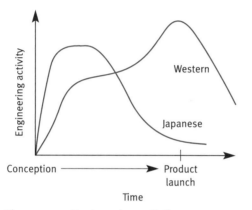

Figure 5.27 Engineering activity

telling them what to make is potentially very different from what goes in at the start of the process ('Chinese-whispers' syndrome – Fig. 5.26).

- Due to the constant process revision that is required, engineering changes are often made very late in the development process. These cause enormous disruption, in particular delay.

It was seen by many who visited Japan and investigated its automotive industry that the level of design changes and engineering activity had a very different profile. The Japanese model was focused on getting the product 'right first time', with the result as shown in Fig. 5.27. As can be seen, the amount of activity declines as the product nears production. The importance of time-to-market has been shown recently to be responsible for over 30 per cent of the total profit to be made from a product during its life-cycle. The reduction in long-term costs has also been shown to be significant if instead of arranging activities to occur sequentially, as would be the simplest arrangement, they are overlapped. Concurrent engineering is used.

The arrangement of product development into a process stream, with all the necessary parties involved at all stages to prevent the cycle of work and rework

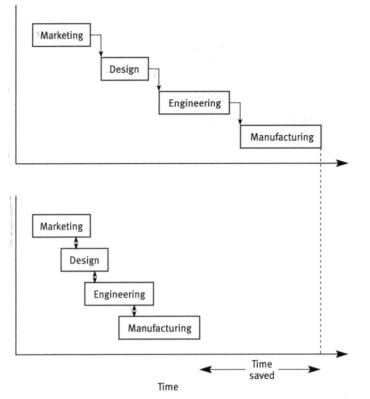

Figure 5.28 Sequential versus concurrent models of new product development

of ideas, has the natural effect of allowing activities to run alongside one another (concurrently) as opposed to one after the other (sequentially). This is shown in Fig. 5.28.

The advantages of a concurrent engineering approach are shown by the ability of the Japanese automotive producers to bring new vehicles to market every three to four years, while Western manufacturers have been taking five to seven years. (The results of a study of the effects of concurrent engineering can be found in Maylor, 2001.) The benefits for projects in general can be summarised as potential for:

- reduced project time;
- reduced project costs – due to the reduction in reworking between each stage.

The disadvantages of applying this method of working include:

- increased overheads – as the teams require their own administration support;
- costs of co-location – people being relocated away from their functions to be with the team with which they are working;
- cultural resistance;
- inappropriate application – it is no panacea for other project problems.

The role of running activities to some extent in parallel is to induce cooperation during planning (not necessarily involving co-location) and high levels of communication during the activity phases. It has proved to be beneficial (as shown in the case at the end of this chapter), but as the following example shows, the application needs careful consideration.

Chicago's Millennium Park

The idea of saving time by organising sequential activities to run concurrently is highly appealing. The reality can be far less attractive. Chicago's Millennium Park is one of many millennium projects around the world that have run into problems. Now running at over double its original US$150 million budget and likely to open three years late, it has suffered from a process that didn't work. The fast-track idea was applied to this project to allow construction work to start on converting the former railway yard into a park before the design work had been completed. The problem appears to have been that the designers, developers and various contractors before the start of works had not agreed the overall scheme for the park. As a result, features were added, then removed, work had to be done and then redone when the designs were changed, and the city found itself in contractual wranglings with its contractors.

As for all 'good ideas', fast-track needs to be considered in context. In such a scenario, there is often great benefit to be gained from having contractors, designers and engineers working together from the outset, to ensure that what is being designed is feasible and can be constructed. There is, however, a logical order to these processes, and continuing without a good basis to work on is futile. The example illustrates what many people know from experience – that the quality of the final job is determined by the level of preparation undertaken. In this case, early resolution of the inherent conflicts with the project should have been undertaken.

5.10 Relevant Areas of the Bodies of Knowledge

The bodies of knowledge (Tables 5.2 and 5.3) are very different in this respect, with the PMI being relatively comprehensive concerning the nature of the processes involved here and the accompanying tools and techniques. It would be possible in either to lose the reason for carrying out the planning process – to enable optimisation of the project processes and the prevention of problems.

Table 5.2 Relevant areas of the APM body of knowledge

Relevant section	Title	Summary
31	Time scheduling/ phasing	This topic is broadly defined and includes activity definition, sequencing, estimating, schedule development & control. The issue of phasing – termed *'the strategic pacing'* of the project – is given some prominence (see *Fast-track Projects*) and the many techniques including Gantt charts, A-o-A, A-o-N and CPA are identified.
32	Resource management	It is simply stated that the allocation of resources – be they human, machine or organisational – to a project is a 'fundamental requirement of effective project planning and management'.
42	Estimating	This is identified as an important activity, 'closely related to budgeting and cost management'.

Table 5.3 Relevant areas of the PMI body of knowledge

Relevant section	Title	Summary
6.1	Project time management – activity definition	This process takes in the WBS and all the other project information compiled up to that point. Through consulting with previous similar projects and breaking down the activities further, the outcome is threefold – a list of activities, the information needed to support and define them, and a revised WBS.
6.2	Project time management – activity sequencing	This part of the process considers the activity list, all the constraints on when activities can be carried out, the time requirements for the project. These are used to construct the detailed plans through *precedence diagramming method* (A-o-N), *arrow diagramming method* (A-o-A) or other techniques (see Chapter 8 in this book). As a result of this analysis, the activity lists may have to be updated.
6.3	Project time management – activity duration estimating	It is not clear how this can take place after the sequencing and analysis of 6.2 – these estimates are required to make these decisions. Techniques identified for estimating include *expert judgement, analogous estimating* (termed as . . . but . . . in this chapter) and *quantitatively based* (termed parametric estimating in Chapter 7).
6.4	Project time management – schedule development	This section presents a wide array of tools and techniques for the development of the network diagrams and activity lists (along with all the associated constraints information) into a schedule for the project.

5.11 Summary

The objectives of the planning process are to optimise the project process and to prevent problems in the process. This is achieved through the systematic evaluation of the project's constituent activities, their duration, and logical linkage (sequencing). The use of graphical techniques helps in the presentation of the plan and facilitates its review and revision.

Having identified the activities through the WBS, the next step is arranging them in a logical sequence and then estimating their time requirements. Estimates become more uncertain the further ahead in time is the situation being considered, and range from rough (usually least accurate) to to-finish (usually most accurate). Learning curves show quantitatively how, when activities are repeated, their times reduce.

The most widely used tools for development of schedules are Gantt charts and network techniques. A Gantt chart is a time-scaled graphical planning tool, which gives a static representation of the relationship between activities and their duration. Network techniques provide a graphical means of expressing more complex projects and include activity-on-arrow (A-o-A) and activity-on-node (A-o-N) methods of representation of the verbal statement of activities.

The application of these methods must be in line with the objectives for the process and in themselves they have little merit. The first level of analysis that can be applied to the network diagrams is critical path analysis (CPA). This allows determination of the path of activities where, if there is any delay, the whole project will be delayed. The critical path should therefore be the initial focus for management attention – for the purposes of both shortening and control.

Scheduling is the process that converts the plan into a specific sets of dates for individual activities to be started and finished. One aspect of this is the phasing of the activities. Recently, the idea of fast-tracking projects has been used with mixed results.

Project Management in Practice

Fast-track product redevelopment at Instron

Background

Instron designs and manufactures machines for testing the properties of all types of material. One particular plastics testing instrument has been selling around 250 units per year worldwide. In 1992 at the height of the recession, with margins being squeezed and sales volume dropping, Instron decided to redesign the instrument to reduce its cost and make it easier to manufacture.

The project

Instron began to undertake change in the late 1980s, which included a programme to institute concurrent new product development. This was accompanied by pressure for cost reduction, the introduction of manufacturing changes, and the breaking of the firm into business teams.

Due to this highly transient and changing environment, there were few restrictions on the way the redesign project had to be handled. It was one of the first projects in Instron to be run from the beginning as a concurrent engineering project. A small multi-functional team was formed, consisting of a manufacturing engineer, a design engineer, a marketing engineer and a draughtsman. The design brief was to improve the ease of manufacture of the product such that a cost reduction of 20 per cent could be achieved.

The team was co-located in an area adjacent to the manufacturing facility. Although there was some initial resistance, the comment was made that 'they don't know how they ever worked without it'. The ease of communication and sharing of ideas became a more natural part of working life.

Adverse effects

The principles of concurrency were, in general, favourably accepted by departments downstream of the design process (manufacturing, shopfloor, service) and, with some notable exceptions, unfavourably viewed by the design department. Individuals had concurrency imposed on them in the initial projects selected; first-line managers had decided that it made good business sense, and that it would be tried out. Senior management staff were selected as champions of the cause, with the objective of overcoming the resistance to change that existed. This came in a number of forms:

1 *passive resistance* – summarised as 'don't show reluctance to apply the new ideas, attend all the group meetings, nod in agreement, then carry on as before';
2 *active resistance* – 'do what you like, but don't ask me to do it';
3 *undermining the initiative* – through overstating the apparent problems.

It was not surprising that this resistance existed: people were uncertain about changes in the authority of the designers, an apparently higher workload, compromised design solutions for the sake of manufacturability, unqualified (in design terms) manufacturing engineers having a major input in designs, and the role of the engineering manager being threatened. There were further worries for all concerned, however. These included reduced product performance, loss of personal contacts (resulting from resiting people), loss of key individuals (who would leave the firm) and higher management overhead.

They began by carrying out brainstorming sessions with manufacturing engineers, buyers, members of the shopfloor, suppliers and additional design engineers, to find new and innovative ways to improve the product. The outcome of these investigations was to draw up a list of areas where improvements were thought possible.

The benefits achieved

The results of this team's actions were:

- cost reduced by 49 per cent;
- product range rationalised from 12 to 2 versions;
- unique part count reduced from 141 to 98 (fewer parts to plan, purchase, stock and handle) and total number of parts reduced from 300 to 189 (much reduced assembly effort);
- assembly/machining time reduced by 55 per cent;
- project completed on time, with last version being released in April 1994.

Once operational, few problems were encountered and those that did occur were minor in nature. The success was attributed by the firm to two decisions:

- the selection of the right project – one that made it easy to demonstrate concurrency;
- the selection of the right people – those who were prepared to be open-minded and have some enthusiasm for the changes.

The company now views this as a simple project that restored the profitability of an established product through the use of innovation, ingenuity and new design techniques by the whole concurrent team. What is also clear is that the product was subject to technical change in only one area – the materials used. The other benefits have all been due to the approach that the firm's management has taken to its new product development (NPD) process. The firm felt that the project has been a success and that this method of working would become an institutionalised methodology.

Case discussion

1 What is the evidence to support the claim that this project was a success?
2 Identify the steps the firm took in this project. How did this contribute to the success?
3 How might the main adverse effects be identified and countered?
4 The firm attributed the success to the choice of project and the people selected to carry it out. If a similar way of working is to be more widely adopted, what might usefully be done to ensure that other projects are similarly successful?

Key Terms

revision/refinement	dependency
forward/backward schedule	dummies
Gantt or linked bar chart	critical path
visibility	earliest/latest event times
networks	forward/reverse pass
activity-on-arrow/activity-on-node	slack

Review Questions and Further Exercises

1 You have been put in charge of organising a group trip to visit a company in Japan which has expertise that you and your group are interested in finding out more about. Identify the constituent activities, their sequence and estimate the times that each of the activities will take. Show how you have used forward and backward scheduling to achieve this. Display your plan as using a bar chart or similar method.

2 Discuss why graphical techniques for displaying plans are superior to verbal statements.

3 Describe what is meant by 'precedence' and illustrate your answer with an appropriate example.

4 Show the dissertation case example (Fig. 5.3) as an activity-on-arrow diagram.

5 Illustrate the differences between A-o-A and A-o-N methods.

6 Show the information given in Table 5.4 about a project activity as an A-o-A diagram.

Table 5.4

Activity	Description	Duration (weeks)	Preceding activity
A	Select software	4	–
B	Select hardware	3	A
C	Install hardware	6	B
D	Install software	2	C
E	Test software	3	D
F	Train staff	5	E
G	System run-up	1	F

(a) From your diagram identify the total project duration.
(b) Show which activities you feel could be run alongside others (in parallel, rather than sequentially). Redraw the network diagram and calculate the new project duration.
(c) What further benefits may arise from using parallel activities, rather than sequential?

7 Show the information given in Table 5.5 about project activities as an A-o-A diagram, using the notation of Fig. 5.13.

(a) From your diagram, do the forward pass and calculate the minimum project duration.
(b) Do the reverse pass and calculate the latest event times.
(c) Show the critical path activities using the notation suggested.

Table 5.5

Activity	Description	Duration (weeks)	Preceding activity
A	Select software	4	–
B	Upgrade office network	3	A
C	Install hardware	6	A
D	Test software	2	B
E	Structure database	3	B
F	Train staff	5	C, D
G	System run-up	1	E, F

(d) Assuming that the completion time is critical, identify which activities you would suggest should be the focus for management attention.

8 Table 5.6 considers the development of a short course in project management. From the information, construct the network diagram.

Table 5.6

Activity	Description	Duration (weeks)	Preceding activity
A	Design course overview and publicity	4	–
B	Identify potential staff to teach on course	2	–
C	Construct detailed syllabus	6	–
D	Send out publicity and application forms	10	A
E	Confirm staff availability	2	B
F	Select staff to teach on course	1	C, E
G	Acknowledge student applications	3	D
H	Identify course written material	2	F
J	Preparation of teaching material	20	G, H
K	Prepare room for the course	1	G

(a) Determine the ESTs, the LSTs, the project duration and the critical path activities.
(b) Show the slack for each activity.
(c) What further factors should be considered in order to give a better view of the realistic timescale for the organisation of the course?

9 Discuss the relative merits of each of the methods for determining the time content of activities.

References

BS 6079: Part 2: 2000, *Project Management – Vocabulary*.

Drucker, P. (1955) *Management*, Butterworth-Heinemann, Oxford.

Maylor, H. (2001) 'Assessing the Relationship Between Practice Changes and Process Improvement in New Product Development', *Omega: The International Journal of Management Science*, Vol. 29, No. 1, pp. 85–96.

Price, F. (1984) *Right First Time*, Gower, Aldershot.

Further Information

Badiru, A.B. (1993) *Quantitative Models for Project Planning, Scheduling and Control*, Quorum, London.

Lock, D. (2000) *Project Management*, 7th edition, Gower, Aldershot, chapters 7–14.

Lockyer, K. and Gordon, J. (1991) *Critical Path Analysis and Other Project Network Techniques*, 5th edition, Financial Times Pitman Publishing, London.

Randolf, W.A. and Posner, B.Z. (1988) *Effective Planning and Management: Getting the Job Done*, Prentice Hall, Englewood Cliffs, NJ.

Reiss, G. (1992) *Project Management Demystified: Today's Tools and Techniques*, Chapman & Hall, London.

Sapolsky, H.M. (1972) *The Polaris System Development: Bureaucratic and Programmatic Success in Government*, Harvard University Press, Cambridge, MA.

Major project planning software

Supplier	Product name	URL and comments
Microsoft Corporation	Project	http://www.microsoft.com/office/project/default.htm and see the cases of applications at http://www.microsoft.com/office/project/CaseStudies.htm
Primavera Systems Inc.	Primavera	www.primavera.com
Asta Development Corporation	PowerProject	http://www.astadev.com/content/indexm.htm
CFM Inc.	Teamflow	www.teamflow.com – a non-traditional approach to project planning which focuses on information flow
ProChain Solutions Inc.	Prochain	www.prochain.com – lots of good information on this site and useful discussions on critical chain project management

6 Critical chain project management

Why should there be need for other methods for Project Management to replace or maybe enhance CPM/PERT? Self-evidently, CPM/PERT frequently does not work. (Rand, 2000, p. 175)

Given the level of project failures identified in previous chapters, the need to find the causes and provide solutions has significant economic importance. Chapter 3 identified some of the strategy-related problem areas. In this chapter, some of the operational problems associated with the current systems for planning and resource allocation are identified. One of the groups of solutions comes from the Theory of Constraints. As will be seen, this provided significant benefit in repetitive operations, and there is growing evidence that the application of these principles can yield benefit in project management.

To determine whether this is indeed applicable, the first step is to identify the problems that individuals and organisations are facing. Following this, the background to critical chain methods is explored, and then their application in the project environment. The Project Management in Practice section at the end of this chapter shows how this generated improvements for one business.

Unlike the other chapters, there is no section on the relevant areas of the bodies of knowledge. This is because, at the time of writing (2002), the approach was not recognised in either body of knowledge.

Contents

Learning Objectives

By the time you have completed this chapter, you should be able to:
- Understand the weaknesses of the PERT/CPM approach to planning and scheduling projects and recognise the need for alternative methods;
- Demonstrate the principles of the Theory of Constraints approach;
- Apply basic analysis to allow generation of buffered programmes;
- Design alternative control measures for monitoring the progress of projects.

6.1 The Effects

Projects that run late, overbudget, or fail to meet key needs of their stakeholders cause considerable problems for businesses, governments and individuals. A basic analysis suggests that either the methods being used for project management or their application or both must be at fault. In Chapter 3 the problems of what Deming termed 'the system' were considered, and it was demonstrated how many organisations have started to come to terms with these problems through a new approach to strategy. This has the potential to remove one group of problems. It is not sufficient on its own, however, to change project performance radically. That is because the operational problems will inevitably resurface where conventional techniques are used.

The problems that we see regularly happening are centred around one fact: projects contain fundamental uncertainties – particularly in as . . . but . . . s and first-timer projects, but also in some painting-by-numbers projects. These may be related to the process (how will we deliver this?) or the outcome (what is it that we achieve?). The challenge is that in many cases, 'we don't know what we will find until we get there'. This applies to technological developments, groundworks on construction sites, or even writing books.

The response to this uncertainty has not helped, for example:

- in large projects in particular, despite the configuration management and change control procedures, many projects are incapable of handling change;
- when working under pressure, people tend to jettison the system, and fall back on wishful thinking – the system does not have credibility with its users;
- similarly, under pressure, people focus on the short-term objectives of completing activities, losing sight of the impact of this on the project as a whole;
- when things do go wrong, review will reveal that there were procedural deficiencies. Adding further procedures often does not help the system;

- the longer the project duration, the greater the chance for changes to be required, which traditional methods seem very poor at handling – as stated above.

These are symptoms of the fact that the methods used are not sufficiently *robust*. Moreover, many of the traditional methods of project planning such as PERT (an extension of network techniques – see Chapter 8) have never been the subject of any evaluation – not least because, until recently, there was no alternative. As for many management initiatives, the methods associated with PERT came out of large organisations with an interest in promoting their usage. Success was selectively measured, and further applications justified on the basis of this 'success'.

One engineer who had worked on the Polaris missile programme in the UK told how PERT charts had been forced on them by their American partners in the project. He further related how the only time that the PERT plans were consulted was just before a visit from one of the American partners. The project was running significantly late and overbudget, but the charts would then be 'updated' to show that the project was in fact running to the latest version of the plan. Original baselines were conveniently forgotten.

These are the effects. The causes can be unpacked from these.

6.2 The Causes

Chapter 5 presented some detailed planning techniques for time – in particular the basics of the critical path method (CPM). Having spent some time getting to grips with these techniques, you now encounter a chapter that states that these techniques do not work (opening quotation). The obvious question arises as to why these were covered at all in the first place. There are two reasons:

- In order to understand the shortcomings of the techniques and search for potential solutions, you must first understand the techniques themselves;
- Many organisations still require the use of the original techniques and have not yet adopted the solutions that are presented here.

The statement that the techniques of CPM and PERT do not work requires some justification. Seven issues are identified which demonstrate the problems associated with the CPM approach to planning and controlling. These are:

1 All goals are based on estimates, which contain uncertainties. We are poor at meeting these goals because the underlying methods of planning contain basic flaws. These include the myth of the Gaussian distribution in planning – that activities will have a most likely time and the actual time taken could be either side of this. The reality is that activities will sometimes run to time, often late, but almost never early (see Parkinson's Law later in this chapter).

2 Estimates of activity times generally include a large safety margin – people will estimate according to their worst past experience of that type of activity but, as will be shown below, this safety margin at each activity does not help in achieving on-time completion.

3   Network diagrams (A-o-N) usually contain a latest start time for activities. For non-critical activities, this builds in slack at the start of activities. Perversely, this creates the situation where these activities, if started at their latest start times (as cash-flow pressures often wrongly dictate), also become critical. The more critical paths in a project, the greater the chance of failing to meet time goals, and the less chance of 'focus' that the project manager will have.

4   Because of this method of scheduling activities, the situation arises where '. . . a delay in one step is passed on in full to the next step. An advance in one step is usually wasted.' (Goldratt, 1997, p. 121). Worse still, where there are parallel activities, regardless of an early finish in one of the paths, the biggest delay is passed on to the subsequent activities.

5   The way that we measure progress is in error – generally by the time that a project manager is notified of a problem it is already too late to prevent it having an impact. This is represented in another piece of project folklore – that a project will spend 90 per cent of its time 90 per cent complete. It is possible to ignore problems when measures indicate that progress is satisfactory, particularly those that rely on managers' estimates of per cent complete.

6   Related to 3 and 4 above, *student syndrome* is identified as where, despite people being given extra time (slack) for an activity, the extra time is wasted at the front end, and often won't start the activity until the latest possible time.

7   It is usual in business projects for people to have to multi-task. The effect of this is to increase the lead-time for all the projects – see below.

Bad multi-tasking

Goldratt (1997) demonstrates this phenomenon very simply in the following example. Imagine that you have three projects to work on – A, B and C. Each is going to take 10 days for you to do your part of the work. If you do them in sequence, the lead-time (start to finish) is shown in Fig. 6.1.

This is simple enough. In the scenario described above, each of these projects was being broken down into smaller units. Let us see the effect of breaking each project in two, doing half of each then returning to finish the remainder, in Fig. 6.2.

The immediate effect is to make projects take considerably longer than they need to. In the case of the development team mentioned above, one can only imagine the effects of having an average of 12 projects per person

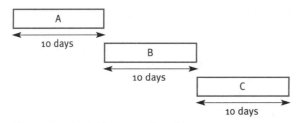

Figure 6.1 Activities completed in sequence

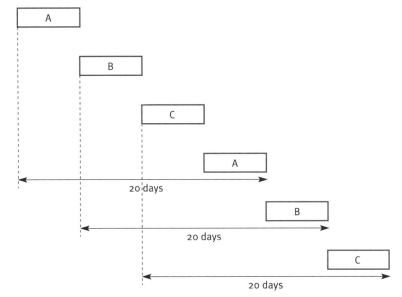

Figure 6.2 The effect of multi-tasking

ongoing at any one time. The reality is, therefore, worse than in the simple example given above as the simple model includes the assumption that people can put down and pick up a project without any loss of time. Where bad multi-tasking was evident in a software company (see the case on the website), programmers would regularly lose 1–2 days of work, refamiliarising themselves with the logic of the task that they were undertaking. These days was lost because of the inefficiency of the system in which they were working. The management system should have identified this and worked to prevent such a waste of time.

There are, of course, some projects where there are delays in getting information or results, where some multi-tasking is inevitable. For instance, in the lighting industry, fluorescent lamps are often guaranteed for 10 000 hours of operation. In one year there are 8762 hours, meaning that testing can take several years, with no realistic means to accelerate such life-tests. It would be pointless waiting for test results to come through before starting on other work – the development team have to move on to other projects.

The above requires planning to take account of human behavioural actions in planning and estimating, and to find ways to either amend the behaviour or mitigate its effects. Some further explanation of the problems of estimating are initially discussed, followed by an elaboration of the remaining points raised above.

Problems with estimates

Typical problems with estimates include:

- Inappropriate use of estimates – people being asked for rough estimates as to how long a particular activity will take, only to find that this becomes the target time enshrined in a committed plan;
- Inappropriate data used to build estimates – people either taking unrepresentative previous experience or not checking whether this was in fact a good representation of the reality of carrying out the task (it is not unusual for such situations to exist for many years where there is a lack of review);
- The estimates are used out of context – having given an estimate of time required to do some work, this is then used despite significant changes having been made to where and how the work is to be carried out.

As commented in the previous chapter, estimates are a guess as to how long an activity or sub-project will take. They should not then be imbued with more certainty than they deserve!

The estimating process

We can view the construction of estimates as being made up of a number of elements as shown in Fig. 6.3. Consider that you are asked how long it will take to prepare a 1500-word report on a subject with which you are familiar. You know from previous experience that the actual task time is probably no more than 2 days, but you know that to promise this would be dangerous. In order to make sure that you have a chance of finishing this in time, you add to the task time. These may be, say, one day for other things that you had already planned to do at that time, another day for interruptions (phone calls, e-mails and other daily tasks) and say, another half-day just in case there are any problems with the project, the computer crashing or the copier not working. Our 2-day activity now takes $4\frac{1}{2}$ days – better say 5 days, just to be sure!

Task time	Other tasks	Interruptions	Safety

Figure 6.3 Building a time estimate

If we now look at what happens to that estimate when the time comes to do the work, we see that there are a number of things that happen. The first is that now we have 5 days to do the job – it will almost certainly take 5 days, and usually more. Does this make us bad estimators? Well, there are certain other factors that intervene:

- Parkinson's Law – an activity will expand to fill the time available;
- Human nature for many of us is also to leave the project until the last possible minute (called *student syndrome* for some reason!) – meaning that the 2 days of real work doesn't need to be started until day 4. We start on day 4 and what happens . . . ?
- The unexpected computer crash (that we had allowed time for initially happens). The problem is that now the time that would have allowed us to recover this has

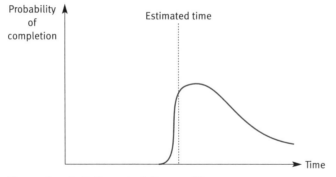

Figure 6.4 Activity completion profile

been used. The activity is almost certain to be late. The safety was used at the start of the activity and did not provide the necessary 'buffer' between the task and the completion date.

The result of this is that time has been wasted on the project – the task still took only $2\frac{1}{2}$ days (2 days for the activity and half a day for the computer crash), but the activity time seen is $5\frac{1}{2}$ days. This is typical and results in an activity profile for completion of projects as shown in Fig. 6.4.

Figure 6.4 shows the chances of early completion of an activity to be very low – we know this from practice. In the unlikely event that someone does finish some work early, they are unlikely to announce the fact for a number of reasons:

- They provided the estimate and do not want to be seen to have overestimated the task time;
- They know that this shorter time will become the 'expected time' for the activity and do not want to have their own margin of safety reduced in future, which might thereby compromise their own perceived performance.

So this early completion does not benefit the project as a whole.

This leads us to the fourth point – that delays will accumulate, but early finish benefits are not passed on. Delays accumulate through the late completion of activities on the critical path of a project, causing delay on the project as a whole. Indeed, if you analyse the chance of lateness of a project, far from the certainties implied by CPM, the only certainty is that the project will run late. For instance, if there are four activities on the critical path of a project and it is known that each has a 30 per cent chance of running late (practitioners usually estimate this to be much higher – nearer 50 per cent), the effect on the project is that there is only a 24 per cent chance that the project will finish on time. The mathematics of how this statement was achieved is unimportant – the result is of the greatest importance. Most projects have considerably more than four activities on the critical path and require rather more certainty than 24 per cent chances of on-time completion. It will be seen in Chapter 8 that a major time risk is where there are long critical paths, with many activities on them. These are particularly susceptible to overrun.

The fifth point is that project managers often use per cent complete measures for estimating progress. This point will be discussed further in Chapter 11, but it does not provide them with the control information that they need to make decisions as to whether any intervention is required to keep the project on schedule.

The above discussion provides some clues as to why such high proportions of projects are late. The challenge now is to analyse the behaviour discussed and determine whether there are alternative methods that may have a better chance of success.

6.3 Background to a Possible Solution – TOC

The Theory of Constraints (TOC) was the result of the application of a structured logic approach to the problems of a manufacturing environment. Specifically, it targeted the way in which production lines were scheduled and the flow of goods was managed. A fundamental of this is to manage systems by focusing on the *constraint* (also termed the *bottleneck*). In a production system, the bottleneck can usually be identified by the pile of inventory waiting to be processed by that part of the process. The importance of the constraint is that it determines the ability of the system to do work and thereby earn revenue. This focus on *throughput* is the factor that differentiated it from other inventory control ideas at the time. It is this focus that will be carried forward to the next section to examine the potential application in projects.

Before continuing to consider whether this is likely to yield any benefit, some understanding of the principles of application of this is necessary. The stages of the TOC approach are as follows:

1 Identify the constraint – the critical path and the critical resources;
2 Exploit the system constraint;
3 Subordinate everything else to the constraint;
4 Elevate the constraint;
5 Go back and find new constraints, repeating the process.

In a production situation, identifying the constraint provided an immediate benefit. New manufacturing technology requires significant investment, and there is no point in adding this to a part of the system that is not a constraint. The focus on the constraint provided an alternative to the conventions of line balancing that had proved so unhelpful. Many firms applied the principles to a range of scenarios, with apparent benefit – particularly to the early adopters. TOC in manufacturing never had the widespread impact on practices that it could have. Perhaps the conflict with the existing planning and scheduling tools that could not handle the approach provided the barrier, or perhaps it was just too different from what had been used previously. The first of these was certainly a barrier to its wider adoption, and it is only recently that widely used software, including SAP, have included TOC as part of their scheduling algorithms. So did it work? There were many successful applications, but just as many where no improvements were gained. This does not provide for an uncritical approach to the application in project management, but there are as many lessons for implementation of such changes, as for the changes themselves. (For a description of these see Leach, 2001.)

6.4 Application of TOC to Project Management

The situation of manufacturing scheduling at the time of publication of *The Goal* (Goldratt and Cox, 1984) has a number of similarities with project management today. First, there was the tendency to try to solve all perceived practitioner problems using increasingly complex heuristics. This led to the promotion of MRPII[1] in manufacturing, and ever more complex planning and scheduling software for project managers. Second, manufacturing was a subject that was unfashionable and rooted in a reactive rather than a strategic mode. The success of the first of these was undoubtedly limited, and to a great extent, the problems were removed through the application of TOC and JIT. The second of these was tackled by the creation of set of strategic frameworks for manufacturing, which would bring the discussion to the boardroom. In project management, journal articles regularly promote one or other new algorithm or method for planning, but without any real attempt to solve the root causes of the problems that project managers face. These are enshrined in the popular software packages that have become the focus of so much project management activity.

The five focusing steps applied to projects are as follows.

The constraint

In a project system, the constraint can be:

- the critical path of the project;
- the resources that are on the critical paths of one or more projects;
- dates that are fixed into the schedule and cannot be moved.

In such a system the constraint is not so immediately obvious, though often the inventory will be in the form of work waiting to be processed piled on someone's desk. In addition to a physical constraint, this weakest point in the system might be a policy of the firm, which will need addressing in the same manner. The critical path was identified in the previous chapter. Further constraints are then added when resources are added to the discussion. Consider the following example.

A marketing firm has two main teams, A and B, to carry out different parts of their projects. There are a number of activities that need to be undertaken and in this case, two activities need the same resource – Team A, as shown in Fig. 6.5.

Many projects run entirely on scheduled dates with every date being a constraint. This is not a happy situation and the result is often significant lateness in many activities and poor performance of the project overall. Despite this, many organisations still seem deeply committed to the system of scheduling everything by fixed dates. This merely compounds the problem of delays accumulating and prevents the usage of early finishes.

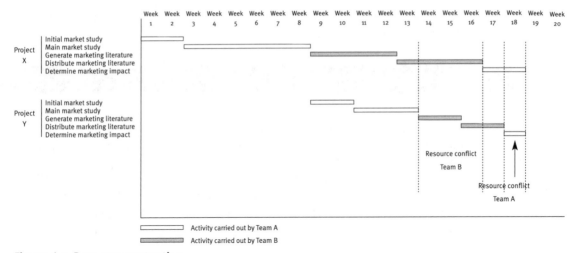

Figure 6.5 Resource contention

Exploit the constraint

Having identified the constraint as the weakest point in the system, exploiting means that anything that prevents that part of the system performing to its maximum potential is to be removed. For instance, one road-building project identified the final surfacing as a constraint activity and the one machine that could do this as a constraining resource. Any delay to the work that this machine carried out delayed the project, causing significant additional costs. The surfacing machine was potentially the weakest link here, as it would frequently break down. The project manager took the decision to have another machine on standby at the site should the first break down. The constraint of the machine being available was protected, and therefore exploited. The cost of the additional rental of the machine was more than offset by the additional certainty that the project would not run late for this reason.

Subordinate everything to the constraint

The next step is subordination – it is pointless having local optima in a system. Therefore, make the constraint the point around which schedules are based and ignore local efficiencies that do not consider the constraint of the system as a whole. For instance, a firm that analysed their processes found that a particular designer was the constraint for many projects – all projects required at least some work to be undertaken by him. It was imperative that work was ready for him and that he was not kept waiting or disturbed during this work. Another firm highlighted critical resources or people performing critical tasks by placing a bright orange beach ball on the desk of that person. This seemingly ludicrous practice made the tasks highly visible, and indicated that that person must not be interrupted until the task was complete. It sounds extreme, but at least no-one was in any doubt as to what was going on.

Elevate the constraint

Elevating the constraint means increasing the flow through that part of the system – removing that as a constraint. In the two examples given above, the road surfacer and the designer need to have their work capacities increased if the system is required to work any faster – either through working longer or through adding extra help to them (e.g. adding another active machine or designer).

The last part is to go back and find the new system constraint, which will probably now be elsewhere in the project. The same rules apply and will ensure that projects are completed as rapidly as possible. Further discussion of these rules is contained in the following section.

6.5 Planning

Are there any differences in the planning process under the critical chain method? Well, the starting point is suggested to be that the true consequences of a late finish should be properly evaluated in financial terms. It is often not a simple process, as the boxes below show.

Road builders

A project to refurbish bridges over a stretch of motorway was being planned. It had been allowed a 4-week duration and the client had required that the project finish on the last working day before the Christmas break. This gave the team planning the project very little time to do any pre-preparation or any of the normal surveying work before the project started. It was handed to the project manager as a JFDI – Just Do It – project. The project was costing the client £300 000 and the industry norm for the profit to be made on it was in the region of 6 per cent. The potential profit was therefore £18 000, provided it was completed on time. If it was not, the penalty clauses in the contract specified £3000 per day to be paid to the client. In addition, the costs of keeping the site going were £3000 per day. This was not unusual, but the Christmas break (the industry closes down for 2 weeks) meant that if the project was running even 24 hours behind schedule the losses would be a minimum of 14 days of penalty clauses (14 × £3000) plus the additional site days. This represented a minimum loss of £42 000, and the chances of running late were substantial. This more than outweighed the potential profit on the project. There was a pressing need to do something different in the management of this project to ensure that it would be completed on time.[2]

This does prove that there is not always a penalty for a late finish. A leisure centre was being constructed for a district council and was completed 2 months late. The council incurred the displeasure of the voters of the region and wanted some redress from the contractors. The problem was determining the extent of the loss that the council had suffered as a result of the lateness. Leisure centres usually require a substantial ongoing subsidy from local government to remain viable. The late opening meant that the council had not had to start paying the subsidy, so the late opening had in fact saved them a considerable sum of money.

Having determined these costs provides the justification for the additional work that follows in the planning stage. The next task is to tackle how estimates are constructed.

Estimates

First, the principles:

- Estimates (both initial and to-finish) should be based on the activity times only, with no safety added. This relies on a number of underlying changes (see later discussion) including buy-in from all people estimating and a commitment to acceptance that 50 per cent of activities will finish early and 50 per cent late. Finishing late is therefore to be expected for half of all activities, necessitating removal of the stigma of a late finish.
- Safety should be included at the end of a critical path – not before. Where there are feeder paths (parallel activities that lead on to the critical path), the safety buffer should be placed at the point where the feeder joins the critical path (see Fig. 6.6).
- Time plans establish precedence relationships but should be treated as overviews only. The nature of project management needs to reflect the dynamic of the actual situation, and accommodate changes as they occur. Furthermore, given the uncertainty of plans, it is vital that all the parties involved are given regular updates on when their input is required. This statement, albeit trite, reflects the need for greater communication to ensure that critical activities can proceed without incurring any delay.
- Progress should be monitored by the critical path – rather than per cent complete, a time to finish is now required from sub-project managers. This can be represented by the state of the project buffer (the slack time at the end of the project).

The constraint may be outside the firm – for instance, with suppliers or customers. It is not unusual in construction or software engineering for delays to be caused by work provided by the client not being ready on time. Suppliers may have

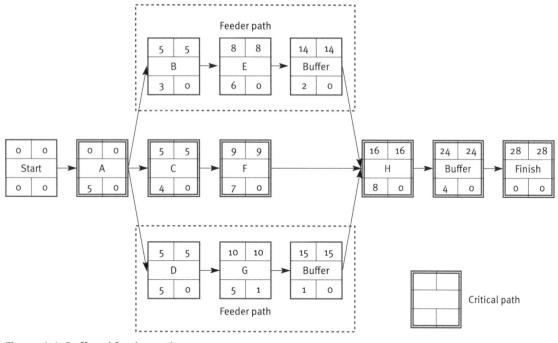

Figure 6.6 Buffered feeder paths

a similar problem – unable to start their part of the project until they have been provided with the necessary information. Using the same approach provides benefits to all parties – we identify that there may be a constraint and buffer it accordingly.

One of the major challenges for a project manager is in keeping plans up to date. They may replan the project on a daily basis and reissue copies to everyone in the project whenever there are changes. This can become very unsettling for everyone concerned, as the whole situation lacks any stability and is not robust to the inevitable changes that will start the minute the project commences. Critical chain project plans with buffers as described and due-date constraints removed from activities wherever possible are far more stable. This stability (as demonstrated in the Project Management in Practice at the end of the chapter) is a major benefit of critical chain scheduling.

Moreover, when a non-critical activity becomes critical it is only necessary to reconsider the criticality as far as the point that the paths merge. Non-critical activities often become critical due to resource contentions. These resources (a person, a department, an external organisation or a piece of technology) are now the constraint, and should be protected by a buffer (some time-slack in front of them). The same rules of managing constraints apply to these constraints, and they should be managed by going through the same five steps in section 6.3.

This added complication to the critical path represents the formation of compound series of activities – often involving different paths – which has been termed *the critical chain*. The TOC approach does result in a new approach to performance, particularly at a local (activity) level. This alone has considerable potential benefit.

6.6 Controlling Projects

So what is the role of the project manager in control, and how is it different under critical chain methods? The answer to the first part of the question is that the project manager has ultimate responsibility for control – by determining the issues of importance, their measures and then devising the system by which they will be monitored and corrective action implemented where necessary. A full description of this process is contained in Chapter 11.

Before we continue, the break with due-dates has been identified as one of the features of critical chain methods. The better alternative is that instead of waiting for a due-date to arrive before starting an activity, that it continues directly from the completion of a subsequent activity. The analogy that describes this best is that of a relay race – where the runners are lined up ready to receive the baton before continuing with their leg of the race. Where due-dates are used, there is no requirement nor incentive for an early finish. Under critical chain, this must be used and any early finish added to the buffers. The role of the project manager therefore changes. Far from watching the dates, the issue becomes one of managing the hand-overs between activities – ensuring that early finishes are encouraged and that subsequent activities are ready to start. This is a major information-handling and communications role, and is one that many project managers undertake anyway, albeit without the framework to gain benefits from the early finish.

6.7 Summary

Goldratt's solution is sufficiently different from previous approaches to warrant some further attention, and uses the same logical basis – the Theory of Constraints (TOC) that has been successfully applied in manufacturing. References to applications are currently limited but as applications increase and software support improves this solution is likely to be more widely used and open to further evaluation.

Project Management in Practice

Balfour Beatty introduce critical chain project management

Balfour Beatty is a large PLC within the construction sector. The case is divided into two parts – the overview and a more detailed consideration. The involvement with the TOC approach starts in 1995 as part of the efforts of their Business Improvement Team. The case charts their experience of the method through to how it is being used today.

The overview

The Business Process Improvement Team identified the possibility of using the approach outlined in *The Goal* in early 1995. During April 1995, two of the team leaders attended the Goldratt Institute's Management Skills Workshop (MSW). They did much analysis of the problems that the firm was facing, including the core problem that 'We don't work to programme'. Projects were regularly delivered late; indeed it was noted that late delivery was expected in the industry. Focusing on their project, they used the problem analysis techniques on the sub-projects in which each of them was involved. They came up with a new approach that was termed 'programme management', which eventually led to what we know today as 'the critical chain'.

In order to make the new approach work a number of senior people went on a two-day programme at the Goldratt Institute in September 1995 to train them in the methods. They returned to work on the A13 project (5.2 km of dual carriageway including three major viaducts, two major junctions and various environmental challenges), which was already under way, but setting up a new 15-month programme. The methods used to support the approach included creating six multifunctional teams who were tasked with working out their own schedules. These were integrated by the site engineer to allow calculation of the critical chain.

The outcome of the project was considered a major success for the company. Over the 15 months of the programme, the firm achieved more than 95 per cent completion of weekly schedules despite significant changes introduced by the client during this period. This compared with an historical average nearer 50 per cent. Other bonuses came in the form of considerably reduced weekend working. The logic for this was simple – don't work overtime where buffers are not under threat. Weekend working was a feature of the industry, and its reduction had a number of beneficial knock-on effects. These included:

- increase in labour productivity;
- reduction in accident frequency rate;
- the job receiving commendation from the client for its high quality.

In addition, as the project was performing so well, staff and contractors achieved their targets and were paid bonuses. In many cases this compensated them for the reduction in overtime.

It appeared that the scenario promised by TOC – that of win–win – had materialised on this project. As commented by Barber *et al.* (1999), 'It [the TOC approach] is not the only approach, but it did prove effective in this instance'.

On this basis, it is often taken that the method should be applicable elsewhere and that the successes are therefore imitable. Further consideration of the case reveals that there are many other contingent factors that should be included in any analysis. These include some consideration of the overall impact on the business since the original implementation.

Further consideration

The issues were revisited with the firm during 2000. This permitted a longer-term view of the approach to be established. It will be shown that despite initial successes, the method ran into heavy resistance, and that the resources which enabled the success were subsequently removed.

During the Management Skills Workshop the participants learned the basics of applying a structured logic approach to the problems that they faced, for identification and solution. These were used by the teams running the project. The project manager commented that this had removed the excuses for poor performance within the teams and had changed the mindset from that of 'we always run late' to that of 'we can complete on time'. However, there were a number of challenges that were faced in this project. The first was that there was only a six-week buffer at the end of the project. This represents only 5–10 per cent of the schedule and is considerably less than recommended for this method of planning (this does not imply non-lean planning – as noted above, simply the 50:50 early:late risk). Second, there was no software available at the time to assist in the planning, requiring a mixture of manual planning and extensive use of 'dummies'. Third, the buffer became a resource for shortening the project for senior managers who did not understand the approach. Given that the stated objective was to '. . . sell the idea that we could complete on time and show the effect of client changes on the schedule' this was particularly counter-productive.

In addition, it required a change in the role of the managers on the site. As the project manager commented, 'it is an information tool – it provides you with the information on which to react. The programme is there to plan management actions, not just construction events.' Furthermore, 'An important part is how you react to the news that the buffer is being shrunk and you have to spend some money'. Given that this was new, many of the middle managers on the sites felt exposed by the approach. On-site, one of the senior foremen commented: 'I thought that this was what we were supposed to be doing anyway,' indicating that at an activity level the changes were not significant.

In the scheduling of resources, particular changes worked well. These included a change in the way that priorities were allocated. The project manager cited the example of the batching plant and the temporary works coordinator, both of which could be bottlenecks in the process. While there were several calls on the batching plant for concrete each day, only one or occasionally two could be handled at any one time. Those that received priority would regularly be those associated with 'those that shouted loudest'. Under the new approach, the highest priority was given to the job associated with the activity with the shortest buffer. In addition, the temporary works coordinator would always have a backlog of work, but now this was prioritised by buffer length associated with the activity.

Other changes were also made. These included:

- delayering the management structure – there were only three (maximum four) layers between the project director and the workforce;
- the cross-functional teams (maximum size 12 people);
- team leaders chosen for leadership rather than seniority or technical prowess;
- changes to assessments to reflect the need to manage not only an individual's own area of work but also how these interface with others;
- supporting actions were demonstrated for the changes that were being made through the 'transition trees' (termed 'action plans' at the firm).

It took 2–3 months to get over the problems of buffer conflicts and the new way of resolving them. The changes were supported by a weekly 'critical events meeting' at which each of the team leaders presented their own programmes. There was agreement not to change any activities due to the likely impact on resource constraints once the programme had been fixed. Feeder paths became separate projects in their own right.

Subsequent to this, the approach was implemented on their next project – the A30/A35. The project manager was not convinced and there appeared to be a considerable resistance to the approach, consistent with a not-invented-here mentality. The notion that 'we've been doing it for the last 20 years and we've never finished on time' prevailed. The project was not completed on time.

Today, the firm is involved predominantly in joint ventures and so is not able to put the TOC approach into practice. In addition, the original business improvement team was disbanded by a new managing director, the firm losing the knowledge as well as the resource to implement the approach.

Case discussion

1 What is the evidence to support the claim that this change was a success?
2 Identify the steps the firm took in this project. How did this contribute to the success?
3 Why would the removal of the supporting resource cause the method to be used in subsequent projects?

Key Terms

TOC	uncertainty
robust planning	Parkinson's Law
student syndrome	multi-tasking
safety	bottleneck
throughput	resource contentions/conflicts
buffered schedules	

Review Questions and Further Exercises

1 Why is there a need for a new consideration – such as through TOC?

2 What are the constraints in projects? How would you recognise them?

3 Carry out estimating on some tasks that you do regularly – the trip to work or place of study, for instance. Compare your estimates with the times you actually take. What do you notice about your estimates?

4 Why might it be necessary to shorten some activities, even if someone has given you an estimate for their time?

5 Where should buffers be placed? Using an example of a personal project, show how the use of a buffer would help.

6 How would you deal with the argument that 'our project is too short to be including buffers into it'?

7 If this is such a good idea how come every project organisation is not using it?

References

Barber, P., Tomkins, C. and Graves, A. (1999) 'Decentralised Site Management – A Case Study', *International Journal of Project Management*, Vol. 17, No. 2, pp. 113–120.

Brown, S., Blackmon, K., Cousins, P. and Maylor, H. (2001) *Operations Management: policy, practice and performance improvement*, Butterworth-Heinemann, Oxford.

Goldratt, E.M. (1997) *The Critical Chain*, North River Press, New York.

Goldratt, E.M. and Cox, J. (1984) *The Goal*, North River Press, New York.

Leach, L. (2001) *Critical Chain Project Management*, Artech House Publishing, Norwood, MA.

Rand, G. (2000) 'Critical chain: the theory of constraints applied to project management', *International Journal of Project Management*, Vol. 18, pp. 173–177.

Further Information

www.prochain.com – good website with lots of discussions of critical chain and regular newsletters. Software works with MS Project to allow the necessary additional features required to construct buffered schedules.

Leach, L.P. (1999) 'Critical Chain Project Management Improves Project Performance', *Project Management Journal*, Vol. 30, No. 2, pp. 39–51.

Newbold, R. (1997) *Project Management in the Fast Lane*, St Lucie Press, Boca Raton, FL.

Rahman, S. (1998) 'Theory of Constraints: A Review of the Philosophy and its Applications', *International Journal of Operations and Production Management*, Vol. 18, No. 4, pp. 336–355.

Schragenheim, E. (1999) *Management Dilemmas: The TOC Approach to Problem Identification and Solution*, St Lucie Press, Boca Raton, FL.

Notes

1 For a description of MRPII, JIT and the application of TOC in manufacturing see Brown *et al.* (2001).

2 Predictably, the project ran considerably over time, and cost what the firm termed 'a significant amount of money'.

7 Cost and quality planning

Time planning was covered before cost and quality planning – does that make it more important? Not necessarily. The importance, as described previously, depends on the project strategy. The order in which the issues are dealt with in practice makes little difference. The three issues of time, cost and quality planning are all interdependent – a decision made in one has an impact on one or both of the other two. They will need to be revised and refined, as described for time planning, through an iterative cycle.

In cost planning, the nature of the costing process will be considered as this determines the process for what follows. Some estimating techniques are described and the costs built up into overall figures. Lastly, the estimates, in many cases after amendment, become the project budget – the financial criterion against which you are assessed.

In quality planning, the definition of the relevant characteristics for the project is followed by the management of both conformance and performance aspects. Treating the project as a service rather than just a product can have benefits here.

Contents

Learning Objectives

By the time you have completed this chapter, you should be able to:
- Identify the priority and role of costs in a project;
- Identify elements of cost and the process of their compilation;
- Demonstrate the role of budgets and how plans impact these;
- Define appropriate characteristics for quality;
- Establish how both conformance aspects and performance aspects of projects can be managed.

7.1   Cost Planning Process

The Sydney Olympics were widely regarded as one of the best games of modern times. In this case the objectives were very carefully considered in terms of the trade-offs identified in Chapter 3, those of time, cost and quality. The strategy in that case was that the games had to be delivered on time (there was absolutely no possibility of postponement) with quality as the next driver and cost as the third priority. This did not sideline the issue – it just put in place the necessary strategy from which decisions could follow. When the organising committee had to return to the Australian Government in 1999 for further funding following the loss of some key sponsors, the argument was clear – if you want the games to be delivered in the way planned it is going to cost more money. Given that the alternative was a compromise on the quality of the facilities or experience for people attending the games this was not an attractive option. The games received the additional funding required. By contrast, 'I want the highest quality output from the project, at no cost, delivered tomorrow' is an all too typical statement of the real requirements of a project and is not a great starting point.

The first stage in this cost planning process, therefore, is to know the importance that is placed on the costs and the potential for trade-offs with other commodities in the project. This will determine what follows.

As a process, cost planning resembles the iterative steps of the time planning process described in Chapter 5. It differs in that there is a further uncertainty with projects of several years' duration. Not only do we not know exactly what the activities will be that far into the project or how long they will take, but we also are susceptible to the vagaries of changes in costs over time as a result of currency fluctuations, inflation and base material costs. We also need to know the basis of the relationship between cost, price and profit in the project that we are undertaking. This will be determined by the context in which we are working.

The role of costing

The basic relationship between price, cost and profit can be expressed in a number of ways:

$$\left. \begin{array}{l} \text{cost} + \text{profit} = \text{price} \\ \text{price} - \text{profit} = \text{cost} \\ \text{price} - \text{cost} = \text{profit} \end{array} \right\} \text{same equation} - \text{different meaning}$$

Which one applied depends on whether price, cost or profit is fixed first. These differences can be explained as follows:

- in the first case the price is fixed through legislation, for example, or in the case of a *target costing* system (see below), through market analysis;
- in the second the cost is fixed, generally through contract purchase which guarantees that goods will be supplied to you at a particular price. This fixes your costs while your selling price and profits can be varied;
- some agreements state the profit that a company is allowed to make through the system known as *cost-plus* or *reimbursable* pricing.

Target costing is being used increasingly in the automotive and aerospace industries, among others. The target price for a complete vehicle or aircraft is established that will give it competitiveness in the intended market and the margin determined by corporate decision. That leaves a figure of the target cost. Designers work back from that figure to the individual component or system costs. The main implication is for component suppliers, who are subsequently set target costs to achieve on their components or systems.

It was normal in the defence industry until a few years ago for everyone to work on a cost-plus basis. This required very detailed time and material cost estimates (and subsequently, records) for a project to be submitted to the purchaser for vetting. Should a supplier be awarded a contract it would be on the basis of direct costs plus a percentage towards overheads and profit. The procedures were lengthy, involved massive bureaucracy and, most importantly, did not encourage suppliers to improve their performance. If costs overran they would still be paid. The changes in the relationships between the various national military procurement agencies and their suppliers mean that contracts are now most likely to be awarded on the basis of competitive tendering with fixed costs for the delivery required. The supplier knows how much they will be paid if awarded the contracts, and has a vested interest in ensuring costs are minimised.

Not everyone welcomed the demise of cost-plus – as one veteran of the era said: 'When we worked to cost-plus, you would do the job properly and know you'd get paid for doing a proper job. Now we have to watch every bean. Previously, the engineers had control over these projects, now it's the accountants.' Reimbursable contracts are still in evidence in some sectors, particularly construction.

In projects that are not direct revenue earners the method of costing is rarely transparent to the uninitiated, but is usually based on the same techniques of estimates, which become budgets against which you have to control. This makes cost planning less of a one-off activity and more something that will be ongoing throughout the rest of the project. The techniques for estimating are discussed in the following section.

7.2 Cost-estimating Techniques

There are two basic approaches to the preparation of costing information:

- bottom-up costing – the estimates of each level in the work breakdown structure are compiled and added together by each level of supervision in the project hierarchy – as would be the case for reimbursable contracts;
- top-down costing – you are allocated a certain amount of money to complete the project activities and this has to be split between the sub-projects. The allocation is based on either senior management's estimates or the use of target costing.

The two systems are illustrated in Fig. 7.1. The advantage of bottom-up costing is that the estimates are prepared by the people who will carry out the activities or their supervisor. This gives some notion of commitment to achieving these figures if the costs are accepted unmodified by the project manager. Where it is common for costing proposals to be cut by project managers the activity level costs generally become artificially inflated, as staff try to remove the effect of such cuts. The process consequently loses credibility. This method is not particularly good at generating accurate estimates. Top-down costing involves the allocation of the costs to the sub-activities. This creates a degree of competition between the supervisors of the activities for resources which many view as being beneficial.

Having determined the nature of the costing process it is now necessary to identify the elements of cost. This is the subject of the following section. The methods for putting numbers to these elements are then discussed, leading on to how they are accumulated into a final cost estimate.

Elements of cost

The major elements of cost are:

- time – the direct input of labour into activities;
- materials – consumables and other items used in the process;

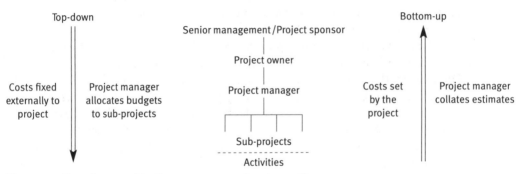

Figure 7.1 Top-down and bottom-up approaches to costing

- capital equipment – the purchase of the means of providing the conversion process, or part of its cost, maintenance, running and depreciation offset against activities;
- indirect expenses – e.g. transportation, training;
- overheads – provision of an office, financial and legal support, managers and other non-direct staff.

Materials can be included in the costings, either at the cost to the company or with a margin added. Capital equipment may have to be purchased specially, in which case its entire cost, or part of it, will need to be offset against the project. Where the equipment will have potential further use after the project has finished with it, it may attract a residual value. Indirect expenses are those not directly related to the value-adding activities, but which are considered necessary to support the project. Overheads are carried by all organisations and include the running of the headquarters and the provision of central services.

To determine the cost of particular elements in advance of the project (i.e. compile estimates), there are a number of techniques that can be employed:

- parametric estimating;
- as . . . but . . . s;
- forecasts;
- synthetic estimation;
- using learning curve effects
- wishful thinking.

Parametric estimating

This type of estimating works well where there is considerable experience of a particular type of project. The project is broken down into a unit that can be readily estimated – for instance, this could be lines of code in a computer program (see Brooks, 1995), hours of contact for a training programme or cost per mile of resurfacing a road. This provides a number to start from with your estimates as shown in the following illustration.

A builder was asked to provide a cost estimate for an extension to a house. The architect had estimated £30 000 for the building works. The builder worked on the basis of £1200 per square metre of additional ground area. The additional ground area was 60 square metres and so there was a considerable variation between the two (£30 000 versus £72 000). Arbitration came from a detailed estimate carried out by a quantity surveyor, who confirmed the builder's estimate by making a very detailed study of the likely hours and materials involved. The parametric version provided a highly robust estimation process.

As . . . but . . . s

As . . . but . . . s are where you or your organisation has experience of doing a similar job previously. The use of previous costs as a baseline for future estimation assumes that these were in some way validated by the previous experience. Given the statement made in Chapter 2 that so many projects are not reviewed in any meaningful way, this is an assumption worth challenging. Indeed, unless there is some method of tracking the actual costings and these are compared with the originals there is considerable doubt as to the validity of such records. Hedgehog syndrome will rule the day. Provided there is some logic to back the continued use of such estimates, they are a good basis from which to start.

Forecasts

These are statements of where it is believed that a particular cost influence will be during the life of the project. It is illustrated by the case below.

Forecasting a conference

The 8th International European Operations Management Association (EurOMA) conference was held in Bath, UK, on 3–5 June 2001. The budget on which the conference was based had been approved at the EurOMA board meeting in June 1999. It had been approved with all the income in euros and all the expenses in pounds. The conference organiser included some allowance for the variable number of delegates (no-one knew until they registered exactly how many would attend – which created a problem in deciding the fixed-cost allocation per head), and in particular for the potential for currency fluctuation. The reality was that the euro depreciated by 17 per cent relative to the pound during the period. This was outside the envelope of uncertainty allowed by the organiser. No more money was forthcoming from the association and no increase in delegate fees was approved. Where now? The organisers had to turn to a range of sponsors to make up the potential shortfall if numbers were low.

For very large projects it is not unknown for the organisation to become involved in currency speculation – either buying the necessary amount of currency when the rates appear favourable, or agreeing exchange deals at particular rates. Where key materials are commodities they may also take an interest in the relevant commodity market. Whatever the case, projects having a currency risk have to factor this into their risk analysis (see Chapter 8).

Synthetic estimates

Where there are considerable items of repetitive work in a project the times for people to carry out certain activities can be analysed to provide a generic set of actions and consequent timings. New activities can be deconstructed into these generic actions and the timings added accordingly. Little or no direct measurement of the workplace needs subsequently to be carried out. This is based on the practices of work measurement, and can be used with some reliability off-line to give indications of the scale of effort required to perform particular tasks.

Time estimation – learning curve effects

Watching a skilled craftsperson at work shows how a highly intricate task can be learned and carried out so that it is made to look easy. Gaining such a level of skill requires years of training and practice (and many mistakes). A project rarely has such an opportunity to gain advantage through repetition. There will, however, be repetitive elements to any activity, particularly during the execution phase. Where this occurs, the time taken each time the task is carried out will decrease as the person becomes familiar with the methods. Subsequent improvements in speed are seen to become smaller over time. This can be quantified using the following formula:

$$Y_x = Kx^n$$

where

x = the number of times the task has been carried out
Y_x = time taken to carry out the task the xth time
K = time taken to carry out the task the first time
n = log b/log 2 where b = learning rate

Learning curves and painting-by-numbers projects

A team is set up to carry out a quality audit of ten departments. The first audit takes four days as the auditors are unfamiliar with the procedures. The second audit takes three. After a period of time, the minimum audit time is reached, and very little further improvement is seen. We can plot this progression as shown in Fig. 7.2.

If we wish to find out how long the eighth audit will take we need to calculate the learning rate, b. The following values can be assigned from the above information:

x = the number of times the task has been carried out = 2
Y_x = time taken to carry out the task the xth time = 3
K = time taken to carry out the task the first time = 4
n can be calculated

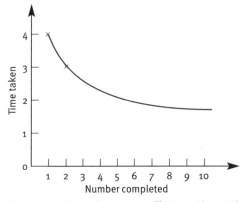

Figure 7.2 Learning curve effect on time taken

Putting these values in:

$$3 = 4(2)^n$$
$$2^n = 3/4$$
$$n \cdot \log 2 = \log(3/4)$$
$$n = -0.1249/0.4149$$

$$n = \log b/\log 2 = -0.4149$$
$$\log b = -0.1249$$
$$b = 0.75$$

From this we can say that the project has a 75 per cent learning curve.

This can also be seen intuitively as another way of expressing the learning curve is to say that every time the total number of audits completed doubles the time taken for the last audit will be the learning percentage multiplied by the original time. In this case as the number of audits doubled from 1 to 2, the time decreased from 4 to 3. The percentage is therefore 3/4 = 75 per cent. As the number of times the audit is done increases, the times taken will decrease as shown in Table 7.1.

Table 7.1

Audit no.	Time taken (days)
1	4
2	3
3	2.54
4	2.25
5	2.05
6	1.90
7	1.78
8	1.69

To complete this example, the time figures can then be put into the kind of cost build-up calculations described in the following section.

Wishful thinking

You are unlikely to find this in any company procedure manual, but the instances of this occurring in practice are legion in most organisations. The prime causes for 'costing by wishful thinking' are:

- Political – for instance, in the Channel Tunnel project, the total cost escalated from £5 billion to £10 billion. Some of the people who worked on the estimating for that project always maintained that the costs would be £10 billion, but that such a figure was not politically acceptable on either side of the Channel. The need to have the fixed transport link was a matter of European integration, with that objective placed above the costs.
- Improper use of estimates – where 'ballpark figures' become official estimates without any checking or further development (see Verzuh, 1999). For instance, you are asked by a colleague how much time it would take to do a particular task just so they can do some preliminary costings. Without any further referral to you the original request is changed, but your figures are still used in preparing a detailed estimate. The latest version of the work is far more involved than you had been led to believe and it is too late to change the figures.
- Failure to be systematic about planning – through either complacency or certainty that they will not actually be called on to do the work being discussed people are vague and give an unqualified estimate to 'get the request off their desks'.

There are many other reasons that are found through review for wishful thinking in this area. Reference to a systematic revision–refinement cycle, particularly for medium or large projects, will help.

The above techniques are used to provide a means of arriving at elements of project cost, with the objective of avoiding wishful thinking. As has been said many times already, however, the answers from even the best techniques are only estimates, and errors made at this stage are multiplied many times.

7.3 Cost Build-up

We decided to employ a researcher for 6 months to do some data collection and analysis. The direct cost of employing the person was calculated at £12 000. The expenses involved in carrying out the work were in the region of £5000. The total mini-project budget ended up at an incredible £52 000 by the time overheads, sundry expenses, administrative assistance and office space costs had been taken into account.

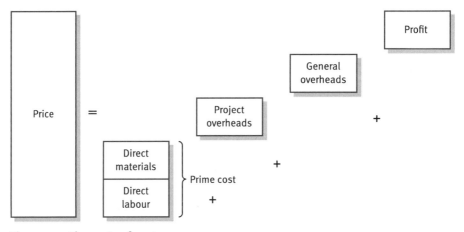

Figure 7.3 Elements of cost

The process so far has identified particular elements of cost. So how do we end up with the final cost? The process can seem quite baffling, and as shown above, relatively small pieces of work can look very expensive once they have been fully calculated. The elements of cost are added as shown in Fig. 7.3.

The following example illustrates the cost build-up principle.

Training course – how much?

The course coordinator wishes to advertise the course but needs to know how much will have to be charged in order to make a profit. The time estimates are made based on the proposed course length – determined by first considering what it could usefully achieve in given times. These are correlated with the necessary labour input to ascertain the direct cost. The programme requires a consultant to do three days' training which costs £250 per day, to be supported by an administrator, whose time is costed at £90 per day. The direct costs (fixed, i.e. regardless of how many delegates attend) are therefore £1020. The course requires the provision of printed materials and stationery, which are a variable cost (the more delegates, the greater the cost) of £60 per delegate. Assuming the course is fully subscribed and can accommodate 15 delegates, a further £900 needs to be added to the estimate. The total of these is the prime cost. Indirect labour and materials include administrative time arranging the course (say eight days at £90 per day), and general overheads would be the ongoing 'fixed costs' of providing the building, heating, lighting and functions such as finance to provide the funds, and procurement in raising the necessary purchase orders. The overhead is added to the total cost at a rate of 60 per cent.

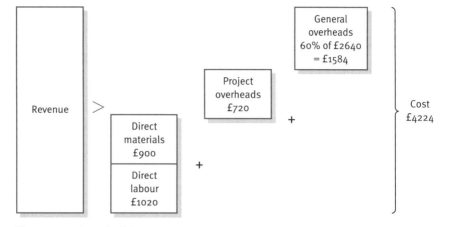

Figure 7. 4 Cost build-up

The cost build-up is as Fig. 7.4. This does not include the profit for the organisation. The minimum rate per delegate should be the total cost (£4224) divided by the number of delegates (15). This gives £281.60. To this should be added a profit margin and a contingency figure in case the course is undersubscribed.

Reliance on this form of allocating overheads does cause anomalies in costing, which can be very damaging to the profitability of the organisation as a whole. These anomalies cast doubts on the merits of conventional cost accounting, though it is still the most-used system. Where, for example, new methods are introduced which speed the flow of tasks through a department, the revenue for that area falls – it is doing the same work only faster, but revenue depends on hours spent on 'doing'. The improved methods therefore generate less revenue for that department, which is unlikely to encourage improvement.

These cost estimates are used in a number of ways. At the outset of the project they will provide a rough idea as to whether the project is viable – that is, the returns will justify the investment. If the project progresses to detail planning, these estimates will have to be revised to show the increased level of consideration that has gone into compiling the estimates. If approved, this spend becomes the budget, though often not without being 'trimmed'. It is this budget that is the subject of the next section, and the basis for control – in particular through earned value (see Chapter 11).

7.4 Cost Management: Budgets

Collins English Dictionary defines a budget as:

a written statement of money: where it is drawn from, its amount, how it is to be spent

Most organisations require managers to perform budgetary analysis at least annually and project managers are in a perpetual cycle of seeking approval and then allocating funds. The following are categories generally found in budget applications/grants. They are more explicit statements of the categories of costs identified above:

- labour;
- materials;
- consumables;
- cap-ex (capital expenditure);
- travel;
- subsistence.

In developing bottom-up costs, these are the basic elements that should be considered. Further elements should be added as appropriate. In addition, it is usual for these to provide headings within project codes which activities can draw against. The boxed example/case at the end of this section questions whether this kind of artificial division of resources really helps progress or project monitoring and control, or simply makes the accounting system neater.

Budgets in public sector environments can be allocated using *zero-base* budgeting. Where activities are ongoing but are reviewed on an annual or similar basis this approach takes into account previous performance. Where progress can be demonstrated, funding may be made available. Where progress is deemed to be unsatisfactory, the remaining activities may either be denied funding altogether or be cut. This has been the case where stipulations of attracting private funding to supplement government grants have been made.

The discussion of budgeting would not be complete without looking at how costs are tracked as the project progresses. In the majority of industries, direct labour and materials would be allocated and costs tracked through a job-costing system. For the purpose of accounting, the job could be issued a code against which charges are made. When costs are incurred, they are noted against these codes. The construction and defence industries use this method extensively. There is usually a budget holder (often the project manager) who periodically checks that what has been recorded is an accurate record.

In considering the value added by the budgetary system there are two problems that frequently arise:

- What should happen to funds left in a budget at the end a project or accounting period?
- What should happen when one category of expenditure is exhausted, but project activities still need funding in that category?

Residual funds at the ends of projects or accounting periods are often spent to prevent their being 'lost' back into the accounting system. This results in unnecessary purchases or in acquisitions being rushed through to beat deadlines. This is unlikely to encourage good use of resources. Underspend through cost efficiency goes unrewarded under conventional systems of budgeting. Alternatives to this include the reward of cost efficiency through greater allocations of funds in the future.

The imposition of constraints, concerning the movement of funds between budget categories, causes anomalies and can result in wasted money (see example below).

Four senior engineers working on the development of a new motor system at a UK plant required a face-to-face meeting with colleagues in Switzerland. This was a reasonable request, but it was pointed out that the budget for air travel had been exhausted. Normally, they could have flown out and back in the same day but that was not possible. There was, however, money left in the accommodation budget and travel by road could be subsidised from general funds. The four hired a car, drove to the ferry and to Switzerland, overnighting on both outward and return journeys, with the round trip taking three days. Flights would have cost in the region of £800, and used four person-days of time. The total, including accommodation and subsistence for the three-day trip, was also £800. The time used, however, was 12 person-days – which represented a considerable additional, but hidden, cost. Adhering to the rules of a budgeting system, which was designed to help cost control, caused considerable unnecessary additional costs to be incurred to the organisation. All in the cause of keeping the accounts in order.

Relative to budgets, the total amount of spend in any one category and against any one activity is of interest. For many organisations, there is a further constraint to the pattern of spend – that of cash-flow.

Cash-flow

Most people have to manage their own cash-flow and there are a number of techniques for doing this. One student, with great discipline, would only draw out a certain amount of money from the cashpoint each week. Once this was gone, nothing further could be purchased. (He is one of the few people I have ever heard about who left university without an overdraft!) This fixed approach to cash-flow is not irrelevant to the project manager, as it is not unusual for funds to be capped and expenditure limited in any one financial period – a quarter or a year.

The size of the budget can be meaningless if you cannot gain access to the funds at the time that they are needed. Part of the challenge of the scheduling process is to ensure that the cash-flow issues do not provide a constraint to the project and that suppliers, for instance, can be paid. Stopping a project because you are waiting for goods that are being witheld by a supplier due to late payment of their last bill not only provides unnecessary delay but is likely to damage your relationship with that supplier.

Other cash-flow issues for project managers include:

1 Where large complex projects are being carried out it is usual for stage payments to be made on completion of certain project milestones. These are vital points in the project for supplier organisations and their business survival can depend on this.
2 The project schedule may have to be revised to reflect the transition from one accounting period to another – a purchase for the project delayed or brought forward to meet other project needs.

Methods of tracking project spend

How do we know what has been spent on a project? The costs of purchases and commitments to purchase (either items ordered and not yet delivered, or delivered and not yet invoiced) have to be tracked and this can be directly attributed to your project budget. The labour input can be tracked through:

- Direct work measurement of the time input – timesheets are completed by individuals showing on which activities they spent what time working. These are then aggregated and the total costs charged against project budgets by the accounting system. This is the basis of the system of *activity-based costing* and is used by many organisations including consultants to determine who will pay for each unit of a person's time – either hourly or on a day-rate basis.
- Work sampling – random samples are taken of what individuals are doing over a period of time, usually several weeks. These data are representative of how the individual proportionally spends their entire time. From this proportion the input of that individual to a project can be estimated and fed into the costing system as for direct work measurements.

7.5 The Quality Planning Process

The quality planning process should follow the structure shown in Fig. 7.5. There are a number of elements to this figure, centring around the first step in any quality process – that of definition. Quality is a term that has so many different meanings for different people that it must be subject to some further definition before we can in any sense manage it. The two major inputs are from organisational strategy and from customer requirements. Customer requirements may be explicitly stated in direct value-adding projects through the terms of the contract or, in many cases, will have to be determined through discussions. The strategy input should help to determine the kind of quality that we are trying to achieve – for instance, technical excellence or meeting certain external standards. These two inputs can be put into context by considering the alternative approaches to defining and managing quality and can be summarised in the manufacturing and service paradigms as shown in Table 7.2.

The manufacturing approach to quality championed conformance to specification as the metric for success. This relied on quality being definable through a precisely measurable set of characteristics. This is applicable to large-scale engineering projects,

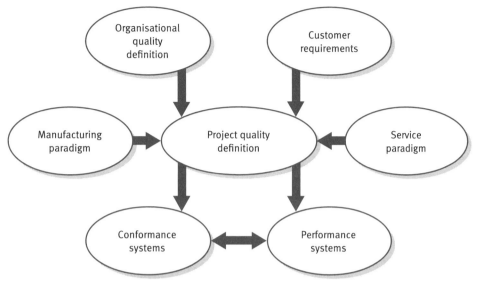

Figure 7.5 Quality planning process

Table 7.2 Manufacturing and service approaches to quality

	Manufacturing	*Service*
Definition	Product-based – a precise and measurable set of characteristics	Based on stakeholders' expectations and perceptions
Attributes	Performance, conformance, features, reliability, durability, serviceability, perceived quality and aesthetics (Garvin, 1984)	Access, communication, competence, courtesy, credibility, reliability, responsiveness, security, tangibles, understanding/knowing the customer (Parasuraman *et al.*, 1985)

for instance. Outside this environment, there are many types of projects that require a much higher degree of customer orientation, considering management of both perceptions and expectations. Furthermore, many modern projects do not have tangible outputs. Rather than applying product-based measures of quality in such instances, service-based definitions and derived measures are far more appropriate. These feed into the two sets of actions that have to be planned at this stage – developing systems that ensure conformance and performance. These two issues are the subjects of the next two sections.

7.6 Quality Conformance Planning

Since the 1950s quality conformance planning – otherwise referred to as quality assurance – has been used to ensure that minimum standards are maintained in a wide array of activities. There is a considerable literature on it (see Further Information at the end of this chapter). The discussion here will focus on the use of a *project manual* as a means of not only *planning* for achieving what you have set out to do in quality terms but also *demonstrating* that you have planned to achieve what you set out to do in quality terms. This is no small difference, particularly when it comes to legal liability issues or preparing the information for a review process. The project manual, as the contents list below demonstrates, is not just about quality. It is about bringing all project information – including that about time and cost – into one place.

A contents list might include the following:

- Introduction – the reasoning behind the project.
- Planning – including the objectives, priorities, scope statement and WBS (as described in Chapter 4), and all the detailed plans – those for time and cost, both in summary and detail, contingencies and risk analysis (see Chapter 8). These are the basis for reference when decisions are required.[1]
- Execution details – including the schedules, the responsibilities (see below), relevant procedures, standard forms and organisational structure that will be used.
- Records – minutes of relevant meetings, notes of problems that have arisen and how they were dealt with, changes requested and made, status reports, other correspondence.
- Miscellaneous information – including contact points for all people involved in the project, sources of technical reference material.

For relatively small, low-complexity projects such a definition may seem excessive, and indeed it can be reduced to a minimum. As one events manager who used a project manual routinely for her work commented, 'If I fall under a bus tomorrow, someone could walk in here and pick up the project, and get up to speed with it fairly quickly'.

Responsibility allocation

A major task for the project manager concerns the allocation of resources to different parts of the project. These may be to different parts of their own firm or even to different organisations. Before plans can go forward for analysis it is vital that the part of the organisation has the resources available to carry out the tasks that have been assigned to them. Inevitably, some parts of the organisation will have little problem meeting the objectives with the resources under their control. Others will be put under considerable strain. If the plans are to have any credibility, they must consider the limitations imposed by the availability of people and equipment.

The allocation of tasks to a project team can be eased by the use of a responsibility matrix. Where there are clear skills requirements for tasks these should be met first, with the less constrained resources matched to the remaining tasks – as was demonstrated in Chapter 6. A responsibility matrix is shown in Fig. 7.6.

All the above provides the basis for having the necessary documentation in place to demonstrate that you have done everything possible to ensure that the project delivers as conforming to the stated requirements. Many organisations do legislate the type and style of documentation required, and this is demonstrated both in the Project Management in Practice at the end of this chapter and in the Appendix. For

Activity Person	1	2	3	4
A		◉	○	○
B	○		○	
C	○	○	○	○
D			◉	
E	○			○
F		○		◉

◉ Person having primary responsibility

○ Some involvement

Figure 7.6 Responsibility matrix

large-scale projects the documentation is a significant workload in itself – and one potential role for a project office. The compilation and sharing of information through a project manual is a task that can be shared using modern IT – Lotus Notes, for instance. Many organisations and individuals do still prefer the project manual to be a physical document, and for this to be available for use and inspection by any of the project team or other stakeholders in the area where the work is being carried out. Does all this make your stakeholders – customers in particular – happy or delighted? The answer to this is that if you do not have it, it will make them very unhappy, but it does not in itself cause delight. Having satisfied the conformance requirements, what can the project manager do to ensure good quality performance?

7.7 Quality Performance Planning

In the Project Management in Practice at the end of Chapter 3 (the University of Rummidge in Splot case) there are several key stakeholder groups, all with different requirements. Compare, for example, the requirements of the council of Splot with those of the staff of Rummidge. At the outset, it would be useful to ensure that there was at least some resolution of the conflict between the objective to have a university based in Splot and the wish of the staff of Rummidge not to have to travel the 40 minutes or more to the new campus. For instance, additional time and travelling allowances could be offered that would counter some of the staff's objections. There are two further aspects that need consideration here:

1 the nature of satisfaction;
2 how then to manage the process by which service provided by the project is delivered.

The nature of satisfaction

Some general principles of stakeholder management come from an appreciation of basic customer behaviour. One part of this concerns the nature of satisfaction. Here, Maister's (1993) first law of service is useful, namely that:

satisfaction = perception – expectation

That is, the satisfaction is determined by the difference between how the project is perceived or viewed by a stakeholder and how they expected it to perform. One of the greatest causes of dissatisfaction is the creation of unrealistic expectations. Where competitive tendering is required for obtaining a contract, firms have to push the limits of what they could achieve. This should be limited, however, as it does set the level of expectations against which they will later be judged. Even where there is no competitive element of bidding for resources, many people still take a very optimistic view of the project outcome. This needs to be considered carefully.

Perceptions can to a certain extent be managed. A useful consideration of this element is to provide customer *cues* – points where the stakeholder's attention is drawn to favourable aspects of the project process or outcome. These are from the stakeholder's own experience, but importantly can be reinforced by external factors such as publicity material. Rather than relying on the assumption that 'quality speaks for itself' and that customers are able unambiguously to evaluate the quality of the outcome or the process, the project manager has a number of channels of communication that can be used to 'manage' consumer perceptions. The publicity element of the marketing communications programme potentially affects the information available to stakeholders – as demonstrated by the following example.

Stakeholder management – the road builders

It seems that wherever you go in the world people moan about the state of their country's roads. The UK is no different in this respect. When a local council decided to resurface the road leading to a major tourist area in the height of the summer the anger turned from the state of the road to the stupidity of doing such work during the period of highest demand. For weeks the road was in turmoil, with significant delays being encountered during very hot weather. Local residents were horrified at the amount of work being done during 'anti-social hours' – creating noise from the works and substantial additional heavy traffic, bringing in machinery and materials to the site. Yet this all seemed to be forgotten when the project was completed and notices were posted at the side of the road stating that:

'XYZ contractors, working in conjunction with your local council, are pleased to announce the completion of the road up-grade scheme, 6 full weeks ahead of schedule.'

Even the local paper was impressed. How about this for stakeholder management?!

A further level in the consideration of the management of perceptions was identified in section 7.5. This concerns the nature of the attribute of the outcome of the project as either a product or a service. As was shown then, services can be considered to have a wider array of characteristics that a customer or group of customers will consider. For instance, the outcome of a project may be the construction of a building or the preparation of a document. Both of these have tangible qualities that can readily be assessed and will form part of the expectations and perceptions of stakeholders. There are also intangible elements of the process. These include:

- *responsiveness* – the speed of reply to requests for information or changes;
- *communication* – how readily the project team provided information;
- *competence/professionalism* – the apparent ability of the project organisation to deliver the outcomes;
- *courtesy* – the style of the treatment received by stakeholders;
- *accessibility* – the ease with which individuals could be identified and contacted when information was required.

These elements may not represent the *core product* of the project – the building or the document. There may be *peripheral* elements – documentation for the building or support information from a document on a website. Project managers therefore also need to consider which elements of the project are core and which are peripheral. While the core should take the majority of the resources, you may find that provided it is achieved in a satisfactory manner, it is the peripheral product of the project on which you will be judged.

Table 7.3 provides a summary of these issues for the project manager. It shows elements of the process and outcomes from the project, and how the expectations and perceptions can be managed in each case. This is a major improvement on the normal system, where managers simply use customer complaints as a measure of the success or otherwise of their actions. However, even if your project performs satisfactorily, do not expect customers to be pleased. You will have to find elements – maybe of the peripheral product – which can be used to provide the excess of perception over expectation. If project management is to move to a more proactive approach to such issues, it is vital that they are considered at the strategy stage.

So how do we ensure that we communicate with stakeholders and that key individuals are kept 'in the loop'? Four-field maps/deployment flow-charts do help with

Table 7.3 Management of expectations and perceptions

	Process	*Outcome*
Expectations	Provide samples of process documentation; do not overpromise	Determine actual requirements; do not overpromise
Perceptions	Provide regular reports of progress	Promote positive aspects of outcome – *cues*

Table 7.4 Communication plan

Stakeholder	Communication	Timing	Format	Distribution	Person responsible
Project sponsor	Monthly	Week 1 each month	Short report	E-mail	Project manager
Accounts department	Monthly spend schedule	2 weeks before start of month	Short budget	E-mail	Administrator
Client department	Monthly	Week 1 each month	1-page report	E-mail and noticeboard	Liason officer

this process, and ensure that those directly affected are included. Many project managers also like to include a specific communications plan as part of the planning process, and indeed this is part of both PRINCE2 methods and the PMI body of knowledge. As a tool, it is probably most useful for medium–large-scale complexity projects, particularly where there is a diverse stakeholder group.

Communications planning

A common technique for communications management centres on the use of a table to identify the nature of the communication (what will be told to whom and in what format), the timing and who is responsible for doing it. We are not considering daily communication or simple information-sharing activities, which while vital, are not the type of 'grand communications' being considered here – typically key reports, announcements of achievements, technical updates etc.

To help structure this the basic stakeholder analysis carried out as part of the project strategy formulation process is expanded in Table 7.4.

While IT can assist in the distribution of information, many managers suffer from e-mail overload, restricting not only their efficiency but also the effectiveness of the communication. Other, more visible, methods of reporting are therefore preferable, as will be shown in Chapter 11.

7.8 Relevant Areas of the Bodies of Knowledge

Under the cost heading, both bodies of knowledge in Tables 7.5 and 7.6 recognise the extensive systems that are already in place in organisations used to dealing with large projects for managing such endeavours. Neither recognises the problems of having to establish such systems in other organisations, nor the costs associated with running such systems. Also, while both bodies of knowledge acknowledge the performance aspects of quality management, both focus on the conformance aspects.

Table 7.5 Relevant areas of the APM body of knowledge

Relevant section	Title	Summary
24	Quality management	The basics of quality planning and control are outlined, as they were for *conformance management* in this chapter. The *performance management* issues are covered under the heading of Total Quality Management – TQM.
33	Budgeting and cost management	This is also relevant to Chapter 11 of this book. The role of the budget as the means by which a project is judged is outlined, along with some of the measures that are associated with the measuring conformance to this.

Table 7.6 Relevant areas of the PMI body of knowledge

Relevant section	Title	Summary
7.1	Project cost management – resource planning	Having determined the activities, how long they will take and other resource requirements, the resource planning stage pulls all this together prior to the start of cost estimating.
7.2	Project cost management – cost estimating	The inputs to the process include several elements not previously discussed – including estimating publications (containing cost rates for different tasks) and risks (discussed in the next chapter in this text). Tools for estimating are identified, including *analogous estimating* (top-down) and use of computerised tools.
7.3	Project cost management – cost budgeting	'Cost budgeting involves allocating the overall cost estimates to individual activities or work packages to establish a cost baseline for measuring project performance.'
8.1	Project quality management – quality planning	This includes discussion of the role of the organisational quality policy into the process, and the role of quality in any trade-off decisions (as discussed in the context of project strategy). Other issues include the role of prevention versus inspection. Conformance to requirements is treated as conformance management, and *fitness for purpose* alludes to some of the performance issues identified in this chapter. A significant alignment with ISO 9000 is evident. Lots of tools and techniques suggested as relevant, including Design of Experiments (Taguchi – see Bicheno, 1998).
8.2	Project quality management – quality assurance	Focusing back onto conformance issues, the main tools and techniques here are quality planning, and quality audit. One of the results of quality assurance is quality improvement – a useful theme in this context.

7.9 Summary

This chapter has been divided into two issues that are well developed in most project organisations – cost and quality. For almost all projects some consideration of these is highly relevant. Both cost and quality planning rely to some extent on the time planning – hence preceding these in the life-cycle. They are, however, interdependent.

For cost planning the issue here is to determine its importance, and through the iterative process outlined to come to some decisions as to the likely costs (and hence price and profit) on the project. This also determines the project viability. There are many techniques for cost estimation, although there is a 'wishful thinking' element to some estimates. Through the idea of cost build-up, all the elements are integrated and when approved, these become the budget against which your project will be assessed.

For quality, the process considered the two main inputs of strategy and customer requirements, and the outputs of a process to consider assurance – or conformance to requirements, and a process to work towards customer satisfaction/delight. This would be through first considering the definition of quality that the organisation had as relevant and the needs of the customers. This definitional issue is highly significant due to the diversity of meanings of 'quality' and this is facilitated through the application of both product and service definitions to core and peripheral outputs from the project. In managing conformance, the importance of documented systems including the use of a project manual was covered. The managing of perceptions includes the use of active cues and a communications plan.

Project Managment in Practice

Adopting a standard for project planning – useful discipline or unnecessary constraint?

Should all the project plans produced in an organisation conform to a particular set of rules as to how they should be constructed such as:

- the notation used in diagrams;
- the use of timescaled axes (the left-to-right scale where distance on the diagram is proportional to time);
- the units to be used;
- who can construct the diagrams;
- what procedure, if any, should be used for checking the plans prior to their issue;
- the filing, storage and control of plans to ensure that only the current version is being worked to;
- the format of reports;

. . . or is this just creating unnecessary bureaucracy?

There was a clear divide among the project managers who were questioned on this issue, which can be summarised in the following composite cases.

Example 1 Makesure Electronics

There are very tight controls as to how project plans may be drawn up. The bureaucracy of the company is considered necessary to ensure that the end-customers of the projects are kept happy (generally military procurement agencies). The correct paperwork is essential to the project and would be returned to the originator if all the boxes on the accompanying forms are not fully completed. It is generally felt that the process prevents any dynamic activity taking place, but that is appropriate for their market.

Example 2 Internal consultancy in a public service industry

The role of the consultancy is one of a team that moves in to help a department solve a particular problem before moving on to the next. The team is required to be dynamic and respond quickly to changes. Plans are mainly for the use of the team in structuring how they tackle the problem. No particular convention is adhered to and there are no rules which the team believe would constrain the problem-solving process. This often causes problems with their 'customers', many of whom believe in the benefits of the more formalised approach but who nonetheless are generally satisfied with the results of their work.

The arguments for and against using a highly formalised approach may be summarised as follows:

For formalisation
- ensures that everyone is working to the same standard – gives the best chance that the plans are universally understood;
- imposes a degree of discipline on the process;
- can be used as a marketing feature for the project organisation;
- is a requirement for some markets, e.g. some construction tenders, government contracts;
- covers your back.

Against formalisation
- restricts creative activity;
- standardisation is to some extent taken care of by the use of a common project planning software package;
- can mask problems of disorder;
- costly to implement and maintain systems;
- it is very unusual for two organisations to work to the same standard or set of rules – does not improve inter-organisational communication.

Key Terms

cost / price / profit	target costing
cost-plus / reimbursable	bottom-up
top-down	parametric estimates

as . . . but . . . s	forecasts
synthetic estimates	learning curves
cost build-up	budgets
cash-flow	work sampling
activity-based costing	conformance / performance
manufacturing/service paradigms	project manual
responsibility matrix	satisfaction
perception versus expectations	communications plan

Review Questions and Further Exercises

1 Identify the different roles that cost, price and profit can play in determining project costs.

2 In costing proposals, discuss the differences between top-down and bottom-up approaches.

3 Describe the major elements of cost in a proposal to:

(a) implement a new computer system for the administration of a college or university

(b) construct a new theme park

(c) introduce a new range of non-paracetamol headache tablets.

4 Identify the benefits and potential disadvantages of a budget system.

5 'Evans the Steam' has set up a new business and secured a contract to build 32 locomotives for mountain railways, which are being reopened as tourist attractions. The order is to be fulfilled in two batches of 16. The first locomotive takes 30 days to assemble with seven people working full-time on it. The daily rate for a locomotive fitter is £80 and the overheads are estimated to be 50 per cent on top of the labour rate. Evans is confident that an 80 per cent learning curve is possible. The first batch has been priced with a labour estimate of £16 000 per locomotive and the last 16 with a labour cost of £10 000. Comment on the pricing of the labour content and show whether the rates per locomotive are sufficient to cover the likely actual costs.

6 Draw up a table of potential costing methods, and show where each might be appropriate, giving examples.

7 What is 'quality?'

8 What is the difference between a 'product' and a 'service?'

9 Carry out a web search of companies to see if you can find their quality policy and any relevant quality documentation. What do you notice about the procedural documents?

10 A firm has very poor quality performance and is contemplating what it must do next to improve its situation. Devise a 10-point plan to improve its quality performance.

References

Bicheno, J. (1998) *The Quality 60*, Picsie Books, Buckingham.

Brooks, R. (1995) *The Mythical Man-month*, 2nd edition, Addison-Wesley, Harlow.

BS–ISO 10006 (1997) Quality Management – Guidelines to quality in project management.

Dimancescu, D. (1995) *The Seamless Enterprise: Making Cross Functional Management Work*, Wiley, New York.

Drucker, P. (1955) *Management*, Butterworth-Heinemann, Oxford.

Garvin, D. (1984) 'What Does Product Quality Really Mean?' *Sloan Management Review*, Vol. 25, No. 3, pp. 25–36.

Maister, D.H. (1993) *Managing the Professional Service Firm*, Free Press, New York.

Parasuraman, V. *et al.* (1985) 'A Conceptual Model of Service Quality and its Implications for Future Research', *Journal of Marketing*, Vol. 49, Fall, pp. 41–50.

Verzuh, E. (1999) *The Fast Forward MBA in Project Management*, Wiley, Chichester.

Further Information

Badiru, A.B. (1993) *Quantitative Models for Project Planning, Scheduling and Control*, Quorum, London.

Chase, R.B. and Stewart, D.M. (1994) 'Make Your Service Fail Safe', *Sloan Management Review*, Vol. 35, No. 3.

Feigenbaum, A.V. (1956) 'Total Quality Control', *Harvard Business Review*, November–December, pp. 93–101.

Goodpasture, J.C. (2001) 'Make Kano Analysis Part of Your New Product Requirements', *PM Network*, May, pp. 42–45.

Gummesson, E. (1991) 'Truths and Myths in Service Quality', *International Journal of Service Industry Management*, Vol. 2, No. 3, pp. 7–16.

Heskett, J.L. *et al.* (1997) *The Service Profit Chain*, Free Press, New York.

Kleim, R.L. and Rudlin, I.S. (1993) *The Noah Project: The Secrets of Practical Project Management*, Gower, Aldershot.

Maylor, H. (2000) 'Strategic Quality Management', in *Strategic Management in Tourism*, Moutinho, L. (ed.), CABI Publishing.

Smith, N. (1995) *Project Cost Estimating*, Thomas Telford, London.

Zeithaml, V. *et al.* (1990) *Delivering Service Quality: Balancing Customer Perceptions & Expectations*, Free Press, New York.

www.asqc.org – the American Society for Quality Control – some useful publications
International Journal of Quality & Reliability Management, Emerald Press.

Note

1 ISO 10006 contains specifications for the content of quality plans – see the Appendix.

8 Plan analysis and risk management

An individual or organisation will wish to pursue a portfolio of projects that will yield the greatest benefits, and so requires systematic methods for assessing proposals. These methods should be reflected in the preparation of proposals and the assessment of those proposals.

Much of the assessment of proposals used to be carried out by specialists, especially financial justification. Twenty years ago, engineers, for example, would not have been expected to be able to complete the financial elements of a proposal. Project management skills today should include the ability to speak the language of the financial analyst. Proposals can be produced and amended with this financial element in mind. Strategic investment decisions are identified as an area in which the normal rules of appraisal do not apply and where new methods are being sought.

This chapter considers the basic skills required in such analysis. Specifically, the plans for time, cost and quality can be examined in a number of ways. Where elements are identified that need reconsideration (e.g. shortening the duration), these can be integrated into the analysis. In addition, risk management is a key element of the planning and ongoing management of projects, and the methods for this are well developed. This is only part of the picture, however. The planning must consider not only what might go wrong and how this is to be handled but also the opportunities that projects present as the process is progressing.

Contents

Further information
Notes

Learning Objectives

By the time you have completed this chapter, you should be able to:
- Carry out basic analysis of plans with the objective of maximising the performance of the project;
- Demonstrate how the negative potential of the project can be minimised through effective risk management.

8.1 Analysing Time Plans

It is remarkable how often project managers spend large amounts of time compiling time plans without then analysing what they have done to see if the process could be improved. It was stated in Chapter 5 that the key objectives of the planning process were first to optimise the process, then to remove potential problems. The role of critical chain methods in this have been discussed, and indeed are one of the main means by which this process should be attempted. There are other basic approaches that also need to be considered.

In Chapter 5 the issues of *slack* and *critical paths* were also discussed. Their optimisation provided one level of analysis. The project manager now needs to determine whether these are significant issues. Specifically, the first task is to calculate whether the project can be completed within the required time period.

As part of the analysis of the time and resource plan you have prepared the issue frequently arises as to how all or part of the project could be carried out in less time. There are few projects of any scale that have the benefit of significant slack. Even if they do have slack as the project proceeds, unforeseen challenges arise and time needs to be clawed back from a subsequent activity. Even with critical chain scheduling, when the buffer enters the 'action' zone, there is a need to shorten the remainder of the critical chain.

There are a number of ways in which activities can be shortened:

- provide an incentive for the work to be completed early – for example, through offering monetary bonuses to contractors for an early finish;
- add additional resources such as extra people or machine capacity, provide overtime, additional contracts, etc.;
- parallel activities – reduce the risk of overrun by providing parallel means of obtaining an output;
- reduce the level of technological change – use existing technology;
- remove the constraints to activities starting – for example, through modifying the dependency relationship between activities allowing part of an activity to start before the previous part is completely finished.

Clearly, there is a decision to be made here – either to compromise the output in terms of time or specification or to commit extra resources. Good project managers often find ways of circumventing such challenges, for example through:

- personal supervision of one or more activities, which can ensure an early completion;
- meeting with the project sponsor to find the time at which the output was required in reality (the absolute latest time) as opposed to what had been given in the brief;
- discussion with the members of the project to find areas that have been conservatively estimated and therefore provide scope for shortening.

Any of these can be achieved, usually at minimal visible cost. Where there is a formalised solution required, the addition of further resources will be needed to crash the project.

Crashing

There is a limit with most activities as to how much they can be crashed as physical limits are reached, for example drying time of concrete in construction projects or the number of people who can work on one activity at any one time.[1]

The trade-off between cost and time should be balanced such that the minimum cost schedule is achieved, i.e. the activities are crashed in a systematic way – the ones that cost the least being the first to be crashed. The following sequence should be followed once the critical path has been established.

1 The following data will be needed for calculating the minimum cost schedule:

Normal time t_n
Normal cost C_n
Crashed time t_c (the shortest possible time an activity can take)
Crashed cost C_c (the cost to achieve the shortest possible time)

2 Calculate the cost per unit time to crash each activity (the relationship between cost and time will be assumed to be linear):

$$= \frac{C_c - C_n}{t_n - t_c}$$

3 Select those activities on the critical path as the first to be crashed.
4 Select the one with the lowest costs per unit time (beware parallel paths!).
5 Reduce this by one time unit.
6 Recalculate the critical path.
7 If total time needs shortening further, go to step 3.

Table 8.1 shows the way in which sequential crashing of activities can be achieved. The network diagram is given in Fig. 8.1, along with the critical path calculated from the normal times.

Table 8.1

Activity	Normal time t_n (days)	Normal cost C_n	Crashed time t_c (days)	Crashed cost C_c	Crash cost per day
A	5	300	3	600	150
B	6	700	5	775	75
C	7	500	4	650	50
D	5	400	3	600	100
E	4	700	3	1000	300

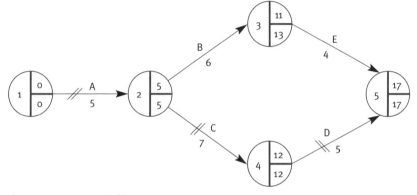

Figure 8.1 Network diagram

The project duration with the normal activity times is 17 days. Table 8.2 shows the optimal route for taking one day at a time out of the schedule, following the seven-step method given above to achieve the minimum cost schedule. The activities cannot now be crashed any further – the absolute minimum time that the project could take is 11 days.

It may be possible to avoid the need for any crashing, and indeed it may simply not be possible to achieve what is being asked within the given constraints. Where such an eventuality does arise, this method will at least give you the evidence as to why it cannot be done, which may persuade the project sponsors to ease one or more of the constraints.

Having determined the new schedule, the new costs will have to be added to the cost schedule, and the following analysis of those costs.

8.2 Analysing Cost Plans

The financial appraisal of project proposals will consider the potential rewards of carrying out a project against the predicted costs. The form of this evaluation will depend on:

- the size of the project being considered;
- the timespan over which the costs and benefits are going to be spread.

Table 8.2

Project duration	Crashed activities	Marginal crash cost	Total crash cost	New critical path	Notes
17	None	–		ACD	1
16	C – 1	50	50	ACD	2
15	C – 2	50	100	ABCDE	3
14	C – 3, B – 1	125	225	ABCDE	
13	C – 3, B – 1, A – 1	150	375	ABCDE	4
12	A – 2, C – 3, B – 1	150	525	ABCDE	
11	A – 2, B – 1, C – 3, D – 1, E – 1	400	925	ABCDE	5

Notes:

(1) + (2) The cheapest of the critical path activities to crash is C, therefore crash this one.

(3) All the activities now lie on the critical path and so to take one unit out of the system either take one day out of A or one day out of B–E and C–D. Costs are:

Option 1: A – £150
Option 2: B–E (cheapest is B) – £75; C–D (cheapest is C) – £50 = £125

therefore option 2 is cheaper at £125.

(4) C cannot be shortened any further – neither can B. Option now is

one unit out of A – cost £150

or

one unit out of E *and* one out of D – cost £100 + £300 = £400.

(5) A cannot now be crashed further, therefore take one unit out of E and one from D – cost £400.

Once the cost of completing the project has been determined from the WBS (bottom-up) or senior management (top-down) system the justification is that the return will at least exceed the amount spent. This return or payback can be analysed in a number of ways to determine feasibility or net benefit:

- payback analysis – simply considers the cash-flow of costs and benefits;
- discounted cash-flow – considers the 'time value' of cash-flows;
- internal rates of return – set basic return criteria on time value of money.

Payback

The most basic method of financial evaluation is simply to compare the income that will be generated with the initial investment. From this a payback period can be determined, i.e. the amount of time the revenue will need to be generated to cancel out the investment. For instance, an initial investment of £30 million will be paid back in five years if the revenue generated is £6 million per year. Many companies set this time period as a hurdle for projects. Some examples of payback times for various items are as follows:

Manufacturing company (Western) production hardware	5 years
Manufacturing company (Japanese) production hardware	10 years
Computer facilities	3 years
McDonald's franchise burger production	12 years

While this method has inherent simplicity it ignores:

- the total life-cycle cost of an item and only considers costs within the payback period (if there are major items outside this period to be considered, e.g. high disposal or decommissioning costs, the analysis does not provide a good financial model of reality);
- the time value of money (see below).

Discounted cash-flow

Where the timespan extends over more than one financial period and certainly where it is over many years, this 'time value of money' will need to be taken into account, through techniques known as *discounting*. The basis of the technique is the comparison between the value of the return on an investment and the value of the same sum of money had it been deposited in a bank account at a given rate of interest for the same period. The technique therefore considers the opportunity cost of the project (i.e. the cost of not doing something else with the resources).

Example

A project proposal aims to spend £100 000 on information technology and £20 000 a year to maintain it for four years. The return is £50 000 per year in terms of labour savings and extra revenue generated. Would the project be worth pursuing or should other options be considered?

The payback model shows that the project would generate £200 000 in revenue from an expenditure of £180 000, and so looks plausible. However, if the money was deposited in a bank account, at say 7 per cent interest p.a., the account would show a balance of £226 120 at the end of year 4 (see later work for how the calculation was carried out). It is clearly better to leave the money in the bank rather than risk it on this project.

The concept of discounting is applied to the cash-flows (not just profits) to determine whether or not the projected costs and benefits are going to yield the necessary results and is called discounted cash-flow.

Compound interest or 'to those that have shall be given . . .'

When a sum of money is left on deposit in a bank account it accrues interest. If the interest is paid into the account then in the following period there will be interest paid on the original amount plus interest on the first period's interest. As time progresses the amount on which interest is being paid grows, hence in the following period more interest is paid, and so on. This phenomenon is known as compound interest and was described by Einstein as the eighth wonder of the modern world! If you are in a situation where you have money in the bank it is a great invention. Of course, the converse is also true, that if you borrow money, you will accrue interest charges not only on the capital amount but also on the unpaid interest levied on the amount.

Discounting is the opposite of compounding. All values are considered in today's terms – called the present value (PV). We can calculate the value of the sum that would have to be deposited at a given rate of interest for a certain period to yield a stated end value.

Example

If you wanted to have a final value of £2012 in 12 years' time with a rate of return (called the discount rate) of 6 per cent, the present value (the amount that would have to be deposited) is £1000. The calculation is done through:

$$PV = \frac{C_n}{(1+i)^n}$$

where

C_n = future value of the investment n years hence
i = discounting rate

(Check the above example by putting $C_n = 2012$, $i = 0.06$ and $n = 12$.)

This basic calculation is applied to the benefits, which must then be offset against the costs. This figure is called the net present value (NPV):

Net present value = present value of benefits – present value of costs

Example

If a project requires the expenditure of £100 000 now and will yield £200 000 in 6 years, how will the manager evaluate whether or not this is viable (assuming a 10 per cent discount rate)?

$$\text{The PV of the benefits} = \frac{200\ 000}{(1+i)^n}$$
$$= \frac{200\ 000}{(1+0.1)^6}$$
$$= 112\ 800$$

The PV of the costs = 100 000
∴ the NPV = 112 800 – 100 000 = 12 800

The minimum criterion for project selection is that the NPV ≥ 0 at a given discounting rate. The project therefore meets this basic criterion and could be allowed to proceed.

The discounting rate can be taken as the interest rate which could be earned from a bank. It is more usual for the rate to be stated according to the type of project and allied to the cost of borrowing that money. A consequently higher rate than the normal bank rates is set, for example one manufacturing company had a discounting rate of 20 per cent. The effect was that it was correspondingly harder for projects to meet the minimum criterion of having an NPV of zero.

It is usual for the revenues and costs to be occurring over a period of years. More complex examples such as the following can be evaluated.

Example

You have been asked to evaluate the following proposal. Apply the technique of discounted cash flow to the figures to show whether or not this is worth pursuing. The applicable discount rate is 12 per cent.

	Now	Year 1	Year 2	Year 3
Start-up costs	£50 000			
Running costs (rent, rates, staffing, etc.)		£30 000	£45 000	£45 000
Revenues		£40 000	£50 000	£60 000
Sale of business				£70 000

$$\text{NPV(project)} = \text{NPV(year 1)} + \text{NPV(year 2)} + \text{NPV(year 3)}$$

$$= (-50\ 000) + \frac{(-30\ 000 + 40\ 000)}{(1 + 0.12)^1} + \frac{(-45\ 000 + 50\ 000)}{(1 + 0.12)^2}$$

$$+ \frac{(-45\ 000 + 60\ 000 + 70\ 000)}{(1 + 0.12)^3}$$

$$= -50\ 000 + 8928 + 3986 + 60\ 501$$

$$= £23\ 415$$

The project on this basis is worth pursuing.

Future value (FV)

The future value of an investment is the value of that money C if deposited for n years at an interest rate of i and is given by:

$$FV = C(1 + i)^n$$

Rule of 72

There is a 'rule of thumb' called the 'rule of 72'. If you invest at a per cent for b years, where $a \times b = 72$, your money will roughly double, e.g. if you invest £1000 at a fixed rate of 6 per cent for 12 years, the balance at the end of the 12th year ($6 \times 12 = 72$) will be roughly £2000 (actually £2012), and if the rate was 18 per cent and the term 4 years the balance would be the same (actually £1938).

The internal rate of return (IRR)

A related technique is to calculate the IRR of a project, i.e. the discount rate for which the NPV = 0. This can be done mathematically involving a number of iterations (working out the NPV with a variety of discount rates and gradually getting to the point where NPV = 0), or graphically. This does depend on the problem to solve being limited.

Example

A sum of £100 000 is invested over six years with a potential yield of £200 000 at the end of the sixth year. What is the IRR of the project? As a starting point, an arbitrary rate of 10 per cent is chosen.

$$NPV_{10\%} = \frac{200\ 000}{(1 + 0.1)^6} - 100\ 000$$

$$= 112\ 895 - 100\ 000 = 12\ 895$$

The discount rate in this case is clearly too low (the PV of the benefits is too high); try 14 per cent:

$$NPV_{14\%} = \frac{200\ 000}{(1 + 0.14)^6} - 100\ 000$$

$$= -8883$$

This rate is too high (the PV of the benefits is too low). Having two points for the NPV, each on either side of the zero NPV target, the value must be somewhere between the two. This is shown graphically in Fig. 8.2. As can be seen, the

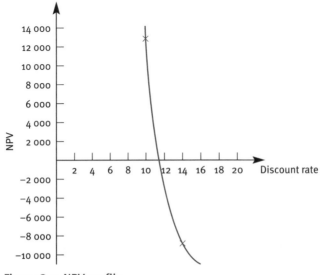

Figure 8.2 NPV profile

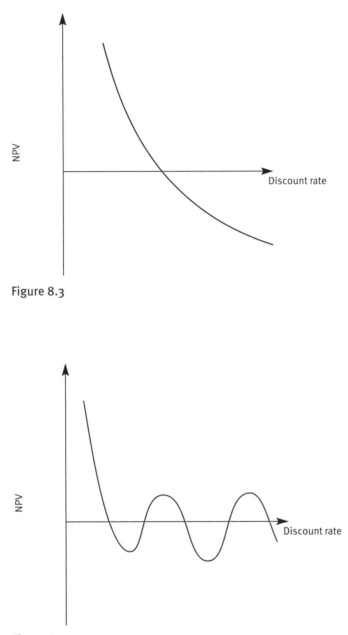

Figure 8.3

Figure 8.4

relationship within small changes in the discount rate can often be approximated to linear. Over a larger range, the change is as shown in Fig. 8.3. As the number of benefit points and payout points increases, there will be multiple IRRs. This is shown in Fig. 8.4, there being one change in direction of the curve (point of inflection) for each change in the sign (+ to −, or − to +) in the NPV analysis.

Using IRR

Using the percentage rate from an IRR calculation has a certain appeal. It also gets over the need to choose a discount rate for a project, which can save considerable debate. On the other hand, two projects may have the same IRR but yield very different NPVs, e.g. if two proposals have the same IRR but one has a much higher NPV, the one with the high NPV is clearly preferable (risk and availability of funds allowing). The IRR also cannot cope with changes in the discount rate over time. This would have been particularly problematic over the last 10 years when bank rates have varied by as much as 10 per cent.

Using discounted cash flow (DCF)

Originally it was only accountants who would be given the knowledge for the use and application of DCF, and would be the ones to accept/reject projects. Its use is now widespread and built into most financial appraisal systems and there are powerful functions in most spreadsheets (including Lotus and Excel) to assist in this analysis (see Appendix 8.2). Almost anyone can run a project through the financial constraints without needing to submit a project plan formally. This has numerous benefits to the project manager, as they can build not only time-based models of the project but also financial ones. The use of financial models has similar benefits to written project plans:

- the model can be interpreted by a non-financial expert to make changes where necessary to components of the model and evaluate the impact of those changes;
- no third-party intervention is necessary until a well-developed plan has been constructed.

It does have certain limitations, however:

- how to determine the interest rate to use – as the late 1980s showed, just about anything can happen where this is concerned. In 4 years, interest rates have fluctuated by as much as 10 per cent;
- the process of forecasting cash-flow years into the future involves a high degree of uncertainty;
- defining the cash-flows – they are different from the data generally presented in a balance sheet – write-off values, for example, are treated very differently.

For many firms, this is an important area of intersection between the financial controllers, management accountants and project managers. In order for everyone to understand the process of financial evaluation of projects better, many organisations provide simple spreadsheet-based evaluation packages, available on intranets or on-line, that can be used by project managers for the purposes of doing initial financial evaluation to see if ideas are worth pursuing. As will be discussed later in this chapter, having such models readily available for people to try out ideas quickly and easily is one of the keys to innovation in both products and processes.

Determining cash-flow figures for DCR and IRR calculations

In order to present the most accurate picture of the financial health or otherwise of the proposal the following rules should be applied (see Hogg, 1994):

- cash-flows, not profit figures, should be used;
- sunk costs (those already incurred) should be ignored;
- only costs arising directly from the project should be included (fixed costs, which would be incurred whether or not the project goes ahead, should be excluded);
- opportunity costs must be taken into account (developing one area of a business to the detriment of another).

Determining the discount rate

It is more usual for the project manager to have discount rates set as part of organisational policy. There are a number of methods for obtaining values for the discount rate – this one determines the risk adjusted discount rate (RADR).

There are three factors that determine the discount rate:

(a) = the rate charged for the use of the capital;
(b) = the rate due to inflation (so that the purchasing power is not reduced);
(c) = a premium factor due to the fact that the investor is taking a risk that the capital amount may never be repaid.

These are selected as follows:

$$(\text{overall rate}) = (1 + a)(1 + b)(1 + c)$$

Cash-flow considerations

The rejection or deferral of a project proposal may have nothing to do with its intrinsic merit. The decision will be based on the availability or otherwise of the necessary cash. A project is almost certain to be competing against others for scarce resources, and as the project manager will have to balance the trade-offs inherent in a project, so the project sponsor will have to balance the cost–benefit trade-offs of a number of proposals.

In large projects, the timing of payments may be critical for both the project organisation and its customers. For this reason it is necessary for both to know when expenditures are going to be made. In order to ease cash-flow, projects may involve stage payments. This is common both in construction and large-scale engineering. While all the necessary credit checks can and should be carried out, it is still a matter of risk for both parties when large contracts are entered into.

Investment appraisal

The previous section was concerned with conventional theoretical approaches to the appraisal of projects. These are particularly problematic where:

- there is no guaranteed return;
- the benefit is made in terms of reduction of labour – some companies do not see this as being in line with their philosophy;
- the project is considered to be 'strategic' in nature.

A good example of these is in new manufacturing technology. Very often the justification will be made in terms of increased flexibility or capability – both of which are very difficult to assign a monetary value to.

Similarly, for a service industry a new computer system may help speed the transfer of information and encourage the organisation to become more integrated, but will be challenged to show a cash return.

Other countries, particularly Germany and Japan, appear to set less demanding payback criteria where longer-term objectives are served by the investment. As Charles Handy (1994) commented:

> The Japanese put long-term growth above short- or even medium-term profits, indeed the profitability calculations hardly figure in some of their strategic decisions. To keep IBM at bay, Fujitsu won the computer contract for the water-distribution system of Hiroshima City with a bid of just one yen. The required rate of return for a 10 year R&D (research and development) project averages 8.7 per cent in Japan compared with 20.3 per cent in the US and 23.7 per cent in the UK. As a result, there is more investment in the future in Japan than in other countries.

Some projects do have to have a 'leap of faith' attached to them – the founder of the Kentucky Fried Chicken fast-food chain presented a proposal that was not attractive to hundreds of banks (over 600 said 'no'). There are many other pieces of business folklore that initially did not meet the conventional criteria. Indeed, as companies strive to find competitive advantage, conventional solutions are less likely to provide them. This is far more likely to be provided by those that challenge the limits of appraisal systems, though as the bursting of the dot-com bubble showed, there is no getting around some business basics concerning expenditure and return.

8.3 Analysing Quality Plans

Project quality assurance is an emerging issue for many, and an established one for those in the fields of public contracts, defence, pharmaceuticals, information technology, automotive or construction sectors. The compilation of a quality log will be discussed in Appendix A2 as part of the requirements of PRINCE2. At a high level, there need to be plans for determining customers' expectations of the project and guiding them as to what can realistically be expected. At a systems level, there must be a set of procedures for determining how these will be met. These should be product driven – that is, they should relate to the achievement of specific elements of the project outcomes.

As was demonstrated in the financial analysis, there is a set of well-developed tools that allow at least the principles of analysis to be agreed. Quality considerations

Table 8.3 Example of 'tick-sheet' approach to process quality plans

Activity	Standard/procedure	Completed	Date	Exception report?
Planning	Prepare PID	✓	12/05	N
	Get sign-off from sponsor	✓	10/06	N
Stage 1 data collection	Use standard forms for recording interview data for study	✓	30/05	Y

are similarly well developed and likewise the practices and requirements vary widely from industry to industry and from one organisation to another. As a minimum, the standards that should be scrutinised at this stage are those that were identified in the mapping stage of the overview process (see Chapter 4). Other criteria are included in standards such as the ISO 9000 series (see Appendix 1).

At the procedural level, however, there is much to recommend the 'tick-box' approach to assessing quality plans. This involves the planning tasks relative to achieving the desired level of quality being listed for each individual or group and a procedure being agreed for identifying that it has been completed satisfactorily. These will obviously only work if the higher-level objectives for quality are agreed and if the procedures are in line with achieving these objectives. Otherwise, they add little value. An example of a sheet that could be used to show the satisfactory completion of parts of the project is shown in Table 8.3. Each activity has a standard or procedure associated with it. When these are completed, they can be ticked, or more usually signed off. Where there are problems that need to be notified, an exception report (also called an *issue* in PRINCE) can be prepared. In Table 8.3 there was a problem with an activity that was noted and a short report would have been appended to state the nature of the exception and how it was dealt with.

The example in Table 8.3 is brief, but shows the ease with which information can be presented in summary tables. These tables should be a working tool at the activity level in the project. Apart from the utility from a management perspective, it can also provide a degree of traceability (ability to demonstrate that procedures were followed). Providing these in the form of a project manual in advance of activities shows that the issue of quality assurance is being taken seriously, and the compilation of this was discussed in Chapter 4. At a procedural level, therefore, the manager can assess whether the sub-projects have adequate assurance activities in place before starting project execution.

8.4 Risk Management

An evaluation of potential risks can show at an early stage whether or not a proposal is worth pursuing. Furthermore, there are well-developed procedures for managing risk as an ongoing process throughout a project. The practices are most well developed in industries where the projects are typically very large (such as heavy engineering), or where there is a significant technical risk element (aerospace projects). There is also a significant body of knowledge on financial risk management, which is separate from the discussion here. Instead we will focus on managing process and outcome risks. The application of active risk management is applicable and beneficial to all projects – right from small, one-person projects up to the very large complex projects that were the origin of many of the techniques. Many eventualities, given the right framework, can be identified in advance to give the project manager a chance to determine the necessary course of action.

The nature of risk

The possibility of suffering harm or loss. (PMI)
Uncertainty inherent in plans and the possibility of something happening (i.e. a contingency) that can affect the prospects of achieving business or project goals. (BS 6079)

The first is very broad as a definition and causes some issue as to what then can be managed, as the possibilities for harm or loss at the extreme are almost limitless for even small projects. Risk management therefore needs to incorporate some means of not only identifying potential risks but also analysing the potential of each so that the most significant ones can be 'managed' on an ongoing basis. The second definition considers the fundamental of any looking into the future – as happens in project planning – that there is *uncertainty*. The objective here is not to eliminate uncertainty or risk. Indeed, an accepted notion in many aspects of business life is that risk is proportional to return. The greater the risk that you run, the larger the return could be (if all goes well, etc.). However, this does apply in some respects to projects and their management.

Risk as a trade-off

Saving money on one activity by using a cheaper method of performing that activity, for instance, may result in the work having to be redone. There is the chance, of course, that it won't. The saved money trades off against the increased risk that the cheaper method presents. This trade-off can be identified with other objectives – time and quality. It is the job of the project manager, through identification of the organisational objectives or product objectives to take some of the decisions.[2] There is also the personal view of risk – what are you as an individual prepared to accept in terms of the potential costs and benefits of taking that risk? The costs to you of a high level of risk may be much greater stress levels during the project, as you have to deal with the consequences of your decision. Whatever the process, this is one area where, outside relatively few projects where any project risk is considered unacceptable (e.g. some nuclear industry projects), the treatment of risk is based less on fact but more on partial knowledge and instinct of the project manager and those around them. Science, it certainly isn't, but there are some frameworks and tools to help.

Framework for risk management

We shall divide the activity of risk management into three main areas – identification, quantification and response control or mitigation. There are many

Figure 8.5 Risk management schema

accompanying tools and techniques for each part of this, and some attributes of each are shown in Fig. 8.5.

Risk identification

Key risk symptoms

Key risk symptoms are those elements of the project that are likely to be indicators that something is going wrong in a project. For example, if an interim report is not received from part of the project team, the likelihood is that there are problems with that part of the project. These are usually generated by a project team. What we really need to know at this stage, however, is not the symptoms but the outcome, so that it can be quantified in the next stage of the analysis. The analysis is therefore concerned with the effects rather than the likely causes at this stage.

External sources

In addition to in-house brainstorming and consultation activities, it is possible to seek wider opinions. During the evaluation of research grant applications, for instance, experts in the relevant subject area will be asked for their opinions of the application and its chances of success. While such a *peer review* process can work against proposals that are more speculative in nature, it is one way of getting expert input.[3] This is only at a high level and is unlikely to be sufficiently systematic on its own. Reference to the WBS provides some further system, and then looking to the time, cost and quality plans for further issues at a detailed level.

TCQ analysis

Carrying out an analysis of TCQ plans has been discussed earlier in this chapter. The likely outcomes are that there is the possibility of missing key objectives, (unexpected) changes from stakeholders, technological problems, or staffing changes. These can be generated by a brainstorming exercise with the team – though they are generally fairly gloomy affairs! An alternative is to consider how it could be made to go wrong – looking at the behaviour that would conspire to cause the failure.

This is generally far more productive as people are required to consider how parties to the project might behave, rather than simply what might happen almost passively to the project. Some particular aspects to consider are:

- Time – the critical path or critical chain provide one unit for analysis, as do activities where there is uncertainty, particularly where there is novelty involved. Other key areas to check are time plans for the risky activities that might not even be on the critical path at the start but could easily escalate if there are problems;
- Cost – the estimates have uncertainty attached to them. How good are they – for instance, if the project is a first-timer?
- Quality – do we have assurance of all our processes or is a key part of the project (e.g. work being carried out by a supplier or customer) outside our control systems?

Assumptions

Key assumptions are also worth checking at this point. A project that will change the way a company operates and is therefore going to save itself some money needs to ensure that it does not simply add the cost somewhere else. The logistics firm that installed satellite tracking devices on its vehicles because it was useful to keep track of them at all times did not factor in the costs of operating the satellite system, which more than outweighed any cost advantage that came from the availability of such information. The system, once installed, was left switched off. The assumptions of ongoing costs had not been checked.

The trick is not to stop here, however, as the box below shows.

It's going to be OK – we've done the identification . . .

One IT firm, considering a new product that was going through development, went through the identification phase and came up with 152 risk events. These included many features of the product not being to the customers' liking to problems with the process, such as not recognising risks early enough and not controlling the specification as the project progressed. This would have been highly productive had the process been followed through with some quantification and mitigation. Unfortunately, this having been achieved, the team left the hotel where they had brainstormed this and during the next two years, over 80 per cent of their risk events actually occurred! The project was a disaster of such proportions that it almost finished the company.[4]

The output of the first phase of this risk management process is a list of key risks that will be passed on for the next stage – quantification.

Quantification

The question that we are trying to answer here is 'just how risky is an event or activity?' The traditional approach to this includes a number of techniques to assess the level of risk. They have a similar approach of:

1 Assessing how likely the event is to occur – somewhere on a scale from improbable to highly likely;
2 Determining the extent of the effect of the event – for instance, is the effect likely to be:
    – critical – will cause the total failure of one or more parts of a project?
    – major – will hold up or increase costs in one or more areas?
    – minor – will cause inconvenience but not set the project back financially or in time?

A third factor has been introduced here – that of *hideability*. This has been introduced because it is often noted that the reasons for failure of projects are not the mainstream risks that were identified during analysis but ones that have emerged because their progress, for instance, was not visible. This factor measures how easy it would be for one party to the project to conceal the fact that things were going very wrong with part of the project. This would mean that the problems cannot be detected until it is too late.

These can be done in many ways and the quantification techniques described in the following section allow for the project manager to determine which of the risk events are going to be managed (it is improbable that all can be managed). This leads on to the final and ongoing phase of the risk management process – response control or mitigation.

Response control/mitigation

Having identified the risk elements to be managed, some procedures are required to ensure that either the likelihood is reduced of that event occurring or the effects managed or *mitigated* in some way. For example, the risk of a critical activity running late can be reduced either through reduction in the scale of the activity or by ensuring that there is sufficient buffer at the end of the project to deal with the outcome – the project being delayed. These two approaches cover the main items in Fig. 8.5 of corrective action, and contingencies and reserves. The last issue to consider is the nature of the opportunities that arise as a result of the project.

Opportunities and threats

One of 3M's most successful and enduring projects has been the Post-It note. It is well described in 3M folklore how this was the by-product of another research project which produced an adhesive that was not sufficiently sticky. Had there not been a process for exploiting such a finding the discovery might have been lost. One of their developers applied the glue to small pieces of paper, which he then used to mark the very thin pages of his hymn book. Other people started asking him to make some for them for a whole range of different applications. Again the invention might have stopped there had 3M not had a process for developing such ideas. As it was, they did have such a process, and the new product was rapidly brought to market. Many great ideas are lost every day by teams and individuals because there is no route for them to be exploited. And yet, it is noted by many people who specialise in the management of innovation that it is rare that the best products are the result of a development process that started out with that objective in mind. They are the result of there being some scope in the process for such development, and have been discussed in Chapter 4. At this stage, it is worth reconsidering the issue, as it is essential that there is a route not only for threats to the project (as is the negative side of risks) but also for the exploitation of opportunities.

It is not possible to envisage every possible action or turn that the project might take, but some evaluation of the top 20 per cent of risks (those that are likely to cause 80 per cent of the delays or overrun) is going to be beneficial. When a significant risk is encountered, it is normal for some form of contingency plan to be put in place for that eventuality. Such plans should form part of the project proposal.

Formal use of risk analysis techniques may be required by:

- company policy;
- clients (especially for defence contracts).

The benefits are considered to be:

- providing a vehicle for improving project plans and better reflecting reality;
- highlighting areas for attention and contingency planning at the planning stage;
- attempting to harness much of the 'gut-feel element' of risk assessment and use this vital intuition as a starting point for further analysis;
- allowing the quantification of risk to build up experience in a structured way and allowing this factor to be traced historically for future benefit in other projects.

The following section considers some of the most widely used techniques for risk quantification, though it is stressed that this is only part of the process. It needs to be followed through with response control or mitigation, and by ensuring that this is not a one-off activity, as risks inevitably emerge during a project.

8.5 Risk Quantification Techniques

As for planning, risk analysis is an attempt to provide a mathematical model of the scenario in an attempt to allow the brain to comprehend the effect of a large number of variables on the outcome. Other risk quantification techniques that will be discussed here are:

- expected value;
- sensitivity analysis;
- Monte Carlo simulation;

- failure mode effect analysis;
- PERT.

Of these, PERT is the most widely accepted, with expected value, sensitivity analysis and Monte Carlo simulation also widely used.

Expected value

The expected value of an event is the possible outcome times the probability of its occurrence, e.g. if a project has a 50 per cent chance of yielding a profit of £30 million, the expected value is 0.5×30 million = £15 million. This provides a basic tool for evaluating different project proposals as an investment decision-maker. Two projects require funding – one has a potential return of £200 million and the other a return of £150 million. The first has a 50 per cent chance of yielding this, while the second has a 70 per cent chance. The expected value calculations yield £100 million for the first and £105 million for the second – on this basis the second is more attractive.

Sensitivity analysis

This works similarly to PERT analysis – an expected value for the main inputs to the project is put into the calculations of the outcome as well as an optimistic (in this case $+n$ per cent) and pessimistic ($-n$ per cent) value (value of n is often 10). This will show the effect on the outcome of a change in the variable considered and can show where management control attention should be focused.

The price of materials and labour for a project is likely to fluctuate. As the contract price needs to be fixed in advance, the project manager needs to see the effect of fluctuations on bottom-line performance. The material is one of the major contributors to the cost of the project. Overheads are calculated on the basis of 175 per cent of direct labour.

Costs:
Materials – £0.60m
Direct labour – £0.20m
Contribution to overheads – £0.35m
Revenues: fixed at £1.2m

The calculations are carried out in Table 8.4 as follows:

  revenue
– material costs
– combined labour and overhead costs
  ─────────────────────────────
= profit

As can be seen, the effect of the changes in costs means that although on initial inspection this looks viable, the figures indicate that should materials increase by 10 per cent, unless there is a drop in the labour costs of the project it will make a loss.

Table 8.4 Sensitivity analysis

		−10%	Materials Expected	+10%
Labour + overheads	−10%	1.2	1.2	1.2
		−0.54	−0.6	−0.66
		−0.495	−0.495	−0.495
		0.165	+0.105	+0.045
	Expected	1.2	1.2	1.2
		−0.54	−0.6	−0.66
		−0.55	−0.55	−0.55
		+0.11	+0.05	−0.01
	+10%	1.2	1.2	1.2
		−0.54	−0.6	−0.66
		−0.605	−0.605	−0.605
		+0.055	−0.005	−0.065

Monte Carlo simulation

This method requires the use of a computer to be practicable, and uses a range of values or distribution, rather than single values, for time, cost and other estimates, and then shows the effect on the finances or other critical project factors.

Monte Carlo simulation is available as an extension to most popular spreadsheet packages (including Lotus and Excel), as well as dedicated pieces of software (see Further Information at the end of this chapter).

PERT provides an in-built level of risk assessment, considering as it does three values for time estimates (optimistic, most likely and pessimistic). It does not tell you how likely these are to occur or their effects. Considering this alone results in only a partial picture of the situation.

The objective of the risk analysis is to enable the project manager to include *contingencies*, that is, having identified the most risky elements of the project, to put some actions in place to make sure that the risk is minimised.

Failure mode effect analysis

One of the most useful tools, which has been used extensively in industry for many years and is readily applied to projects, is *failure mode effect analysis*. This considers three elements of each activity or path through the activities. These were described above as likelihood, severity and hideability. Each of these can be analysed individually, though a practical method is to consider the total risk to be the product of these three elements. Each can be rated on a 1–10 scale and the total risk is:

Table 8.5 FMEA analysis

Activity	Severity	Hideability	Likelihood	Total
Development carried out by contractors	8	9	2	144
Development carried out in-house	8	2	7	112

(likelihood) × (severity) × (hideability)

Two activities are analysed as in Table 8.5.

The opportunity exists for development work to be carried out in-house or by contractors. The risk analysis shows that there is potential for failure here – and that the failure would be severe to the project.

The criteria in the example are relative to quality objectives. The method works equally well for time plans. Activities from the critical path (or those with little slack) can be subject to the same criteria and then action taken based on the activities' relative totals. This is the basis of the team-based risk assessment, described in the Project Management in Practice at the end of this chapter.

Programme evaluation and review technique (PERT)

Programme evaluation and review technique (PERT) was developed for use in the Polaris project in the USA in 1958. Due to the claimed success of the technique in this case, it was for a long time held up as the model that everyone should work to in planning projects (though see the note on PERT in Chapter 6). The technique is intended to deal with the likelihood that the single value given as the estimated time for completion of activities is going to have a degree of error associated with it. Instead of taking a single time, three time estimates for each activity are required:

- optimistic time – how long the activity would take if the conditions were ideal;
- most probable time – time if conditions were 'normal';
- pessimistic time – how long the activity would take if a significant proportion of the things that could go wrong did go wrong.

There is an infinite number of possibilities as to how this range is distributed, e.g. optimistic and most probable times may be close together with the pessimistic time considerably different from the other two, or all three may be very close together. This flexibility in the distribution that is applied is one of the major appeals of the technique. The analysis that can be applied can be very simple or go into complex statistics that require the use of a computer. The following example can be done without the need for this. The project that was planned in the critical path analysis section was further examined, and the times estimated for each of the activities expanded to include an optimistic and a pessimistic element. The result is shown in Fig. 8.6.

The activity arrows now have three figures associated with each in the order optimistic, most likely, pessimistic, e.g. for activity A:

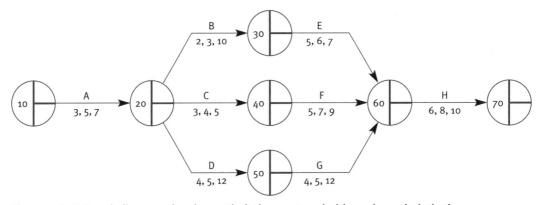

Figure 8.6 Network diagram showing optimistic, most probable and pessimistic times

optimistic time $= o = 3$
most likely time $= m = 5$
pessimistic time $= p = 7$

In order to schedule these activities, it is necessary to calculate the expected time for each activity. This is done by calculating:

expected time $= [o + 4m + p]/6$

In the case of activity A, the expected time $= [3 + [4 \times 5] + 7]/6 = 5$.

For activity B, the expected time $= [2 + [4 \times 3] + 10]/6 = 4$.

This distribution can be represented by Fig. 8.7.

The example is now completed using the expected times shown in Table 8.6 instead of the most likely times and a critical path analysis carried out. Putting these figures into the network diagram and carrying out the forward pass gives a project expected duration of 25 days. This is not considerably different from the 24 days that the original analysis revealed. The reverse pass reveals that the critical path has

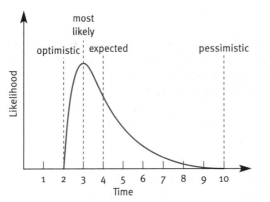

Figure 8.7 Distribution of estimated times for an activity

Table 8.6

Activity	Optimistic time o	Most likely time m	Pessimistic time p	Expected time
A	3	5	7	5
B	2	3	10	4
C	3	4	5	4
D	4	5	12	6
E	5	6	7	6
F	5	7	9	7
G	4	5	12	6
H	6	8	10	8

changed. Originally it was ACFH, but with the consideration of the ranges of times, it is now ADGH.

In order to save drawing the distribution each time, it is possible to compare activities in terms of a variance measure. This is calculated as follows:

$$\text{variance of activity time} = [[p - o]/6]^2$$

Explanation

The standard deviation of each activity's time is approximated to one sixth of the difference between the optimistic and pessimistic times. The variance = [standard deviation]^2. The standard deviation is the normal measure of spread in a set of numbers, and is represented by the Greek symbol σ or sigma. It is a characteristic of a normal distribution that 99.7 per cent of the numbers being analysed (called the 'population') fall within $\pm3\sigma$ of the mean (the average of the population).

In this case, the extremes of the distribution are represented by the optimistic and pessimistic times. The normal distribution is applied and the approximation is made that between these two values, 99.7 per cent (practically all) of other values will lie. The upper limit (mean $+3\sigma$) and the lower limit (mean -3σ) are equated to the pessimistic and optimistic times respectively.

The distribution that is being considered is the beta distribution, a generic form of which the normal distribution is a special case. Unlike the normal distribution (represented by a bell-shaped curve) the beta distribution need not be symmetrical about the mean, i.e. it can be skewed. It therefore encompasses the effects of one of the values of o and p being further from m than the other.

Applying this to the example:

$$\text{variance for activity B} = [[10 - 2]/6]^2 = 1.78$$
$$\text{for activity A} = [[7 - 3]/6]^2 = 0.44$$

Thus we have a mathematical measure for what can be seen from the figures, that the variance (as a measure of uncertainty with this activity) is much higher for activity B than for A, i.e. there is more uncertainty in the completion of B than A.

Figures such as the variance are of greatest practical use in estimating the likelihood that a set of activities will be completed within a certain time. The steps involved are as follows.

1 Calculate the variance for each activity.
2 Calculate the variance for each path (a sequence of activities that will take you from the first event to the last – there are generally many paths through networks) in the network diagram. This is done by summing the variances of all the activities on the path.
3 Calculate the standard deviation for that path:

σ_{path} = square root of the variance.

4 Identify the time within which you wish to complete the activities.
5 Calculate the value for z determined by:

z = [specified time – expected time]/σ_{path}.

6 Refer to Appendix 8.1 at the end of this chapter – the value of z corresponds to a probability (expressed between 0 and 1). This is the probability that the activity path will be completed within the time identified in 4.
7 The probability that all the paths that have been considered will be finished in the given time is found by multiplying the probabilities for each of the paths together.

This method is best illustrated by an example. If the middle section of the previous example is used, and the events 20–60 considered, the steps are as follows:

1 Calculate the variance for each activity (shown in Table 8.7).
2 Now it is necessary to identify the paths. There are several rules regarding the selection of paths for this process:
   • Each activity must be on only one path – where activities are shared between several paths, the one that is the critical path should be used;
   • Activities on different paths need to be independent – there should be no unwritten logic relationship between activities on different paths.

Table 8.7

Activity	Optimistic time o	Most likely time m	Pessimistic time p	Variance
B	2	3	10	1.78
C	3	4	5	0.11
D	4	5	12	1.78
E	5	6	7	0.11
F	5	7	9	0.44
G	4	5	12	1.78

Table 8.8

Path	Path variance	Standard deviation	z	Probability of completion in 11 days
B–E	1.78 + 0.11 = 1.89	1.37	[11 – 10]/1.37 = 0.73	0.7673
C–F	0.11 + 0.44 = 0.55	0.74	[11 – 11]/0.74 = 0.0	0.5000
D–G	1.78 + 1.78 = 3.56	1.87	[11 – 12]/1.87 = –0.53	0.2981

With these in mind the three paths that need to be considered here are:

B–E
C–F
D–G

The following steps are calculated in Table 8.8. The variances are then summed for each path.

3 The standard deviations are then calculated.
4 The time required for completion is arbitrarily 11 days.
5 The z values are added.
6 The probabilities are derived from Table 8.6.
7 The probability of each of these times being achieved is clearly highest where the expected time was less than the time required for completion (path B–E). These values are now required to find the probability that all three paths will be completed in 11 days. This is achieved through the multiplication of the three probabilities. In this case, the probability that the three paths will all be completed in 11 days is:

$$0.7673 \times 0.5000 \times 0.2981 = 0.1143$$

i.e. there is less than a 12 per cent chance that this part of the project will be completed in 11 days.

Many authors choose to use PERT as the generic title for network techniques. This is perfectly valid – the original CPA that was carried out using a single value for the estimated time can be taken as a special case of PERT, where the most likely = optimistic = pessimistic time.

The use of PERT in practice

As mentioned at the beginning of this chapter, PERT was very popular in the 1960s. It appears to be less well used today as many project managers feel that the additional complexity is not justified by the return in the accuracy of the plans produced. Also, it was suggested that in organisations where this kind of planning is prevalent, the use of PERT can encourage people to be less accurate in their forecasting. This said, for many very large-scale projects and particularly in the defence sector, this technique remains popular. For smaller projects, there is likely to be little benefit in attempting the kind of analysis that PERT permits.

8.6 Relevant Areas of the Bodies of Knowledge

Both bodies of knowledge in Tables 8.9 and 8.10 are clear about the nature of risk and risk management, and the importance that this issue has for the successful management of projects. The PMI body of knowledge is far more extensive in its coverage of specific techniques and the role of systems to deal with risk on an ongoing basis. In other respects, neither of the bodies of knowledge is particularly strong on the analysis of plans, though both make it clear the need and role of a business case.

Table 8.9 Relevant areas of the APM body of knowledge

Relevant section	Title	Summary
23	Risk management	The identification of risk and its management is stated as a key part of managing projects. Alongside the identification, quantification and mitigation discussed in this chapter, the issue of risk transfer is also mentioned – whereby the impact of the risk is reduced by another party taking responsibility for that. Risks are not only downside, but upside as well. 'Risk management should balance the upside opportunities with downside risks, doing so in an open, clear and formal manner.'

8.7 Summary

The analysis of plans provides the opportunity for problem prevention as well as performance maximisation. The issues of time, cost and quality are central to this, but are not the only criteria for which plans should be analysed. For instance, environmental impact assessment plans, or human resource performance plans, might be appropriate for particular projects. In time analysis, the basic issue is whether there is sufficient time to perform the project. Often there will need to be compressions of that time period, and the methods for time compression, including crashing to a minimum cost schedule have been discussed. Cost analysis is central to this stage of the analysis, and there is a wide range of tools available to carry this out. Last but not least of the main three objectives is quality. Assessing quality plans can be done through checking the process designs to determine whether procedures for assurance and performance are in place.

Table 8.10 Relevant areas of the PMI body of knowledge

Relevant section	Title	Summary
11.1	Project risk management – risk management planning	Treating risk in the same way as TCQ is a comprehensive means of dealing with the subject. The consideration of organisational policies both explicit and inferred (inferred from actions of the organisation) and the roles of individuals in the process shows the potential scope of such an activity in a large project. The risk management plan developed includes the *risk tolerance* of the organisation.
11.2	Project risk management – risk identification	From the risk plan, there are number of methods that can be employed for risk identification. These are largely as described in this chapter. In addition, *triggers* are identified as 'indications that a risk has occurred or is about to occur'. These are specific outputs from the risk-identification process.
11.3	Project risk management – qualitative risk analysis	The quality of the data provided through the risk identification is first established. Then a number of techniques are applied to determine in qualitative terms (low, medium, high, for instance) the nature of the severity and likelihood of occurrence. The final stage of this process can be to turn these into a quantitative assessment, to feed into a quantitative analysis.
11.4	Project risk management – quantitative risk analysis	This section focuses on the use of quantitative techniques to determine the magnitude of particular risks and their impact on the schedules and costs. PERT and Monte Carlo simulation are mentioned, and the probability distributions for such analysis discussed.
11.5	Project risk management – risk response planning	The objective of this part of the risk management process is to ensure that there is some action as a result of a particular risk being identified. By assigning an 'owner' to each risk, and then putting in place plans to avoid, transfer, mitigate or accept that particular risk outcome, the outcome is a risk response plan. This may include the apportionment of contingency funds or time, or changes to plans, contracts or set in train other processes.
11.6	Project risk management – risk monitoring and control	This section reinforces the nature of risk management as an ongoing process, linked in to the control systems for other objectives of the project. The compilation of a risk database is suggested, as is the use of checklists to manage the feeding of risk knowledge gained to future projects.

The issue of risk is central to the consideration of projects. There is always risk with any endeavour, and how this is managed will have a large impact on the success or otherwise of the project. The basic process of identification, quantification and mitigation, provides a structure for this activity, and the main tools for risk management are described.

It's a risky business

Four friends wanted to start a business. After much discussion, they had hit upon the idea of launch a mail-order toys and games business. They were in the development stage of their business plan and wanted to be sure that they had been thorough with their planning. To reinforce this, they had just received a letter from a group of venture capitalists, agreeing to fund the start-up. It concluded its review of their plan by stating:

> The business plan presents a credible opportunity for all involved and we are prepared to approve the funding request, subject to a risk analysis being carried out on the project to start the business.

The group were stunned – the funding that they had been hoping for was suddenly a reality. Just one thing stood in their way – that damned risk analysis process.

They started with identifying the key risk elements that could face the business during its start-up phase. They considered the process between the time that they received the funding and day one of trading. What could possibly go wrong? Lots of things. They brainstormed the possibilities and recorded them. They then considered the effect that these would have on the project as a whole. The list they generated provided them with too much to do – they would spend all their time trying to prevent things going wrong and not enough making sure that the positive steps towards the business opening were happening. They needed to prioritise the events. As importantly, what would happen, when they eventually occurred? Who would be responsible for each of them? on what basis could they rank each risk, in order to identify the most important risks for which they would develop mitigation and ownership?

They decided to use a table to show the risk event, the likelihood, the severity and by multiplying the two providing a risk priority number (RPN). This would then allow ranking of the risk elements. For the three highest ranked elements, the group then generate a mitigation process with someone in the group taking ownership of that process. The result of their deliberations is shown in Table 8.11.

As can be seen, the top three risks were identified and mitigation tasks put in place to either prevent the risk event happening or to reduce its effect. The initials of the 'owners' of that risk in the last column show who has agreed to monitor that set of events and ensure that the mitigation is put into place before the project suffers from that event occurring.

Case discussion

1 What further methods could have been used to generate ideas for the identification part of the risk process?

2 How scientific can the method that was used to rank the risks claim to be?

3 What should happen as the project progresses to manage risk? Suggest a plan for the remainder of the project (the three months up to the business launch).

Table 8.11 Simple risk management table

Risk event	Likelihood	Severity	RPN (rank)	Mitigation	Owner
Brochure not ready in time for business launch	4	8	32 (2)	Identify rapid printing firms; develop artwork early	AL
Website not ready in time for business launch	4	9	36 (1)	Website to be ready 3 weeks prior to launch for testing; use simple version first	SL
Banking facilities not ready	2	10	20 (5)		
Initial stock not ready	3	8	24 (3)	Place orders immediately for opening stock	KM
Group cannot agree on items to be sold	3	7	21 (4)		
Loss of one of group members	1	10	10 (6)		

Key Terms

crashing
minimum cost schedule
resource smoothing/levelling
payback
discounting
internal rate of return (IRR)
PERT
quantification
opportunity cost
compound interest
risk database

net present value (NPV)
risk-adjusted discount rate
expected value
sensitivity analysis
Monte Carlo analysis
failure mode effect analysis (FMEA)
identification
mitigation
contingency
stage payments
risk transferral

Review Questions and Further Exercises

1 From the network diagram shown in Fig. 8.8, identify the critical path and show the project duration. In Table 8.12 the crash cost per day is given along with the crash time. Use the information to show the sponsor of this project the most economical way of taking two days out of the plan. You should explain all the terms used.

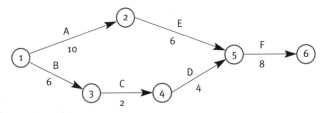

Figure 8.8 Network diagram

Table 8.12

Activity	Normal time (days)	Crash cost per day	Crash time (days)
A	10	50	6
B	6	30	3
C	2	–	2
D	4	40	2
E	6	80	4
F	8	100	5

2 In the development of the Sinclair C5 (a recumbent, electrically assisted tricycle) there was the opportunity to develop both new power supplies and new motors, but both required additional development time. The decision was taken to proceed with existing technology – in this case a conventional car battery and the motor from a truck engine cooling fan. Intended performance was significantly compromised as a result.

Evaluate the risks that the company ran by pursuing this course of action and suggest alternative means by which a better technical result might have been achieved.

3 Evaluate, using discounting techniques, which option, lease or buy, is most financially beneficial in the scenario given in Table 8.13. You should consider the discount rate to be 10 per cent and the period of consideration to be five years.

Table 8.13

	Buy	Lease
Purchase/lease cost	£50 000	£10 000 per year
Annual operating cost	£4000 per year	£4000 per year
Maintenance cost	£2000 per year	Maintained by leasing co.
Salvage value at the end of five years	£20 000	not applicable

4 The purchase of new office furniture for a boardroom has caused conflict between two factions within a company. One faction argues that the company should buy modern furniture, which will cost £12 000, and can be scrapped

(replaced with zero salvage costs) in six years' time. The other favours the purchase of antique furniture which costs £30 000, but can be sold for £30 000 in six years' time. The modern furniture will cost £500 in maintenance and the antique £1000. You have been asked to arbitrate the decision and resolve the conflict using financial methods (calculate the net present value of each scheme, using the company discount rate of 12 per cent).

5 Discuss the three main pricing strategies and indicate which one you feel provides the greatest benefits to customers and which to suppliers.

6 What are the benefits of the 'tick-box approach' to quality assurance at a procedural level in a project for both the project team and the manager?

7 What are contingencies and why should the project manager identify these?

8 Consider a project which may be carried out for reasons other than profit, such as building a non-toll road. How might the benefits of such a project be assessed to provide a justification for its being carried out?

9 Considering the critical path alone for the project Table 8.14, calculate the activity variances and the total variance of the critical path. From this, calculate the standard deviation. Determine the probability of the project being completed within the following times:

(a) 30 days.
(b) 40 days.
(c) 42 days.

Table 8.14

Activity	Optimistic time	Most likely time	Pessimistic time
A	3	4	11
B	1	2	3
C	3	10	11
D	8	10	18
E	1	2	3
F	1	3	5
G	2	3	4
H	2	6	10
J	16	20	30
K	1	1	1

10 A construction project requires five major pieces of work to be completed which are independent. These five paths have variances as given in Table 8.15.
    Determine the probability that the project will be completed within:

(a) 18 weeks.
(b) 16 weeks.
(c) 13 weeks.

Table 8.15

Path	Expected duration (weeks)	Variance
A	10	1.21
B	8	2.00
C	12	1.00
D	15	2.89
E	14	1.44

11 You are in charge of a new product launch. This will be a formal press launch, where the product is introduced by your managing director and the press and major customers have the opportunity to see the product for the first time.

The formalities are to be preceded by a buffet. Before hiring the catering service it is necessary to identify the guest list and invite them to determine numbers. Because of tied arrangements between certain venues and the caterers, you will have to select the venue, then select the caterers. The launch publicity materials will need to be designed, and artwork carried out before brochures can be printed. These must be available on the day. The promotional boards to be placed around the launch room should be constructed once the publicity materials have been designed. No artwork is required for these. A sound system is required and must be hired once the venue has been identified.

The activities are included in Table 8.16, together with the best estimates for optimistic, pessimistic and most likely times. The MD has asked you to set the launch date (all times are in weeks). Show the criteria that you have used, and include the network diagram.

Table 8.16

Activity	Description time	Optimistic time	Most likely	Pessimistic time
A	Select launch venue	1	2	3
B	Design launch publicity	2	3	4
C	Have artwork prepared	2	3	5
D	Print brochures	1	2	4
E	Construct promotion stand	1	2	3
F	Order sound system	0.5	1	1.5
G	Select caterers	1	2	3
H	Develop invite list	1	1	1
J	Invite and get replies	2	3	5

References

Handy, C. (1994) *The Empty Raincoat*, Hutchinson, London.

Hogg, N. (1994) *Business Forecasting Using Financial Models*, Financial Times Pitman Publishing, London.

Monden, Y. (1992) *Cost Management in the New Manufacturing Age*, Productivity Press, New York.

Waldron, D. and Galloway, D. (1988) 'Accounting – The Need for a New Language for Manufacturing', *Management Accounting*, Vol. 66, No. 10, November, pp. 34–5.

Further Information

BS 6079: Part 3: 2000, Guide to the Management of Business Related Project Risk.

Chapman, C. and Ward, S. (1997) *Project Risk Management: Processes, Techniques and Insights*, Wiley, Chichester.

Chicken, J. (1998) *The Philosophy of Risk*, Thomas Telford, London.

Gray, C.F. and Larson, E.W. (2000) *Project Management: The Managerial Process*, McGraw-Hill, Singapore, Chapter 5.

Kaplan, R.S. and Atkinson, A.A. (1989) *Advanced Management Accounting*, 2nd edition, Prentice Hall, Englewood Cliffs, NJ.

Leach, L. (2001) 'Putting Quality in Project Risk Management', *PM Network*:
Part 1: February 2001, pp. 35–40
Part 2: March 2001, pp. 47–52

Lumby, S. (1991) *Investment Appraisal and Financial Decisions*, 4th edition, Chapman & Hall, London.

Pender, S. (2000) 'Managing Incomplete Knowledge: Why Risk Management is Not Sufficient', *International Journal of Project Management*, Vol. 19, pp. 79–87.

Williams, T.M. (1995) 'A Classified Bibliography of Recent Research Relating to Project Risk Management', *European Journal of Operational Research*, Issue 85, pp. 18–38.

www.cs-solutions.com – for information about Risk+ software
www.predict.com – for information about Predict Risk management software
www.pertmaster.com – for information about Pertmaster software

Notes

1 There is a saying that 'no matter how many people you put on the job, it still takes 9 months to have a baby.'

2 I am grateful to Paul Walley of Warwick Business School for sharing his thoughts on this subject.

3 For a further listing of such tools and techniques, see BS 6079:2000: Part 3, Annex B.

4 See Project Management in Practice – the VCS case – at the end of Chapter 14.

Appendix 8.1 PERT Factor Tables

Table A.1(a) Areas under the standardised normal curve from $-\infty$ to $-z$

0.09	0.08	0.07	0.06	0.05	0.04	0.03	0.02	0.01	0.00	z
0.0002	0.0003	0.0003	0.0003	0.0003	0.0003	0.0003	0.0003	0.0003	0.0003	−3.4
0.0003	0.0004	0.0004	0.0004	0.0004	0.0004	0.0004	0.0005	0.0005	0.0005	−3.3
0.0005	0.0005	0.0005	0.0006	0.0006	0.0006	0.0006	0.0006	0.0007	0.0007	−3.2
0.0007	0.0007	0.0008	0.0008	0.0008	0.0008	0.0009	0.0009	0.0009	0.0010	−3.1
0.0010	0.0010	0.0011	0.0011	0.0011	0.0012	0.0012	0.0013	0.0013	0.0013	−3.0
0.0014	0.0014	0.0015	0.0015	0.0016	0.0016	0.0017	0.0018	0.0018	0.0019	−2.9
0.0019	0.0020	0.0021	0.0021	0.0022	0.0023	0.0023	0.0024	0.0025	0.0026	−2.8
0.0026	0.0027	0.0028	0.0029	0.0030	0.0031	0.0032	0.0033	0.0034	0.0035	−2.7
0.0036	0.0037	0.0038	0.0039	0.0040	0.0041	0.0043	0.0044	0.0045	0.0047	−2.6
0.0048	0.0049	0.0051	0.0052	0.0054	0.0055	0.0057	0.0059	0.0060	0.0062	−2.5
0.0064	0.0066	0.0068	0.0069	0.0071	0.0073	0.0075	0.0078	0.0080	0.0082	−2.4
0.0084	0.0087	0.0089	0.0091	0.0094	0.0096	0.0099	0.0102	0.0104	0.0107	−2.3
0.0110	0.0113	0.0116	0.0119	0.0122	0.0125	0.0129	0.0132	0.0136	0.0139	−2.2
0.0143	0.0146	0.0150	0.0154	0.0158	0.0162	0.0166	0.0170	0.0174	0.0179	−2.1
0.0183	0.0188	0.0192	0.0197	0.0202	0.0207	0.0212	0.0217	0.0222	0.0228	−2.0
0.0233	0.0239	0.0244	0.0250	0.0256	0.0262	0.0268	0.0274	0.0281	0.0287	−1.9
0.0294	0.0301	0.0307	0.0314	0.0322	0.0329	0.0336	0.0344	0.0351	0.0359	−1.8
0.0367	0.0375	0.0384	0.0392	0.0401	0.0409	0.0418	0.0427	0.0436	0.0446	−1.7
0.0455	0.0465	0.0475	0.0485	0.0495	0.0505	0.0516	0.0526	0.0537	0.0548	−1.6
0.0559	0.0571	0.0582	0.0594	0.0606	0.0618	0.0630	0.0643	0.0655	0.0668	−1.5
0.0681	0.0694	0.0708	0.0721	0.0735	0.0749	0.0764	0.0778	0.0793	0.0808	−1.4
0.0823	0.0838	0.0853	0.0869	0.0885	0.0901	0.0918	0.0934	0.0951	0.0968	−1.3
0.0985	0.1003	0.1020	0.1038	0.1056	0.1075	0.1093	0.1112	0.1131	0.1151	−1.2
0.1170	0.1190	0.1210	0.1230	0.1251	0.1271	0.1292	0.1314	0.1335	0.1357	−1.1
0.1379	0.1401	0.1423	0.1446	0.1469	0.1492	0.1515	0.1539	0.1562	0.1587	−1.0
0.1611	0.1635	0.1660	0.1685	0.1711	0.1736	0.1762	0.1788	0.1814	0.1841	−0.9
0.1867	0.1894	0.1922	0.1949	0.1977	0.2005	0.2033	0.2061	0.2090	0.2119	−0.8
0.2148	0.2177	0.2206	0.2236	0.2266	0.2296	0.2327	0.2358	0.2389	0.2420	−0.7
0.2451	0.2483	0.2514	0.2546	0.2578	0.2611	0.2643	0.2676	0.2709	0.2743	−0.6
0.2776	0.2810	0.2843	0.2877	0.2912	0.2946	0.2981	0.3015	0.3050	0.3085	−0.5
0.3121	0.3156	0.3192	0.3228	0.3264	0.3300	0.3336	0.3372	0.3409	0.3446	−0.4
0.3483	0.3520	0.3557	0.3594	0.3632	0.3669	0.3707	0.3745	0.3783	0.3821	−0.3
0.3859	0.3897	0.3936	0.3974	0.4013	0.4052	0.4090	0.4129	0.4168	0.4207	−0.2
0.4247	0.4286	0.4325	0.4364	0.4404	0.4443	0.4483	0.4522	0.4562	0.4602	−0.1
0.4641	0.4681	0.4721	0.4761	0.4801	0.4840	0.4880	0.4920	0.4960	0.5000	−0.0

Table A.1(b) Areas under the standardised normal curve from $-\infty$ to $-z$

z	0.00	0.01	0.02	0.03	0.04	0.05	0.06	0.07	0.08	0.09
0.0	0.5000	0.5040	0.5080	0.5120	0.5160	0.5199	0.5239	0.5279	0.5319	0.5359
0.1	0.5398	0.5438	0.5478	0.5517	0.5557	0.5596	0.5636	0.5675	0.5714	0.5753
0.2	0.5793	0.5832	0.5871	0.5910	0.5948	0.5987	0.6026	0.6064	0.6103	0.6141
0.3	0.6179	0.6217	0.6255	0.6293	0.6331	0.6368	0.6406	0.6443	0.6480	0.6517
0.4	0.6554	0.6591	0.6628	0.6664	0.6700	0.6736	0.6772	0.6808	0.6844	0.6879
0.5	0.6915	0.6950	0.6985	0.7019	0.7054	0.7088	0.7123	0.7157	0.7190	0.7224
0.6	0.7257	0.7291	0.7324	0.7357	0.7389	0.7422	0.7454	0.7486	0.7517	0.7549
0.7	0.7580	0.7611	0.7642	0.7673	0.7703	0.7734	0.7764	0.7794	0.7823	0.7852
0.8	0.7881	0.7910	0.7939	0.7967	0.7995	0.8023	0.8051	0.8078	0.8106	0.8133
0.9	0.8159	0.8186	0.8212	0.8238	0.8264	0.8289	0.8315	0.8340	0.8365	0.8389
1.0	0.8413	0.8438	0.8461	0.8485	0.8508	0.8531	0.8554	0.8577	0.8599	0.8621
1.1	0.8643	0.8665	0.8686	0.8708	0.8729	0.8749	0.8770	0.8790	0.8810	0.8830
1.2	0.8849	0.8869	0.8888	0.8907	0.8925	0.8944	0.8962	0.8980	0.8997	0.9015
1.3	0.9032	0.9049	0.9066	0.9082	0.9099	0.9115	0.9131	0.9147	0.9162	0.9177
1.4	0.9192	0.9207	0.9222	0.9236	0.9251	0.9265	0.9279	0.9292	0.9306	0.9319
1.5	0.9332	0.9345	0.9357	0.9370	0.9382	0.9394	0.9406	0.9418	0.9429	0.9441
1.6	0.9452	0.9463	0.9474	0.9484	0.9495	0.9505	0.9515	0.9525	0.9535	0.9545
1.7	0.9554	0.9564	0.9573	0.9582	0.9591	0.9599	0.9608	0.9616	0.9625	0.9633
1.8	0.9641	0.9649	0.9656	0.9664	0.9671	0.9678	0.9686	0.9693	0.9699	0.9706
1.9	0.9713	0.9719	0.9726	0.9732	0.9738	0.9744	0.9750	0.9756	0.9761	0.9767
2.0	0.9772	0.9778	0.9783	0.9788	0.9793	0.9798	0.9803	0.9808	0.9812	0.9817
2.1	0.9821	0.9826	0.9830	0.9834	0.9838	0.9842	0.9846	0.9850	0.9854	0.9857
2.2	0.9861	0.9864	0.9868	0.9871	0.9875	0.9878	0.9881	0.9884	0.9887	0.9890
2.3	0.9893	0.9896	0.9898	0.9901	0.9904	0.9906	0.9909	0.9911	0.9913	0.9916
2.4	0.9918	0.9920	0.9922	0.9925	0.9927	0.9929	0.9931	0.9932	0.9934	0.9936
2.5	0.9938	0.9940	0.9941	0.9943	0.9945	0.9946	0.9948	0.9949	0.9951	0.9952
2.6	0.9953	0.9955	0.9956	0.9957	0.9959	0.9960	0.9961	0.9962	0.9963	0.9964
2.7	0.9965	0.9966	0.9967	0.9968	0.9969	0.9970	0.9971	0.9972	0.9973	0.9974
2.8	0.9974	0.9975	0.9976	0.9977	0.9977	0.9978	0.9979	0.9979	0.9980	0.9981
2.9	0.9981	0.9982	0.9982	0.9983	0.9984	0.9984	0.9985	0.9985	0.9986	0.9986
3.0	0.9987	0.9987	0.9987	0.9988	0.9988	0.9989	0.9989	0.9989	0.9990	0.9990
3.1	0.9990	0.9991	0.9991	0.9991	0.9991	0.9992	0.9992	0.9992	0.9993	0.9993
3.2	0.9993	0.9993	0.9994	0.9994	0.9994	0.9994	0.9994	0.9995	0.9995	0.9995
3.3	0.9995	0.9995	0.9995	0.9996	0.9996	0.9996	0.9996	0.9996	0.9996	0.9997
3.4	0.9997	0.9997	0.9997	0.9997	0.9997	0.9997	0.9997	0.9997	0.9997	0.9998

Appendix 8.2 **Present Value of £1**

Year	1%	2%	3%	4%	5%	Discount rate 6%	7%	8%	9%	10%	12%	14%	15%
1	0.990	0.980	0.971	0.962	0.952	0.943	0.935	0.926	0.917	0.909	0.893	0.877	0.870
2	0.980	0.961	0.943	0.925	0.907	0.890	0.873	0.857	0.842	0.826	0.797	0.769	0.756
3	0.971	0.942	0.915	0.889	0.864	0.840	0.816	0.794	0.772	0.751	0.712	0.675	0.658
4	0.961	0.924	0.889	0.855	0.823	0.792	0.763	0.735	0.708	0.683	0.636	0.592	0.572
5	0.951	0.906	0.863	0.822	0.784	0.747	0.713	0.681	0.650	0.621	0.567	0.519	0.497
6	0.942	0.888	0.838	0.790	0.746	0.705	0.666	0.630	0.596	0.564	0.507	0.456	0.432
7	0.933	0.871	0.813	0.760	0.711	0.665	0.623	0.583	0.547	0.513	0.452	0.400	0.376
8	0.923	0.853	0.789	0.731	0.677	0.627	0.582	0.540	0.502	0.467	0.404	0.351	0.327
9	0.914	0.837	0.766	0.703	0.645	0.592	0.544	0.500	0.460	0.424	0.361	0.308	0.284
10	0.905	0.820	0.744	0.676	0.614	0.558	0.508	0.463	0.422	0.386	0.322	0.270	0.247
11	0.896	0.804	0.722	0.650	0.585	0.527	0.475	0.429	0.388	0.350	0.287	0.237	0.215
12	0.887	0.788	0.701	0.625	0.557	0.497	0.444	0.397	0.356	0.319	0.257	0.208	0.187
13	0.879	0.773	0.681	0.601	0.530	0.469	0.415	0.368	0.326	0.290	0.229	0.182	0.163
14	0.870	0.758	0.661	0.577	0.505	0.442	0.388	0.340	0.299	0.263	0.205	0.160	0.141
15	0.861	0.743	0.642	0.555	0.481	0.417	0.362	0.315	0.275	0.239	0.183	0.140	0.123
16	0.853	0.728	0.623	0.534	0.458	0.394	0.339	0.292	0.252	0.218	0.163	0.123	0.107
17	0.844	0.714	0.605	0.513	0.436	0.371	0.317	0.270	0.231	0.198	0.146	0.108	0.093
18	0.836	0.700	0.587	0.494	0.416	0.350	0.296	0.250	0.212	0.180	0.130	0.095	0.081
19	0.828	0.686	0.570	0.475	0.396	0.331	0.276	0.232	0.194	0.164	0.116	0.083	0.070
20	0.820	0.673	0.554	0.456	0.377	0.312	0.258	0.215	0.178	0.149	0.104	0.073	0.061
25	0.780	0.610	0.478	0.375	0.295	0.233	0.184	0.146	0.116	0.092	0.059	0.038	0.030
30	0.742	0.552	0.412	0.308	0.231	0.174	0.131	0.099	0.075	0.057	0.033	0.020	0.015

Year	16%	18%	20%	24%	28%	Discount rate 32%	36%	40%	50%	60%	70%	80%	90%
1	0.862	0.847	0.833	0.806	0.781	0.758	0.735	0.714	0.667	0.625	0.588	0.556	0.526
2	0.743	0.718	0.694	0.650	0.610	0.574	0.541	0.510	0.444	0.391	0.346	0.309	0.277
3	0.641	0.609	0.579	0.524	0.477	0.435	0.398	0.364	0.296	0.244	0.204	0.171	0.146
4	0.552	0.516	0.482	0.423	0.373	0.329	0.292	0.260	0.198	0.153	0.120	0.095	0.077
5	0.476	0.437	0.402	0.341	0.291	0.250	0.215	0.186	0.132	0.095	0.070	0.053	0.040
6	0.410	0.370	0.335	0.275	0.227	0.189	0.158	0.133	0.088	0.060	0.041	0.029	0.021
7	0.354	0.314	0.279	0.222	0.178	0.143	0.116	0.095	0.059	0.037	0.024	0.016	0.011
8	0.305	0.266	0.233	0.179	0.139	0.108	0.085	0.068	0.039	0.023	0.014	0.009	0.006
9	0.263	0.226	0.194	0.144	0.108	0.082	0.063	0.048	0.026	0.015	0.008	0.005	0.003
10	0.227	0.191	0.162	0.116	0.085	0.062	0.046	0.035	0.017	0.009	0.005	0.003	0.002
11	0.195	0.162	0.135	0.094	0.066	0.047	0.034	0.025	0.012	0.006	0.003	0.002	0.001
12	0.168	0.137	0.112	0.076	0.052	0.036	0.025	0.018	0.008	0.004	0.002	0.001	0.001
13	0.145	0.116	0.093	0.061	0.040	0.027	0.018	0.013	0.005	0.002	0.001	0.001	0.000
14	0.125	0.099	0.078	0.049	0.032	0.021	0.014	0.009	0.003	0.001	0.001	0.000	0.000
15	0.108	0.084	0.065	0.040	0.025	0.016	0.010	0.006	0.002	0.001	0.000	0.000	0.000
16	0.093	0.071	0.054	0.032	0.019	0.012	0.007	0.005	0.002	0.001	0.000	0.000	
17	0.080	0.060	0.045	0.026	0.015	0.009	0.005	0.003	0.001	0.000	0.000		
18	0.069	0.051	0.038	0.021	0.012	0.007	0.004	0.002	0.001	0.000	0.000		
19	0.060	0.043	0.031	0.017	0.009	0.005	0.003	0.002	0.000	0.000			
20	0.051	0.037	0.026	0.014	0.007	0.004	0.002	0.001	0.000	0.000			
25	0.024	0.016	0.010	0.005	0.002	0.001	0.000	0.000					
30	0.012	0.007	0.004	0.002	0.001	0.000	0.000						

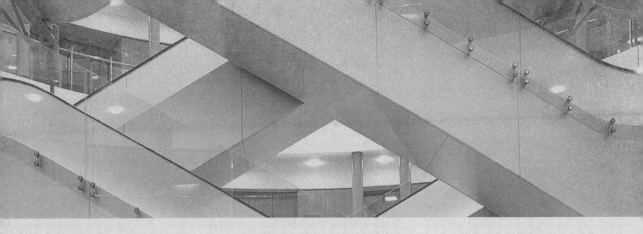

Phase Three
Deliver the Project
(Do It!)

9 Project organisation: structures and teams

The gathering together of individuals with the aim of making them a cohesive whole and ensuring the benefit of all stakeholders is a fundamental role of most project managers. This is at best likely to be a very hit-and-miss process (very few will naturally achieve both good social interaction and commercial success) and, at worst, financially disastrous. There have been many attempts to describe the best mixture of personalities that will ensure that the group dynamics are right and some of these will be discussed here. These are project issues. A strategic issue is how the project management structure fits in with the structure of the organisation as a whole. The various forms of matrix are also discussed.

Project teams are increasingly being formed not just from within one organisation but from multiple organisations (such as in joint ventures) and often geographically separate locations. This presents an extra set of challenges to the project manager and the team. Some of the ways that organisations have dealt with these challenges are covered.

Contents

Key terms
Review questions and further exercises
References
Further information
Note

Learning Objectives

By the time you have completed this chapter, you should be able to:
- Consider the role of teams in achieving project objectives;
- Understand the impact that the choice of structure will have on the achievement of project objectives;
- Provide a framework for the project manager to guide understanding of some of the personnel issues that they will face.

9.1 The Role of Teams

The organisation of people into *ad hoc* groups takes advantage of bringing together individuals from different specialisms (marketing, engineering, etc.) as needed for a project task. It is notable that as organisational size increases, the degree of specialism of individuals is increased. Since the days of Henry Ford, large organisations have been organised by functional specialism into 'chimneys' (see Fig. 9.1). The notion is that by grouping all the specialisms together, the arrangement is very efficient, as when you need that function to be performed, there is an obvious resource to draw on. Quite reasonably, from the point of view of the individual, career paths are well defined and basic administration systems are geared to this way of working. Give a group the task of setting up and running their own business and, 99 per cent of the time, the first task they set themselves is to allocate roles as heads of the various line functions. This arrangement prevails in many traditional industries, but has been shown to be detrimental to the creativity of individuals and the responsiveness of the organisation to changing market needs.

However, as discussed in Chapter 1, one single function will rarely provide a customer's entire need or want. To do this requires cross-functional activity, i.e. the linking of the activities of more than one functional area. Functional arrangements

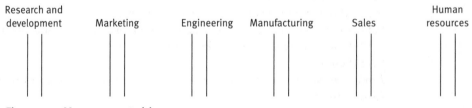

Figure 9.1 Management chimneys

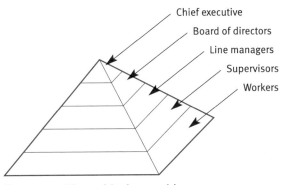

Figure 9.2 Hierarchical pyramid

tend to lead individual managers to build their own empires by creating work for themselves – regardless of whether this is value-adding for the organisation as a whole. Departmental head-count is considered to be a measure of the status of the individual manager and the importance of their function.

The conventional management hierarchy or pyramid (see Fig. 9.2) has provided the basis on which the majority of organisations are ordered. The style is militaristic and there may be eleven or more layers in the chain of command (foot-soldier to top-ranking general).

For many organisations today, this has been the subject of recent change, with de-layering and corporate restructuring attempting to minimise the number of layers in the organisation. These 'flatter' structures may only have three to five levels (instead of eleven or more previously). Organisations that have done this claim that it simplifies decision-making, as well as removing a considerable overhead cost to the organisation.

Other structures include organisation by:

- product group;
- customer type (e.g. military/civil);
- geographical area (of their operations or the customers they serve);
- the function they perform.

It is common to see a mixture of these forms of organisation being employed – depending on the nature of the business and the degree of vertical integration in the supply stream (how many of the suppliers/customers are owned by the same organisation).

Where a project can be defined as having more than one function involved (which systems and strategy projects are almost bound to have) it is emerging as one of the roles of the project management specialist to define possible organisational forms. Many authors note that project managers themselves rarely have a choice about how the project organisation is arranged and, consequently, have to use what are often inappropriate structures. The emerging strategic importance of the project manager means that they are likely to have more input in determining the structures within which they work in the future.

The nature of the work organisation is important as it:

- defines responsibility and authority;
- outlines reporting arrangements;
- determines the management overhead (costs);
- sets the structure behind the organisational culture;
- determines one group of stakeholders in project activities.

As organisations have expanded, so the functions have often become less integrated by, for example, geographical separation. Walls, both literal and metaphorical, are constructed around them. In order to try to enforce communication between departments, many organisations use 'dotted-line responsibility'. Here an individual may have a responsibility to one functional manager, with a dotted-line responsibility to another. This device has been used frequently to ensure that certain individuals do not engage in empire-building. In the manufacturing industry, this was done by manufacturing directors who wanted to ensure that they retained responsibility for the running of the entire manufacturing operation. Consequently, when it became fashionable to employ a quality manager they were not given any direct staff but inspection and other quality staff would work for the manufacturing manager while given a dotted-line responsibility to the quality manager (indicating that they were linked to the goals of this part of the operation). It did still leave power in the hands of the manufacturing people. . . .

In addition to the dotted-line responsibility, detailed administrative procedures are introduced to ensure that some form of integration takes place. Often involving interminable meetings and mountains of bureaucracy, they are an attempt to make the organisation perform acts which it is not designed to do, i.e. integrate. Sloan's General Motors in the USA of the 1930s was run using considerable command-and-control structures – based on the premise that 'whoever holds the purse strings, commands'.

9.2 The Pure Project Organisation

To move away from the functional chimneys to the project-based organisation is a major step. It is a structure that predominates in the construction industry (see Fig. 9.3). At the highest levels in the organisation there are staff posts – senior

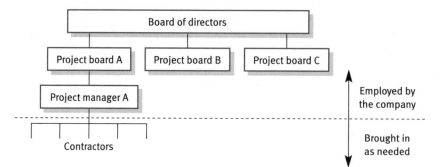

Figure 9.3 Project organisation

managers, directors, administrative staff, etc. (called the 'project board'). The next level down is a series of project managers who have control over one or more projects at a time. The constitution of the project team depends on the stage in the life-cycle of the project, e.g. at the planning stage there will be architects, structural engineers, quantity surveyors, and various other technical specialities such as groundwater engineers and legal advisers. These will be replaced by various contractors who are brought in to carry out specific tasks (such as steel fixers, electricians and heating/ventilation engineers) as the project moves through the operational phase. Once the particular task is completed, the team in each case is disbanded. The project manager may be retained to move on to other projects.

The advantages of such an arrangement are that:

- the labour force is highly flexible – labour can generally be attracted as and when required, without providing a labour burden or overhead for the rest of the time;
- the main company only has to administer the employment of its own staff – saving on the costs of directly employing others.

The disadvantages are significant:

- the project team is only temporary and so these people have no commitment to its success. The pay on a piece-rate basis may encourage the speed of work, but does little to ensure high quality or solve problems ahead of time. Paying on a time rate only encourages people to drag out jobs over a longer period of time. The only one who has an interest in the achievement of time:cost:quality objectives is the project manager;
- when there is a boom in a particular area in an industry, there is a shortage of labour, increasing labour rates and making hiring of the necessary resources problematic;
- where there are significant events occurring in a project, it is very hard for the lessons of these to be passed on to future projects as the people who have carried out the 'do' part of the project are not around for the 'review'. They cannot benefit, therefore, from the review process. Progress in improving work methods is likely to be slower.

9.3 Matrix Management

Matrix management was invented as a way of achieving some of the benefits of the project organisation without the disadvantages. There are three situations where a matrix management structure is appropriate (Mullins, 1999):

- where there is more than one orientation to the activities of the operation, e.g. multiple customers or geographical differences in markets served;
- where there is the need to process simultaneously large amounts of information;
- where there is the need to share resources – one function or project cannot justify the expenditure on a dedicated resource.

A matrix organisation can be defined as (Davis and Lawrence, 1977):

matrix structure + matrix systems + matrix culture + matrix behaviour

The matrix structure and the variations on the theme are included below. Matrix systems include the activities of management in planning, organising, directing, controlling and motivating within the structure. The culture requires acceptance of the system by the people who have to work within it, and the behaviour required is the ability to understand and work with overlapping boundaries.

The organisation of the matrix follows one of three models:

1 **The lightweight matrix**   In this arrangement the project manager acts as a co-ordinator of the work of the project and chairs meetings of the representatives of all the departments involved. Responsibility is shared for the success of the project between the departments. This is regarded as being the weakest form of matrix structure, as there is little commitment to project success from anyone and the project manager is relatively impotent compared to the functional managers. The project meetings can be either led off-course or totally discredited by the inclusion of people of too high/low levels of authority respectively in the group.

2 **The balanced model**   This is an attempt to balance the power of the project manager with that of the line manager. The administration of the organisation is such that the line manager needs the activities of the project manager to balance their resources, i.e. the project provides a means of securing part of the income of that function. The emergence of a second line of command – the project and the line manager – over any member of the team is the crucial drawback of this model. The person will have project responsibilities in addition to their line responsibilities.

3 **The 'heavyweight matrix'**   Functional departments have the role of providing resources through seconding people on a full-time basis to the project team. On completion of the project, they return to the line function. In this way it is possible to have the resources available to bring in technical specialists without the project being saddled with their cost on a continuous basis. Such an arrangement is feasible where the project is of vital importance to the organisation. Drawbacks include the discontinuity of tasks for the individual and the resident department.

The success of application of the above models depends on:

- the training given to both managers and team members on working in such environments;
- the support systems – administrative, informational and career-wise;
- the nature of the individual – in particular, their tolerance level for role ambiguity. Working in the uncertain environment of the project, and with career progression allied to the department rather than the project, means that there are often conflicting priorities.

9.4 Structure Selection

It was noted in Chapter 2, in the discussion of the 7-S of issues facing the project manager, that the selection of structure was important. It is not uncommon, however, to find projects run using structures that are wholly inappropriate for their importance to the organisation. The previous discussion has outlined the options available. The choice should refer to the critical objectives of each project that an organisation is undertaking. A summary is provided in Table 9.1 of the relationship between structure and objectives for the project.

While Table 9.1 infers a degree of certainty on the choice of structure, there are additional factors to be considered. These include the predominant technology of the firm and the potential resource conflicts that heavyweight teams cause. The choice of structure is therefore a decision that should not be taken in isolation. This again highlights the importance for an organisation of the aggregate project plan and the project being given a definable priority. It is neither feasible nor practical

Table 9.1 Relating project structures to project objectives

	Functional organisation	*Lightweight project organisation*	*Heavyweight project organisation*	*Project organisation*
Example of usage	Minor change to existing product	Implementing change to work organisation, e.g. IT system	Major innovation project	Large construction projects
Advantages	Quality through depth of specialisation possible within functions, possible to 'hide' project costs	Quality maintained	Speed and quality (improvement) through use of relatively 'stable' organisation as a base	Speed highest through dedicated resources; organisation design dependent only on project strategy
Disadvantages	Relatively slow as a process	Some cost disadvantage due to additional coordination expense of the matrix	Adverse reaction from line managers; additional coordination and administration costs	Can incur significant additional cost due to the relative expense of contractors; quality may not improve over time; instability for staff
Issues for the project manager	Integration of functions within the organisation	Two bosses problem	Two bosses problem	Management of knowledge

Adapted from Ulrich and Eppinger (2000)

for all projects in the firm to have a heavyweight matrix structure. As a simple rule, those with the highest levels of priority should have the heaviest weight structures.

One of the drawbacks identified in Table 9.1 is the *two bosses problem* – a team member must report to the project manager in addition to the line manager of the function in which they normally work. This leads some[1] to the conclusion that matrix management is unwieldy and practically unworkable and even the comment that 'matrices become hopelessly complicated bureaucracies and gut the emotional energy and ownership of those closest to the marketplace' (Peters, 1992). The dual command leads to power struggles between the two managers and a selection of the following problems (Davis and Lawrence, 1977):

- anarchy – people perceive that as soon as a team actually starts to work together, they are disbanded to go to work on another project;
- groupitis – decision making is removed from the individual who will not take a decision without group approval;
- overhead that is imposed is excessively costly – heavyweight structures in particular often have their own coordination and administration alongside that of the functions in an organisation;
- decision strangling – so much time is spent trying to get consensus that any individual flair is stifled and the group becomes a barrier to any rapid progress.

Having stated all these potential problems, it is understandable that many organisations avoid the matrix form. There are, however, others who use it to good effect, proving that there is not one single way of managing a project that is applicable in all situations. The model that is chosen must be on a contingent basis, i.e. it responds to the needs of the organisation at that moment in time. In contrast it has been stated that

> A new management agenda lies ahead . . . one piece of that agenda [is] the weaving together of companywide teams that gather strength by understanding the whole endeavour to which they are connected. This frees them to function independently of the artificial labels and boundaries constructed around them. It also frees them to tap the collective genius of the group, rather than simply cementing individually conceived parts into a lesser whole (Dimancescu, 1995).

Having observed the best Japanese companies' management practices, Dimancescu's view is that the future for project management in large functionally based organisations is to encourage cross-function teaming and communication. However, it still does not solve the two bosses problem, other than to say that the normal situation is for the project process to take precedence over the function. This is the operationalisation of the view stated above – that to do anything in an organisation which meets a customer's need involves many functions.

The cross-function teams that Dimancescu studied consisted of members from all functions regardless of seniority. The tasks would typically be meeting customer quality requirements, controlling costs or ensuring that deadlines were met (see Fig. 9.4).

Traditional planning tools such as CPA or PERT do not state information requirements that are very often met informally through impromptu corridor

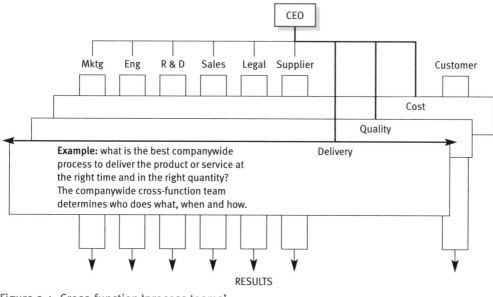

Figure 9.4 Cross-function 'process teams'
(*Source*: Dimancescu, 1995)

meetings, for example. The promise of information technology to overcome this deficiency (in identifying information requirements) has not been realised in the majority of organisations. Information provision is frequently hampered by different departments working on different hardware and software, with compatibility between the two being non-existent. Better solutions look to come from improved use of people rather than any increase in the use of technology.

Process mapping, as discussed in Chapter 4, is part of the toolkit that can enable the management of cross-functional teams. It is decided at the planning stage who needs information and who needs to be involved at the various stages in a project. This is by nature an integrator – a tool that can be used to keep the overall objectives in view. It can also point to the kind of structure that will be appropriate during the different phases.

9.5 Mixed Organisational Structures and Coordination

The above discussion considers the options open to the project manager where a single, homogeneous team is needed. Increasingly, particularly where a project has a high degree of organisational complexity, project managers are being required to use mixed organisational structures and additional coordination mechanisms to help make the structures effective. A recent product development project had the structure shown in Fig. 9.5 which allowed the project manager a high degree of flexibility in resourcing the requirements of the project, but also good use of internal expertise – particularly product knowledge.

In Fig. 9.5 the project manager has direct control over the heavyweight team working within the organisation and the contractors being employed on the project. They will have less direct control (usually) over staff members of other organisations, though this devolved authority does form part of some joint-venture contracts. In

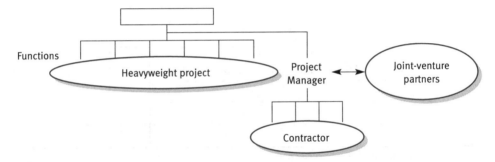

Figure 9.5 Mixed organisational structure

such a case, staff from one organisation may be working directly for a manager from an entirely different organisation.

The other issue arising from such complex structures is how to ensure that parts of the project being undertaken by different functions will actually work together. In the case of the London Underground refurbishment where the new trains would not fit into the tunnels (see Chapter 4), the two functions clearly did not work together on aspects of mutual interest. While it is an additional overhead for the project, many projects use an *integrator* – someone who works with both functions and ensures that areas of overlap are addressed. Functions may also swap staff or temporarily relocate them as another means of ensuring that this happens.

9.6 Teamwork

The distinction between the terms 'team' and 'group' is made to indicate the differences in operating characteristics of each. A group is simply a collection of people. A team meets the following criteria:

- the output of the group is greater than the sum of the outputs of the individuals, e.g. a team can engage in creative processes (idea generation) far more effectively than a collection of individuals;
- a greater range of options can be considered by exploiting differences in individual thought processes;
- decision-making by the team is likely to be better (see Chapter 13).

The purpose of studying the role of teamwork in the project environment is:

- to help the project manager in the design and selection of the workgroup;
- to enable the monitoring of the degree to which the team is functioning effectively;
- to provide feedback to the team to help improve effectiveness.

The above assumes that in the first instance the project manager has the luxury of a free hand in the selection of who should form their project team. In reality, the team or group is more likely to be 'inherited' rather than designed. The study of teamworking will raise awareness of what is possible through teaming and the symptoms and consequences of the process not being managed to best effect.

Other characteristics of teams include:

- more openness to taking risks, as the risk is shared between the team rather than carried by one individual;
- higher overall level of motivation, as there is an inherent responsibility to others in the team and a desire not to let them down;
- better support for the individuals within the team, who are more likely to be included in a greater range of activities than they would normally be exposed to, but without their having to work alone.

Typically a team consists of two to twenty people, though many managers suggest that effectiveness will decrease once the numbers go above ten. Larger teams are managed in the same way as large projects – by breaking down the big team into smaller, more manageable groups. As for the work breakdown structure, such an organisational breakdown must have the appropriate coordination mechanisms in place between the smaller teams.

9.7 Life-cycles of Teams

Teams, like projects, can be seen as having various stages of development. These can broadly be defined as collection, entrenchment, resolution/accommodation and synergy, followed almost inevitably by decline. At some point, the team will be disbanded because either they have reached a point at which it is no longer feasible for them to carry on working together or the task they are working on has been accomplished. The characteristics of each phase are shown in Table 9.2 and the effectiveness profile during the life-cycle is shown in Fig. 9.6.

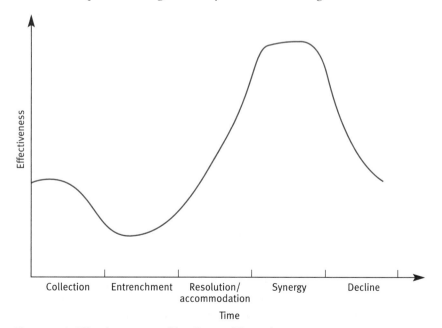

Figure 9.6 Effectiveness profile of team life-cycle

Table 9.2 Team life-cycle

Stage	Characteristics
Collection	The bringing together of individuals into a group with a collective task or problem to solve. The participants have a degree of eagerness and initial enthusiasm and generally rely on the authority and hierarchy to provide a degree of certainty in this uncertain environment. They will use this initial phase to establish themselves and find what is expected of them.
Entrenchment	As the group starts work they begin to find out where each person stands on various issues. The entrenchment comes when people arrive with preconceived ideas as to how the project should be proceeding and are unwilling to be persuaded of the merits of allowing the group to decide on the course of action. This phase can be very destructive and is generally fairly unproductive. The reasons for this unproductiveness are issues such as disillusionment with the goals of the project, competition for power or attention within the group, or general confusion as the work being undertaken bears little relationship to the goals of the project.
Resolution/ accommodation	The disagreements begin to be resolved, and characteristics such as mutual trust, harmony, self-esteem and confidence are seen. This is where the team starts to put aside the negative social effects and move to being more productive.
Synergy	Based on Ansoff (1968), synergy is defined as when the output of the whole is greater than what would be obtained from the component parts, otherwise stated as $2 + 2 = 5$. This is the peak of effectiveness of the team, leadership is shared, and there is a new motivation to complete the tasks at hand.
Decline	At some point the team will meet an event when its effectiveness starts to decline – this can be through the nature of the task being undertaken not changing or the focus of the activities being allowed to move towards a social group.
Break-up	If this occurs naturally before the task is finished, there can be problems in getting a new team to take up the remaining work. They will be expected to get 'up to speed' very quickly and have an additional pressure on them. Where the group finishes its task and it is during one of the earlier stages of development, either in resolution or synergy, the effects on future projects can be highly beneficial as the participants go away with good memories of the work they have done.

Using this knowledge, the project manager can identify the stage at which their team is operating, ensuring that the decline phase is held back for as long as possible. This may be done through changing the composition of the team to take the development back a little or expanding the range or scope of the tasks being undertaken to add a new challenge. The important point is, though, that teams do have a natural life-cycle and this should be recognised and used to advantage.

Life-cycle of quality circles

Quality circles have been a very popular management tool for encouraging people from all parts of organisations to work together to solve problems. They are a move to get people who only previously had limited responsibilities to use their natural creativity and have the opportunity to innovate. The idea was promoted very heavily during the 1980s by the UK's Department of Trade and Industry for use in all organisations. The frequently quoted example was that of a trade delegation to Japan who were amazed to find the extent of the use of quality circles in industry, and even more to find it in service industries – including a restaurant where the waiters had formed their own quality circle.

The initiative was taken up by a large number of companies. Quality circle meetings would often take place in the workers' own time, though generally they were given worktime at the start to set up the circles. It was notable that within a very short period (often less than 12 months) these project teams were being disbanded and the idea of quality circles discontinued. Initial results were generally found to be excellent – the biggest problems were tackled first by the newly integrated groups and considerable savings were made. Then they started to decline. As was found by Lawler and Mohrman (1985):

> During this period, groups meet less often, they become less productive, and the resources committed to the program dwindle. The main reason the groups continue at all is because of the social satisfaction and pleasure the members experience rather than the group's problem-solving effectiveness. As managers begin to recognise this they cut back further on resources. As a result, the program shrinks. The people who all along have resisted the program recognise that it is less powerful than it once was, and they openly reject and resist the ideas it generates.

As was demonstrated by the above, the idea of using quality circles over an extended timeframe neglects to take account of the natural life-cycles of teams. The alternatives are as follows:

1 Have the team assembled for the purpose of solving one single problem, then to be disbanded once it has been solved.
2 Provide a path for the development of the role of the team from solving one or a small number of low-level problems into semi-autonomous workgroups. This will require other changes (in management reporting arrangements, for example) and considerable development of the team through education and training.

9.8 Managing Personalities in Teams

It is stated above that the project manager can benefit from an understanding of the ways in which individuals behave in group situations. These situations have been studied by social scientists for a long time and the results of these studies form a significant part of the sociological and management literature. Managing the process is discussed in the following section, while here it is useful to consider the role of the individual.

In order to determine the character of an individual (the 'personality profile') there are hundreds of commercially available psychometric tests that can be used. Many claim to be the 'definitive and only possible test you will need to find that ideal candidate for your team', but most can be bluffed by an intelligent candidate and few are totally applicable to people other than graduates. They can also be expensive to administer and often require expert guidance to interpret the results. The *curriculum vitae* and interview, though maligned, is still the normal mode for recruiting in most project environments.

In designing your team there are certain basic requirements you may wish key players to have, e.g. qualifications or relevant experience. These determine their eligibility for the job. The suitability can be determined through assessing how they are likely to fit in with the rest of the team, and whether or not the team has a balanced portfolio of characteristics relative to the task being undertaken. Belbin (1993, 2000) has shown that a structure based on a greater number of classifications than those given above can prove useful in both the selection and ongoing management of the project. The characteristics that Belbin identifies are shown in Fig. 9.7.

Having categorised the individual's personalities, it is worth considering the effect this has on their behaviour. Belbin cites this as consisting of six factors:

- personality – as determined through testing;
- mental abilities – e.g. critical reasoning;
- current values and motivations (determined by all sorts of personal factors – the weather, family situation, how well the Blues did on Saturday, etc.);
- field constraints – those rules and procedures that affect behaviour from the environment in which you are working;
- experience – prior events which have left varying degrees of impression on the individual;
- role-learning – the ease with which an individual can take on one of the roles listed in Fig. 9.7, but which is not their natural role – this increases their role versatility.

The effects on the design of the team are that there can be a degree of scientific method applied to the selection of individuals – though how *scientific* tests (like the Belbin role profiling) are is open to debate. They are liked by many project managers not just for their use in selection (making sure that there is the right balance of people in the team) but also as part of team development. Understanding the roles of individuals in the team can have a very positive effect on the interactions between team members.

	Roles and descriptions – team-role contribution	Allowable weaknesses
	**Plant:** creative, imaginative, unorthodox. Solves difficult problems.	Ignores details. Too pre-occupied to communicate effectively.
	**Resource investigator:** extrovert, enthusiastic, communicative. Explores opportunities. Develops contacts.	Overoptimistic. Loses interest once initial enthusiasm has passed.
	**Coordinator:** mature, confident, a good chairperson. Clarifies goals, promotes decision-making, delegates well.	Can be seen as manipulative. Delegates personal work.
	**Shaper:** challenging, dynamic, thrives on pressure. Has the drive and courage to overcome obstacles.	Can provoke others. Hurts people's feelings.
	**Monitor evaluator:** sober, strategic and discerning. Sees all options. Judges accurately.	Lacks drive and ability to inspire others. Overly critical.
	**Teamworker:** cooperative, mild, perceptive and diplomatic. Listens, builds, averts friction, calms the waters.	Indecisive in crunch situations. Can be easily influenced.
	**Implementer:** disciplined, reliable, conservative and efficient. Turns ideas into practical actions.	Somewhat inflexible. Slow to respond to new possibilities.
	**Completer:** painstaking, conscientious, anxious. Searches out errors and omissions. Delivers on time.	Inclined to worry unduly. Reluctant to delegate. Can be a nit-picker.
	**Specialist:** single-minded, self-starting, dedicated. Provides knowledge and skills in rare supply.	Contributes on only a narrow front. Dwells on technicalities. Overlooks the 'big picture'.

Strength of contribution in any one of the roles is commonly associated with particular weaknesses. These are called allowable weaknesses.

Executives are seldom strong in all nine team roles.

Figure 9.7 The nine team roles
(*Source*: Belbin, 1993. Reprinted with permission of Butterworth-Heinemann, a division of Reed Educational and Professional Publishing)

9.9 Effective Teamwork

You have cleared some of the structural barriers to success – as identified in previous chapters. You have planned the project using the best available methods. You now want to make sure that the project teamwork makes a positive contribution to the success of the project. Eight characteristics, most of which are under the control of the project manager, have been identified (see Larson and LaFasto, 1989). These are as follows:

- a clear, elevating goal – a sense of mission must be created through the development of an objective which is understood, important, worthwhile and personally or collectively challenging;
- provide a results-driven structure – the structure and composition of the team should be commensurate with the task being undertaken (see below);
- competent team members – need to balance personal with technical competence;
- unified commitment – create the environment of 'doing what has to be done to succeed';
- foster a collaborative climate – encourage reliance on others within the team;
- standards of excellence – through individual standards, team pressure, knowledge of the consequences of failure;
- external support and recognition – where good work is performed, recognise it. It is likely to be absent from the other stakeholders, so it will be the responsibility of the project manager to provide it;
- institute principled leadership – see Chapter 10.

The first point is stated in virtually every consideration of this subject. Indeed, many go as far as to say that demanding performance which is challenging is an integral part of the way of creating a team. In addition, the first tasks that the team carries out will set the scene for the entire project, in particular through the definition of roles and rules of behaviour.

The structure of the team and its composition are broken down into three basic categories – creative, tactical and problem-resolution. The use of each can be related to the appropriate or most likely phase in the project life-cycle. The requirements of the structure of each are shown in Table 9.3.

How teams/groups work can be seen in Fig. 9.8. At one end of the spectrum is the disintegrated group, where there is no agreement between the team members and complete breakdown of the decision-making processes. At the other end is the integrated team, which has complete consensus on all matters, but which has 'gone over the edge' in terms of effectiveness. Their processes can be categorised by what is termed group-think, otherwise described by 'they've beaten the defence, but no one can bang the ball into the back of the net without discussing it with the group first'. Generally this results in ludicrous decisions being made – the ill-fated charge of the Light Brigade resulted from a group of generals who sat around and agreed with each other, rather than upset the working of the group by disagreeing with the decision!

Table 9.3 Requirements of team structure

Category	Likely phase of project life-cycle	Characteristics of team structure
Creative	Planning	Needs to have a high degree of autonomy in order to explore the widest range of possibilities and alternatives. Needs to be independent of systems and procedures and requires independent thinkers and people who are self-starters.
Tactical	Doing	Needs a well-defined plan, hence unambiguous role definitions and clarity of objectives for the individual members. The team members should have loyalty and a sense of urgency.
Problem solving	Doing (when problems arise)	Will focus on problem resolution rather than any predetermined conclusions – these must be eliminated. The desirable characteristic of the people involved is that they are intelligent and have people sensitivity.

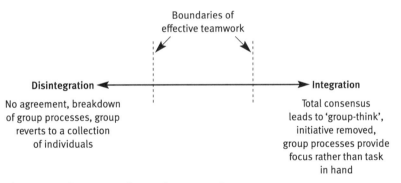

Figure 9.8 Spectrum of team/group performance

9.10 Managing the Team – Running Effective Meetings

Manager 1: 'I'm really not in favour of the Scorpion Project – it certainly won't do what my department wants.'

Manager 2: 'Mine neither. Don't worry, I'll just make sure that the meetings go nowhere. They'll soon drop it!'

The project manager will often have to chair meetings, so a discussion of the good practice concerning how they should be run is very relevant. This is an exceptional management skill, yet it is so basic that most people assume that they know how to do it. In practice, this is rarely the case and meetings often break up without any progress being made – as is occasionally intended and demonstrated by the quotation at the start of this section. This short section is intended to provide only a few guidance notes as to what constitutes good practice.

1 Confirm the purpose of the meeting – there has to be a reason why you need to bring people together. This should be very specific so as to help eliminate spurious issues that can detract from the main purpose.
2 Deciding who should be invited with the minimum requirement of including anyone who would be offended if they were left out. It is often worth checking by asking the individual concerned if you are in doubt.
3 The pre-meeting preparation – the location and timing, agenda, and any reports providing background information on the topic under discussion should be circulated in advance.
4 Running the meeting – provide a forum for constructive debate while limiting the scope of discussion to the matter in hand. Do not allow repetition of points or any one member to dominate the discussions. Regularly summarise progress and ask for conclusions to be drawn based on the discussions. The project manager should have in mind that the level of attention of most people declines rapidly after the first 20 minutes, and after two hours there is unlikely to be any constructive progress. People will often agree to anything at this point simply to get out of the meeting. Obtaining consensus is an art, which the skilful chair of a meeting will aim to achieve. This ensures that the entire meeting has 'bought-in' to a decision and makes carrying it out far easier than with a number of dissenters.
5 Post-meeting follow-up – send copies of the minutes with action points and who should carry them out listed against each. Most meetings can have their conclusions and action points stated on one side of A4 paper – they have a high chance of being read in this form, rather than 'filed'. These minutes and action points must then form the basis of the next meeting's early discussions, ensuring that whoever said they would carry out a task has a natural responsibility to the meeting to do it. They also know that should they fail to carry out an action, this will be identified at the next meeting.

There are many excellent management skills courses which develop the above ideas, including some of the more complex aspects such as conflict resolution, and aspiring project managers should avail themselves of these. The Further Information at the end of this chapter contains several texts which provide an expansion of the subject.

9.11 Managing the Team – Working with Geographically Remote People and Groups

All the above good ideas about working with teams are fine where everyone is 'drinking from the same watercooler/coffee machine'. That is, they are geographically close. Many project managers today, even for projects of medium complexity, are having to work with other organisations, often at a distance. Among the reasons for this is the increase in outsourcing (see Chapter 12) and in the number of collaborative projects as a result of organisations working more closely together.

For example, one project to develop a new magnetic tape drive at Hewlett-Packard required work to be undertaken at their plants at Greeley (USA), Bristol (UK) and Japan. The obvious problems concern:

- Language and culture – each of these operating units had their own way of working and despite the fact that two of these three nominally had English as their first language, there was much work to be done to ensure that communication was effective;
- Where each group placed this project in their priorities – each operating unit had its own set of priorities, and the product had a very different relative importance for each site;
- The time-zone – relative to the UK, the US plant was 6 hours behind and the Japanese plant 8 hours ahead. This meant that there was no time in the day when all parties would naturally be at work;
- Standards – due to the different requirements of each market that each plant served, they had different standards and tests that would have to be undertaken on the product. This had the potential to create technical conflict.

As you can see even from such a superficial analysis, there is plenty of potential for problems and it is very difficult to conceptualise the management task in this environment. More generally, problems that arise include:

- obtaining buy-in to objectives from remote teams and individuals;
- poor development and communication of plans;
- no clarity as to who is responsible for what and to whom;
- lack of sharing of problems as and when they arise;
- delays caused by support systems – in particular, incompatibilities between administrative systems (e.g. where procedures for allocating and handling budgets may be very different).

Add these to the feelings of isolation of individuals working in such environments and the effects can be contrary to the expectations of high-performing teamwork. To counter these the first stage for the project manager is recognition that such problems arise and that it is only through more active management that they will be avoided or at least minimised. Typically, other devices that managers use to help in such environments include:

- Formal project start-up meeting – North American firms often use an all-singing and dancing roadshow to 'rev the team up'. Quite how effective this is in other cultures is debatable;
- Regular face-to-face meetings to ensure that communications are working and to keep the team engaged with the project;
- Establishing regular video-conferences where face-to-face meetings are not possible – use the same guidelines for meetings as in the previous section;
- Judicious use of e-mail in the circulation of project information, that is, keep people 'in the loop' but don't add to their drowning in unnecessary data. Also being aware of the problems that people 'reading between the lines' in what is a relatively informal communications medium can have;

- Working with senior managers to clear the way for project staff in remote locations to be supported in their project work, including assessment and rewards;
- Establish some rules for dealing with particular scenarios – e.g. where conflicts arise in the team, and how these should be handled;
- Create highly visible progress measures that can be viewed by all the project team in real time (see Chapter 11);
- Don't expect to get full productivity from a team that is so diverse – many managers have found that 75–85 per cent is the most that can be expected, due to all the reasons given above. This may require longer schedules or additional resources to be employed, but is at least realistic.

The above list again shows that project management, far from being a mundane and routine task, is one of the most challenging that we face. There are no hard and fast rules here – just some structures and guidelines that warn of potential problems that are known to arise under particular circumstances, and the actions of some managers in dealing with them. The gap between that and practice is to be filled by the individual manager, using their knowledge and creativity, to find ways of working that fit the context and meet their particular set of challenges.

9.12 Relevant Areas of the Bodies of Knowledge

The PMI approach in particular (see Tables 9.4 and 9.5) suggests that there should be a highly planned and formalised process for all these stages. The reality for many

Table 9.4 Relevant area of the APM body of knowledge

Relevant section	Title	Summary
66	Organisational structure	The point is made that the organisational structure defines the reporting and authority relationships in the project. Three basic kinds of organisation are defined (functional, project, matrix), and it is noted that this may change through the project life-cycle.
70	Communications	The many forms of communications are identified, including the need for particular meetings to be conducted – e.g. a kick-off meeting at the start of the project.
71	Teamwork	The importance of the project team is discussed and the principles outlined that motivation and conflict resolution are important aspects of this. In addition, it is stated that 'Cultural characteristics of team members should be given full consideration: different cultures create different working needs.'
75	Personnel management	The recruitment, development, safety and welfare of staff is identified as a specialist skill set, where the project manager has some responsibility.

Table 9.5 Relevant area of the PMI body of knowledge

Relevant section	Title	Summary
9.1	Project human resource management – organizational planning	This is counted as part of the project planning phase, where the structure is determined in advance, and jobs designed into the structures. This is a very involved process that results in the production of an organisation chart for the project, along with job descriptions and identified needs for staff development.
9.2	Project human resource management – staff acquisition	The characteristics of the individuals required should be determined to include their experience, interests, characteristics, availability and competencies. They are then recruited through negotiation with functional heads, or procurement from outside sources.
9.3	Project human resource management – team development	'Development as a team is critical to the project's ability to meet its objectives.' This activity should be in line with the needs of the project therefore, and the tools for doing this include team-building activities, general management skills enhancement and training, reward and recognition and, interestingly, co-location.

project managers is that they are handed a team, an imperfect structure and told to 'get on with it'. These are good guidelines, however, but present a significant upfront workload to the project manager. They do contribute to problem prevention, development of *human capital* and recognition of competence.

9.13 Summary

The conventional approach to designing organisations is to have the key functions arranged into 'chimneys' with people who perform a similar set of tasks grouped together with their own hierarchies. These are very convenient, but are not the most appropriate for achieving results through projects. The pure project organisation is possibly the most flexible and far removed from the conventional approach to management – people are brought in on a contract basis for the project and no other task. The hiring organisation does not then have a further labour overhead when there is no work to be done. Matrix management is an attempt by conventional organisations to give some degree of authority to the project manager while retaining the benefits of the functional organisation. The three different types of matrix model represent increasing levels of authority given to the project manager – namely lightweight, balanced and heavyweight. Matrix management is extensively used but does suffer from the problem of one person having two bosses. The choice of the structure to be used is dependent on, among other criteria, the strategic objectives of the project.

One representation of the heavyweight matrix – called *the seamless enterprise* – exists when the functional chimneys are seen as being subordinate to key business processes. The use of tools such as process mapping can help to make this a reality by stimulating cross-function communication and activity.

Forming groups of individuals into teams is a complex process. There are many productivity and effectiveness benefits (synergy) to be gained from teamwork over that of a group. Teams have a natural life-cycle which has recognisable characteristics to each part. The project manager can have a role in controlling both the emergence of the various phases and the management of negative effects when the team goes 'over the hill'.

Belbin, among others, has provided managers with a tool for identifying the personalities of individuals which can provide a guide as to the nature of the person or mixture of people who will be required for particular tasks within a particular team. Classifications such as Belbin's do provide a useful avenue for team development activities. However, in order to get the most from a team, the manager can draw on the experience of others. Providing a clear and elevating goal is one of the most important points. The nature of the team can also be managed through the categorisation of the task to be carried out – creative, tactical or problem solving. Running meetings – as for most of project management – is a skill that can be learned, and there are many issues to be resolved when a team is geographically spread, and become *virtual teams*.

Overall, getting the most from an organisation of individuals does require that they work in a structure that is appropriate to the task being undertaken, and that their local environment is managed as part of the process. This is a whole area of study in its own right.

Project Management in Practice

Matrix management at Cardiff Bay Development Corporation

As a government-funded body the corporation is one of a number of UK regional development corporations charged with the regeneration of specific areas. It is a predominantly project-based organisation – the life-span of the corporation was generally fixed at its inception. Its roles include the promotion of the area and the bringing in of business, housing and the necessary infrastructural changes to make it all work. Aside from London's Docklands development, the Cardiff Bay development is one of the most ambitious schemes currently running. It includes the construction of a barrage across the estuaries of the rivers Taff and Ely, which will form a freshwater lagoon when completed. The 2200 acres of land that will be directly adjacent to the lagoon are under the control of a number of owners, with around 60 per cent of it being under contract or negotiation for redevelopment.

When founded in 1987, the corporation was divided into functional groups – engineering, commercial, finance and administration, each under the control of a director. As the work of the corporation grew, it was decided that this was becoming unwieldy and that in order to simplify matters, a matrix (overlay) structure would be adopted. The directors maintained overall charge and the team members were drawn in as needed. The overlay consisted of eight horizontal functions, divided into geographical areas.

As the engineering director commented:

> This proved to be too complicated as people found themselves on too many teams. They lost sight of the corporate objectives – the teams ended up competing against each other for developers to take plots of land, regardless of who was most suitable for that site. What we needed to do was to maintain that competitive spirit, but channel it more constructively. The sale of sites was also problematic as the revenue generated would technically be earned by the teams, but would go back into a central pot for use by all.

The experiment with this form of matrix management was abandoned. The current structure keeps the power of the functions intact but looks at four key areas through the business processes that are carried out in those areas. In this way, it now more closely follows the seamless ideas than those of the conventional matrix.

Project Management in Practice

Semco

Semco is an unusual company. Based in Brazil, it has gone through the worst of Brazil's economic mayhem, survived (800 per cent-plus inflation, the government seizing large proportions of available cash, and at times an almost non-existent home market for its goods) and still grown. It has done this through the evolution of a new management structure – known as the satellite or networked organisation. The case is an example of taking the project management organisation to an extreme.

Semco was a traditional, hierarchically oriented manufacturing business which was run by its founder. When the business passed to his son, the changes started. The recession in Brazil meant that there would have to be major redundancies or the firm would close. This presented a unique opportunity to the company. Employment legislation in Brazil meant that severance pay was very high. Their services would still be required, however, in some measure, particularly those of the direct employees. By selecting the workers who could handle the break, the company helped these people to set themselves up in their own businesses, providing the company (and any others who might wish to use their services) with the service they had previously provided as employees. Often this would be on the very hardware that they had used previously, but which was now leased or owned by them. This idea was applied to all areas of their operations – legal, accountancy as well as some manufacturing. No guarantees were given on either side, a strategy which was intended to make sure that both parties could remain competitive and flexible. The structure is shown in Fig. 9.9.

Treating people who were previously employees as contractors had the necessary effect of reducing the fixed labour overhead. In addition, people view problems

Figure 9.9 Satellite organisation

differently when working for themselves. Too often project managers would be left with other people's problems because they had no stake in solving them. Now they have the same interest in the achievement of an end-result as does the project manager. Encouraging people to take control of their working lives through self-employment is a major break – a person is now paid for what they do, rather than what their job title is worth.

What Semco has done is to hive off much of the line-management responsibility and become purely project focused – removing the constraints of processes and procedures. Its core business is a small amount of assembly work, with the coordination of innovation being the central aim of the core. This is an example of what Handy (1989) calls the 'shamrock organisation', and does away with conventional structures in favour of something far less easily comprehended, but which meets the needs of the modern business in achieving the necessary strategic flexibility. Such a form is clearly the ultimate expression of that current management buzzword – empowerment.

Key Terms

functional chimneys
cross-functional activities
dotted-line responsibility
matrix management
seamless enterprise
teamwork

collection/entrenchment/resolution/
synergy/decline/break-up
personality profile
group-think
meetings

Review Questions and Further Exercises

1 Why is the functional organisation prevalent in modern business?

2 What are the disadvantages of the functional organisation?

3 Briefly list the other ways in which an organisation may be structured.

4 Why is the subject of organisational structure so important?

5 Why is the 'pure project' organisation a useful structure?

6 Why should an organisation use the matrix structure?

7 Briefly describe the three basic types of matrix organisation.

8 Why should an organisation consider it very carefully before attempting to use matrix management?

9 How do the ideas of the 'seamless enterprise' differ from those of matrix management and those of functional management?

10 Why should project managers concern themselves with the way the groups they are working with interact?

11 How might a knowledge of the life-cycle of teams help the project manager?

12 Using Belbin's character profiles, indicate which of these you feel best applies to you. You may like to apply this to a group in which you are working by then analysing each other's characteristics.

13 What actions can the project manager take to try to ensure effective teamwork?

14 Discuss the statement that 'project meetings regularly take up too much time and achieve very little'.

References

Ansoff, H.I. (1968) *Corporate Strategy*, Penguin Books, New York.

Bartlett, A. and Ghoshal, S. (1990) '"Matrix Management" – Not a Structure, a Frame of Mind', *Harvard Business Review*, July–August, pp. 138–45.

Belbin, R.M. (1993) *Team Roles at Work*, Butterworth-Heinemann, Oxford, p. 23.

Belbin, R.M. (2000) *Beyond The Team*, Butterworth-Heinemann, Oxford.

Davis, S.M. and Lawrence, P.R. (1977) *Matrix*, Addison-Wesley, Reading, MA, pp. 18–19.

Dimancescu, D. (1995) *The Seamless Enterprise: Making Cross Functional Management Work*, Wiley, New York.

Handy, C. (1989) *The Age of Unreason*, Arrow, London.

Knight, K. (ed.) (1977) *Matrix Management – A Cross Functional Approach to Organisations*, Gower, Aldershot.

Larson, C.E. and LaFasto, F.M.J. (1989) *Team Work*, Sage, London.

Lawler, E.E. and Mohrman, S.A. (1985) 'Quality Circles After the Fad', *Harvard Business Review*, January–February, pp. 65–71.

Mullins, L.J. (1999) *Management and Organisational Behaviour*, 5th edition, Financial Times Pitman Publishing, London, pp. 542–3.

Peters, T. (1987) *Thriving on Chaos*, Macmillan, London.

Peters, T. (1992) *Liberation Management*, Macmillan, London.

Semler, R. (1993) *Maverick! The Success Story Behind the World's Most Unusual Workplace*, Century, London.

Ulrich, K.T. and Eppinger, S.D. (2000) *Product Design and Development*, 2nd edition, McGraw-Hill, New York.

Further Information

Berne, E. (1967) *Games People Play: The Psychology of Human Relationships*, Penguin, Harmondsworth.

Bishop, S.K. (1999) 'Cross-Functional Project Teams in Functionally Aligned Organisations,' *Project Management Journal*, September, pp. 6–12.

Blanchard, K., Carew, D. and Parisi-Carew, E. (1992) *The One Minute Manager Builds High Performing Teams*, HarperCollins, London.

DeMarco, T. and Lister, T. (1999) *Peopleware: Productive Projects and Teams*, 2nd edition, Dorset House, London.

Katzenbach, J.R. and Smith, D.K. (1993) *The Wisdom of Teams*, Harvard Business School Press, Cambridge, MA.

Kerzner, H. and Cleland, D.I. (1985) *Project/Matrix Management, Policy and Strategy, Cases and Situations*, Van Nostrand Reinhold, New York.

www.belbin.com – Belbin Associates website and on-line role profiling.

Note

1 See the results of research carried out by Bartlett and Ghoshal (1990), and the anecdotal evidence of Peters (1987, 1992).

10 Management and leadership in project environments

The literature on the subject of management and leadership is vast. A search of a single university library yielded in excess of 6000 references – the system simply did not bother to count beyond this. The subject is well studied in many disciplines and so provides for an overlap with the organisational behaviour and the human resources management specialisms. There is also a substantial literature which is practitioner based that has much to offer the practising manager and student alike.

This chapter considers the basics of management and leadership and cites some of the key historical developments in this area. A structure is provided for the literature and the role of new management theories or 'paradigms' is considered. The need for the manager to show leadership and treat time as a valuable resource is highlighted through the consideration of time management.

Contents

Learning Objectives

By the time that you have completed this chapter, you should be able to:
- Identify the differing roles of leadership and management in the project environment;
- Show the impact of the individual manager on the performance of the group of people that they are managing;
- Discuss the role of changes in management thinking and the implications of these for practitioners.

10.1 The Role of Leadership and Management in Projects

The structure employed for these discussions is shown in Fig. 10.1. The assumption is made that management has a positive role to play in the achievement of project goals. The figure shows the major contributory factors in this. At the highest level, the generic ideas concerning project management are deconstructed into three major components which all have an input into the individual project manager/leader's role:

- management – the technical discipline of applying and administering authority over others which is given through the formalised structural arrangement of the organisation;
- leadership – the quality of obtaining results from others through personal influence;
- individual skills and attitudes which the project manager possesses.

Figure 10.1 shows the components of the individual project manager's role in planning, organising, directing, controlling and motivating the people concerned with the achievement of the task. Apart from the three characteristics already mentioned, the nature of the task being undertaken, the motivations of the individuals in the team, the organisational structure and the elusive notion of 'culture' are all inputs to determining the role that the project manager should play. This in turn determines the style that will be adopted, which leads to the concept of each project or task being a 'test of management effectiveness'. Should the factors that the project manager uses prove to have been used effectively then there will be a positive influence on the outcome. This is not to say simplistically that the outcome itself will be positive, as there are many external factors that can have a more significant effect. Therefore, the discussion of the role of management in this chapter is limited to the factors that are internal to the organisation or the project team itself.

Managing is a term that implies capability to direct and administer the work of others. It does not imply technical specialism, though this is often required, but the term 'manager' should imply a knowledge of the issues involved in 'managing'. The definition of management has been stated to include a measure of power or authority

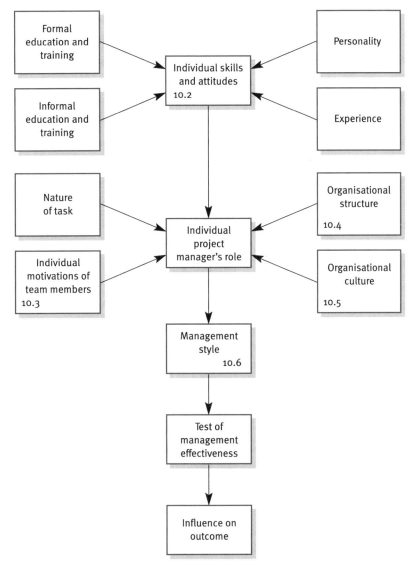

Figure 10.1 The role of leadership and management

given by the organisational structure. Managing is therefore considered to be task-related.

As Drucker (1955) commented:

The manager is the dynamic, life-giving element in every business. Without his leadership, the resources of production remain resources and never become production. In a competitive economy above all, the quality and performance of the managers determine the success of the business, indeed they determine its survival. For the quality and performance of its managers is the only effective advantage an enterprise in a competitive economy can have.

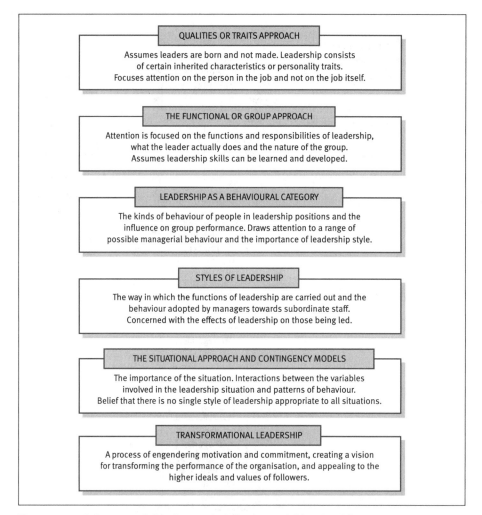

Figure 10.2 A framework for the study of managerial leadership
(*Source*: Mullins, L.J., 1999, *Management and Organisational Behaviour*, 5th edition, Financial Times Pitman Publishing, p. 260. Reproduced with permission)

Leadership

Leadership involves the influencing of others through the personality or actions of the individual. The definition is therefore people-related. A framework for the study of managerial leadership is given in Fig. 10.2.

The earliest approach to leadership was the 'traits' approach. The context was militaristic, aligned to the notion that born leaders are the type of people who could lead a group out of the trenches and into attack. The idea that 'leaders are born and not made' is contentious and highly dubious. Great leaders in all spheres of human endeavour have developed their skills and attributes to the point needed for the task they are undertaking. Both of these are teachable – provided the individual wishes to learn. Intelligence is one of the few characteristics that cannot be taught, though this has rarely been a constraint on success. Much of the research into establishing the precise characteristics of a leader has been inconclusive or contradictory. The more recent approaches (functional or group approach, leadership as a behavioural category, style) have to some extent followed the same pattern. The emergence of the 'contingency' models recognises what might have been expected, that there is no single 'recipe for leadership' which, if followed, will make you instantly successful. Transformational leadership is the most recent and most change-focused of the approaches, involving a more human-centred attitude to management issues.

The following quotation questions whether it is possible for an individual to be both a manager and a leader in the same context:

> What is the best way to develop leadership? Every society provides its own answer to this question, and each, groping for answers, defines its deepest concerns about the purposes, distributions and uses of power. Business has contributed its answer to the leadership question by evolving a new breed called the manager. Simultaneously, business has established a new power ethic that favours collective over individual leadership, the cult of the group over that of personality. While ensuring the competence, control and the balance of power relations among groups with the potential for rivalry, managerial leadership unfortunately does not necessarily ensure imagination, creativity, or ethical behaviour in guiding the destinies of corporate enterprise. (Zaleznik, 1977)

While there is clearly a role for both project managers and leaders, the term management will be used from here on to denote both the management of the task and the leadership of the people involved.

10.2 Individual Skills and Attitudes

The model in Fig. 10.1 shows the inputs of personality (discussed in Chapter 9), experience (from previous activities within and outside the work environment) and (in)formal methods of training and education (see below).

Many of the skills required of the project management are learnable, in particular personal management (the management of yourself, as opposed to personnel management which is the management of people) and the ability to motivate a team. Personal management will be discussed here and motivation in section 10.3.

The basis of the study of personal skills management is the application of Deming's fifth point:

> Improve constantly and forever every aspect of product and service provision.

The best place to start with any management change is yourself. Most managers would like to have extra time, and no matter what project you are involved in, time is one resource that is not replenishable. The successful project manager has learned to apply some form of structured method to the allocation of that resource. While there are many excellent proprietary time management systems, the discussion here will be on the general principles rather than the characteristics of any one particular example.

A study showed that for a sample of American managers who had not had any time management training (De Woot, quoted in Godefroy and Clark, 1989):

49 per cent of their time is spent on tasks that could be done by their secretaries;
5 per cent is spent on tasks that could be delegated to subordinates;
43 per cent is spent on tasks that could be delegated to colleagues;
3 per cent is spent on tasks which justify the input of their talents and abilities.

Many project managers work long hours, with their own work always being subject to delays and fitting the description 'running to stand still'. This leads to poor decision-making as time is not properly allocated to the analysis and consideration of the issues involved. Their work assumes a pattern where they have no basis for making the decision as to whether to accept or reject further tasks and so undertake more than they can realistically handle. For many people, this is a way of remaining useful as they are seen to be busy, but in reality they are rarely effective.

Time allocation fits three broad categories:

- proactive – working on plans that are beyond the timeframe of 'that which needs to be done immediately' with the emphasis on 'problem prevention'. If one considers management to be a process and have a 'management product', the quality of that product will be determined by the effect that it has on both the short- and long-term performance of the project they are managing;
- reactive – there is a problem, work to solve it. This is also known as 'firefighting' or 'busy work' and is a style of management which can be very rewarding in that the constant attention of that manager is required (Zeus culture) but stress is high and progress on innovative matters haphazard;
- inactive – resting between the bouts of proactive and reactive work. Does not include thinking time, but does include time spent outside work.

The basis of any time management system is that it provides a logical base to work from in deciding how to prioritise time between the three categories. The effects of good or bad time management are shown in Fig. 10.3.

Figure 10.3 Effects of time management on the behaviour of individuals

One of the major effects of poor performance in management is stress. This is pressure which, through the natural reactions of the human body, generates in the individual symptoms ranging from anxiety to death. The body generates adrenalin (for 'fight or flight') which is not worked off by the body – particularly in sedentary occupations. While a certain amount of pressure is beneficial and leads to enhanced performance as an individual rises to a challenge, the negative side is 'stress'. By far the most helpful guide to the individual managing stress has come in the form of the 'four Ps':

- plan your way out of the situation that is causing you the stress;
- pace yourself – don't try to do everything at once;
- pamper yourself – reward yourself for goals accomplished or plans completed;
- piss yourself laughing – the healing power of laughter is enormous.

The approach to improving time management involves taking a little of that commodity to plan and involves the classical business strategy development cycle:

- Analyse the current situation – the best way of doing this is to chart the amount of time that you spend during a period of several weeks on certain tasks – record them in a table such as Table 10.1. This is generally a fairly depressing exercise, especially when you refer to the next section. The priority column should rank the importance of the item being considered from 1 (will contribute to long-term objectives) to 5 (totally irrelevant diversion).
- Set goals and targets for short-, medium- and long-term (broken down into professional, financial, personal and any other) objectives, which must be SMART:
  S – specific and written down – this is a fundamental starting point for both personal and project management, defining, specifically where it is that you want to be (discussion of the need to set objectives often uses the metaphor of a journey – you would not start out unless you knew where it was you were going);
  M – measurable – there should be a definable point at which it can be objectively determined that the goal has been achieved;
  A – achievable – the objective must be physically possible;

Table 10.1 Time usage analysis

Start time	Activity	Time taken	Priority	Comments

R – realistic – for yourself to achieve this, without being too conservative (goal should be uplifting – see Chapter 6);

T – time-framed – having a limit on the date by which it will be achieved.

Where there is a discrepancy between the objectives you have set for yourself and the way in which time is allocated, the plan to achieve those objectives must be changed as follows:

1 Set the plan in place as to how to achieve those goals – there is a certain amount of time that we have to allocate to each of the above areas of activity. This amount of time should reflect the priority that each takes, e.g. the time outside contracted working hours – is that to be spent doing extra work, time with family, in front of the television or on social or sporting activities? Most people can put these in a ranking. The achievement of a certain goal should be associated with the allocation of a certain amount of time to it.

2 Use specific techniques to keep to the above (see Table 10.2).

3 Constantly review your performance – the use of a diary along with the repetition of the time evaluation form from time to time can show the magnitude of improvement. Some of the most successful people keep a 'journal'. This is a record of their performance, both good and bad, written at regular intervals (daily/weekly). This form of honest self-analysis is excellent for charting progress, particularly over a period of years and providing support to the idea that taking charge of your time can yield enormous benefits. As one very successful

Table 10.2 Techniques to keep to a plan

Use a diary or other form of time-planner ('the shortest pencil is better than the longest memory') – record activities rather than trying to remember them – this only takes up valuable space in your mind.

Say 'no' to non-goal-achieving tasks – do not add to your current task list.

Handle each piece of paper once only – this rule avoids the little time-bombs (memos that required action by a date which is approaching rapidly) that sit in an office because you have not got round to tackling them.

Use checklists and to-do lists to save you having to remember events and to enable you to sequence them rationally. Do not avoid difficult or unpleasant tasks. Get them done and out of the way so that your time may then be more positively employed.

Make telephone calls with a fixed duration – e.g. by calling five minutes before a meeting you limit the time of the conversation to five minutes.

When you talk to someone have your agenda written down and record the results of the discussion. Don't handle information twice.

Allow people to make and implement decisions for themselves – they do not need to bring all basic issues to you – the rules for making the decisions should be established.

Do not allow interruptions to disturb meetings or periods when you need to be engaged in proactive work.

Do not be constrained by the normal work practices of time and place (if allowable).

project manager put it, 'What better way of showing that you are ready for the responsibility of managing other people than by taking effective control of your own time? How on earth can you hope to be an effective manager of other people, if you are incapable of managing yourself?'

One thing at a time – the idea of focus that has been applied to such effect in the development of organisational strategy (the operation that focuses on meeting a narrow range of needs will be more successful than that which tries to meet a wider range) is also applicable to personal time management. Focusing on the goals to be achieved and eliminating distractions can clear the way of unwanted activities.

The last two Ps are vital if you are to be successful as a project manager. The former takes on the ideas of balance in your life as a whole through sport or other recreation, while having fun is a major spur to better performance as well as a great stress reliever. Peters (1992) quotes a Californian marketing company as having a number of strategies to encourage the 'fun' back into work, including regular water-pistol fights in the accounts department (see also Schrage, 1999; Peters, 1999; Firth, 1996).

Having cited these methods for improving your time management, these kinds of skills are only the basis of a longer period of sustained self-improvement. Formal post-experience education for managers is a major industry and most forward-looking organisations promote individuals taking time to study through providing study leave or flexible working arrangements. Some organisations have gone as far as creating their own study centres (e.g. Unipart University in the UK). Informal methods of learning are just as valuable such as reading new books and journals, in addition to sharing knowledge and ideas with colleagues and people from other organisations (often referred to as 'networking').

10.3 Individual Motivation

The modern project manager has a responsibility both to the organisation and to the team members to ensure that they are provided with a high level of motivation. People work better and faster when they have pride in their work. The individual will need to gain satisfaction from the tasks they are assigned, as work generally occupies a significant part of their lives (call this a 'social duty'). By providing for the needs of an individual, their performance can be made less uncertain and, to a degree, managed for benefit to both the individual and the organisation. The major theories of work motivation are shown in Fig. 10.4.

Scientific management

Figure 10.4 includes the work of Frederick Taylor (1911) in the development of the principles of scientific management. This is included as its importance is largely historic, but it had an unprecedented effect on management thinking. Despite the principles being nearly a century old, there is still much evidence of their application.

The principles of scientific management or 'Taylorism' are most applicable to repetitive work. They are as follows.

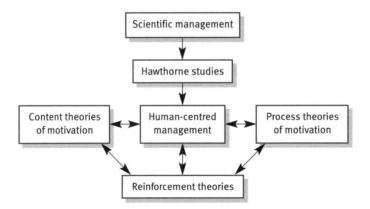

Figure 10.4 Main theories of work motivation

1 Work should be studied scientifically to determine in quantitative terms how it should be divided and how each segment should be done. The aim is to maximise efficiency of the activity and is achieved through measurement, recording and subsequent analysis.
2 The worker should be matched scientifically to the job, e.g. where a task has a physical input to it, the physique of the individual should match the requirements of that task by, for example, using a well-built person to move heavy loads.
3 The person carrying out a task should be trained to do it as per the results of the analysis – it must be carried out exactly as designed and closely supervised.
4 The person carrying out the task should be rewarded for following the prescribed method exactly by a substantial monetary bonus.

The result of Taylorism is the separation of the work task from any thinking process by the individual. Any attempt at motivation is purely financially based. Support activities are carried out by trained individuals. The advantage of the system for working is that the task is made very simple, which means that an individual can become very proficient at it and can be replaced with relative ease. The downsides are considerable, however, with the person being alienated from the task they are doing and having no real input to the conversion process. This alienation can be passive in the form of losing of interest in the process ('don't care' attitude) ranging to destructive (pilfering, sabotage, deliberate waste, bomb threats, militant union action).

The Hawthorne studies

The Hawthorne studies were carried out to assess the impact of working conditions (temperature, light, noise) on the motivation and hence the productivity of individuals (Roethlisberger and Dickson, 1939). They focused on a group of production workers and showed that initially, when the lighting level was increased, the level of productivity of the people also increased. The link was made – improving the lighting–improves the motivation–improves productivity. The lighting was increased on subsequent occasions with the same result. The lighting level was now returned to its original level and the productivity still increased. This caused the initial hypothesis to be rejected – there was a much more important factor at work. There is a fundamental rule of measurement – check that the measurement process does not affect the performance of what you are trying to measure. While the measurement process was relatively unobtrusive, what was causing the change was the attention being paid to this group of workers. This finding was far more significant than the finding about physical conditions. There is a clear implication for practical application here – paying attention to groups improves the likelihood of good performance.

Figure 10.4 shows three paradigms of modern motivation theory/management behaviour:

- content theories – focuses on what motivates an individual at work. Key theories include the 'hierarchy of needs' and 'motivation–hygiene';
- process theories – focuses on how particular behaviour is initiated, or the process of motivation. Key theories include 'expectancy';
- reinforcement – focuses on how desirable patterns of behaviour can be reinforced.

Content theories

Maslow published his theory on the 'hierarchy of needs' in 1943 (see also Maslow, 1970) and these are shown in Fig. 10.5. This analysis of needs is based on the notion that individuals will have basic requirements to be content at one level. Once these are met on an ongoing basis, their needs move to the next level, and so on. As Maslow stated, 'Man is a wanting animal and rarely reaches a state of complete satisfaction except for a short time. As one desire is satisfied, another pops up to take its place.' This theory has intrinsic appeal, as it enables the person designing a working environment to meet the needs of an individual at an appropriate level – providing the elusive motivation through an individual pursuing as yet unmet needs.

The first set of needs are physiological – food, shelter, etc. Maslow argues that until the basics are met, someone will not be looking for higher-order needs, such as

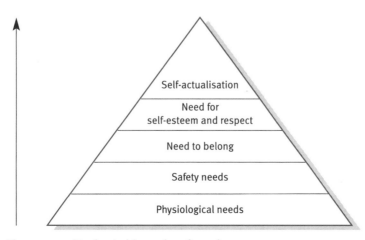

Figure 10.5 Maslow's hierarchy of needs

recognition. Safety needs are the next level up the hierarchy where the provision of the basic needs is seen to be enduring rather than transitory. Above this is the need to belong, which represents 'man the social animal'. This may be to a social group or to a recognisable team, something which will give them an identity. The need for self-esteem and respect comes next, with the thoughts of others about an individual counting in their own self-image. The need for self-actualisation – or to be the best person you can be – is the highest level of needs. Maslow did recognise that this order was not universal and that individuals would have their own hierarchies.

Herzberg's work to produce his 'motivation–hygiene' theory focused on the provision of rewards to the individual. He categorised needs from the task as either 'hygiene' factors or 'motivational'. Hygiene factors are those needs that, unless satisfied, will have a negative effect on motivation. Once a level of satisfaction is reached, increasing the level still further will not increase motivation. Pay is considered to be one such factor for many people. Motivators are those factors which result in higher motivation the better they are met. Recognition is one such factor.

Process theories

Vroom (1964) first developed one of the main theories in this category – that of 'expectancy'. The theory considers that people have a choice regarding the amount of effort they expend (termed the 'motivational force') in a certain situation. This will depend on their perception of the likelihood of their receiving a desired outcome from this. The first-level outcomes are performance-related (the results from the task directly – the satisfaction of doing a good job, for example). The second level is the extrinsic benefits that are achieved, such as praise from a colleague or superior, promotion or pay rise. This motivational force is translated into effective work, through the skills and abilities of the individual.

Further revisions of this work have taken place, all building in more or different factors to try to provide a theory which is universally applicable. Human behavioural processes are far more complex than the models can allow, particularly where science dictates that a single exception disproves a rule. Such theories in practical application may help in explanatory roles, but are rarely effective in a predictive mode.

Reinforcement

Reinforcement as a means of influencing behaviour is often, somewhat cynically, related closely to the manipulation of people. It forms a significant part of popular 'how to manage' books and is summarised by the way in which good behaviour can be positively reinforced. The five rules for providing this are as follows (see Skinner, 1985):

1 Be specific – praise should refer to specific achievements and be backed up with current information.
2 Be immediate – do the praising as soon as the good performance becomes obvious. This will enable the individual to make the link between the good action and the praising.

3 Make targets achievable – help individuals to break down tasks so that they consist of a series of achievable and recognisable milestones (or even 'inch-stones' or their metric equivalent) and praise on the completion of each.
4 Remember the intangible – praise may be more of a motivator to future performance than pay or status.
5 Make it unpredictable – the passing comment of praise can be far more rewarding than the expected 'pat on the back'.

There is, however, an underlying assumption of rationality in the above theories – that an individual's environment can be logically designed and their needs met on an individual basis. While this is clearly desirable, not only the environment but also the system of reward (usually based on promotion and the pay system) have to be designed. Doing so in a large organisation will obviously be an immensely time-consuming activity if the principle that 'the system of reward should be designed to meet the motivation system of the individual' is adhered to. Practically stated, if the individual is motivated by purely financial considerations (which is only a few per cent of the population), then their reward system should be financially based. If they are seeking recognition through status or title, then this should be provided (or offered as a potential reward).

Other factors that affect the motivation of the individual include the following:

• Location – there are differences between the motivation systems and expectations of traditional rural communities and those from urban backgrounds.
• Length of service of the individual – someone with long service (beyond two to five years) is going to have different needs from someone new in a job. If a project is being run with a new team, the focus for early management action should be to provide guidance and early feedback so that expectations of the individual are defined. Working with uncertain assessment criteria is very unsettling as you have nothing to rate yourself against. As was stated in Chapter 3:

> Tell me how you measure me and I will tell you how I will behave. If you measure me in an illogical way, do not complain about illogical behaviour (Goldratt, 1990).

• Previous work environment – people react and mould to the constraints placed on them. Man is a surprisingly versatile animal. Change in attitude and role does not always come with changing jobs or joining a new project team. For this reason, many new manufacturing companies have placed age restrictions on new employees who are going to work in line environments. The objective is that they required people who had not been sullied by the intense management–union fighting at the end of the 1970s or whose spirit had not been broken by too many years in a Tayloristic environment.

The literature is probably most fragmented in the area of motivation. Vroom cites over 500 different studies on the impacts of various factors on motivation back in 1964. What the figure for 2002 would be. . . .

10.4 Structural Implications for Project Managers

The role of organisational structure has already been discussed in Chapter 9. The following section considers some of the cultural implications of the applications of various organisational structures. The application of Taylorism required a highly developed organisational functional hierarchy. The evolution of the more modern management paradigms has changed this considerably. There are implications of structure for motivation of the individual. The issue has already been raised of the system of promotion for project managers and how this is often not as clear as for line personnel.

Taiichi Ohno is widely accredited as the designer behind the Toyota production system. His role in the development of project engineering (as Womack *et al.*, 1990, showed) has been significant as was shown by comparing the way in which Western car producers organise their product design teams with those of the lean producers (all Japanese). The Western approach is to organise people by functional group, e.g. engine designers would have graduated from being component designers and, if successful, may hope to progress to powertrain design. This provides a clear progression path for individuals, but a designer simply progresses as a designer with no increasing appreciation of the implications of their work on the manufacturing process. As was commented:

> Ohno and Toyota, by contrast, decided early on that product engineering inherently encompassed both process and industrial engineering. Thus they formed teams with strong leaders that contained all the relevant expertise. Career paths were structured so that rewards went to strong team players rather than to those displaying genius in a single area of product, process, or industrial engineering, but without regard to their function as a team (Womack *et al.*, 1990).

The subject of promotion is rather cynically summarised by the statement that:

> 'In a hierarchy, anyone will be promoted to their level of incompetence.'

This is known as 'the Peter principle' (Peter and Hull, 1970) and was used by its originators to explain why, in their experience, so many managers appeared to be lacking in the basic qualities needed for the task of managing. Their theory relates to the above very closely – they noted that competence in a line task would generally be rewarded by further promotion up the line of authority. The further they were promoted, the further they moved from the specialism for which they had first been promoted for being competent. As noted earlier in this text, project management does not escape this particular principle.

10.5 Cultural Implications for Project Managers

Culture itself is almost impossible to define. This is because of the number of different cultures that exist within any one organisation and the fact that even the most

Table 10.3 Culture of organisations

Name	Description of culture	Characteristics	Advantages	Disadvantages
Apollo	Role	Formalised, rule-based, focused on individual specialisms	Stable, predictable, visible	Stable, predictable
Zeus	Club	Entrepreneurial, focused on single leader, autocratic style	Little structure to prevent dynamism	Little logic to what is done, total dependence on one person
Athena	Task	Group gathered with common purpose	Creative, dynamic	Expensive to maintain, needs constant stream of new tasks and highly qualified people
Dionysus	Existential	Organisation that shares resources but where people are not dependent on each other	Allows each to be self-determining, little structure	Relies on individual responsibilities and risks, needs high level of personal development

detailed deconstruction would provide an inaccurate picture of the totality. At the simplest level, the culture of a group or team can be described as relating to one or more of the Greek gods – Apollo, Zeus, Athena and Dionysus. These ideas were developed by Handy (1985) and show how the nature of the group will need to influence the style of management that is practised if the two are not to clash. The styles, their characteristics and the advantages and disadvantages of each are shown in Table 10.3.

This table is of interest in providing the kind of managerial overview that is often more useful than an academic description of the same issues. When the 'so-what' test is applied, some further amplification of the effect of culture in attaining management success is required. The fundamental principles are that the culture should reflect the team membership and the task, and the management style should be in line with that culture.

In a project environment, it is almost inevitable that the role of the project manager will have much in common with that of a line or operations manager for periods of time, e.g. in the execution phase of a project to develop a new material there was much testing and retesting of samples to be undertaken. Similarly, at all levels in all projects there will be routine tasks that have to be performed, documentation being a good example. In this situation, the Apollo culture prevails. Using a group which is best described as having an Athena culture (a motivated, highly trained taskforce) to carry out such tasks will cause disinterest due to the lack of scope in the task for creativity.

In the Zeus organisation, an autocratic boss rules by their word alone. Many businesses are run in this way – usually small ones. This kind of boss makes the decisions for their people and will control absolutely, jealously guarding their knowledge of how the business operates. Projects run in this way may get the task achieved, but often at the expense of the project team and other stakeholders. Where the task is anything other than the simplest, attempting to get one person to consider all the issues involved is impossible. There are times, though, for example when a project is running behind and desperate measures are called for, when short-term gains may be made by taking this approach.

The Apollo organisation is highly structured – relying on the idea that breaking down the task into small units creates pockets of specialism. Many organisations have this kind of culture – government departments, large companies. The roles of departments and individuals have already been discussed under the topic of line management. As previously stated, one of the major drawbacks is the lack of creativity that this engenders, in addition to a degree of bureaucracy. Bureaucracy is often typified by a kind of behaviour that obstructs progress. A storekeeper at a major company refused to allow a project manager to have the equipment he needed for a crucial part of his project, as he claimed that the item was not logged on the computer system. When the manager pointed it out to him on the shelves in the store, the storekeeper would still not release the equipment, as without the necessary listing on the computer system the correct paperwork could not be generated. Following an investigation of the business processes, the storekeepers were abolished and the stores run on a take-as-needed basis, with key suppliers filling the shelves directly.

The Dionysus and Athena cultures rely more heavily on the role of the individual than the other two. The Dionysus culture is represented in some ways by the university culture in the UK. Staff are seen as groups with very loose ties that are bonded to the organisational nucleus by the need for the services that they provide – such as administration, buildings and maintenance, technology provision and, mostly, funding for both individual activities and collective projects. Other professions have a similar culture – the medical profession (particularly hospitals) where the sharing is of central facilities.

Consequently it should be no surprise that certain problems have arisen:

- Quality systems have been shown to be less applied in organisations that have Athena, Dionysus or Zeus cultures. Such systems invariably lead to a degree of preceduralisation that would fit well with an Apollo culture, but again it is an example of the characteristics of one being superimposed onto another.
- Matrix management often fails to yield the results planned – the Apollo culture of the functional organisation is overlaid with an Athena culture which is task-centred.

The effect of the early work on the planning of projects should be taken into account. The ideas of work breakdown structure are likely to lead to a functional arrangement and the kindling of an Apollo culture. The project may be far more dynamic than this and require more of an Athena approach.

Parkinson's Law of 1000 is that once you have a corporate staff of 1000 people, they can become totally self-sustaining in work generated within the company without any need for external interaction. That is, they can generate enough work to keep themselves busy (generally by paying people to read reports that you have paid others to generate) without adding one penny of value.

10.6 Management Style

Cooperation–coercion scale

Cooperation is based on educating the individual as to the reasons why it is in their interests to participate in your venture as an active contributor. This is the focus of the humanistic movement and works well in ventures which require active participation rather than grudging acceptance. The style of management that is required is accommodating – ensuring that the needs of the individual are met through the activities and the group support.

Coercion is based on using whatever functional devices and authority exist to force the individual to carry out a particular task – the basis of Taylorism. This works well in the short term where there is a specific task to be carried out. The style of management is confrontational, as there is no commonality of purpose between the individual and their superior.

10.7 The Development of Management Thinking

There are two distinct approaches to management thinking. They can be broadly categorised as either academic or popularist. There was a time when academic thinking was based on the work of a few key individuals whose theories had been proved through limited trials. As is often the case, some of the most advantageous work was done first. The application of psychology and other sciences to management actions has resulted in the wide literature that was referred to in the introduction.

All the above discussions on the academic literature can be summarised in a move from Taylorism at the start of the twentieth century to a new humanism at the end (see Table 10.4). The emergence of humanism is the result of society demanding a new management agenda, the reversal of fortunes of Taylorism (the industrial strife at the end of the 1970s showed that while the Tayloristic systems had provided the Western world with an unprecedented standard of living, it had gone past the point where it was going to continue to be beneficial) and the study of world-class performers in all sectors. Those companies that were showing world-class traits invariably were those that had the greatest ability to harness the creativity of all the individuals within their organisation. In addition, modern expectations, as gleaned in schools, mean that people are far less likely to agree to work under such conditions. The new management is not universal, nor is it without critics or opponents. The move to what has been termed 'anthropocentric management' is also not easy. Letting go of hard-won control sits uneasily with people used to working in Zeus or Apollo cultures. It is almost certain that future organisations will move away from these structures.

Table 10.4 The Tayloristic versus the humanistic agenda

	Tayloristic agenda	*Humanistic agenda*
Level of needs met	Most basic level – physiological and possibly safety	Higher level – need to belong up to self-actualisation
Role of individual	Automaton carrying out specialised task under stated rules	Individual with freedom and autonomy
Advantages for system	Predictability of outcomes	Intrinsically motivated individuals, providing caring creativity
Advantages for individual	Unchallenging, safe, ordered existence	Challenging role with chance for self-determination
Role of management	Designer and controller of work tasks	Provider of scenarios and facilitator
Responsibility for outcomes	Lay with project manager	Shared between all members of the team

The popularists are characterised by books and articles based on either personal management experience (such as Harvey-Jones, 1988) or that of a collective of organisations (including *In Search of Excellence* and others by Tom Peters). The basics are the sharing of what the authors consider to be elements of good practice that have wider application. These are often distilled into principles that one is tempted to treat like laws of physics – fundamental and immovable, which all guarantee a management revolution. However, if there is one lesson to be learned from these texts, it is that the ability to remain flexible and customer-focused are the only constants. *In Search of Excellence* was notable in that many of the companies that were studied and considered to be excellent soon ran into financial trouble. These popularist texts have an important role to play in the ongoing development of managers and maintaining an interest in how the virtues of customer (or stakeholder) focus and flexiblity can best be applied.

10.8 The Development of New Management Paradigms

The modern manager who reads widely would be forgiven for being confused by the range of management paradigms or theories which all appear to have universal application. The temptation is either to go ahead and try the ideas or just to get on with what you are doing and hope that, like many fads, they will pass. Total quality management, the lean paradigm and business process re-engineering are among the most significant and influential to emerge over the last ten years. What is clear from the literature examining the success of such changes in management thinking is that success is far more likely to come from adaptation of a particular idea rather than its wholesale adoption. The role of the successful project manager will be to keep up to date with changes in management thinking, but to take an intelligent approach as to which changes will add value. In summary, any new idea should be

- adopted only after careful consideration;
- purged of unnecessary buzzwords and clichés;
- judged by their practical consequences;
- tied to the here and now;
- rooted in genuine problems;
- adapted to suit particular people and circumstances;
- adaptable to changing and unforeseen circumstances;
- tested and refined through active experimentation;
- discarded when they are no longer useful.

This concept of constantly making small changes and observing the results on a continuous treadmill of improvement is possibly the most significant. The project manager is especially well positioned to adopt this approach, as their role is central to achieving predetermined outcomes – particularly with organisational change projects. For many, the adoption of project management methods fits with this discussion (see Chapter 15).

As Sir John Harvey-Jones (1988) commented:

> Increasingly companies will only survive if they meet the needs of the individuals who serve in them; not just the question of payment, important as this may be, but people's true inner needs, which they may even be reluctant to express to themselves. People want jobs which have continual interest and enable them to grow personally. It goes without saying that they want adequate rewards, but in my experience people are less greedy, and far less motivated by reward, than capitalist theory would suggest. It is certain that every individual not only expects, but should be entitled to a reward which recognises his contribution. The needs of one's people are also wider than just the paypacket. They wish to feel that they are doing a worthwhile job which makes some contribution to society.

10.9 Relevant Areas of the Bodies of Knowledge

The APM body of knowledge starts with the behavioural characteristics of project management professionals: attitude, common sense, openmindedness, adaptability, inventiveness, 'prudent risk taker', fairness and commitment. These present an interesting wish-list of characteristics, without showing how these would be detected or developed in individuals. None of these are tested (or indeed, are testable) empirically. Both bodies of knowledge (Tables 10.5 and 10.6) appear to demonstrate that this an emerging area, with far fewer rules than in other areas such as planning, and therefore less ability for either to be prescriptive.

Table 10.5 Relevant area of the APM body of knowledge

Relevant section	Title	Summary
72	Leadership	The distinction is drawn here between management (involving organising, directing and controlling) and leadership (providing the conditions for high levels of motivation of the team). Project leaders are differentiated from other roles, including the champion and the sponsor.

Table 10.6 Relevant areas of the PMI body of knowledge

Relevant section	Title	Summary
2.4	Key general management skills	The skills of a general manager are very broad, requiring ability to manage functions, structures, work relationships, and oneself. These aspects are elaborated at some length, including the aspect of negotiation (not covered in this text).

10.10 Summary

So – what are the skills and attributes of a good project manager or leader? The skills and attitudes of the project manager will be determined by personality, experience, and both formal and informal education and training, and there are a number of structures that can be applied to help with the understanding of this area. It is important to the organisation and to individuals as the project manager can have a significant impact on the achievement of outcomes for all stakeholders.

Leadership is categorised by the hopefully positive influence of the individual on people, whereas management is centred on people being treated as one of a number of resources. For the individual manager or leader, time is a non-replenishable resource and must be managed accordingly.

Leadership and motivation are intrinsically linked. Craft-based industries were replaced during the nineteenth century by organisations with tasks designed according to the principles of scientific management. These relied on financial reward as the prime motivator. However, financial reward is only one means that management can provide as a motivator. Meeting certain other needs through the work task can be more beneficial (Maslow) as well as treating people as individuals rather than automatons.

Leadership also involves having a sympathy with the culture of the organisation in which you are working. These may be broadly described as either role (Apollo), club (Zeus), task (Athena) or existential (Dionysus). Each has different roles for management and situations where it is applicable.

Finally, new management paradigms (including the widespread application of project management!) should be screened very carefully before being adopted by the manager. The hype should be eliminated and a realistic evaluation of their ability to add value to the 'management product' carried out.

Doesn't time fly?

It was 7.30 on a Tuesday morning, when John Edwards, general manager of the Jenkins Company's main factory, turned on to the M3 to drive to his office in Basingstoke. The journey took about twenty minutes and gave John an opportunity to reflect on the problems of the plant without interruptions.

The Jenkins Company ran three printing plants and had nationwide clients for its high-quality colour work. There were about 350 employees, almost half of whom were based at Basingtstoke. The head office was also at Basingstoke.

John had started with Jenkins as a fresh graduate ten years previously. He was promoted rapidly and after five years became assistant manager of the smaller plant in Birmingham. Almost two years ago he had been transferred to Basingstoke as assistant manager and when the manager retired he was promoted to this position.

John was in good form this morning. He felt that today was going to be a productive day. He began prioritising work in his mind. Which project was the most important? He decided that unit-scheduling was probably the most important – certainly the most urgent. He had been meaning to give it his attention for the past three months but something else always seemed to crop up.

He began to plan this project in his mind, breaking down the objectives, procedures and installation steps – it gave him a feeling of satisfaction as he calculated the cost savings that would occur once this project was implemented. He assured himself that it was time this project was started and mused that it should have been completed a long time ago. This idea had been conceived two years ago and been given the go-ahead but had been temporarily shelved when John had moved to Basingstoke.

John's thoughts returned to other projects that he was determined to implement: he began to think of a procedure to simplify the transport of materials from the Birmingham plant; he thought of the notes on his desk; the inventory analysis he needed to identify and eliminate some of the slow-moving stock items; the packing controls which needed revision and the need for a new order form to be designed. There were a few other projects he remembered needed looking into and he was sure he would find some time in the day to attend to them. John really felt he was going to have a productive day.

As he entered the plant, John was met by the stock controller who had a problem with a new member of staff not turning up. John sympathised with him and suggested that he got Personnel to call the absentee. The stock controller accepted that action but told John that he needed to find him a person for today. John made a mental note of the problem and headed for his office. His office manager, Mrs James, asked him whether she should send off some samples, or would they need to be inspected? Without waiting for an answer, Mrs James then asked if he could suggest a replacement for the sealing-machine operator, as the normal operator was ill, and told him that Pete, the manufacturing engineer, was waiting to hear from him.

John told Mrs James to send the samples. He noted the need for a sealer-operator and then called Pete, agreeing to meet in his office before lunch.

John started on his routine morning tour of the plant. He asked each supervisor the volumes and types of orders that were being processed that morning, how things were going, and which orders would be run next. He helped one worker to find storage space for a container-load of product which was awaiting dispatch, discussed quality control with an employee who had been producing poor work, arranged to transfer people temporarily to four different departments and talked to the dispatch supervisor regarding pick-ups and special orders which were to be processed that day.

Returning to his office, John reviewed the production reports against his projected targets and found that the plant was running slightly behind schedule. He called in the production foreman and together they went through the machine schedules, making several changes. During this discussion, John was asked by someone else to agree several labelling changes to their products and received a telephone call for the approval of a revised printing schedule.

John next began to put delivery dates on important orders received from customers and the sales force (Mrs James handled the routine ones). While doing this, he had two phone calls, one from a salesperson asking for a better delivery date and one from the personnel manager asking him to book time for an initial induction meeting with a new employee. John then headed for his morning conference at the executive offices. He had to answer the chairman's questions on new orders, complaints and potential new business. The production director also had questions on production and personnel problems. He then had to see the purchasing manager to enquire about the delivery of some cartons and also to place an order for some new paper. On the way back to his office, John was talking to the chief engineer about two current engineering projects. When he reached his desk, he lit a cigarette and looked at his watch – it was ten minutes before lunch.

'Doesn't time fly,' he commented as Mrs James entered his office to put some papers on his desk. 'No,' she replied, 'Time stays, we go.' Wondering about the meaning of this, he headed for the canteen.

After lunch he started again. He began by checking the previous day's production reports and the afternoon followed the pattern of the morning. Another busy day, but how much had he accomplished? All the routine tasks had been managed, but without any creative or special project work being done. He was the last to leave the plant that night.

As he drove home he pondered the role that he was paid to fulfil and wondered where the time to carry out any innovative thinking had gone today. He was sure that he had planned intelligently and delegated his authority. He acknowledged the need for a personal assistant, but saw that as a long-term project as the chairman was having a blitz on the overhead created by non-direct staff.

Case discussion

1 Identify the tasks which John should have done himself and those which he should have delegated.

2 Discuss how he uses his time – what are the main problems?

3 How effective do you feel John's 'management by walking about' is?

4 How could he improve his time planning?

5 Would employing a personal assistant for John really 'add value' or just be another overhead cost on the company?

Key Terms

management and leadership

stress

time management

motivation

scientific management (Taylorism)

hierarchy of needs

humanism

culture

cooperation

coercion

management paradigms

Review Questions and Further Exercises

1 Differentiate between the tasks of leading and managing a project.

2 Show the influences that an individual project manager will bring to the role.

3 What are the influences from within an organisation on the role that a project manager takes?

4 Why might the study of time management be fundamental to a project manager?

5 Using Table 10.1, examine your own time-management performance over the period of one or two days. How does this relate to the goals that you have set yourself?

6 From your analysis in Question 5, show what strategies you are going to use to keep yourself on track to the targets you have set for yourself.

7 Compare the work of the major thinkers on motivation. What influence has each had on modern management?

8 Why is it reasonable to think that as managers, our action can have an effect on a project outcome?

9 Why do people need to have a clear promotion path in their jobs? What other motivators would you provide for people?

10 Distinguish between the four basic types of organisational culture as outlined by Handy (1985). Give examples of each and show how each meets the needs or constraints imposed on the organisation in which they operate.

11 Why is it necessary to ensure that the style of management meets the culture of the organisation?

12 Show how the emergence of humanism changed the way in which people are treated within organisations.

13 Compare one major popularist text (e.g. *In Search of Excellence*) with an academic journal article of your choice. What are the purposes, potential audiences and likely effects of each of these? In your view, what is their role in forming management thinking?

14 How might a project manager differentiate between management paradigms that may prove beneficial and those which are going to be of no benefit?

References

Drucker, P. (1955) *Management*, Butterworth-Heinemann, Oxford (first published in 1955 – many later editions are available and still as relevant to the discussion of the role of management).

Firth, D. (1996) *How to Make Work Fun*, Gower, Aldershot.

Godefroy, C.H. and Clark, J. (1989) *The Complete Time Management System*, Piatkus, London.

Goldratt, E.M. (1990) *The Haystack Syndrome*, North River Press, New York.

Handy, C. (1985) *Gods of Management*, revised edition, Pan Books, London.

Harvey-Jones, J. (1988) *Making It Happen: Reflections on Leadership*, Collins, London, pp. 249–50.

Herzberg, F. (1974) *Work and the Nature of Man*, Granada Publishing, London.

Markham, U. (1989) *The Practical Guide to Using Stress Positively*, Element Books, London.

Maslow, A.H. (1970) *Motivation and Personality*, 2nd edition, Harper & Row, New York.

Mullins, L.J. (1999) *Management and Organisational Behaviour*, 5th edition, Financial Times Pitman Publishing, London.

Nohria, N. and Berkley, J.D. (1994) 'Whatever Happened to the Take-Charge Manager?' *Harvard Business Review*, January–February, pp. 128–37.

Peter, L. and Hull, R. (1970) *The Peter Principle*, Pan Books, London.

Peters, T. (1992) *Liberation Management*, Macmillan, London, p. 602.

Peters, T. (1999) *The Project 50*, Alfred Knopf, New York.

Peters, T.J. and Waterman, R.N. (1982) *In Search of Excellence – Lessons from America's Best-run Companies*, Harper & Row, New York.

Porter, L.W., Lawler, E.E. and Emmet, E. (1968) *Managerial Attitudes and Performance*, Irwin, Homewood, IL.

Roethlisberger, F.J. and Dickson, W.J. (1939) *Management and the Worker*, Harvard University Press, Cambridge, MA.

Schrage, M. (1999) *Serious Play: How the World's Best Companies Stimulate to Innovate*, Harvard Business School Press, Boston, MA.

Skinner, W. (1985) *Manufacturing: The Formidable Competitive Weapon*, Wiley, New York.

Taylor, F.W. (1911) *The Principles of Scientific Management*, Harper, New York.

Vroom, V.H. (1964) *Work and Motivation*, Kreiger Publishing, New York.

Womack, J., Jones, D. and Roos, J. (1990) *The Machine That Changed The World*, Rawson Associates, New York.

Zaleznik, A. (1977) 'Managers and Leaders: Are They Different?' *Harvard Business Review*, May–June, pp. 67–78.

Further Information

Adair, J. (1988) *The Action-Centred Leader and Effective Leadership: A Modern Guide to Developing Leadership Skills*, revised edition, Industrial Society, London.

Alexander, R. (1992) *Commonsense Time Management*, Amacom, New York.

Forsyth, P. (1994) *First Things First, How to Manage Your Time for Maximum Performance*, Institute of Management/Pitman Publishing, London.

Handy, C. (1985) *Understanding Organisations*, 3rd edition, Pelican, London.

Jay, A. (1987) *Management and Machiavelli*, revised edition, Business Books, London.

Kloppenborg, T.J. and Petrick, J.A. (1999) 'Leadership in the Project Life Cycle and Team Character Development', *Project Management Journal*, Vol. 30, No. 2, pp. 8–13.

Pettersen, N. (1991) 'Selecting Project Managers: An Integrated List of Predictors', *Project Management Journal*, Vol. 22, No. 2, pp. 21–26.

Slevin, D.P. and Covin, J.G. (1990) 'Juggling Entrepreneurial Style and Organisational Structure: How to Get Your Act Together', *Sloan Management Review*, Vol. 31, No. 2, pp. 43–53.

Tack, A. (1984) *Motivational Leadership*, Gower, Aldershot.

Thoms, M. and Pinto, J.K. (1999) 'Project Leadership: A Question of Timing', *Project Management Journal*, Vol. 30, No. 1, pp. 19–26.

www.iofl.org – the Institute of Leadership

11

Control of projects

'I love deadlines. I particularly like that whooshing noise they make as they go flying by.' (Author unknown)

So, how's it going? An innocent enough question, but one that causes all sorts of problems for project managers. Where projects are of low complexity it may be possible to apply some basic control without any of the devices described in this chapter. For medium- and high-complexity projects the role of the project manager in establishing and maintaining some system for control is paramount during this 'Do It' phase of the project.

The nature of control is discussed here along with the characteristics that require controlling. We shall again see the influence of strategy when we select what to control, and the development of a number of devices that will assist in the control process. Some of these are very simple, others very involved. Whatever the system, the objective is to maximise the visibility of progress and the performance measures that we use should be chosen with this in mind.

Contents

By the time you have completed this chapter, you should be able to:
- Identify the elements of a control system appropriate to a particular project;
- Determine the key performance measures that will be controlled by the system;
- Select appropriate tools and techniques to enable such control.

11.1 Control Systems

Given that many projects do run late, overbudget or otherwise fail to deliver to customer/stakeholder requirements, the question is often asked – 'how did this happen?' The answer is often that it happened very gradually, with days being lost and money spent, not in one large block but in small amounts. These amounts gradually add up and over the life of most projects will provide significant problems. The only way that we can deal with this is by having systems that will detect such occurrences, and allow the project manager the opportunity to instigate correction actions to bring the project back on track. This assumes, of course, that we know what the particular track is that we are trying to stay on. Where there has been poor use of planning there may be considerable confusion as to whether progress is indeed acceptable or whether intervention from the project manager is required.

While this work on control predominantly takes place during the execution phase of the project, it should be given careful consideration during the planning phase. It must be careful to add value to the project – so many projects become overburdened by the weight of bureaucratic requirements imposed to try to keep the project in order. Such a burden is counterproductive – as people will resist the additional work required and either ignore or find ways around 'the system'. The alternative is to provide control at different levels within the project that relies on simple and easily understood measures that reflect the objectives of the project.

The basic requirements for a control system include:

- defining system characteristics of importance;
- defining *limits* to their variation;
- *measurement* of those characteristics;
- making progress *visible*;
- *feedback* to the team of performance;
- instituting *corrective action* where required.

This constitutes the most basic model of a control system and is shown in Fig. 11.1. In this diagram, the output of a process is monitored by some means to determine the characteristics of the output. These data are interpreted and then fed back in order for the project manager to make the necessary changes to the process. On receipt of this information, adjustments are made to the process. By using this kind of 'feedback control system', the performance of the process can be guided by the application of corrective actions to keep it within certain limits (having defined 'acceptable deviation' from the desired performance).

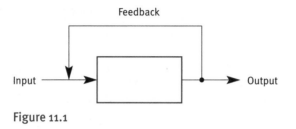

Figure 11.1

Defining system characteristics of importance

So – what characteristics are important? In an ideal world we would be able to say that everything was important and we could devote massive resources to the control effort. If you are NASA, this might be the case. For the rest of the world, we have to prioritise the most important characteristics for control. The most important aspects that need controlling are those that form part of our strategy – typically time, cost and quality. We will know from our strategy which of these is the most important, and should therefore have the greatest attention paid to it. Again here it is vital that project activities and processes are consistent with strategy. The Sydney Olympics, discussed in Chapter 7, had the strategy that time and quality were paramount, and that cost would be sacrificed should the need arise rather than compromise the other two. The greatest efforts were therefore placed on ensuring that the quality and time objectives were met through controlling activities.

We must not assume that TCQ objectives are necessarily the only ones that an organisation will have. Other issues of strategic importance were identified in Chapter 3 and these (legal, ethical, environmental, human resource) and others may also be the subject of control.

Defining *limits* to their variation

The second requirement is to define limits to the variation of the performance in those key areas. We have seen in previous chapters that performance does vary across people and activities, and various methods have been discussed to deal with this variation (see Chapter 6). So, when does a deviation from a requirement become a problem? For some organisations, a 1 per cent deviation from cost targets would be tolerated, while a day's delay would be unacceptable. Others would state their objectives differently. So, what are the limits of variation? The first issue here is that there will always be some variation – but that should be both positive and negative. The theory runs that provided we can harness the positive benefits, they will cancel out the negative issues. That's the theory. For all the reasons discussed in Chapter 6, the reality is that it is often difficult to harness the positive variations, but the negative ones inevitably accumulate. Having accepted this, you immediately put some stability into the process. In reality any negative deviation (activities run-ning over time/cost or failing to meet quality), should trigger further monitoring to ensure that we can keep track of what is happening. There should then be a further zone that triggers action (see box below).

Control using critical chain

As discussed in Chapter 6, there should be a buffer that can be monitored during the project. At regular intervals – daily in many instances – activity managers are asked 'how long to finish?' Their answers can be simply interpreted in terms of the effect that they will have on the buffer – an early finish will add days to it, a late finish will take days from it. This information provides the project manager with a means of deciding what to do next. One method that has proved highly effective is to divide the project buffer up into three regions. If the buffer was, say, 30 days, each of these regions would have 10 days in them. Once there is any erosion of the buffer at all, this puts the project manager into the first zone – that of monitor carefully. Use of 10 days of this buffer puts the project into the next zone – plan. Here plans are drawn up to restore the buffer to its original size (or as a proportion of the time remaining in the project). It is only when 20 days of the buffer has been eroded that the plan is required to be put into action. The three zones are shown in Fig. 11.2.

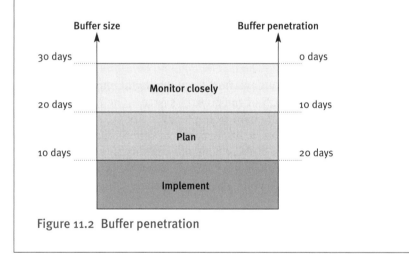

Figure 11.2 Buffer penetration

Measurement of characteristics

What we measure has been defined as part of our reconsideration of strategy. A crucial part of control is when to measure. Here, control activities need to strike a balance. Somewhere between finding out too late to take any action and permanently harassing people to find out how they are progressing lies a position that will satisfy both the needs of control and the needs of the project team to keep the work:reporting ratio right.

Imagine that you are driving a car. This is a good example of a control system. You are sensing characteristics of the environment around you (e.g. seeing a corner ahead) and based on that sensing, making changes to speed and direction to keep the car on the road and away from other cars. While this clearly doesn't apply in the capital cities of most countries, the principle still holds in most other situations. Here you are sensing continuously what is happening around you, unusual for the project situation. What is clear in the driving case is that you need to assess the feedback and take action without delay. Imagine if you only opened your eyes for a second every 10 seconds, or then waited 5 seconds before reacting to the situation in which you found yourself. How long would it be before your 'control' failed? Not long. These two issues are as important in project management – the timing of your observation and speed of reaction to the situation. Time delay in receiving information or implementing action is a killer for any control system.

Making progress visible and feedback of performance

This is an area where there have been many developments in recent years. The principle of visible control was evident in the world-class Japanese manufacturing systems (e.g. *Andon* lights above machines in a factory that would indicate where there was a problem, and continuous monitoring and display of the quantity of output relative to the day's target) were found to be a key factor in their success. The same principles apply very well to project management situations. Given the importance of this, it will be covered in a separate section later in this chapter.

Instituting corrective action

Finding that there is a deviation from what you expected to be happening is only the first part of the job of the control system. The issue then arises of what to do about it. In the critical chain example given above, it is clear what the action to be taken is (monitor, plan or implement). In other situations it may be less clear, but here an important principle of control shows itself: you can only manage the future – what has happened is history. While knowing where you are is important, it is what you do next that will make the difference.

Example of a control system – corrective actions and stability in a physical system

Try balancing a ball in the centre of a tray – start it moving and try to bring it to rest again 10 centimetres away from the start point. Very quickly the movements of the tray get larger and the movement of the ball will generally become anything other than diminishing as it passes over the point without stopping. The system rapidly becomes unstable as the movement of the ball has passed out of control and soon leaves the tray completely. This is the result of instability in the system – the brain cannot make the necesssary corrective action to bring it back to rest and so the control actions get larger as the ball exhibits behaviour which is considerably different from that which is required. The movement of the ball becomes as shown in Fig. 11.3. Programming a machine to do the same task with the application of appropriate control actions can render the system stable in a very short period of time. The pattern of motion is as shown in Fig. 11.4. This system is stable – the movement or response of the system does not go off to infinity or cause the

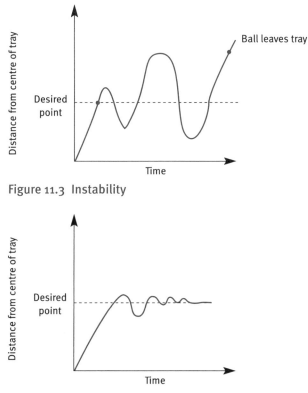

Figure 11.3 Instability

Figure 11.4 Stable system

destruction of the system (as evidenced by the ball finally running off the edge of the tray in the first test), but settles back to an equilibrium (stationary) after the initial disturbance (the move).

The control of projects requires the view that although there is a single event being carried out, it is the product of many interlinked smaller events (within the Work Breakdown Structure) which, like the moving of the ball on the tray, can have their progress monitored and appropriate corrective actions applied to keep them on track.

The system for overall control can be viewed as a series of smaller systems of control, which the project manager interlinks. This overall system of control will expand, the larger the project becomes and, as it does so, more of the control actions will have to be devolved. The system of control systems within systems is shown in Fig. 11.5. In high-complexity projects, the role of the project office as gatherers and processors of data is fundamental.

The control that will be discussed throughout this chapter is a mixture of feed-back control and *feedforward*. A useful way to think of feedforward control is to consider the driving example, where you are not only looking ahead but using your knowledge of the road to make additional changes to speed and direction. For instance, if you knew that there was a particularly dangerous bend ahead, you may take extra care – reducing your speed ahead of the bend. In projects we look ahead

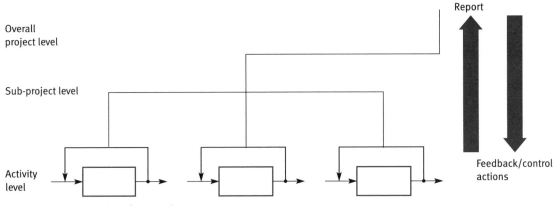

Figure 11.5 Hierarchy of control systems

to see what problems or situations we will be faced with and make changes to protect the project outcomes from the potential of these events. Part of this feedforward control is risk management – performed at the start and ongoing through the project.

11.2 Control of Major Constraints – Quality

The project manager has two roles in the control of quality. These concern the *conformance* of the product and process to agreements (both actual and implied) and the *performance* of the delivery – specifically to manage the stakeholder expectations and perceptions of the project process and outcome.

Conformance

The establishment and management of an effective system to control the quality of products and services is a role of increasing importance in project management. The quality system contains a number of key elements – policies, system description and procedures. The policies for quality control are determined and set out either as part of organisational policy or as required by contractual terms laid down by a client organisation. The systems are then put in place to meet the requirements of these policies and the procedures are what people at all levels of the organisation carry out on a day-to-day basis. The objective of such quality control is:

To provide a formalised system within the project system which ensures that the needs of the customer or the stated objectives of the system are continually being met.

The system needs to be formalised and so requires much of the informality which exists within organisations to be removed. The 'customer' here is anyone who takes the output of the project activities – from an end-user of an artefact or system to a department that receives information from the project team (e.g. accounts or marketing).

There are other reasons for having a quality system in place:

- to protect the project organisation, as far as is possible, from legal liability, most notably professional negligence and product liability claims. The organisation, through its quality system, can demonstrate that it has taken 'every reasonable precaution' to ensure that the project was carried out in a way that ensures that the stated needs were met. This requirement has emerged for many project managers as the business environment in many countries becomes increasingly litigious;
- it is a prerequisite for obtaining business in many markets, including aerospace, defence, public procurement and the motor industry.

The emergence of the importance of quality systems has come as a natural extension of the role of specialisation. In traditional craft industries, the craftsperson would have responsibility for the quality of the output of their process – hence the use of hallmarks in silverware and other forms of labelling of the product, which would allow it to be traced back to the originator. The medieval trade guilds provided a level of quality assurance by regulating their members. As organisations have become more complex and the division of labour has been more extensive (along Tayloristic lines) the role of the quality specialist has emerged.

More recently it has become common to consider not only product (or output) quality but also the 'process' by which that output is delivered. Quality systems provide elements for assuring both of these. One of the recognisable standards for a quality system is ISO 9000 – this is discussed in the Appendix.

Performance

The control of stakeholders' expectations and perceptions has been identified as vital if businesses are to achieve customer satisfaction and retain customers profitably. For a non-revenue-generating project such as organisational change, managing expectations and perceptions is an ongoing challenge. Some issues here are:

- Don't create expectations that cannot be delivered – as a minimum a project should have the characteristic of the paint advert that stated: *It does exactly what it says on the tin.*
- Measure expectations and perceptions – the issue here is vital for control, that throughout the process we recognise the importance of the stakeholders. Where deviations are uncovered, it is often possible to make very small changes that will bring the perceptions back into line. Like other aspects of control, time here is critical – not leaving it too long to measure or to act where unacceptable deviations are uncovered.

11.3 Control of Major Constraints – Cost and Time

This control requires a considerable input from the project manager in their establishment and execution. The attributes of cost and time are interlinked as previously discussed. The need is for practical tools that will identify when corrective actions are required and what they should be. The role of the project manager in cost control may be stated as:

- setting up the cost control system in conjunction with the needs and recommendations of the financial function;
- allocating responsibilities for administration and analysis of financial data;
- ensuring costs are allocated properly (usually against project codes);
- ensuring costs are incurred in the genuine pursuit of project activities;
- ensuring contractors' payments are authorised;
- checking other projects are not using your budget.

The measurement that is often taken to consider progress using cost as a measure is 'sunk costs'. This is the measure of what has been spent to a particular point in time on activities. It is notoriously unreliable as a measure of how much has been achieved, as it is perfectly possible for a project to be 80 per cent complete but to have incurred 95 per cent of the budget allocated to it. Controlling cost overruns clearly needs more than just a raw figure such as expenditure incurred. The 'earned value' concept is one attempt to make the measure more meaningful.

Earned value

For complex projects where warning of problems and an ability to predict final costs and times at completion is required, the use of the concept of earned value can be most useful. This measure brings together time and cost performance elements into a monetary quantity – a unit that is easily understood.

For instance, a project has ten activities to be performed over a period of 10 weeks. The first stage in the earned value assessment process is to set a budget for each of the activities. The activities are identified and the budget for each estimated, based on the estimated time, materials and overhead element (see Chapter 7) for each. These times and costs are shown in Table 11.1. Each of the activities will run sequentially, one after the other.

Table 11.1

Activity	Time	Budget
1	1 week	€5 000
2	1 week	€8 000
3	1 week	€7 000
4	1 week	€12 000
5	1 week	€14 000
6	1 week	€10 000
7	1 week	€13 000
8	1 week	€11 000
9	1 week	€16 000
10	1 week	€4 000
TOTAL	10 weeks	€100 000

The next stage in the measurement of earned value takes place during the project. After a number of weeks, the project manager has a number of ways to address the main question – 'how's it going?' In this case we will consider progress at week five. We need to know how much has been spent on each of the activities (see below for discussion of the difficulty of calculating amounts spent). We also need to know which of the activities have been completed at this point. After 5 weeks, it is found that activities 1–4 have been completed, and that the spend to this time is €36 000. Using a measure that simply looked at the spend, the target was to have completed five activities during this time and therefore the spend should be:

€5000 + €8000 + €7000 + €12 000 + €14 000 = €46 000

We have spent only €36 000, so this is good, isn't it? Planned spend of €46 000, actual spend of €36 000 means that we are running €10 000 under budget. Don't start to plan the post-project party just yet. The earned value measures tell us a different story.

The project manager does the following calculations. The first is to determine the earned value. 'Value' is 'earned' by the completion of activities and the budget for each activity is the value that is earned. In this case it would be the sum of the budgets for the completed activities 1–4:

$$\text{Earned value after completion of activities } 1{-}4 = €5000 + €8000 + €7000 + €12\ 000$$
$$= €32\ 000$$

So now we have an array of measures:

Actual spend: €36 000
Planned spend: €46 000
Earned value: €32 000

How do we interpret these? The first is to consider the cost performance. This is done by comparing the earned value with the actual spend. In this case we can see that the earned value is €4000 less than the actual spend – this is not good. We can state that there is a variance of €4000 between these two. Another way to state this is to provide a ratio of the two measures – known as the *cost performance indicator*.

$$\text{Cost performance indicator} = \text{earned value/actual spend}$$
$$= 32\ 000/36\ 000$$
$$= 0.889$$

Next we can consider time performance. To do this we compare the earned value with the planned spend at that point in time. There is a considerable variance here. Earned value of €32 000 compared with the planned spend of €46 000 – a variance of €14 000. Another way to state this is to provide a ratio of these two measures – known as the *schedule performance indicator*.

Schedule performance indicator = earned value/planned spend

= 32 000/46 000

= 0.696

Both the schedule performance indicator and the cost performance indicator show that there are problems here – as they are both considerably less than 100 per cent. More than this, they provide the project manager with a predictive capability. This will show the likely effect on the overall completion of the project *if nothing is changed*. In this case we can provide a forecast of both the likely cost and time to complete the project.

The cost is calculated from the cost performance indicator and the original project budget as follows:

Estimated cost at completion = Original budget/cost performance indicator

= €100 000/0.889

= €112 500

Similarly, we can calculate the time of completion as follows:

Estimated time of completion = Original time estimate/schedule performance indicator

= 10 weeks/0.696

= 14.4 weeks

Both of these are useful calculations and with the assistance of simple spreadsheets can provide good information on the likely effects of the current state of performance on the project overall. The project manager can then decide on appropriate action to take.

These measures can be summarised in the form of reports which provide the input to problem-solving processes (see Chapter 13). The information needs to be collated by a timing coordinator who can do so in one of the following ways:

- obtaining a verbal report on progress from the person or team carrying out that section of work;
- sending out and collecting a form of progress questionnaire, which outlines the activities and the original targets for them which the team members complete and return to the coordinator with the current status recorded;
- detailed internal measure of progress – an assessor viewing progress as a semi-independent arbiter;
- an external assessor carrying out some form of audit on the project, with widespread powers of access to project data.

Clearly the last two are useful where independent checking of information is required, but it tends to infer a lack of trust of the people doing the work. The point is that whatever data is collected must be reliable (it is not unusual for problems to go hidden or undisclosed due to an individual's fear of retribution if poor performance is discovered). Verbal reports are fine but they can obscure important information through either of two extremes – a person who complains about 'problems' even though progress is good, and the person who will say things are OK simply because 'it is not as bad as it could be/as it was last time we did this'. The project manager must be aware of these and look for evidence to corroborate the information received from other sources. Thus the cost information should be matched with verbal reports of time progress from several members of the same team, in addition to gleaning opinion from other teams.

The climate for reporting should be set to provide a balance:

- people require feedback on how they are performing;
- people need to be clear what information to report, in what format (and what to leave out);
- the project manager needs to have a positive statement that progress is being made according to plan;
- *but* the major reports need to be the exceptions – where there is a clear deviation from acceptable performance in meeting any of the constraints imposed on an activity.

This focus on the exception is vital and must be reflected in the importance that the various reports are given. The bureaucracy of 'paying someone to read reports that you have paid someone else to write' is partially eliminated by this focus on exception.

The factor not so far discussed in relation to the reporting and feedback loop is *timeliness*. If the information or feedback is held up for any period of time, the control action will have to be more severe than if the deviation had been spotted and acted on earlier. The analogy of trying to control a car showed this problem.

There are many measures that can be used by the project manager and there are many ways to make these visible. The following section shows some methods for doing this.

11.4 Visual Control

If you can see what is happening you can control it, runs the theory. There is certainly plenty of evidence to support this, as the measurement and assessment part of the control system is easily achieved. Compare, for instance, the control of the construction of a building with the writing of software. The construction project has one great advantage in terms of control – you can see what is happening (or at least a trained person could determine whether progress was being made). Obtaining some notion of progress when writing a complex piece of software, on the other hand, is more difficult, as the progress will be determined by the finished result only.

To guide progress, the number of lines of code written may be checked or the product modularised so that the unit of control (the element that you are controlling) is made smaller. Either way, the measure is not so easy to construct. How then would you control a scientific research project – say, one of the projects working on the cure for a disease? The result may not be achievable, so this is not a good measure, and is too far away to provide a useful point for control. In such a case, the method of control is on the process rather than the outcome. For instance, the number of experiments performed or the number of ideas generated that would lead to testable formulations for drugs could be monitored. Whatever the circumstance, some measures are needed.

To make the control visible there are a number of systems used. The Gantt chart frequently has a role to play (see the Project Management in Practice at the end of this chapter). One firm needed to track the progress of critical jobs through an office. They did this by placing a large orange beachball on the desk of the person working on the critical task at that time. This had a number of effects. First, it made progress highly visible – simply look for the beachball to determine to which stage the project had progressed. Second, it reinforced the importance of the critical path – that any delay here would delay the entire project. The message to others of 'keep away – this person is working on a critical activity' was most effective. Other systems include traffic lights and various computer-based 'digital dashboards'. The latter are particularly effective where teams are spread out over a number of sites or locations and make extensive use of computers. A part of the computer desktop (the working area of the screen) is given over to indicators that show how particular activities and sub-projects are progressing.

Real-time control

The availability of cost-effective network communications has given rise to the possibility that control information can be reported as it happens, with people making reports on progress several times a day. This data is fed to a central processing unit (one of the possible roles for a project office) and added to data from other activities. The reporting is far less formal, and the results fed back to the users immediately. This gives the opportunity for small corrective measures to be applied, either where activities are running ahead of time (and subsequent activities should be alerted to the possibility of an early start) or where they are running late (where the application of further resources would bring it back into control).

However, there are other ways of making the progress of a project visible. These include using a whiteboard in the centre of the area in which the project team are working. Ongoing activities are listed and ticked off as they are completed. Here we can also apply the traffic lights idea:

Project within 2 per cent of cost and budget	Green or ☺
Project within 10 per cent of cost and budget	Amber or ☺
Project not within 10 per cent of cost and budget	Red or ☹

These do, however, rely on the information collected through the kind of systems that we have discussed above, and are intended to demonstrate how we are conforming rather than performing.

11.5 Last Planner

There are many ways to perform the detailed planning on a project. However, it is often seen to be a weakness and a reason for failure that this was not well carried out. One way to do this detailed planning is to have a central planning office that undertakes such work. Putting the planner at a distance from the work itself is thought by some to provide a degree of independence of the estimate, making it therefore more accurate. Consistent with all the current management thinking and approaches to empowerment, the alternative of allowing the detailed planning to be carried out by those who perform the activities being planned has become popular. This has been promoted by the Lean Construction Institute in the USA, and published as the Last Planner (Ballard, 1994). The method involves the production of look-ahead schedules (consistent with feedforward control) for 4–6 weeks in advance. These contain the details of activities and provide an opportunity to explore the detailed dependencies between activities that are frequently not identified at higher levels of planning. This is of benefit in itself. The main issue for control here is the use of weekly schedules. These are prepared from the look-ahead schedules and contain all the work activities, broken down into half-day units or less. This feature is important – that the work unit size is small (around half a day) and consistent between the different activities. These are listed in a table, and Table 11.2 shows how the preparation of part of a report and presentation by a team with the activities is broken down in this way.

The following week they were able to review their progress simply by taking the same table and adding two extra columns – one for whether the activity was complete or not (just a simple yes or no) and where an activity had not been completed why this was the case. Table 11.3 shows the result that the group achieved for this week.

The table shows the basic analysis that can be performed weekly – and the main measure that is used is that of Planned Percent Complete. This is calculated as:

PPC = activities completed / intended completed activities

In this case 12 of the 18 activities were completed this week – giving a PPC measure of 67 per cent.

The PPC measure works well where there are a number of activities going on at any one time. Weekly review meetings provide the forum for discussing progress, but most importantly is that this tool provides for ongoing problem-solving. Where a group is working together week on week, this provides a means by which review can be carried out every week, and the project process improved as the project progresses. In the above example, the group could meet and discuss the causes of the problems that were faced that week – in this case by the non-completion of the project analysis. Why was this – was it not planned well? Were the time estimates too short? Was the information not made available by someone from within or outside the group? Whatever the reason, the weekly meeting provides an opportunity to

Table 11.2

Activity	When	Who	Notes
Write outline of chapter 4	Mon a.m.	All	
Write section 4.1	Mon p.m.	HT & MR	
Complete graphics for chapter 3	Mon p.m.	WF	
Complete telephone interviews	Mon p.m.	KR	
Write section 4.2	Tues a.m.	HT & WF	Relies on 4.1 being complete
Outline presentation	Tues a.m.	MR	
Write section 4.3	Tues p.m.	HT & WF	Relies on 4.2 being complete
Transcribe telephone interview data	Tues p.m.	KR & MR	Relies on interviews being complete
Analyse interview data	Wed a.m.	KR & WF	Relies on transcription being complete
Write section 4.4	Wed a.m.	HT & MR	Relies on section 4.3 being complete
Write conclusion to chapter 4	Wed p.m.	HT & MR	Needs all 4 sections complete
Outline chapter 5 – data analysis	Thurs a.m.	All	Relies on chapter 4 and the data analysis being complete
Write up data analysis	Thurs p.m.	KR & MR	
Extract key findings into presentation	Thurs p.m.	HT & WF	
Prepare graphics for chapter 5 and presentation	Fri a.m.	WF	
Compile report and check flow	Fri a.m.	HT, KR & MR	Needs all sections complete, graphics to be inserted for chapter 5 later
Integrate chapter 5 graphics and print report	Fri p.m.	All	
Practice presentation	Fri p.m.	All	

make sure that problems are solved at this level, and not left until the post-project review (see Chapter 14) to be resolved. Week by week, we should expect the PPC measure to improve. This is a highly visible and easily understood measure and very powerful in communicating with teams.

Table 11.3

Activity	Complete	Reason for incomplete
Write outline of chapter 4	y	
Write section 4.1	y	
Complete graphics for chapter 3	y	
Complete telephone interviews	y	
Write section 4.2	y	
Outline presentation	y	
Write section 4.3	y	
Transcribe telephone interview data	y	
Analyse interview data	y	
Write section 4.4	y	
Write conclusion to chapter 4	y	
Outline chapter 5 – data analysis	y	
Write up data analysis	n	Analysis not completed in time
Extract key findings into presentation	n	Analysis not completed in time
Prepare graphics for chapter 5 and presentation	n	Analysis not completed in time
Compile report and check flow	n	Awaiting chapter 5
Integrate chapter 5 graphics and print report	n	Awaiting chapter 5
Practice presentation	n	Conclusions not yet ready
PLANNED PERCENT COMPLETE (PPC)	67%	

11.6 Technical Performance Monitoring

As was stated in Chapter 3, the nearer to completion the project gets, the easier it becomes to forecast what the final result will be – in terms not just of cost and time but also of the technical performance of the result. A 'technical performance measure' can provide an objective and visible means of comparing the actual-to-predicted performance. This should be a part of the regular project review procedure, as it allows other estimates based on this to be re-evaluated.

Scientific research projects – how do you control them?

The problem with scientific research projects is that there is not an output that can be easily measured for the project manager. Bodies that fund science (national governments, trusts, the EU and private firms) are reasonable for asking for some control measures over the money that is invested in the research work. Typically, a project can be evaluated post-completion by the number and quality of publications that are generated. This might be of scientific interest, but is of little help to the manager – the control loop is simply too long, as the findings may take many years to be published. *Peer review* is frequently used, both of such publications and of the process, as a means of monitoring 'how it's going'. Other measures include the number of pieces of experimentation carried out, number of additional avenues for further research identified, or number of aspects of the matter explored to a certain stage. Linking these to budgetary control can give measures of progress. One twist has generated some discussion. EU-funded projects now pay only the final stage payments for research on submission of acceptable final reports. This provides a considerable incentive for scientists to complete work and submit final reports.

11.7 The Role of Project Management Information Systems (PMIS)

The control and distribution of information to the project team members and other stakeholders form a significant part of the responsibility of the project manager. They are particularly vital if the stakeholders' expectations are to be managed effectively. The cycle of events that leads to the generation of reports should be as follows:

measure–record–analyse–act

If an attribute is to be measured for control purposes it should be recorded, ideally in the form in which it was collected and without any interpretation. This and other measures should be combined and analysed before action is formalised. Not proceeding with the cycle at any point wastes the previous actions. To prevent this waste, if data is not going to form part of an analysis and subsequent possible action, it should not be collected.

Computer-based PMIS are the most commonly used and allow the regular updating of schedules to provide a basis for management action. The bar charts produced

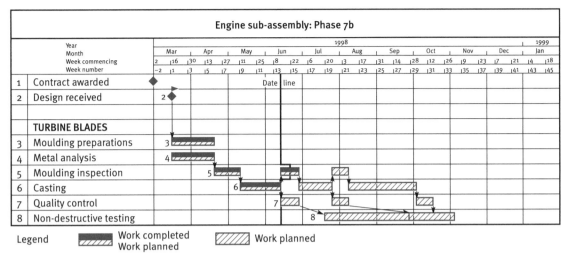

Figure 11.6 Bar chart showing work completed

by the planning system are a convenient tool for continuous monitoring and updating of plans (see Fig. 11.6). The work completed is shown as the top half of the bars in the chart and is indicated by dark shading. The purveyors of project management software like to help their customers believe that impressive-looking systems can be the panacea in control. This reliance on computers can lead to the following problems:

- computer paralysis – the project manager spends all day at the computer updating the project data. This is not a value-adding or problem-solving activity;
- PMIS verification – selective treatment of data can hide problems very effectively;
- data overload – there is too much for anyone to make sense of and hence act effectively;
- isolation – the project manager becomes a slave to the computer and detached from what is really happening;
- dependence – apparently removes the role of problem analysis and decision-making from managers, leading to less effective actions and removal of proactive problem-solving;
- misdirection – the effects of problems are tackled rather than the inherent causes (see Thambain, 1987).

The role of the system should be to identify exceptions (as above) and provide timely control information. The decision in setting up the systems should ask 'at what point does the difference between expected and actual performance merit a control action?' This needs to take into account the fact that in any activity there will be a degree of variability. It is the role of the decision-maker to set limits (called 'control limits') at which it is determined that the deviation from desired performance is significant (i.e. would not have occurred through natural variation). The concept of applying control limits to projects is shown in Fig. 11.7.

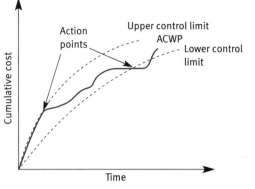

Figure 11.7 Control limits applied to progress in budget spend

11.8 Change Control

> This business would be fine if it wasn't for our clients. . . .

Stakeholders change their views about their requirements of the outcome of projects. The cause cannot always be eliminated, at least not without eliminating the clients themselves. The control system has to have the capability to change the inputs to the process based on changed requirements by one or more of the stakeholders. The typical system is shown in Fig. 11.8.

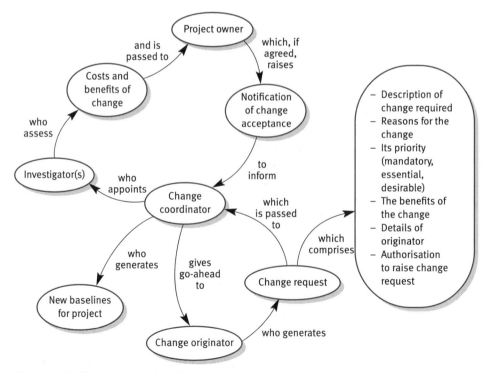

Figure 11.8 Change control system

The originator of the change may be any one of the downstream processes from your own project, e.g. in product development it is not unusual for products to have relatively major changes in the final stages of their development, particularly as they are about to go into production. The engineers raise change requests, which are passed through a system for evaluating:

- costs and benefits;
- the priority attached to the change (whether it is cosmetic or fundamental);
- the effects of the change on other processes;
- the effects on other assumptions – particularly cost.

It is usual for this to be completed on a proforma and to be circulated until the necessary approvals have been obtained. Such a bureaucratic system can provide benefits for medium- and high-complexity projects, and can help avoid the problems of *scope creep* that have been previously discussed.

11.9 Control of the Work of Development Projects – Intellectual Property

Intellectual property is the same as other forms of ownership in law. The role of intellectual property legislation is such that individuals or companies that develop new ideas have the opportunity to exploit them without fear of someone else copying their work. The main form of intellectual property protection is the 'patent'. If you wish to maintain control of the ownership of the product or process that you have developed (note – not software) then patenting is the major route open to you.

There is another fundamental role of the patent information for the development organisation, that of a 'design database'. Over 80 per cent of the records held in the Patent Office have expired, i.e. they are either more than twenty years old or the renewal fees have not been paid. It is estimated that as much as 30 per cent of development work duplicates that which has been done already. To avoid this, a relatively cheap search of Patent Office records can be the alternative to months of expensive development activity. Some major companies (including Sony and Hitachi) have representatives employed to scan filed applications for patents. These will often not go through the full process to become patented and so enter the public domain.

Once a development has been made, the granting of a patent depends on it fulfilling the following four criteria:

- must involve an inventive step – not be an immediately obvious derivation of an existing idea;
- not have been previously disclosed – through publication or discussion with others, for example;
- be capable of commercial exploitation – the only reason that patents are granted is to enable the inventor to have the right to exploit the idea commercially;
- not be excluded – designs for new nuclear weapons, for example, are excluded, as it would not be desirable to have them on public display in the Patent Office!

Once a patent has been granted, you have the exclusive rights to:

- exploit this through commercialisation of the idea;
- licence a third party to commercialise the idea, usually for a fee;
- grant a number of parties non-exclusive licences to the technology.

11.10 Relevant Areas of the Bodies of Knowledge

There is some similarity in the areas considered by the two bodies of knowledge, with the emphasis on the systemic needs for managing this area. Less emphasis is placed on the visual and communications aspects of control than has been suggested is necessary in this chapter.

Table 11.4 Relevant area of the APM body of knowledge

Relevant section	Title	Summary
34	Change control	This recognises the inevitability of change during projects, and the requirement for this to involve the full array of stakeholders to the project. A documented change control system should be in place to allow the impact of changes to be assessed.
35	Earned value management	The concept of earned value is explained, with the requirement for project managers to report cost to completion at various stages during the project.
46	Configuration management	This is described as an assurance function for the project deliverables. A major issue is change control.

Table 11.5 Relevant areas of the PMI body of knowledge

Relevant section	Title	Summary
4.3	Integrated change control	Establish how changes will occur, how they are to be evaluated and accepted or rejected, implemented, and assess their impact on scope and performance. Updated plans to be produced and distributed where changes are accepted.
5.5	Scope change control	When a change is requested, from wherever it comes, a set of procedures are required to determine the impact on the original scope statement. This may mean reworking the WBS, for instance.

Table 11.5 (*cont'd*)

Relevant section	Title	Summary
6.5	Schedule control	Provide a means to keep the project consistent with original objectives, but recognising that changes will occur during the process. This system should be able to show the impact of events, both possible and actual, to assist in decision-making. It should also be capable of keeping stakeholders informed of progress and future plans.
7.4	Cost control	A system is required to track costs, the effects of changes and report these to the necessary people. Typically this might include assessments of the Earned Value of the project and updates to budgets.
8.3	Quality control	The application of the principles of manufacturing quality control to a project processes, including defect prevention, inspection, and reporting of quality issues.
10.3	Performance reporting	A system for gathering performance data and then reporting it should be established. This will indicate the current state of the project and provide forecasts for the effects of deviations in performance to the necessary stakeholders.
11.6	Risk monitoring and control	A system for identifying, quantifying and mitigating risks as they emerge through the life of the project. This will involve the updating of the risk log/register and interface with other control systems – all those given above.

11.11 Summary

So, how's it going? It probably started as a very simple question at the start of this chapter, but the execution phase of the project is a complex task even in relatively simple projects if control is to be applied effectively. Given the history of projects failing and its incremental nature in the majority of cases, this clearly deserves some attention. There are some relatively new approaches that appear to be generating benefits – Last Planner and other methods to increase the visibility of progress, in particular.

The most basic approach to control centres around a feedback control system. This requires monitoring of the project at the activity level, processing the information to determine if there is a significant variation from desired performance, and then instigating corrective action to the process itself. The nature of the feedback determines whether or not the system is stable and timeliness is essential in the provision of feedback. The focus of control is on those aspects that were defined by the project strategy as being the most important.

Among other techniques, costs can be monitored through the application of the 'earned value' concept. Technical performance monitoring provides an ongoing input to future forecasts of the outcome of the project activities and Project Management Information Systems (PMIS) provide the means for achieving the measure–record–analyse–act system for ensuring minimisation of waste in the control system. Change control is needed to check that the effects of changes (in particular, the cumulative effects of many small changes) are considered before they are implemented.

In the development of new products or processes, patent records are a source of design data, and patenting provides legal protection for the results of the design process.

Project Management in Practice

The Lifter project

In 1998 the Lifter Company saw that the market potential existed for a new model in its range. Following some problems during the project, the plans were redrafted, as shown in Fig. 11.9. The decision needs to be made now as to whether the project is likely to be delivered on time or whether the launch dates need to be moved further back. (Homologation is not an issue here, as it will be done in each country in which the product is launched as an ongoing activity.)

At this time (August 2000) it was decided to allocate further resources to the project. However, analysis of the costs incurred was produced for the next quarterly review in October. The effects of the additional resources can be seen on the cost curve in Fig. 11.10. The company directors are concerned about the cost overrun, but the project manager thinks that this will be minimal. Again, a decision is required as to whether this is realistic, as it will have significant implications for the budget of the firm.

Case discussion

1 From the plans of Fig. 11.9 and the history of the project to date, is it realistic to think that the project will be completed with only a small amount of slippage? How do you know and could you say this with any certainty?
2 What data, other than costs incurred and estimated times, might help the project manager to form a better overall picture of progress?
3 How might the data better demonstrate progress in this project?

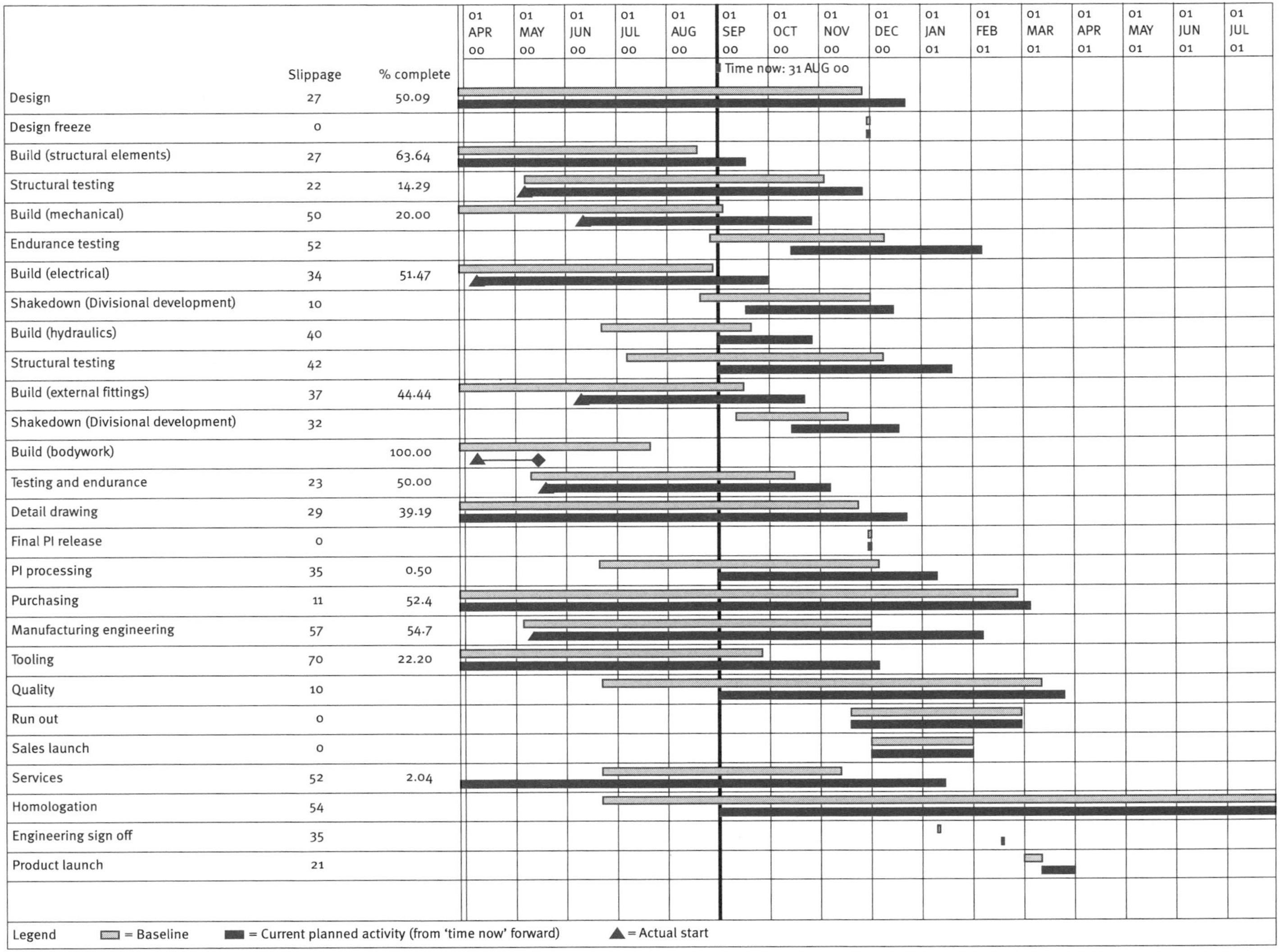

The following is a data table associated with the Gantt chart:

	Slippage	% complete
Design	27	50.09
Design freeze	0	
Build (structural elements)	27	63.64
Structural testing	22	14.29
Build (mechanical)	50	20.00
Endurance testing	52	
Build (electrical)	34	51.47
Shakedown (Divisional development)	10	
Build (hydraulics)	40	
Structural testing	42	
Build (external fittings)	37	44.44
Shakedown (Divisional development)	32	
Build (bodywork)		100.00
Testing and endurance	23	50.00
Detail drawing	29	39.19
Final PI release	0	
PI processing	35	0.50
Purchasing	11	52.4
Manufacturing engineering	57	54.7
Tooling	70	22.20
Quality	10	
Run out	0	
Sales launch	0	
Services	52	2.04
Homologation	54	
Engineering sign off	35	
Product launch	21	

Legend: ▨ = Baseline   ▮ = Current planned activity (from 'time now' forward)   ▲ = Actual start

Time now: 31 AUG 00

Figure 11.9 A summary of the project against the baseline set on 22/06/00

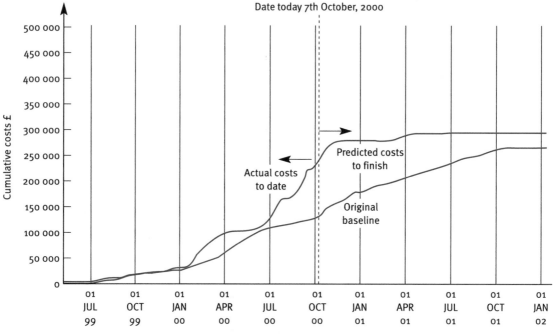

Figure 11.10 Cost control curves for Lifter project

Key Terms

feedback control systems	actual cost of work performed (ACWP)
corrective/control action	budgeted cost of work performed (BCWP)
Last Planner	variance
Planned Percent Complete	estimated cost at completion (ECAC)
technical performance measure (TPM)	budgeted cost of work scheduled (BCWS)
audit and review	intellectual property
earned value	patents

Review Questions and Further Exercises

1 What is *control* in the context of project management?

2 Why is making progress visible so important?

3 How do measures of *conformance* and *performance* differ?

4 Carry out an internet search for examples of *earned value* being used in practice. What are the limitations of this technique?

5 What are the potential advantages of the *Last Planner* approach to project control? Are all members of a project team likely to be so happy with such *micro-level* planning and control? If not, what would you do about this?

6 Why is configuration management and change control so important to the project manager?

7 Carry out a search of patents relating to an object that you have recently purchased using the www.patent.gov.uk website.

References

Ballard, G. (1994) *The Last Planner*, see www.leanconstruction.org

Thambain, H.J. (1987) 'The New Project Management Software and Its Impact on Management Style', *Project Management Journal*, August.

Further Information

Archibald, R.D. (1992) *Managing High Technology Progams and Projects*, 2nd edition, Wiley, Chichester.

Brandon, D.M. Jr (1998) 'Implementing Earned Value Easily and Effectively', *Project Management Journal*, Vol. 29, No. 2, pp. 11–18.

Fleming, Q.W. and Hoppelman, J.M. (1996) *Earned Value Project Management*, PMI, Upper Darby, PA.

Goldratt, E.M. (1990) *The Haystack Syndrome: Sifting Information Out of the Data Ocean*, North River Press, New York.

www.patent.gov.uk – The Patent Office

12 Supply chain issues

Most of the goods and services that we buy are not the result of one individual or firm but the product of a supply chain. The same applies to a large proportion of project work – and hence the importance of the area. This is the result of a relatively recent trend for firms to outsource major parts of their business (have it provided by external firms, rather than carry out the work by direct employees of the firm). Indeed, for many organisations today the relationships that are developed between themselves and other parties in the their supply chains are vital to their survival.

Contents

Learning Objectives

By the time you have completed this chapter, you should be able to:
- Identify the role of the supply chain in project management and its importance in ensuring project success;
- Discuss the evolution of the approaches to provision of bought-in products and services, from purchasing to the current state of supply chain management;
- Describe the nature of the supply chain relationships that can exist;
- Identify the use and limitations of contracts in modern supply chain relationships.

12.1 Introduction to Supply Chain Management

A project is only as good as the weakest part of the process. We can commit considerable resources to ensuring that the processes within our organisation are the best that they can be, but the outcome will be poor if this excellence does not also exist in our supply chains.

The subject of supply chain management has evolved considerably in recent years. Twenty years ago, the central issue was that of purchasing, and many firms had specialist buyers and purchasing staff. This function was almost entirely reactive and usually had a very simple objective – obtaining the necessary goods and services at the lowest possible price. While this appeared to provide the necessary short-term needs of the firm, it was becoming clear that there were many different approaches being used. In particular, the performance of the Japanese automotive producers was being studied, including the work of the IMVP at MIT[1] in the USA. These studies will be referred to further in Chapter 15. They showed that the Japanese automotive producers had significantly different relationships with their suppliers from their Western counterparts. These were much closer – relying far less on contract for control and far more on trust and long-term relationships. These differences were resulting is a much higher level of performance of the supply chain – shorter development times for new products, much lower levels of inventory and higher levels of quality. These differences are illustrated through the examples given in the boxes below and throughout this chapter we will consider how these issues from repetitive (manufacturing) industries can be applied in the project environment.

Scenario A – The construction manager

'The contract is everything to us. It defines what we will do and how we will do it. We rely on it because the client will always change their mind, which results in 'extras.' These extras are where we make our money. We also regularly end up in court at the end of a project to see who will pay for different things (called *claims*). The problem there is that the only people who make any money out of that are the lawyers!'

Scenario B – The sales manager – aerospace components company

'For us the contract is a formality. It is kept in the bottom drawer. We know that if we have to resort to the contract terms and conditions, we are in trouble. We rely on mutual goals – we help the assembler (their immediate customer) to develop their product, and then supply, fit and help maintain those components and systems over the life of the aircraft. In many cases, we are the sole supplier of particular products to that firm. We need them, and they need us.'

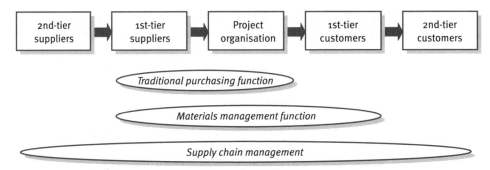

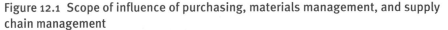

Figure 12.1 Scope of influence of purchasing, materials management, and supply chain management

As demonstrated in these cases, the approach to the role of purchasing and supply management is very different. This is reflected in the differences in the role and scope of influence of the purchasing and supply professionals and departments. These are shown in Fig. 12.1.

As the figure shows, there is a large scope difference between the different roles. At one extreme, the traditional purchasing department is purely concerned with the relationship with first-tier suppliers – those who supply the project organisation directly. *Materials* management, though restricted to a concern with physical goods, does look after the logistics aspects of the flow between first-tier suppliers, through the project organisation, through to the first-tier customers. In materials management, a *product breakdown structure* will provide the physical material requirements for the project, in the same way that the work breakdown structure provided the activity list for the project. This product breakdown structure is also called a *bill of materials* and will often be managed through a system of Materials Requirements Planning.[2]

At the most extensive, supply chain management involves issues concerned with the strategic and operational in projects, from primary industry (where applicable) to end-user. Its influence can go beyond the second-tier suppliers indicated in Fig. 12.1. Table 12.1 shows examples of supply chains in some medium- and high-complexity projects.

Having identified the supply chain that is relevant to the project, how important is it to the success of the project? The answer to this depends on the following:

- the value of the bought-in products or services relative to the total value of the project;
- the criticality of the items being purchased – do they represent key parts of the project outcome?
- the timing of the work being purchased;
- the impact of the quality level of work purchased.

Some organisations today conduct relatively little of their own project work, preferring to have it carried out by specialist consultants or contractors. This is typical in many parts of the IT industry, construction and manufacturing. The level of

Table 12.1 Examples of supply chains

Project	Second-tier supplier	First-tier supplier	Integrator	First-tier customer	Second-tier customer
IS implementation project	Computer components supply	Hardware supplier	System implementer	IT department of client firm	Users in client firm
Construction of new houses	Raw material extractor	Material manufacturers	House-building firm	Sales department of house-building firm	House buyers
New product development in pharmaceutical firm	Private research institute	Formulation testing firm	Pharmaceutical firm	Distributors of drugs – shops and pharmacies	End-users
Consulting firm advise a firm on improving customer service	Providers of knowledge, e.g. research firm, regulatory bodies	Contracted consultants	Consulting firm	Immediate client wishing to improve customer service	Customers of immediate client

importance of the supplier can therefore be rated according to the above four characteristics. Where a firm is using or has the scope to use the same suppliers over a period of time, and the suppliers rate highly on these four characteristics, the organisation should be investing considerable time and effort, developing their relationships with the suppliers.

Where large firms are being supplied by relatively small firms, this may include direct investment and knowledge-sharing. Many automotive and electronics firms require their suppliers to undergo particular training and to have particular processes in place. This is highly intrusive for the suppliers, but results in a very different relationship between themselves and their customers. This is described further in the following sections.

Before we consider the nature of the relationships between different parts of a project supply chain, we shall discuss the fundamentals of purchasing.

12.2 Purchasing

As identified above, there are many instances where a significant part of the value of a project is spent with suppliers and contractors. Indeed, some organisations only exist as 'management shells', having no direct capability to deliver the projects from which they earn their revenue. These include businesses from most sectors. The ability to coordinate the delivery of the project and take part of the revenue for this service provides the business rationale. This increase in the role of outsourcing is

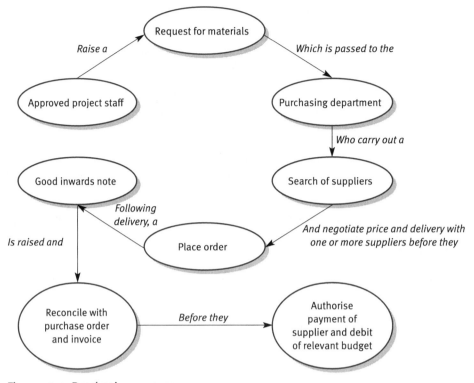

Figure 12.2 Purchasing process

also not limited to large projects. Many organisations have reduced the size of their human resources function significantly by buying-in training resource from consultants rather than trying to maintain it in-house. Similarly for IT – there was a trend at the start of the 1990s (since reversed in many firms) to outsource all the IT provision and support. Therefore, not only are direct costs the subject of outsourcing, but also many of the indirect or overhead costs – including project managers in some firms.

Who does the purchasing and what is involved? The diversity of activities covered by this term is illustrated by the following example. In one firm, £20 million of purchases were made each year by a purchasing department of two people. In another, it took 20 people to achieve the same value of purchases. Why should this be so? The traditional purchasing process involves the steps shown in Fig. 12.2. It is the number of these steps that they are involved with that determines the workload, in addition to the size of each order (several large or many small orders), the size of the supply base and the ease of placing an order (electronic data interchange versus having to create vast quantities of paperwork).

As shown in Fig. 12.2, only authorised staff can make purchases – this provides the central point of control for many projects. A formal request for a purchase leads the purchasing department to carry out a search for a suitable supplier. Where this is a regular item purchased or one that is part of a standard range, this may be a relatively short process. For large capital purchases, the process of seeking and selecting suppliers is extensive. Having determined the supplier and negotiated prices (see below) an order is placed. This can be in a number of forms, from an e-mail or fax, and as a minimum, most organisations require an *order number*. This is a unique identifier for the order that allows its origin and all other information relating to it to be traceable. On arrival of the materials, another document is triggered – the goods inwards note. This must be reconciled with the delivery note from the supplier, the purchase order, and eventually the invoice or request for payment from the supplier. Provided these all agree, the invoice can be passed for payment. When the process is largely automated and the suppliers consistent, it is possible for the scenario with two people to be feasible. With the number of activities that need to be carried out and pieces of documentation that must be reconciled, there is clearly scope here for twenty to be perfectly feasible too.

There are many decisions to be made and issues to be understood with regard to purchasing in projects. These include the nature of the organisation that can carry out the purchasing role, the purchasing objectives and the nature and role of contracts established.

The organisation of purchasing

For large project organisations, the decision will have to be made as to the nature of the purchasing organisation. While the design and control of the purchasing function is clearly a management specialism in its own right, the project manager should be aware of the implications of the design chosen for the organisation. The two extremes of purchasing organisation are shown in Table 12.2 – centralised and localised. For a firm, centralising the purchasing organisation means that all projects place their requirements through one purchasing office that has control of all the requirements for all the business. At the other extreme, a project manager can employ or use the services of a local purchasing officer. In other cases, it is not uncommon for the purchasing function to be outsourced to an external provider.

It is not uncommon for there also to be mixed purchasing arrangements. For instance, large or standard items can be purchased through a central office. Where local knowledge or a rapid delivery is required, these items can be sourced through local arrangements made by project staff. This does reduce the level of central

Table 12.2 Centralised and localised purchasing

	Centralised purchasing	*Localised purchasing*
Advantages	• Purchasing power due to aggregation of orders • Better materials utilisation and stock management • Economies of staffing • Standardisation of purchasing procedures	• Local knowledge of suppliers • Low organisational inertia • Local management control • Enhanced supplier relationships

control that many organisations seem to like, but it can provide a closer meeting of project needs. In addition, for large capital projects, a *purchasing agent* may be used – an intermediary who specialises in the purchasing of those particular items.

At the most local level, some firms have allowed their employees to purchase materials and services up to certain values, using a company credit card. This allows direct contact between the buyer and supplier, significantly increasing the effectiveness of the information transfer, and simplifies the purchasing process considerably. Billing is also simplified as accounts are provided on one monthly statement, rather than every item having to be processed as a separate transaction.

The credit card schemes that some firms have pursued have provided a lead-in for purchasing to be carried out on-line. As the potential for cost-savings through on-line purchasing have grown (British Telecom was claiming £5 billion savings through e-procurement in 2001, though never bothered to justify how this would be realised in practice) so have the number of firms moving this way. The project environment does present some problems here – not least that items and services purchased may be unique. While automation of the purchase of standard or commodity items through this channel may provide benefits, the case still needs to be made for one-off or special items. This said, there are many project-based industries that do purchase large quantities of standard items, and the opportunities for fast information transfer may actually help in the sourcing of unique items. On-line auctions also provide some firms with opportunities to source products and services globally, for instance buying programmers' time from India or increasing the range of products that may be considered for a particular application (see www.qmx.com). In addition, as was demonstrated by the processes of Fig. 12.2, there is considerable potential for automation of the process, and the use of the Web provides one way of doing this.

Purchasing and project strategy

The objectives of the purchasing activities should be consistent with those of the project. In project strategy (Chapter 3), we considered the objectives for the project to be broadly stated as having time, cost or quality as the primary objective, with the other objectives arranged in priority. In purchasing terms, the strategy is converted into 'the five rights'. These are interdependent characteristics of a supplier or contractor depending on their ability to deliver:

- the right quantity;
- the right quality;
- at the right price;
- at the right time and place; and be . . .
- the right supplier.

Quantity

The quantity of goods or services (contractors are generally assumed to deliver a service) is determined from the schedules drawn up with the plans. Where there have been changes these are built in and the quantity calculated. At one time, *big* orders were considered the way to be – with large volumes incurring large discounts – so buy as much as possible at one time. As will be shown in the following sections and in Chapter 14, the notion that prevails today is that the necessary goods should be provided at the point of need in the quantity required for that piece of work only. This requires very different systems for conveying orders and managing the supply and resupply process in projects where there are repetitive elements of work than where there are single large or high-value items.

Quality

The quality of goods and services may be determined through:

- trial supply of goods or services;
- prior reputation;
- certification or assessment of a supplier's quality system.

There are also other issues to consider such as where contractors are hired on an individual basis, the recruiter may also seek membership of a particular professional body and possibly ask the contractor to provide their own legal indemnity insurance. However, these issues all presume that conformance to standard is the quality that is required. There are many other definitions of quality – such as the quality of service that is provided, the speed of response to enquiries, and other indirect features of a purchased product or service that have a great impact on the overall quality of the project. For instance, the suppliers of hardware for an IT project may have a great influence on the outcome of the project not only through the hardware that they provide but also through the technical support that they give to the software producers and the installers.

The important quality issues for the project manager with purchasing are therefore:

- Assurance – managing the conformance of the supplied goods and services to the necessary levels of quality (technical and service quality);
- Performance – working with the suppliers and customers to obtain the best possible result.

Price

Achieving a purchasing decision at the right price is a challenge. In project organisations there is often the need for long-term relationships to be built up between buyer and supplier, though the relationship for that particular project may be fairly short. There are clearly gains to be made by applying pressure on the price to obtain the cheapest supply. In the long term, however, the supplier may go out of business or may simply economise in ways that cost you money elsewhere. Indeed, Deming's fourth point is:

> End the practice of awarding business on the basis of a price-tag. Purchasing must be combined with design of product, manufacturing and sales to work with the chosen supplier: the aim is to minimise total cost not merely initial cost.

The best supplier may not then be the cheapest, as there is often a trade-off in other areas. As for project strategy, this may be against time, cost or flexibility.

Further parts of this discussion are concerned with the relationship between cost and quantity. For instance, will a supplier of materials assess the discount given depending on the value of each order, or will they simply consider annual volumes of business? Other issues include the cost of purchasing – typically large. One firm divided their total purchasing costs by the number of orders placed with suppliers, and found that their average cost per order was £8. This can be a considerable overhead cost to a project. Section 12.4 considers some of the ways that firms have tried to reduce this.

Time

Achieving the right time and place is the basis of much literature and the predominant complaint that industrial purchasers have about suppliers. The rating of suppliers and regular performance reviews can keep this as an issue for them. It is also one advantage that a degree of centralisation can have for the purchasing function – that of being able to track supplier performance on the basis of criteria such as late delivery. A major point to note is that it is no good blaming a supplier for late delivery if paperwork to place the order takes six weeks to be processed by the purchasing function. Giving suppliers the longest possible time in which to fulfil an order is going to be beneficial to both parties in the long term.

Supplier

Being the right supplier clearly has dependence on the other four categories, but is included to start the discussion as to the way in which one selects suppliers. The choice based on price alone has been shown to provide possible short-term gains, which can be more than countered in the longer term. There are several other factors that should be considered:

- Are choices made on the basis of a 'free lunch'? The expansion of the corporate hospitality industry over the last fifteen years in most countries has been immense. Interestingly, this has been paralleled by efforts by many companies to be seen to be behaving ethically and state publicly that their staff will not accept gifts, however small, from suppliers. There is clearly a contradiction between these two facts. In the UK, The Chartered Institute of Purchasing and Supply (CIPS – see Further Information at the end of this chapter) has a code of conduct for their members which expressly prohibits the acceptance of gifts from suppliers, and other national regulatory bodies do likewise.
- How are orders conveyed, with what frequency and how do the suppliers really know what your requirements are? Also, they often have expertise in both the design of their products and their application, which, as Deming suggests, should be used as a source of knowledge and improvement.

It is obviously not possible to treat the purchase of the smallest-value items in the way suggested above (through partnership rather than adversarial relationships with suppliers). The use of a version of Pareto analysis (see Chapter 13) can identify the 20 per cent of bought-in goods and services that take 80 per cent of the project spend. It is on these that the focus of purchasing attention will rest as they are the areas that will have greatest scope to impact the project's costs. However, where time is the key issue, the consideration of the value of the products or services being provided may be immaterial if they are critical to the project. In such cases the cost focus can be misguided.

One of the activities that many project managers need assistance with is in the negotiation of deals with suppliers and customers alike. In this respect, purchasing staff have often proved invaluable, as, having heard sales pitch after sales pitch, they are less likely, in theory at least, to be influenced by the shine over the substance of the deal. Also, unless you are aware of the games of negotiation, it is a minefield. Some considerable assistance can be provided through the study of some of the specialist publications in that area (see, for instance, Acuff, 1997; Fisher *et al.*, 1997; Kennedy, 1998).

The details of the establishment of contracts between suppliers and purchasers is a topic that concerns many specialist books. Not only are there obvious and large national differences between practices in contract law, there are many sectoral idiosyncrasies with which project managers should familiarise themselves. The books on contract law are filled with horror stories of how contracts drawn up by non-experts have only worked well if they were never questioned or tested. The safest advice, in a commercial environment where litigation is becoming more common, is to rely on professionals in this field. There are some issues that can safely be discussed at a general level that will facilitate understanding of some project environments. The comment will be made again, as stated in section 12.1, that many industries have reduced their reliance on contract as a means of control.

12.3 Contracts

It was stated in section 12.1 that the use of contracts in many industries has changed. The process by which contracts are awarded depends on the nature of the task being contracted, the relationship between the purchaser and supplier and the relative size of each. In addition, industry norms apply, e.g. in construction, the allocation of contracts for trade services, while following basic rules, may be at the discretion of the site manager. There are two issues here for the project manager. The first is the type of contract that they may be working with, and the second is the process for working with contracts – which will be compared between large and small projects.

Some contract types are listed below:

- Fixed price – just what it says – there is this much money agreed for the job to be done, there is no more;
- Time and materials – the customer agrees to pay a particular hourly or daily rate and the cost of the materials. This separation of labour and material may

increase the transparency of the costings, particularly where materials are a large proportion of the activity cost;

- Target cost – where the customer sets a target cost for an item (see Chapter 7) and the supplier is required to work back from this to see what they can provide for that cost;
- Revenue share – this has been used with some success in the aerospace sector, where the selling price of a finished aircraft is determined by its performance. The better it performs, the more it is worth. In an effort to get their systems suppliers (major components, e.g. navigation, instrumentation, flight control etc.) working together, deals were agreed where systems would be sold to the firm on the basis that they would attract a percentage of the final selling price of the aircraft. The more it sold for, the greater the price that the systems suppliers would receive;
- Cost-plus – this is where the customer agrees to reimburse whatever costs the supplier incurs on a project, plus a margin for profit. This was until relatively recently the preferred form of contract for many military development and procurement projects.

The process

Where a contract is being placed for the supply of a major part of the project spend the process shown in Fig. 12.3 may be used. This is a single-stage process – unlike that recommended by the World Bank for development projects, and the major high street banks for human resource development projects. Here a two- or more stage process may be beneficial with a first call to see who has the technical capability and capacity to deliver the project. This identifies potential bidders and may provide considerable insight into how what is being requested can be improved, for instance to reduce cost by making small changes to the requirements. A second phase may

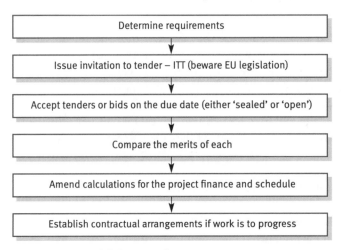

Figure 12.3 Establishment of contracts

then ask the potential bidders to provide detailed costings of their proposals. Such a phased approach does take more time to complete, as there will have to be several rounds of bidding, but it does save time by pre-filtering the bidders by technical capability.

There are further rules – for instance, the value for public contracts (central government, purchase/lease of goods or services), over and above which open European tender (the ITT must be published Europe-wide) is required, is in the region of €140 000 (approximately £90 000). This is not large by the standards of much project management activity. When the bids or tenders arrive, they may be treated as either 'sealed' (not opened until a given time) or 'open' (where the information contained in the bids becomes public at the time the bids are received). The system of sealed bids is often felt to be fairer for larger contracts.

The information contained in the bids should be fed into the project's financial and time calculations and any amendments to budgets or schedules made on this basis. Contractual arrangements are usually based on standard terms and conditions, but establishing whether the supplier's terms and conditions or those of the purchaser apply is a role for legal advisers, due to a process known as *battle of the forms*:

Customer: 'We place the order subject to our terms and conditions.'
Supplier: 'We accept, subject to our terms and conditions.'

The main objective is to ensure that the contracts can be met on both sides. Breaches of contracts and the ensuing litigation rarely benefit either party greatly but the legal industry considerably.

The engineering institutions of the UK have recognised the need to provide a starting point, which can eliminate some of the wrangling between suppliers and purchasers. Various bodies have compiled standard forms of contract, e.g. in the construction industry CIRIA 85 ('Target and Cost Reimbursable Construction Contracts', 1982) provides a standard form for target cost contracts and the Institute of Chemical Engineers has its 'Red Book' ('Model Form of Conditions of Contract for Process Plants: Lump Sum Contracts', 1981).

Other contract issues that project managers should at least be aware of include:

- Role of penalty clauses – used in many sectors to encourage suppliers to do what they said that they would do. In practice, it does appear that these are treated as the point of last resort if they have to be invoked, which leads onto:
- The role of bonds and insurances – if you are providing goods and services to a larger project, the effects of your part of the project going wrong could have implications way beyond the scale of your part of the project. (For example, a building contractor, contracted to do the concreting of the ground floor of a skyscraper, used concrete that didn't cure properly, resulting in a 4-week delay to the opening of the building. The contract value: £80 000. The damages as a result of their 'misfortune': £2.8 million.) Before being awarded contracts, many firms will require insurances to be in place and bonds to be provided. These may require certain quality procedures to be in place as well.

- Retention money – on completion of large projects there are often final pieces of work to be carried out. These may not delay the completion of the contract and payment of the majority of the agreed contract fee, but the customer may insist on retaining some of the money to ensure that the final jobs are completed to their satisfaction.
- Stage payments – in order for suppliers to stay afloat financially, it is usual in many projects for there to be interim payments made on delivery of particular objectives.
- Contracts may get in the way of project start-up. Where days or even weeks are crucial, a supplier who will not start work until a contract is in place may hold up the project considerably. More flexible means of proceeding (letters of intent are often used) do not replace contracts, but may overcome the initial problems.

A final thought before moving on. The most basic piece of contract legislation in place in many countries is that goods and services provided should be what they say that they are, and do what they say that they should do. This may come as a surprise to many firms who have purchased large IT packages. The systems that they were promised at the usually very glitzy sales promotions do not turn up until very late and then only partly work – the remaining features that you needed being 'still in development'. This being the case for so many IT projects, it must be asked how the firms selling such goods manage to do so without any apparent fear of legal action. The answer appears to lie in the nature of what you buy. In the case of software, you usually do not buy the product, which would be subject to such law, but you buy a licence to use the product. This apparently circumvents the usual laws.

12.4 From Buying to Relationship Management

As stated earlier in this chapter, there have been big changes in the nature of the relationships between buyers and suppliers in some sectors. As will be shown, this has moved from short-term arrangements based on contracts to long-term relationships based on trust. This change is by no means universally applicable nor desirable, but the project manager should be aware of the implications of the intentions of the arrangement for decisions and processes in the project.

There are many classifications of relationship available. For the project manager, we shall simply consider three basic types:

- Traditional adversarial – characterised by the reliance on contract, competitive bidding, short-term relationships (as long as the contract), and little by way of process cooperation between the buyer and supplier. The focus of the choice of supplier will be on cost and short-term gain on each side. Orders are conveyed by fax or letter and there will often be several suppliers for each item.
- Partnership – here two firms enter into a long-term agreement, whereby the purchaser agrees to award a firm sole-supplier status in return for process developments being undertaken and closer cooperation on costs (see below) and

Table 12.3 Adversarial versus partnership relationships

Feature	Adversarial	Partnership
Temporal basis	One-off purchase	Ongoing
Commodity	Product	Product, service, knowledge support
Contractual basis	Each purchase negotiated – competitive basis	Long-term deals agreed in advance, trust-based rather than contractually reliant
Communications and involvement	Limited to 'information as necessary' as determined by contract terms; use standard communications – telephone, fax, e-mail	Involved at all relevant stages of the project, as determined by impacts on all parties; may involve staff loan; suppliers involved in scheduling and planning; communicate through linked networks and regular information-sharing sessions
Focus	Our bit of the project is most important – maximise the return from that bit	The performance of the project as a whole is most important

information transfer. Orders may be exchanged by Electronic Data Interchange (EDI) or call-offs from a pre-agreed quantity ('we don't need all of it, this is the amount that is needed now'). Where there is a small supplier for a large firm, this may take the form of direct investment, e.g. in particular equipment or research and development.

- Relationship management – this is where one of the parties in a complex supply network takes on the role of coordinating and developing the entire supply network. This goes way beyond managing a partnership, but may consider all the elements of the supply chain from primary industry to customer. The British Airports Authority is a good example of a project customer taking control of the supply network and getting involved with firms way down the supply chain to ensure that any weak links are strengthened.

Table 12.3 describes the differences between the traditional adversarial approach and the partnering approach that many firms are at least aspiring to today.

The key points of note are the differences in the practices applied in the execution of the work being carried out. Instead of looking around to many suppliers, it is likely that under partnering, a firm will have one supplier for each category of purchase. This has resulted in a significant rationalisation of the supply base by many firms, and a simplification of the purchasing process – as was described in Fig. 12.2. There is another side to this type of relationship that is evident in repetitive industries, and has become apparent in certain project environments (see Larson and Drexler, 1997). This concerns the intrusive nature of the relationship and the tough requirements that are often placed upon suppliers for improvement. As one project-based supplier of components to the automotive sector commented:

> The first year they demanded a 5 per cent reduction in our costs from one project to the next. That was just about achievable – we totally rethought our processes and managed to hit our targets. The second year, we were asked to do the same again. That was really hard and we struggled. The third year, the same was asked again. We asked them to suggest ways to do this, but did not receive any further help from them. We made a loss on the business that year and took the decision to end the relationship. It was all one-way. Possibly, it was because they were a big firm and we were a small one. We have moved out of this sector and concentrated elsewhere, and are now making three times as much profit as we used to make, without any of the aggravation!

As can be seen, the management of relationships is not all win–win and while the principles are admirable, there is clearly considerable effort to be expended with application. As for other 'good ideas' there is plenty of case material on the application which is worth referring to (see Further Information at the end of this chapter).

12.5 Modern Techniques in Supply Chain Management

Open-book accounting

This has been widely used in the automotive industry, particularly where firms are first-tier suppliers to the automotive companies. The principle is that by opening up the accounts of a supplier, the customer can see how much profit is being made out of them. Too little, and the supplier is going to be unable to have the investment necessary to improve its processes in the future. The customer may suggest ways to reduce costs in such a situation. Too much profit, and the customer will be looking for price reductions.

The use of open-book agreements is not universally popular, with many, particularly small, suppliers resenting the intrusion of accountants from the large firms into their business. They also reduce significantly the bargaining power of a supplier in price negotiations, as the customer is privy to their data. In principle, therefore, this is a nice idea, with helpful customers ensuring that their suppliers remain financially healthy. The reality is often far from this, with the costs data simply being a tool for beating suppliers with, rather than helping them directly.

For the project environment, the notion of greater transparency of costs does apply, as it does in repetitive operations.

Vendor-managed inventory

For many organizations the only way to obtain goods for projects was to buy them in bulk in advance of need. For instance, if a building project needed 400 pallets of bricks for the whole job (say, 10 weeks' supply), these would be ordered and delivered at the start of the job – which looks good as the materials are there ready for use, the goods were obtained at a discount price as they were bought in bulk, at least in the short term. If we look closer, this presents a number of problems for both supplier and customer. For the supplier, they have a sudden surge in demand. In order to meet this demand, they may have staff working overtime, and thereby increasing costs. For the customer, what do they do with 400 pallets of bricks? They store them, count them, move them, and probably have to guard them. Theft of such stocks is common. Also, because of the bulk ordering issue, the materials planners have probably overordered to sure make that there are enough for the job. In the construction sector there are many countries where it is normal to over-order by a minimum of 10 per cent. Any materials left at the end of the job are either 'removed' for other jobs by the staff or the firm has to pay to have them taken away.

Such a scenario is common in many sectors, not just construction, and results in considerable waste (see Chapter 15). The principle of vendor-managed inventory (VMI) is that the supplier will work with the customer to determine the amount of that particular type of material that will be needed during different phases of the project. This is made available on-site, and the material is taken as needed for the job. The supplier owns the material (and may even have to pay the customer rental for site-space to store it) until it is used. The supplier will then invoice the user regularly for the material used. The supplier becomes the sole supplier for those items and in doing so gains the maximum share of that business. As importantly, as the sole supplier they will be involved in the planning process to ensure that the necessary materials are available at the time they are needed, and may also provide technical support for the products and advice (for instance, if the same product is available from another manufacturer at a better price). Such arrangements are used in automotive and electronics projects and manufacturing, and are increasingly being used in retailing. It appears to be a win–win for both supplier and customer as:

- the customer now pays only for the material actually used;
- the customer pays only for material when it is used – no advance purchasing costs;
- the number of transactions is drastically reduced – only one bill for all the materials supplied, instead of many (overhead cost reduction);
- the customer eliminates the costs of storage, checking, and moving materials;
- the supplier can provide regular small deliveries rather than having to arrange small numbers of large deliveries;
- the possibilities for partnership between the firms is increased.

The supplier clearly now has a bigger role, managing material as opposed to just being the intermediary between the manufacturer (or their agent) and the user. This is not a transition that many make without problems, but there are plenty of instances of existing practice for them to draw on for knowledge of how to make it work. It appears to have been highly successful in areas of supply such as stationery – see the box below.

The Rapid Pencil Company

When the firm decided to carry out an audit of annual spend they were horrified at the value of purchases of stationery in the year. Some quick parametric estimating, and based on the number of people and the type of work the firm carried out, and they were buying roughly three times the amount of stationery they thought that they would need. This was being passed on to individual projects in the form of overhead costs, so it was considered worth monitoring. In addition to the costs of the items being bought, there was significant time dedicated to the ordering, storing and distribution of items. A short investigation revealed that because the supply line was considered to be unreliable, almost everyone in the organisation kept their own stock of materials. Once 'theirs', these stocks would be far more likely to end up at home.

The Rapid Pencil Company offered the firm the opportunity to remove most of the stocks from the system and to eliminate ordering costs. They did this by providing cupboards on each major office level. These contained an agreed level of stock and were replenished each week. In addition, where there were special requirements, these could be ordered directly via a website. The firm submitted one invoice per month to the firm, rather than one for each separate order. As the financial director of the firm commented, 'It was a step of trust to let them take over this activity from us, but it has worked really well. No more ordering for things that we have run out of – that used to happen almost daily – and just one invoice a month. We now know roughly what the spend should be, and we can simply check against that.'

12.6 Relevant Areas of the Bodies of Knowledge

Both bodies of knowledge (Tables 12.4 and 12.5) are based in the traditional view of purchasing and are focused on the norms for large-scale or first-time projects. They only partially cover the more common scenario of multiple/repeat purchasing and the nature of ongoing relationships with other parties in the supply chain.

Table 12.4 Relevant areas of the APM body of knowledge

Relevant section	Title	Summary
53	Procurement	As the title suggests, this is concerned with the purchasing process, though the scope given for it is wide – to include the support of purchased items, and materials management functions. The role of contracts is stressed.

Table 12.5 Relevant areas of the PMI body of knowledge

Relevant section	Title	Summary
12.1	Procurement planning	Including what to buy (as opposed to do in-house) how much, and when to buy it. Produce specifications for products and services and agree the type of contract to be used.
12.2	Solicitation planning	Provide documents that will invite potential suppliers to tender for the work, determine how they will be selected and keep them up to date with any changes.
12.3	Solicitation	Invite potential suppliers to tender for the work, answer queries related to the work, gather the bids.
12.4	Source selection	Select suppliers and negotiate contracts.
12.5	Contract administration	Control to contract terms key aspects of time, cost and quality performance, administer changes and ensure that invoices provided are correct and passed for payment.
12.6	Contract close-out	Ensure that the contract is completed as required, and when this is achieved, close down the administration system, providing necessary documentation for audit and review. Issue close-out notices.

12.7 Summary

The value of goods and services purchased can make up a major proportion of a project budget. This has been the case for many project-based industries for some time, and the trend to outsource more and more of our businesses has increased the impact of the suppliers on projects as a whole. Partly in response to this change, the role of purchasing or procurement in organisations has changed to incorporate the management of both suppliers and customers with the objective of maximising the performance of the project. This has led to the area being referred to as supply chain management, rather than simply purchasing or procurement. The activity of purchasing is still important, however, and the stages involved in a typical purchasing process have been described with the accompanying documentation that is required by many systems.

A feature of the work of many in the supply chain management area has been the negotiation of contracts. There are many standard procedures to follow and legal issues to navigate – particularly where international trade is concerned. The contract is still the formal basis of some projects, containing the criteria by which it will be assessed. In other projects where the basis of the relationship is different between the parties the contract takes the role of a document 'just in case' it all goes wrong. This is just one feature of the different styles of relationship that can exist between suppliers and customers. At the extremes, the relationship can be adversarial or run on a partnership basis. While the potential advantages of partnering between organisations are clear, there is a considerable downside element to these, particularly where one of the parties is significantly more powerful than the other.

Project Management in Practice

Project partnering at British Airports Authority (BAA)

The construction sector in recent times has not been noted for its high levels of performance. Firms like BAA, who own and operate airports including Heathrow and Gatwick – London's two major airports – rely heavily on their suppliers, including their construction suppliers, for their own performance. Where construction projects are delayed, the financial consequences can be disastrous. Furthermore, the disciplines of working on airport premises, including the security issues, play a significant part in the daily working lives of project staff. New firms bringing new staff onto the airport sites invariably require time to bring them up to speed with the appropriate ways of working. Particular problems include:

- security – all personnel with access to airside parts of the airport (i.e. past passport control) must be security vetted and trained. The vetting process takes six weeks, so firms must prepare project staff in advance;
- deliveries – getting materials into the airport is problematic, due to significant congestion and lack of availability of areas for storage;
- constant use of terminal buildings by passengers – the closing of areas causes problems with passenger capacity. The firms are required to work with the constraints of passengers using the areas around where the work is being carried out and physical and noise intrusion must be kept to a minimum;
- the commercial activities (shops and restaurants) are the economic lifeblood of the business, with large ground-rents. The objective of projects involving these areas is not simply to complete works on time but as early as possible, so that the areas can start to generate rental incomes.

The traditional approach to managing fit-out projects (changing internal layouts to accommodate different facilities and in particular new retail facilities) was that every contract was different, and would be negotiated with different contractors. These would then employ their own sub-contractors to carry out parts of the work. The approach that has worked far better for all concerned has been through the appointment of lead contractors, with long-term contracts – in most cases 10 years – to be the prime supplier of fit-out services to BAA. This particular contract was awarded to MACE. As part of the agreement, BAA has paid for MACE staff to attend training programmes (including work to implement Last Planner – as described in Chapter 11). This has extended further, with help being offered to their suppliers – of both materials and labour – for development. Where particular problems are identified, the supplier can be asked to take part in an improvement programme. Satisfactory completion can result in similar long-term deals (tied to continual improvement) being offered to those suppliers. In some cases the problems – particularly with designs for areas – have been the responsibility of BAA. The mechanisms are now in place to identify these problems and to introduce new practices to avoid them in future.

Case discussion

1 Summarise the arguments for such a policy of partnering with a major supplier such as BAA and MACE have done here.
2 What might be the drawbacks for both parties of such an arrangement?
3 Carry out further research to identify further examples of partnering in projects. How well do they appear to be working?

Key Terms

relationships	contracts
materials management	tiers
PBS/bill of materials	outsourcing
EDI	order number
invoice	reconciliation
centralised/localised	five rights
ITT	bid
battle of the forms	adversarial/partnership
open-book accounting	vendor-managed inventory

Review Questions and Further Exercises

1 Consider the way that you make purchases for yourself. How do you decide from whom to buy? Are there examples of your personal purchasing where you have frequented a particular business and formed a partnership-type relationship?

2 Why is the process for procurement so involved? Figure 12.2 contains significant bureaucracy that surely does not help the objective of getting the project completed. Suggest why these processes are in place and how they might be simplified.

3 Why the trend to outsourcing? Suggest how this might or might not be beneficial to a project organisation.

4 Surely it would be better for project managers simply to deal directly with suppliers? Under what circumstances would such an arrangement be beneficial and when would it be inappropriate?

5 You have been offered tickets to your favourite entertainment event of the year by a major potential supplier. The offer includes full corporate hospitality treatment. Should you accept this offer?

6 What are the likely trade-off issues in the purchasing decision, and how would you resolve these?

7 How is the Internet changing the role of the purchasing function? Carry out a search of software vendors and investigate the kinds of features that are being offered here. What are the possible benefits for project managers of these?

References

Acuff, F. (1997) *How to Negotiate Anything With Anyone Anywhere Around the World*, Amacom.

Association for Project Management (1998) *Contract Strategy for Successful Project Management*, APM, High Wycombe.

Brown, S., Blackmon, K., Cousins, P. and Maylor, H. (2001) *Operations Management: Policy, Practice and Performance Improvement*, Butterworth-Heinemann, Oxford.

Fisher, R., Ury, W. and Patten, B. (1997) *Getting to Yes*, Arrow Books, London.

Kennedy, G. (1998) *New Negotiating Edge – the Behavioural Approach for Results and Relationships*, Nicholas Brealey Publishing, London.

Larson, E. and Drexler, J.A. Jr (1997) 'Barriers to Project Partnering: Report from the Firing Line', *Project Management Journal*, Vol. 28, No. 1, pp. 46–52.

Further Information

Baily, P., Farmer, D., Jessop, D. and Jones, D. (1998) *Purchasing Principles and Management*, Financial Times Prentice Hall, Harlow.

Harland, C.M., Lamming, R.C. and Cousins, P. (1999) 'Developing the Concept of Supply Strategy', *International Journal of Operations and Production Management*, Vol. 19, No. 7.

Hines, P. and Rich, N. (1997) 'The Seven Value Stream Mapping Tools', *International Journal of Operations and Production Management*, Vol. 17, No. 1.

Hines, P., Cousins, P., Lamming, R. *et al.* (2000) *Value Stream Management*, Financial Times Management, Harlow.

Lamming, R. (1993) *Beyond Partnership: Strategies for Innovation and Lean Supply*, Prentice Hall, Harlow.

Lock, D. (2000) *Project Management*, 7th edition, Gower, Aldershot, chapters 15–18.

www.cips.org – The Chartered Institute of Purchasing and Supply

Notes

1 International Motor Vehicle Programme at the Massachusetts Institute of Technology – see http://web.mit.edu/ctpid/www/imvp/index.html

2 For a further description of MRP and other materials management issues, see Brown *et al.* (2001) Chapters 5 and 7.

13 Problem-solving and decision-making

During the execution phase of a project particularly, the project manager will be faced with the need to solve a whole range of problems rapidly and effectively. As it will not be possible to pre-plan all eventualities, the objective of this chapter is to show how such situations can be handled. Most of the techniques meet the criterion of being simple enough to be used by anyone, though some of the mathematics can be considerably more involved. Decision-making is considered as part of a generic problem-solving process.

Price (1984) describes one of the conflicts that exists in management:

> Business is a risky undertaking. According to those who have devoted their lives to the proper study of mankind, Man is a risk-evasive animal. From what I have seen, risk addicted seems closer to the norm. There is excitement in taking risky decisions and it is possible to get hooked on it; it makes you feel good.
>
> Risk, unnecessary risks, are taken by the thousand every day. Often they are unnecessary simply because they are made in the light of inadequate knowledge, but it boosts somebody's self-esteem to make them with an air of omniscience, which is one of the reasons why we are on the whole, such poor quality performers.

There is another view, namely that the modern project manager is overloaded with data rather than information; the information revolution has provided the means to access large quantities of numbers quickly, often without the means to assimilate them. Handling such volume complexity without succumbing to 'data paralysis' is a significant task and one of the value-adding roles that management can play.

The project manager should have the option either to try to provide a structure for making 'rational' decisions or rely on gut-feel and experience and hope that this is appropriate.

Contents

Learning Objectives

By the time you have completed this chapter, you should be able to:
- Provide a structure for the identification, definition and solution of problems;
- Identify appropriate tools which can be brought to bear at different stages of the problem-solving process;
- Show the implications of some of the changes in modern management thinking in the area of decision-making.

13.1   The Problem Framework

One of the key roles of a manager is to handle problems that challenge them in their own role, as well as being a resource for members of the project team to turn to for help. Problem-solving is a core management skill but, like leadership, one that too often is assumed to be an inbred attribute rather than an acquired skill.

For the purposes of this discussion, a problem is defined as:

The gap between an actual situation or the perception of it and the required or expected situation.

The two properties, expectation and perception, are subjective and based on the viewpoint of the individual. Many issues presented to managers fail this definition; people perceive that there is a problem without identifying the gap. Clarifying the reality of the situation with objective measures is a precursor to the problem-solving process. Part of the role of the project manager in this process is the gathering of the possible worldviews. This requires the skill of being involved yet objective.

The nature of the problem determines the point of departure for the manager. This can be categorised as:

- requiring an immediate reaction – the timescale of a decision requires a 'conditioned reflex' rather than a 'considered response'. Such a situation would include the threatening of the wellbeing of an individual;
- response to a crisis – the problem can be considered within a relatively short time period, i.e. an undesirable state of affairs has occurred – you need to do something about it soon;
- emerging problem – some undesirable state of affairs appears likely to happen – what are you going to do to resolve it?
- response to an opportunity (see Reebok in section 13.10 below) – speculative problem-solving or avoidance in advance of an undesirable situation (missed opportunity);
- strategy formulation – the plotting of a course to a desired situation over a period of years.

The time period of the first kind of problem means that the response or intended solution must be either instinctive (such as to run away) or ingrained through training (to remove the source of potential danger). There is scope in the latter for a major component of any discussion on problem-solving – that of proceduralisation. This is not restricted to emergency situations but is a major component of any work situation today. This proceduralisation or systematisation can be defined as:

The enaction of a predetermined reponse to a given set of conditions.

The systematisation of problem resolution depends on identifying the situation. The programmed response is then initiated, as shown in Fig. 13.1.

The preprogramming of actions has a number of advantages:

- once a method has been defined for resolving a situation, it can be refined and improved;
- by removing thought processes from the actions they are, to a great extent, independent of the individual carrying them out;
- if a predetermined procedure is followed, actions are traceable back to the people who carried them out;
- the actions are then the responsibility of the organisation rather than the individual;
- should the procedure fail, the identification of the fail-point is considerably helped, as the steps can be retraced.

The alternative is that the problem-solving cycle is invoked. As for the planning process, the cycle is iterative (involves repetition of steps if the output does not meet recognised or emerging conditions). The remainder of this chapter will consider the possible approaches to problems with a degree of novelty – those that are being solved for the first time and those that are being considered for proceduralisation. There is a downside, not least of which is the removal of the individualism in the performance of that part of the task. No-one has yet achieved an effective procedural description for carrying out the job 'as if you cared personally about the outcome'.

The problem-solving model (Fig. 13.1) shows the process moving from determination whether a standard procedure exists to choosing a definition for the problem. Classical problem-solving focuses very heavily on providing a definition for

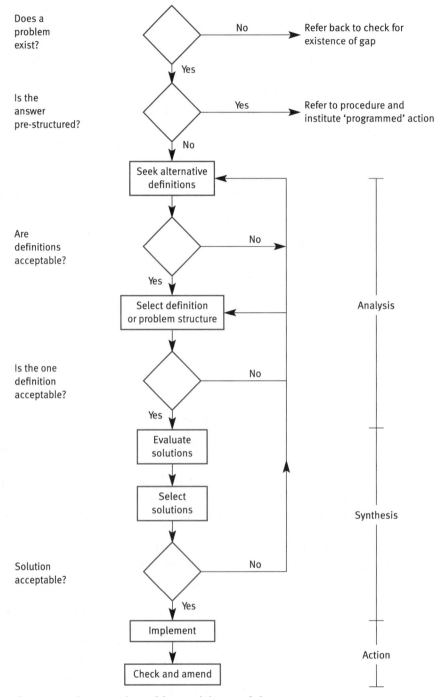

Figure 13.1 Systematic problem-solving model

the problem – indeed, it is often stated that 'if you can define the problem you are working with, you are half-way to a solution'. The definition must include the statement of the gap between the two states: actual/perceived situation and desired/expected situation. Without these two, the problem is said to be 'unbounded'. Once the problem has been defined in this way, the process can move on to the next stage – the construction of various alternatives. At this point the process leaves the analysis of the problem, at least temporarily, and moves to the synthesis phase. This transition involves the first major piece of decision-making. The logic of the process is fairly simple at this point – there needs to be a decision made only if there is a choice of definitions or solutions. Where only one exists the implications need to be considered, but without wasting time on non-decisions.

In Chapter 10 the extremes of management style were identifed as 'coercive' and 'cooperative'. The natures of the decision-making processes are different. For the former, the project manager would be the key decision-maker. In the latter, many of the decisions would be devolved, either to the individual with the most knowledge or responsibility for this part of the project or to the group as a whole. This devolution removes a large part of the decision-making role of the manager. Part of the process of devolution involves seeking ideas from others. This ensures that the set of possible solutions can bridge the problem gap – and includes 'brainstorming'.

Brainstorming

Taking a group out of their normal work situation to ponder a problem can be immensely beneficial to both the organisation and the group. The dynamics of the brainstorming process are aided by adherence to a few rules:

- provide a basic structure to the task of decision-making – groups are generally very bad at looking for structure or logic in decisions;
- the benefit is from the extraction and combination of ideas from a variety of people – the object of the exercise is therefore to facilitate this;
- give people the opportunity to do some pre-thinking on the problem – the subconscious mind has an enormous capacity and can provide solutions without the input of conscious effort;
- at the start of the meeting an ice-breaking exercise will help people to relax and provide a 'safe environment' for the generation of ideas;
- all ideas must be written down – use whiteboards and 3M's Post-It notes, for example;
- express ideas as the participants state them – paraphrasing removes the original meaning and adds a slant of your own. If in doubt as to the veracity of the point being made, seek clarification;
- do not allow any criticism of ideas put forward – this will destroy the credibility of that person and you will be unlikely to gain much more from them;
- do not permit one or a small group of individuals to dominate the proceedings – this will exclude potentially valuable input from others;
- summarise and record the outcome of the brainstorming session and then circulate it to all those concerned – the after-meeting feedback is a further source of solutions and ideas, as people think of all the things that they would like to have contributed during the session.

Decision-making as a process is the period involving the seeking of alternatives through to the end of the comparative evaluation stage. The inputs to this process are:

- strategic – in order for an organisation to retain coherence the decisions made in the projects that it undertakes need to fit with the overall strategy outlined for the organisation;
- fundamental/political – each person brings their own viewpoint to the decision-making process. This will range in form from bias (often undeclared) to a forthright statement of personal beliefs;
- quantitative modelling;
- subconscious elements – obtaining people's legitimate reservations about a decision can be a preventor of 'group-think' provided that an atmosphere can be created in which people feel free to try to elucidate such thoughts.

The nature of the decision-making process depends on the system that the decision concerns. In Chapter 4 a basic overview of systems was given which showed the application of the input/output/constraints and mechanisms model to a project system. Further examination of this is needed to determine whether it is:

- an open system – having interaction with systems outside through the flows of material or information;
- a closed system – being self-sustaining in informational and material terms – operating in isolation.

It is tempting when considering systems to look for the closed-system model. If this is possible, the modelling process involves defining variables from within the system and then optimising these. In most projects, however, this leads to inappropriate models of behaviour being constructed, as they do not show the dynamic nature of the inter-change between the systems and their external environments, i.e. they are open systems.

The use of open-system models is not as attractive, however, as by definition they require the variables from external factors to be continuously introduced and the nature of the environment to be dynamic and inherently unstable. This instability is reflected in a tendency for the behaviour of the system to be unpredictable, and hence the need for the risk management practices and robust planning developed in previous chapters.

13.2 Modelling Systems for Decision-making

Drucker (1956) states the reasons for poor decision-making as being:

- data not properly ordered or structured;
- too much time spent developing answers to problems rather than the statement of the problem;
- an inability on the part of the decision-makers to consider all the variables/factors involved;
- an inability to evaluate the impact of extraneous factors.

The growth of the use of personal computers and the availability of a great range of highly capable software mean that there exists relatively cheap means of processing large quantities of data. There is little excuse now for the data not to be properly ordered or structured. The ease of preparation of graphs and other graphical techniques should have removed this as a cause. The same argument could also be applied to the third of Drucker's points, as the ability to build more data into decision-making models has been greatly enhanced. The second and fourth of the factors are procedurally linked to the decision-making process and are only removed by:

- increased awareness of the potential of both of these to affect the process;
- focus on the removal of the damaging effects of poor decisions, i.e. make the decisions more robust.

There has been a considerable growth in the use of sophisticated models in decision-making. The application of scientific models to the solving of management problems has developed into a specialist branch of management known as 'management science' or 'operational research'. The temptation is to view the output of management science analysis as having a high degree of truth, because the mathematical models that are used are very difficult for a lay person to dispute. In reality, management science is one of the tools that can be employed in decision-making, rather than being the totality of the process.

The model of the system may take on one of many forms, including:

- a descriptive model – using words or graphical means to describe the action or performance of a system, e.g. systemigrams;
- a geometric model – expressing an object in a mathematical form (as used in computer-aided design systems);
- a mechanistic model – determining the inputs to and outputs from a system;
- static predictive – taking a limited picture of the state of a system at a particular point in time and using various mathematical techniques to predict the future performance;
- a dynamic predictive model – a 'real-time system' which takes a constant review of the inputs to a system, providing the most up-to-date forecast of future performance.

Taking a generic view of the modelling process, a model of a system is defined as:

A system which is constructed under controlled conditions, whose behaviour mimics that of another system where it would not be possible for those conditions to be controlled (economically or physically).

The benefits of using modelling during projects are (see Jennings and Wattam, 1994):

- time contraction – it is often possible to speed up events to show the effects of time on a system and use it in the prediction as to what will happen after a period of time, without necessarily waiting that long;
- what-if – the decision-makers have the option to manipulate a model and determine a range of scenarios based on their own individual predictions of the conditions as to what the external environment for the system will be;

- error avoidance/detection – there are many systems that can shadow the decisions made by others and act as a coarse filter for marginal decisions or ones where there has been an error. Such systems are often used both in mechanical design and stock-market trading.

In addition:

- it is possible to examine the fundamental assumptions on which a model was based;
- parameters can be optimised without the need for potentially expensive trial and error with reality;
- the sensitivity to external effects can be measured.

Modelling involves a cycle of activities as used in the project planning cycle – that is, the model is designed, built, tested and then amended based on the comparison of the performance of the real system and the model. The model is then updated based on this performance. The process itself involves:

- making assumptions about the behaviour of systems;
- simplification of the system parameters;
- estimation of the likely values of unrelated variables.

13.3 Handling Uncertainty in Decision-making

There are two basic paradigms associated with handling uncertainty – the mathematical and the managerial. The research literature on improving mathematical models for handling uncertainty is vast. Most requires the input of an expert statistician to be used effectively. This approach tries to impose a degree of certainty on to the system through treating the causes of the uncertainty. The alternative (managerial perspective) is to provide a basis for handling the effects.

As an example, a company is about to launch a new product onto a market in which it has previously operated. It feels that there is a considerable degree of uncertainty as to whether the new product will be a success. There are a number of possible routes open to it:

- first, analyse, using the best data available, the possible sales patterns for this product;
- second, do rough predictions and spend the rest of the time looking for options as to what will happen given various scenarios – both good and bad.

In the former case, the managers are unlikely to have much input to the process by which forecasts are generated, nor faith in the results. In the latter case, the process is visible and the options given market conditions can be evaluated. This also involves setting up frameworks which can be improved on for future product launches – they can review what they decided would happen given a certain set of conditions, then how their reaction to this would work. The first looks at handling the cause of a problem, the uncertainty inherent with product volume forecasting, and tries to remove it. The second accepts that variability exists but focuses on the task of pre-evaluating various management strategies given various sets of conditions.

13.4 Mathematical Modelling Techniques

The use of mathematical models in decision-making is widespread, ranging from basic spreadsheet calculations to the most advanced statistical techniques. Table 13.1 indicates the most-used techniques, a description of their usage and survey results indicating the degree to which they are employed with either frequent or moderate usage in industry (from Forgionne, 1983). Each of these techniques required a different level of mathematical skill to use effectively and each would justify a chapter to itself.[1] The role of simulation, network analysis and decision trees is discussed below.

Table 13.1 The use and level of application of a variety of mathematical modelling techniques in decision-making

Technique	Description	Utilisation (see note below) (%)
Simulation	Computer modelling of a scenario	87.1
Linear programming	Optimal allocation of restricted resources to maximise or minimise a variable (such as price or cost)	74.2
Network analysis through CPM or PERT	Obtaining the logic of both precedence relationships and time requirements in a project environment through graphical means (see Chapters 4 and 5)	74.2
Queueing theory	Shows how a system reacts when faced with a random (stochastic) customer who demands the services of that system	59.7
Decision trees	Graphical method for describing the flow of decisions depending on the possibilities available at each juncture. May be pursued as a statement of possibilities or with statistical analysis	(Not included in this survey) 60 (estimated)
Markow processes	To determine, in a sequential manner, the probability of the occurrence of certain events	(Not included in this survey) 30 (estimated)

Note: Forgionne (1983) shows the percentage of respondents to their survey who indicated frequent or moderate usage of the techniques.

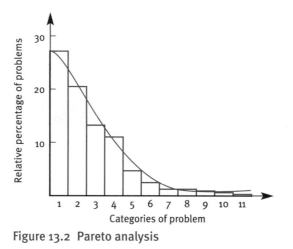

Figure 13.2 Pareto analysis

Problem-solving Tools

The basic problem-solving tools of the project manager include Pareto analysis and Ishikawa/fishbone diagrams.

Pareto analysis

Pareto was an 18th-century economist who found that 80 per cent of the wealth of Milan was held by 20 per cent of the people. This 80/20 'rule' often recurs – many companies find that 80 per cent of their profits are generated by 20 per cent of their products or services (see Fig. 13.2) or that 20 per cent of their clients provide 80 per cent of their business. The Pareto principle applied to problem-solving means that part of the initial analysis is to discover which 20 per cent of causes are causing 80 per cent of the problems. The effort of the problem-solvers can then be focused on establishing solutions to the major factors. Over time, the 80 per cent of problems has been removed, but the principle is still valid, stated simply – apply effort where it is going to yield the greatest result.

Ishikawa/fishbone diagrams

The fishbone diagram is a simple graphical technique which can help to structure a problem and guide a team into seeking further information about the nature of the system under consideration. The effect is shown on the right-hand end of Fig. 13.3. The causes are then broken down into categories and these are then further deconstructed to show what contributes to that problem from those categories.

The problem of late delivery of software to clients is considered in the example shown in Fig. 13.3. As can be seen, the problem is broken down into four main subject areas – management of the team, specification of the software, the people in the development team, and the hardware on which they are working. Each of these is then broken down further. The predominant cause is shown by highlighting the particular area – in this case it is the changing of the specification during development.[2]

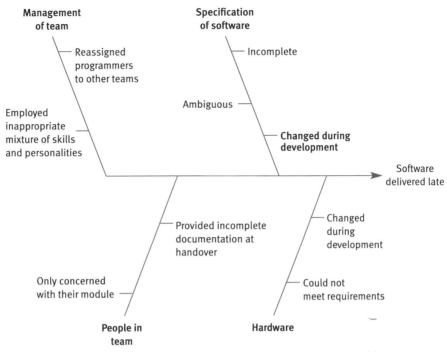

Figure 13.3 Ishikawa/fishbone diagram applied to late delivery problem

13.6 Cause–effect–cause Analysis

Several challenges frequently emerge during the problem-solving process:

- the problem is complex and difficult to structure;
- people enter the discussions with solutions in mind rather than the analysis of the problem itself.

This leads either to stagnation in the process due to the inability to handle the complexity or to inappropriate solutions being given lengthy discussion time. Neither of these is likely to promote good decision-making. Among the problem-solving techniques that have sought to overcome these challenges is cause–effect–cause analysis. This is appropriate where:

- a trained, literate and skilful facilitator is available;
- the group is open to consideration of new problem-solving methods.

The objective is to analyse what the group states to be the undesirable effects of the problem (the gap) to find the root cause or causes. These can then be systematically addressed, rather than attention being focused on the effects. This is an excellent way to bound a problem and come up with a detailed description of its nature. The technique is not novel, but has recently been popularised by Goldratt (1993) in his treatment of it as part of his 'theory of constraints'. Used as above it can be very powerful. It has been found from experience to be less useful for solving tactical problems than for strategic ones, as the skills and rigour of checking the logic of the system are not always available at the lower levels of companies.

The Japanese use the technique of asking why a problem occurs five times (the five whys) – this gets to the root of the problem as they see it, though it is likely to suggest a single root cause rather than, as often happens, several. The process is similar for constructing cause–effect–cause analysis – for the tool to work, the logic has to be preserved in both the reality of the effects listed (do they exist?) and for the linking of causes to effects.

The task order should be completed as follows. It looks odd to start with but, like the construction of network diagrams, will become clear once you have practised using it.

- List the effects of the problem you are tackling – development projects are always delivered late, for example. These must all be real entities, i.e. it must be agreed that these do exist as statements in their own right.
- Start with this as one bubble in the middle of a page (see Fig. 13.4).
- Select another of the effects and show how this relates to the first – either as a cause or an effect. Show the result as in Fig. 13.5. This should then be read as: IF A THEN B, e.g. IF [it rains tomorrow] THEN [we will not be able to complete the site testing].
- Select other effects and build these round the first two. Many will be interlinked, though at first sight they appeared unrelated. Go as far as you can, again each time checking the links you have made to ensure that the logic is followed.
- Where one cause has a number of effects, this should be drawn as in Fig. 13.6.
- Where there is more than one cause linked to an effect, this should be as Fig. 13.7, if there is dependency on both of them, i.e. IF [A] AND [B] THEN [C]. If the dependency is on either [A] OR [B] for [C] to exist, this is drawn without the 'banana' linking the two.

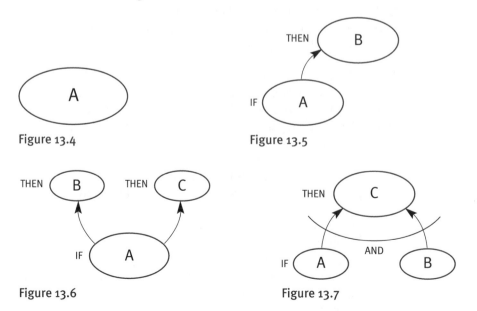

Figure 13.4

Figure 13.5

Figure 13.6

Figure 13.7

It is often necessary during the course of constructing the diagrams both to amend the entities and to add others, e.g. in the example that follows the link between [doesn't allocate time well] and [permanently tired] is not entirely logical. The additional entity [goes to bed late] was added to keep the logic flow. It was obviously necessary to check, as before, that this entity was real. The example shows how a problem concerning the poor performance of a person was analysed. The limited set of effects were listed as:

[Bill's performance at work is poor]
[He works slower]
[He has a bad attitude]
[He is often late]
[He is permanently tired at work]
[He appears more interested in fishing]
[He does not allocate his time well]

These are then formed into the diagram shown in Fig. 13.8. The additional entities and logic links are a matter of opinion to some degree. A further example of how this technique can be used to structure problems is included at the end of this chapter.[3]

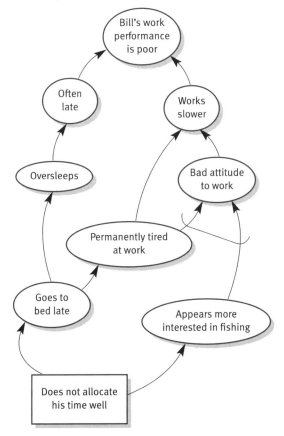

Figure 13.8

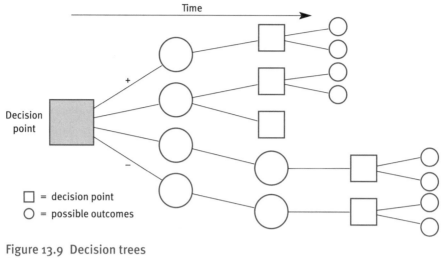

Figure 13.9 Decision trees
(*Source*: Greenwood, 1969)

13.7 Decision Trees

A technique similar in format to the cause–effect–cause analysis, decision trees can be treated at a simple qualitative level or by detailed consideration through the addition of probabilities/distributions to each of the events. A basic format for constructing decision trees is shown in Fig. 13.9.

The decision points are shown as squares while possible outcomes are shown as circles. The possibilities and implications of decisions are therefore clearly identified provided that all the decision points are shown. The qualitative treatment of the structure has merit in its simplicity and speed of construction. Further analysis of the probabilities of the chance events occurring can be made, providing a means for assessing the likelihood of needing contingency plans. The use of 'expected value' measurements can be both derived from and applied to this tool. The likelihood of the outcome of an event is assessed, and the cost/benefit in monetary terms calculated based on this outcome. The expected value of the branches can then be calculated from the sum of the subsequent expected values.

Example

A decision has to be made on whether to fund project X or project Y. Each has two possible outcomes. For X, it has a 75 per cent chance of yielding £100 000 but a 25 per cent chance of yielding only £20 000. For Y, it has a 50 per cent chance of yielding £200 000 and a 50 per cent chance that there will be no yield. The decision tree in Fig. 13.10 illustrates the problem.

The financial decision is based on the sum of the expected values of the yields of each branch of the decision tree:

For project X – expected value = $(0.75 \times 100\ 000) + (0.25 \times 20\ 000) = 80\ 000$
For project Y – expected value = $(0.5 \times 200\ 000) + (0.5 \times 0) = 100\ 000$.

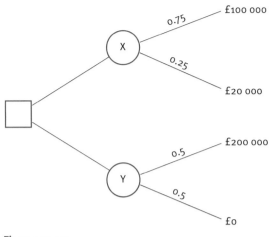

Figure 13.10

The assumption is that we wish to maximise the yield, therefore project Y should be pursued.

This method is attractive in that relatively complex models can be constructed and evaluated quickly. The figures for probabilities and values of return are both a matter of prediction, so the outcome will be determined by the quality of the data with which the model is provided.

13.8 Simple Decision Frameworks

Many complex decisions are best made if they can be broken down into the desirable elements of the outcome of that decision. Techniques for aiding in this process include the use of attribute analysis and force-field analysis.

Attribute analysis involves breaking down the decision into a set of desirable outcomes. These are then placed alongside the choices in the decision process and rated accordingly. For example, a company wishes to choose a supplier for a project. There are five alternative suppliers (A to E) which are arranged across the top of the table, as shown in Table 13.2. The desirable outcomes are arranged down the table (knowledge and experience, reputation, etc.). The manager of the team can then rate the individual suppliers on their perception of how they will perform on each of those outcomes/attributes. The rating is given out of ten, and then totalled for each supplier.

This form of attribute analysis assumes that each of the attributes is of equal importance. Where one is considerably more important than another (e.g. reliability of delivery times may be vital if this is a critical path activity), it can be given an increased weighting – making the score out of 30, say, for that attribute. The totals are viewed in the same way as before. This is clearly a fairly arbitrary means of arriving at the decision, however it is simple to construct and allows a degree of traceability back to how a decision was made. It also enables people to have a discussion on each of the attributes and come up with some relatively objective measure.

Table 13.2 Supplier selection using unweighted attributes

Attribute	A	B	C	D	E
Knowledge and experience	6	7	7	9	8
Reputation	6	6	7	9	10
Prone to strikes/bankruptcy	4	6	9	9	9
Significance of their support	4	8	7	9	9
Design appreciation and conformance	7	7	8	8	9
QA system	5	6	8	9	9
Defects and warranty claims to date	7	6	8	9	10
Reliability of delivery times	6	6	6	9	10
Cost control	7	6	7	6	6
Service level	8	7	8	8	10
Total	60	65	75	85	90

where 1 = very bad, 10 = excellent

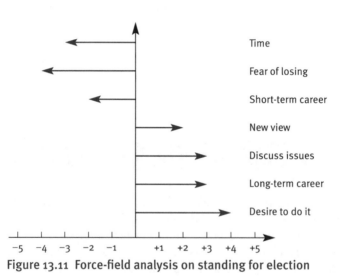

Figure 13.11 Force-field analysis on standing for election

Force-field analysis examines the strengths of different influences on a decision. This is best illustrated through the following example (see Fig. 13.11). The decision to stand for election to a representative body (student's union council, parish or town council, club committee, etc.) has a number of implications. First, the time input to get elected may be substantial and the fear of losing the election significant. There is an opportunity cost – other work has to be put off until after the project is complete (which generally proves to be a poor career move, at least in the short term). There are benefits, such as the requirement to take a new view on a subject and to discuss issues that affect your life. It may improve your CV and career prospects. A major consideration is also whether you want to be elected. These influences can then be rated on a 0–5 scale as being positive (stand for election) or negative (find something better to do). The influences with some numbers assigned are shown in Fig. 13.11. As can be seen by summing the positive (+12) and negative influences (−9) and subtracting the negative from the positive, the decision was positive.

13.9 Decision-support Systems

The principle which decision-support systems embrace is that there is sufficient knowledge existing for the subject to be considered complex, and therefore can be better interpreted through the abilities of computers to deal with large amounts of information. The knowledge must exist within the system, and this is provided through the contribution of experts in the relevant subjects.

The most basic form of decision-support system is a database. The data is structured in 'fields' which the database system can manipulate and structure as required. One example is the database of poisons held at Llandough Hospital in Cardiff – the effects of the poison, and its antidote or appropriate treatment, are held on a central computer which other hospitals can access by telephone. The decision on the appropriate form of treatment is taken without the need for guess-work by the treating doctor. Another use of the information on that database is to track back from the symptoms to the nature of the poison.

A further development of the database is the expert system – otherwise known as artificial intelligence. The expert system takes the expert knowledge, usually gained from an individual or a number of individuals over a period of time. Curtis (1995) states:

An expert system typically:
- incorporates expert knowledge in a particular subject area, usually by storing and representing this as rules or other representative forms (knowledge base);
- separates the general knowledge from the details of a particular case under consideration to which the knowledge base is applied (particular context);
- clearly distinguishes the knowledge from the mechanism of reasoning (inference engine);
- possesses an interactive user interface for providing explanations, justifications and questions to the user;
- provides, as its output, advice or decisions in the area of expertise.

The logic IF [A] THEN [B] is simple for computers to handle. Decision-taking far more often involves the logic IF to a certain extent [A] THEN to a certain extent [B]. This is known as 'fuzzy logic' and needs further examination before it is amenable to computer analysis.

This system of rules can be modelled directly as a system, although for people who do not have this level of programming skills, the use of an expert system 'shell' is likely to be the most beneficial.

13.10 The Importance of the Follow-up Actions

Many poor decisions have been 'rescued' by the work that followed. This process will be aided the more people have 'bought in' to that decision. Gaining that kind of commitment will only work if the style of management is participative – confrontational management will focus the decision back on to the decision-maker.

This can be of benefit if the manager wishes to insulate the team from external elements.

Example Reebok launches 'the pump'

Reebok launched its 'pump' range of sports shoes at a show where it had not planned to do so and despite its marketing plan being incomplete. The pump offered the wearer new levels of comfort due to part of the shoe being inflatable – it would then mould exactly to the contours of the wearer's foot. The case is an excellent example of opportunism – the company's chief executive officer was attending a European trade show and saw that there was little by way of innovative new products being presented. He made the decision to launch the product at that show, without waiting for the normal cycle of development to be completed. This was a bold move which gained the company a great deal of positive publicity – the follow-up action, however, made the decision a good one. The company was then mobilised to carry through the implications of this decision and appears to have managed to do so well. Had the company itself not been so capable, the decision, in retrospect, would have been a very poor one.

13.11 Relevant Areas of the Bodies of Knowledge

While both bodies of knowledge refer to decision-making, neither actively recognises the need for the problem-solving process. To some extent, this is dealt with procedurally through the risk and quality management processes that have been described elsewhere, but there are no specific sections on either of these topics.

13.12 Summary

Problems will arise during projects – that is one certainty that you can rely on! As for other project issues, some structure to the thinking and some tools for the process greatly help the project manager in managing towards a successful conclusion. The first stage in this is to define the issue. We define a problem as the gap between perceptions of an actual situation and that of the expected or required situation. Furthermore, problems may be categorised according to the required reaction time and the nature of the response required – for instance, responses may be predetermined through procedures or reasoned through the problem-solving cycle.

To assist the process, a model may be constructed either qualitatively (through descriptive modelling) or quantitatively (through mathematical modelling) to provide a representation of reality which can be tested under controlled conditions. As we saw during the discussion of risk in Chapter 8, uncertainty can be handled either through statistical means, calculating the most likely set of events, or through managerial action to make the system more robust to the effects of uncertainty. Various mathematical tools can be employed to take away the need for subjective decision-making in some areas, while providing decision support in others. Other methods to help in the problem-solving process include:

- Ishikawa/fishbone diagrams provide a graphical method for structuring problems; Pareto analysis provides a guide as to which problems to tackle first.
- Cause–effect–cause analysis provides a graphical technique for finding the 'root' of a problem through structuring the logic of the situation.
- Decision trees where the route that actions take can be graphically evaluated and probabilities then assigned to each route if required.
- Decision-support systems are normally computer-based and allow expert knowledge to be expressed as a series of rules which are then interpreted by the system.

These do not eliminate the need for gut-feel and experience, however – indeed they should be better at capturing these elements. They have a vital role to play in decision-making – an area that is central to the discussion of 'what managers do'. The management product must be part of the process of continual improvement too.

Project Management in Practice

The use of cause–effect–cause analysis

A board meeting was held at the Mighty Sealing Company. There was growing concern about the competitive environment in which the company was operating. Board members were asked to state what they felt the major problems were. They highlighted eight issues. These were:

1 Existing market is in decline.
2 Sales people do not sell effectively.
3 We have insufficient sales support material.
4 We have an inadequate entry barrier (to the markets in which we operate).
5 We are confused as to which products we should sell.
6 We are unable to exploit new markets.
7 We do not really understand our market environment.
8 There is increasing competition.

These problems or 'undesirable effects' (UDEs) provided the basis for constructing the logic diagram (the 'current reality tree'). Other entities (or logic elements) were introduced to the tree to clarify the logic (see Fig. 13.12). The current reality tree shows that there are many effects (including the most significant – the decline in sales volume), but that there is one major cause over which the company has some control – UDE no. 7 [we do not really understand our market environment]. This finding provided the basis for the next steps.

In order to start to resolve the issues faced, the same form of logic diagramming was used. The result: the 'future reality tree' where the root causes are put in place to result in a particular desired effect (in this case sales volume grows). This is shown in Fig. 13.13.

The method shown allowed a complex problem to be addressed in a systematic way, and initiatives put in place to help understand the processes that were taking place. How these would contribute to the desired objective could then be mapped.

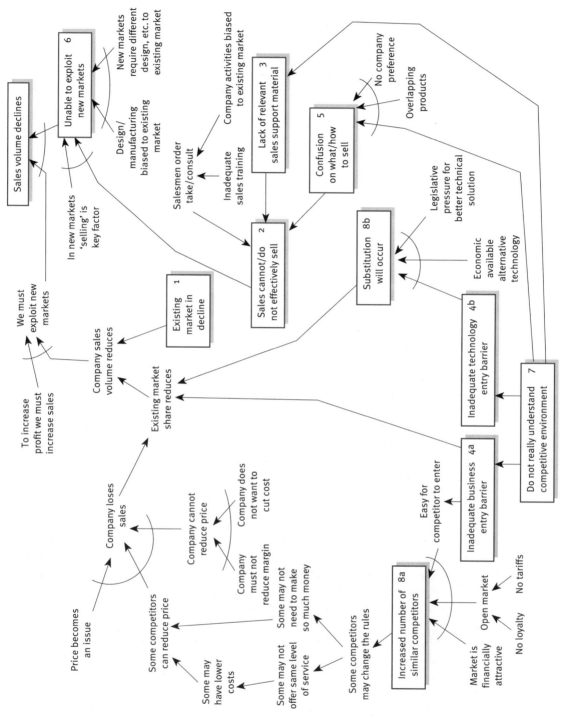

Figure 13.12 Current reality tree

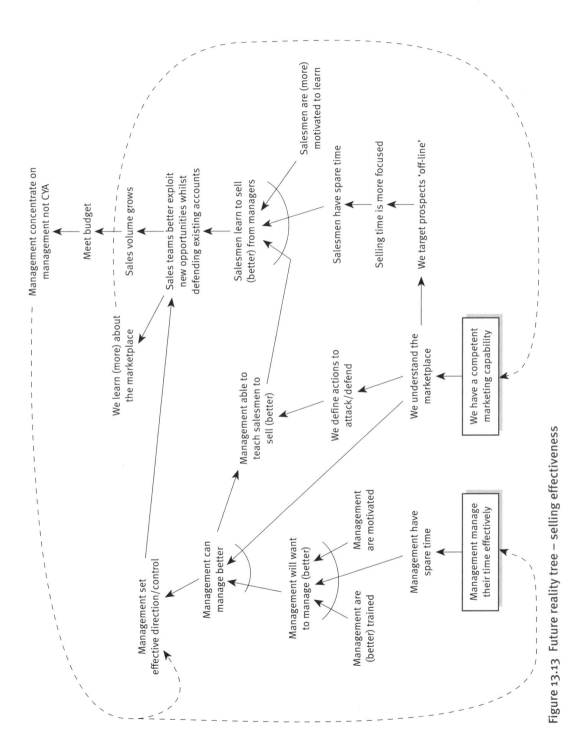

Figure 13.13 Future reality tree – selling effectiveness

Case discussion

1 What is the benefit of constructing a 'current reality tree'?
2 Why is it necessary to insert additional elements into the tree?
3 Why would focusing on 'selling effectiveness' lead to a better understanding of the market?
4 Evaluate the 'future reality tree' – does it resolve the UDEs listed at the start of the exercise?

problem-solving cycle
programmed actions
bounding a problem
brainstorming
management science/operational
  research
what-if analysis
Pareto analysis

Ishikawa/fishbone diagrams
cause–effect–cause analysis
decision frameworks
decision trees
attribute analysis
force-field analysis
decision-support systems
expert systems/artificial intelligence

Review Questions and Further Exercises

1 Discuss the statement made by Price in the introduction to this chapter that 'Man is a risk-addicted animal'.

2 How might the tools outlined in this chapter reduce the risk in decision-making?

3 Show the advantages of having preprogrammed actions:

  (a) as part of a health and safety policy – for example, in the event of a fire
  (b) in the handling of client enquiries
  (c) for the installation of new work procedures.

4 Show the effect of time on problem-solving and give practical examples of each of the different timescales.

5 What is the role of 'brainstorming' and how might it be used to greatest effect?

6 What are the major inputs to the decision-making process and how might these be best harnessed to ensure that the decision-making process is effective?

7 What are the basic forms of systems model? Give an example of each and their role in a project environment.

8 As a project manager in a development activity for a new range of computer software, discuss how uncertainty may be handled.

9 You are the coordinator of a moderately complex project. The following problems have arisen during the execution phase of previous projects with the resulting delays as shown. Use an appropriate technique to show which of the problems you would focus your attention on and show the results of your analysis graphically.

Problem	*Delay (days)*
A Late delivery from suppliers	36
B Last-minute redesign of assembly due to customer change of specification	7
C Suppliers fail to meet the quality levels required in goods supplied	41
D Schedule did not leave enough time for testing	5
E Components did not fit together when assembled	6
F Customer rejected initial trial system	12
G Engineer left team during the project	16
H Office move was scheduled for during the completion phase	5
J Hauliers' firm sacked by customer due to dispute over delivery times	3

10 Select a problem with which you have been involved, and use the Ishikawa/ fishbone diagram to structure the causes of the problem. Indicate what you feel to be the biggest causal factor.

11 State the same problem using cause–effect–cause analysis, showing the relationship between the various facets of the problem. Does the root cause you indicated above still hold?

12 Use a decision-tree model to show the effect on your finances of various decisions regarding the choice of a holiday this summer.

13 Discuss the role that decision-support systems such as expert systems will play in the decision-making of the modern project manager.

14 Discuss the benefits of ensuring that all 'hard' and 'soft' information is included in the decision-making process.

15 Forecast what the home of ten years' time will contain in the way of labour-saving gadgets and entertainment. If there are 30 million homes in the UK by this time, consider how many of these will have taken up this technology. Filter these ideas by considering:

(a) the cost–benefit to the purchaser
(b) whether your view is affected by your enthusiasm for the technology
(c) whether there would be hard statistical evidence which could be drawn on to prove your estimates of the likely take-up of the new technology.

References

Anderson, D.R., Sweeney, D.J. and Williams, T.A. (1991) *An Introduction to Management Science*, 6th edition, West Publishing, St Paul, MN.

Bicheno, J. (1998) *The Quality 60*, Picsie Books, Buckingham.

Curtis, G. (1995) *Business Information Systems*, 2nd edition, Addison-Wesley, Reading, MA, pp. 536–7.

Dennis, T.L. and Dennis, L.B. (1991) *Management Science*, West Publishing, St Paul, MN.

Drucker (1956) *Nation's Business*, The Chamber of Commerce of the US, April.

Forgionne, G. (1983) 'Corporate Management Science Activities: An Update', *Interfaces*, Vol. 13, No. 3, June.

Goldratt, E. (1993) *Theory of Constraints*, North River Press, New York.

Greenwood, W.T. (1969) *Decision Theory and Information Systems*, South Western, pp. 83–104.

Jennings, D. and Wattam, S. (1994) *Decision-Making: An Integrated Approach*, Pitman Publishing, London.

Mizuno, S. (ed.) (1988) *Management for Quality Improvement: The 7 New QC Tools*, Productivity Press, New York.

Price, F. (1984) *Right First Time*, Wildwood House, London, p. 66.

Further Information

Cooke, S. and Slack, N. (1991) *Making Management Decisions*, 2nd edition, Prentice Hall International, Hemel Hempstead.

Goldratt, E. (1995) *It's Not Luck*, North River Press, New York.

Littlechild, S.C. and Shutler, M.F. (eds) (1991) *Operations Research in Management*, Prentice Hall, Englewood Cliffs, NJ.

Rivett, P. (1994) *The Craft of Decision Modelling*, Wiley, Chichester.

Notes

1 For a detailed discussion of linear and integer programming, queueing theory and Markow processes, see, for example, Anderson *et al.* (1991) and Dennis and Dennis (1991).

2 Further problem-solving tools (also called tools of quality control) may be found in Bicheno (1998) and Mizuno (1988).

3 For further developments of this technique, see Goldratt (1993).

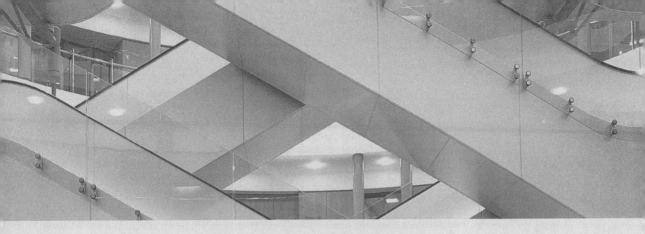

Develop the Process (Do It Better Next Time)

14 Project completion and review

Once the main part of the work is completed, it is very tempting to move on rather than ensure that the work is completed and the maximum benefit yielded from it. How the last phases of 'check and act on the results of the checks' are managed will determine to a large extent the views of stakeholders on the outcomes as well as set the chances for future project success.

These final processes carry a number of challenges, which the project manager will have to address:

- trying to make the review process objective while taking into account a rich picture of the events surrounding project performance;
- relating procedural conformance to project performance;
- the establishment of long-term programmes of improvement while being assessed on short-term measures which are predominantly financial;
- satisfy all the relevant stakeholder groups, while looking ahead to the next project.

Such challenges are not easily resolved, particularly where weak guidance is provided from senior management. These same people may be demanding ever greater performance without providing the means to improve. As will be shown, IF organisations want to take the challenge and significantly improve their project processes, THEN they will have to dedicate some resources in the short term to this. In the longer term, it will be demonstrated that the improvement process becomes self-sustaining, at least in financial terms. Given the poor performance identified during Chapter 1 of the majority of projects and project-based firms, the potential here for financial benefit in the medium to long term is enormous.

Contents

Learning Objectives

By the time that you have completed this chapter, you should be able to:
- Identify the steps required to complete the project and start the final phase – that of process improvement;
- Construct the mechanisms for process improvement;
- Conduct basic reviews of projects using appropriate techniques;
- Provide a business case to justify such activity through analysing cost of quality.

14.1 Project Completion and Handover

The Bangkok skyline is littered with unfinished skyscrapers. These buildings look eerie, with their concrete reinforcing bars sticking up into the sky. The construction of these buildings is over – many will have to be pulled down. For the moment they remain a powerful reminder of the financial crash that has caused so much economic hardship throughout Asia. These projects were stopped simply because the firms building them were not able to raise the necessary capital to complete them.

There are many reasons that work stops on projects. For some, it is because of the successful completion of the task. Some are stopped by their sponsors, due to changing needs or poor project performance, and others, as the skyline of Bangkok today testifies, due to lack of the necessary resources to continue.

Where projects are prematurely terminated it is usual for the staff to be dispersed with no provision for a review. Where projects are completed, there should be no reason for not reviewing. However, many firms do not allow staff time to review project activities, preferring them to stay busy and simply continue to the next project. In Chapter 2, we identified the result of this – *hedgehog syndrome*. Here, mistakes are repeated over and over again, and the rate of improvement of such organisations is poor or non-existent. For the individuals involved this presents much frustration. As we will see in section 14.6, this is a very short-sighted view and the costs of hedgehog syndrome are enormous. Before we get to this stage, however, this is the time when completer–finishers (see the Belbin analysis in Chapter 9) become a highly valuable commodity, and other role types try to run off to start on the next project! Proper completion of projects requires discipline. Carrying out a worthwhile review requires investment of time and resource. This chapter will consider both of these.

The elements that will require the attention of the project manager during this phase are:

- ensuring there is an incentive for the project to be finished and that activities are completed (all projects);
- ensuring documentation of the process is provided to allow review, and of the outcome to facilitate any future support activities (all projects);
- closing down the project systems, particularly the accounting systems (projects where there has been a medium–high organisational complexity and dedicated systems have been used);
- constructing the immediate review of activities – providing a starting point for all improvement activities (all projects);
- appraisal and relocation of staff who have completed their activities and disposal of assets that are surplus to requirements (some projects);
- ensuring that all stakeholders are satisfied – sell your achievements and maximise the business benefit from your project (all projects, every time!).

Completion

The situation the project manager needs to avoid is where a project spends 90 per cent of its life 90 per cent complete. Finishing the activities so that resources can be released for other work and minimising the costs incurred during the close-down phase are vital. There is a trade-off to be considered here – how much time and resource should be put into the closing of activities? At one extreme, there is a temptation to abandon the activities in a great rush to move on to other tasks. Such action risks undue haste and removes the possibilities for maximising the benefit of the review, for example. At the other, a close-down process can become drawn out, nothing is really finished, and the overhead costs of the activities remaining keep escalating. Which approach is taken often depends on the success or otherwise of the project – it is clearly much more desirable to spend time closing a project which is an apparent success, whereas a disaster is more likely to be rapidly abandoned. As already discussed, the review process is equally important in either case, as are the other activities listed above.

In the kind of organisation where people are brought in on contract for the duration of that project alone and are paid a time rate (according to the amount of time they spend working on it), there is little incentive for the work to be finished on time. Indeed, it is in their interests to ensure that things go mildly wrong and result in the plan of work being extended. The provision of some form of bonus for early completion should be considered where personnel have an active input to the result. Contractors and sub-contractors should be treated as suppliers in this respect and be eligible for development effort (as discussed in Chapter 12). In addition, as anyone who has had tradespeople working at their house will know, you find yourself saying, 'While you're here, will you take a quick look at the leak/squeaky board etc.?' This addition to the task list can be a serious additional cost, and one that can disrupt significantly, the main task. That doesn't mean that they should be avoided, just not taken as 'free'.

Documentation

This subject usually elicits groans from practitioners, for whom this is the least exciting part of the project. Project personnel who are used to being very goal focused often have great difficulty getting to grips with this task, and the quality of documentation is often compromised as a result. The purpose of providing documentation is:

- to provide evidence that the project has been completed in a proper manner – increasingly important given the requirements of ISO 9000, to assist avoidance of future litigation and to provide the starting point for review. Section 14.6 demonstrates the importance of the quality of the information that is provided during this phase;
- to give the customer of the output of the project guidance on the operation and maintenance of the item provided – particularly so in the case of a piece of software, a building or a piece of machinery;
- to allow any future work on a similar project to have a good starting point – knowledge of what was done in this project.

In addition the following should be noted:

1 If it is left to the end to write documentation much information can be lost, as staff are already reassigned to other activities and the task gets left to certain individuals to complete. As noted above, this task is one that most people dread. Including this activity as part of the work breakdown structure is vital, rather than hoping that it will be carried out as an unaccounted extra. Where time is short, this activity should not be regarded as the one that can be 'squeezed' to provide slack for other hard-pressed activities or this will immediately signal that it is less important than 'the real work of the project'.

2 The nature of the documentation includes the formal items presented throughout the course of the work and the communication documents and notes of individuals. Individuals need to keep their own logbooks of events, discussions and agreements. The professional institutes require these to be kept during training as the basis for assessment of training programmes. Their long-term use is growing more important as the issue of professional liability becomes more pertinent. Such a document might provide valuable material should an individual be implicated in an inquiry involving professional negligence.

3 Formal documentation includes all project correspondence – including contracts, permissions, letters and memoranda. All documentation with legal ramifications must be kept and the length of time they are to be kept for determined (the life of the product or 7 years, whichever is the longer is used by many organisations for complex projects). A policy should be established for electronic documents and e-mails as to whether these need to be stored in hard-copy form (becoming less likely) and whether the electronic data can be consigned to a data warehouse. In this respect, ISO 9001 states the requirement for record storage: that the organisation should provide a filing system for project data, including a guide as to the whereabouts of any item of information.

The close-down activities should form part of the detailed planning. However, it is often difficult to know exactly what will need finishing due to variations in the project schedule. Some further planning is therefore vital during this phase to ensure that there is some system to the activities being carried out and to minimise the temptation for projects to drift on. A major tool here is *checklists* – to provide a highly visible means of ensuring that the finishing tasks are carried out. Such a checklist is:

- an *aide-mémoire* in addition to formal work allocation;
- evidence that the close-down tasks were planned;
- evidence, when completed, that the tasks were carried out, by whom and when.

Closing down the project systems

The activity curve in Chapter 2 shows that, in general, the level of activity falls off as the project nears completion. This is accompanied by a slowdown in the spending rate – on both labour and materials. As people leave the project team it must be remembered that the systems, in particular the accounting and quality systems, are still operational. For the accounting systems, it is likely that people will know the codes against which items could be charged. Rather than deplete new budgets, there is always the temptation to try to get expenditure set against other budgets. In order to ensure that costs are not run up against project codes, the project manager must ensure that further unauthorised expenditure is curtailed. There will, however, be late invoices being received from suppliers and possibly overhanging administration activities that will need to continue to be charged. These must be paid and are one of the reasons why the financial position at the end of major work does not always provide a good indicator of the financial performance of the project overall. As stated in Chapter 11, assessing the committed spend of large projects is a complex task in itself.

A formal notice of closure is issued in many industries to inform other staff and support systems that there are no further activities to be carried out or charges to be made.

In contract project activities, the legal termination of activities occurs at the time when the customer 'signs off' the project. It is often tempting for work to continue after this has occurred and for the team to provide the customer with 'free' consultancy. Many service projects have this element, in particular in information technology. However, no organisation can afford to:

- cut off the customer completely at this point and ruin the possibilities for future business;
- continue to provide services for which they do not charge.

In reality, if this 'consultancy' is required on an ongoing basis, it is likely to indicate that other aspects of the project execution were less well managed. This could be in particular the handover process or the failure of documentation to identify solutions to problems. Where the completion criteria for projects are left open, you are more likely to end up providing further benefits with possibly no hope of obtaining payment for them.

Further specifics about the nature of the close-down processes are contained in PRINCE2 (see the Appendix) and the bodies of knowledge.

Conducting immediate project reviews

The review system contains key elements, providing further control or corrective actions:

- immediate 'post-mortem' on the activities;
- immediate remedial and improvement action;
- long-term audit and review;
- strategic and procedural changes.

The formal long-term review may prescribe major procedural or strategic changes. The one that is carried out as a completion phase activity is intended to provide rapid feedback on the performance of individuals and systems that the dispersing team members can take away with them. It is the basis for identifying short-term needs, such as procedural changes or changes in skills required by individuals. People need rapid feedback on their own performance – the organisation should provide this in order that:

- they know what aspects of their performance should be repeated;
- managers can identify training or educational requirements;
- the organisation can assess the utility of individuals to future teams.

A further role of the post-mortem is to provide a case-history of the project which is then a guide as to the documentation that will be required, over and above that already compiled, for the long-term audit.

The assessor or reviewer in this case should be someone who can be brought up to date on the context of the project and the challenges that have been faced – physical, political, environmental, financial and personal. The likely reviewers are the sponsor and the manager, though many believe that the manager could not be expected to be sufficiently objective about the process. Other project managers in the organisation can lead a review, and it is a role that can be well taken by staff from the project office (see Chapter 3) or even an external consultant.

One of the tools which is of considerable benefit to short-term improvement is an audit of the management by the team (assumes that the team is managed by an individual rather than being autonomous). Such characteristics as attitude, skills, approachability, openness, ability to delegate authority yet share responsibility, ability to represent the project team to others, and willingness to embrace change, may be assessed. This kind of management questionnaire can demonstrate very clearly that the manager is serious about improving the 'management product' through continuous self-improvement, rather than just preaching the message to others.

The feedback gained by individuals (both managers and team members) provides reinforcement for good skills and behaviours and a path for change where improvement is required. This information is a vital input to the work of the human resources function in identifying satisfaction levels associated with different ways of working and levels of motivation. This is only one type of review. For low-complexity projects, this is likely to be all that is required to feed onto future improvement activities. For medium- and high-complexity projects, a more formal review of the longer-term aspects of the performance is necessary. Such an extended review is discussed later in this chapter.

Appraisal and relocation of staff and disposal of surplus assets

Conducting staff appraisal was mentioned above and is a vital part of nurturing the 'human capital' of project organisations. It is one of the management skills that is often assumed to be present in people because they have the title 'manager'. The reality is that this is part of a skill-set that is not included in any genetic ability, but needs to be trained.

Having carried out appraisal, many project managers will themselves move on to other projects. The relocation of staff is one area where project managers may have little direct influence, but provision of support and help during this process is desirable. Many project managers note the importance of such activities in building a network of good people who can be called upon to carry out particular project activities in the future. Provision of such assistance will strengthen these personal ties.

Assets left at the end of activities include surplus stocks. These represent waste – they were not needed and should not have been supplied. Other project hardware that is not absorbed by the controlling organisation also needs to be disposed of. This is often carried out with the view that as the job is finished, the sooner they are eliminated from the accounts, the site or just from view, the better. Valuable material is put in skips, left to rot or any number of other options that an entrepreneur would baulk at. Trying to encourage people to think of beneficial means of disposal of assets is unnatural for many – they have the attitude that the organisation can afford it and often that 'the paperwork would cost more to raise than would be raised in revenue from its proper sale'. This is, however, more symptomatic of galloping bureaucracy than detachment of the individual from financial results. In such a case, it is possible to outsource the disposal and retain a significant percentage of the market value of such assets.

Ensuring that all stakeholders are satisfied

Marketing influences much of our consumer behaviour, consciously or otherwise, from the clothes that we wear to the brands of groceries we buy. Selling success appears to be an unpopular concept among project professionals, but one that should be considered in enhancing the customers' image of the project organisation. The data for such promotion should come from the review process (for total disasters, the potential and opportunities for improvement come from the same source). The concept of the 'product surround' should be utilised – actual performance is likely to account for 20 per cent of people's perceptions (and hence impact) but costs 80 per cent of the budget to achieve. The 80 per cent of the impact of the work carried out comes from 20 per cent of the spend. Put simply, 'an ounce of image is worth a pound of performance'. Achieving good publicity can have internal benefits as it is seen that items of good performance are being both looked for and recognised – organisations are often regarded as only after 'catching you out for doing something wrong'.

Marketing professionals can and should, therefore, be involved at this stage in the process to maximise the business return on the project work. Trade journals, even national newspapers, may pick up on a particular success story following a press release.

14.2 Structuring Improvement Activities

There is much written on the subject of process improvement from almost any perspective you care to imagine. This provides a degree of confusion for the practitioner, often leading to a kind of *paralysis* where everything looks possible so nothing gets changed. Management paralysis is often seen and can usually be linked to poor strategy and policy deployment on the part of senior management. As was discussed in Chapter 3, strategy provides the essential focus for improvement activities and all our activities should be geared towards these strategic objectives.

With the focus of a clear strategy, the project manager can carry out activities that will improve the performance of future project processes on these criteria. A useful structure is to separate two elements (see Pisano, 1997):

- *learning before doing* – ensuring that the necessary knowledge and skills are available in advance of their need in a project;
- *learning by doing* – those elements that can be learned from previous activities.

The original intention of this structure was concerned with technical elements of processes, though they apply equally to the management elements of processes. It is the *management* of the process that we will be referring to here. The system is shown in Fig. 14.1.

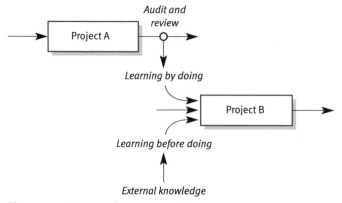

Figure 14.1 Process improvement

Learning before doing is difficult to manage in practice. Identifying sources of ideas for changes that are likely to yield the results that you are seeking takes time and requires a very clear view of the available sources. Two sources for such ideas are the use of consultants (see the following section) and benchmarking (see Chapter 15). Many world-class organisations, however, make far more use of the learning from their own projects. Research recently carried out at one of Hewlett-Packard's plants showed that the review information from previous projects provided a starting point for the planning of future projects. This had been done consistently over a long period, resulting in highly developed processes. This internal learning was often missing at firms that had less well-developed processes and tended to rely on external sources for their process development efforts. As a whole, these were less successful than those generated internally.

The following two sections consider each of the issues of learning before doing and learning by doing in more depth.

14.3 Learning before Doing – the Role of External Knowledge

The main sources of external knowledge that will be considered in this section are through training and education, and the use of consultants.

Training and education

In the area of project management it is frequently seen that firms run training courses for their people, though with very varied rates of success. Having visited the home of a person who had a year previously been on a training course, I was regaled with the excellence of the hotel and the quality of the course notes. 'In fact,' said the friend, 'I've got them here.' He went to his kitchen and reached up above the kitchen units and pulled down a very impressive-looking file. Blowing the dust from it he remarked, 'only wish I could have used the ideas. Nobody at work was really interested.' That course had cost the firm the wages of the person for a week, the course fee and the hotel, plus travelling expenses, and yet had derived no noticeable benefit.

Training therefore needs to have a relatively immediate application if it is to be worthwhile. This includes a group of people who will be able to work in the new method, once the person has been trained. It is rare that one person on their own will be effective in changing methods. They more often are demoralised by the lack of cooperation from colleagues and the processes remain unchanged as a result. Managers must realise that change requires a *critical mass* – that is, it has been suggested that for any change to occur in processes, over 80 per cent of the people working in those processes must be capable and willing to make the necessary changes. This could save a great deal of wasted training time in future and provide a greater focus for improvement activities. Such support and mentoring for change in project processes can be provided by the project office as noted in Chapter 3.

Another external source of knowledge that is used with very varied levels of effectiveness is consultants. The role of consultants is discussed below.

Consultants

There are many large and influential management consultancy firms (e.g. PriceWaterhouseCoopers, McKinsey, Accenture) in addition to legions of individuals, but very little is written on their roles or how their skills can best be applied. The general role of consultants is in the provision of specific services such as accountancy, strategic analysis, human resource development or information technology. The consultant within the project environment can have the following roles:

- an integrator – providing an overall project management service as a single point of contact for a customer. They arrange the allocation of tasks between sub-contractors and are responsible for overseeing progress;
- as an honesty-broker – gaining an external 'independent' viewpoint on a situation can be immensely beneficial. As one consultant commented, 'Sometimes people get too close to the coal face to see the wood for the trees!' People working within the project organisation can be more inclined to accept the views of an outsider on changes than to move from entrenched positions at the behest of a colleague. As importantly, such a solution may allow individuals to 'save face';
- as a change-agent – providing the focus for activities while keeping an overview as to what is happening;
- as a knowledge provider in one or more specific areas or techniques;
- as a resource provider – to allow tasks to be carried out that people from within the organisation would claim that they do not have the time or capability to do (certain documentation activities or specialist technical knowledge);
- as a checker of the way in which the process is being carried out;
- as a trainer – rather than doing the job for the organisation, the knowledge is imparted to the members of the organisation through training. As one consultancy firm advertised, 'Your consultant says "Do this. . . ." You do it. Your consultant says "Now do this. . . ." You do it. Your consultant leaves. What do you do now?'

The first stage in employing consultants is to decide exactly what it is that they are being brought in to achieve. The means of achieving this must be determined either through having the consultants do the job for you or through training. The evaluation of the suitability of one or other firm can be performed through:

- membership of appropriate professional bodies;
- talking to previous clients;
- closely evaluating their capabilities;
- evaluating the costs for the job, in particular whether there is any financial incentive for them to finish the job in a given time, and whether their fee is linked to tangible benefits achieved from their work.

One encounter with a consulting company ended when the two consultants stated that nothing had been written on the area in question. The manager concerned had preprepared for the meeting by going to the local university library and locating two large tomes on the subject, which he duly produced for the meeting. The consultants did not get the assignment.

One of the challenges of employing consultants is how to evaluate the benefit of the service that they have provided. Many consultants in the field of total quality management treated it as heresy if a company employing them evaluates their impact in terms of financial cost and benefit. This may be condoned if there is going to be a definable longer-term benefit, but the mechanisms need to be put in place to ensure that this is achieved. Many managers, when viewing the output of consulting assignments, have made the comment that 'If you give them your watch, they will tell you the time!' This does not mean that the findings had little value – getting someone impartial to state the obvious is as good a means as any of starting the debate on such issues.

One of the benefits of a consultant's study is that it is largely impartial. The allocation of tasks to consultants should be fully in the knowledge of any potential conflicts of interest, e.g. if they also do work for a major competitor or if they are employed at various stages in the project. A consultant may be employed to help in the evaluation of a project proposal. The same consultant could quite reasonably be brought in later in the project if it goes ahead. Therefore they would have a vested interest in its going ahead!

In the future consultants are going to have an important role to play in the management of projects and in the provision of resources that companies are not large enough to have in-house. Their role will need intelligent purchasers of their services if it is to be successful. The lure of the consultant's patter can then be put to good use selling the necessary ideas to those for whom their activities will be value-adding in the longer term. The way that consultants charge for jobs may also be reconsidered. The normal method is currently to work on the basis of a daily rate (one hundred up to several thousand pounds per day per consultant). This does not offer the consultant much incentive to get the job done at any particular speed. Some firms have included clauses in agreements that they will achieve a return in a given period of so many times their fee for a client. This appears to be moving in the right direction.

14.4 Learning by Doing – the Role of Audit and Review

The process of auditing and reviewing activities at a slight time distance from their execution is a part of normal life in some project organisations and an obvious omission from many others. Carrying out audit and review some time after the project has benefit as the results of the actions and the way in which they were undertaken become evident. The return-on-development activities may take even longer to yield the benefits that were attributed to them during the planning process. This should form part of the normal project processes, just as planning does. The process itself requires:

- a reason to exist;
- time;
- information;
- resources;
- credibility.

The reason for reviews is often described as 'praise of the unworthy followed by punishment of the innocent'. The reason must go beyond this and be set out clearly in the terms of reference. The main goal is to ensure that continuous improvement activities are in place and are followed through. It also provides a point at which the responsibility of the project manager can be objectively assessed.

Before continuing to look at some procedural issues associated with review, the first task is to identify the aspects of the project that need reviewing.

Time must be allocated from other activities and an appropriate auditor/reviewer arranged. The project manager should be involved in the process. Information should be provided along with the necessary access and authority to obtain further information. It should be resourced, either from central overhead allocation or from an amount set aside from the project funds to carry it out. As for the manager, the process must be given credibility. The research should be carried out in a manner that is rigorous but fair, and there should be no hidden agendas (praise or punishment).

The auditing process involves:

- establishing the procedures – the formal statement of intent as to how activities should be carried out, whether financial, quality or environmental;
- checking documentation and other records of practice to show that they have been followed;
- presenting a report detailing the areas where there are deficiencies or irregularities.

An audit is often viewed as a negative process, i.e. it is trying to catch people out. However, it is responsible for identifying inconsistencies, double-checking information as well as seeking alternative viewpoints on the proceedings. There will regularly be conflict into which the players may try to draw the audit team.

The review process involves:

- studying overall performance relative to constraints;
- identifying areas where the procedures failed or have otherwise been shown to be inadequate;
- reporting on the areas and suggesting improvements.

It is a real skill and art to carry out a worthwhile review process. Getting the truth, or many versions of it, and attempting to make sense of the conflicts (as for audits, but with a more open mandate) are common tests. It is always going to be a subjective exercise – this factor is worth remembering. Two different teams, given the same project, are likely to produce totally different reports. This will depend on the skills and biases of the individuals. The review should differ from the audit in one further dimension – that of the focus. Audits look internally, while reviews should take into account the impact of the project on the environment as a whole. The changes that were impressed by the environment should also be considered.

The nature of the feedback will differ from the post-mortem type of review. Changes are rarely made to procedure-level events at this stage – procedures may have already been changed considerably and the context is unlikely to be completely the same again. Where the greatest impact will be felt is in strategic issues – the role of the project manager, of suppliers and the imposition or relinquishing of controls on activities can be examined. Above all, it is likely that a full picture of performance indicators will be available by this time and provide a more complete picture of the accuracy of forecasts and the veracity of other planning assumptions.

In the execution of a formal audit or review the criteria under consideration will to some extent determine who should be the auditor or reviewer. Expecting someone without accountancy skills, experience or qualification to carry out a financial audit is unlikely to produce usable or credible results. The criteria for the assessor also require a degree of independence. There is often the tendency in formal organisations that run projects in matrix form for one department or function to assess another's projects and vice versa. This arrangement, while being convenient and usually very cost-effective, can be counter-productive as there is the equal chance of complicity or hidden agendas as the departments have old scores to settle. This 'culture of distrust' is perpetuated by such arrangements and simply adds another degree of paying someone to check the work that you have paid someone else to do in the first place. Although it can expose incompetence, the audit/review procedure has to be seen as a value-adding activity, rather than simply an opportunity to be negative about the work of others.

The implication of the above is that there can be a worthwhile role for the project audit and review process. An assessor works with the project sponsor and manager to look for areas of improvement. In reality, if you want to find the major areas for improvements, the people who are in the best position to provide this information are those that were directly involved with the activities – the project team themselves. This knowledge is collated with the assessor taking a collaborative role rather than an adversarial one, and utilising their experience to be fair and openly objective, rather than having to indulge in political games-playing. The view should be holistic – no one aspect of the project performance should be considered in isolation and data should be corroborated wherever possible. Substantiating the claims of suppliers (both internal and external) by verification with their customers is always a good check of data. Maintaining a focus which looks externally as well as at the internal data sources ensures that the fundamental objective of 'meeting customer requirements at lowest cost' remains on the management agenda.

Table 14.1 shows the nature of both procedural audits and performance reviews that can be used to assess a project. It shows a variety of criteria and their methods

Table 14.1 Review and audit criteria

Criteria	Audit	Review
Financial	Accounting systems	ROI, cost variance
Time	Conformance to plan	Customer satisfaction
Quality	Quality procedures	Customer perceptions
Human resources	Conformance to policy	Team-spirit, motivation
Environmental	Conformance to policy	EI assessment
Planning	Conformance to plan	Cost, techniques used
Control	Systems for control	Basis for improvement

of assessment. As stated during the work on control, if you measure only financial performance measures, do not be surprised if the focus of the project team rests on short-term performance gains. Carrying out such assessment shows the team how seriously the organisation regards the criteria set out. If policy statements at senior management level are not backed up by the allocation of assessment effort *and* resources for improvement as a result of these assessments, the policies will become discredited.

Given that all these are possible, how do you decide which of these is important enough to warrant the effort of a review? The answer comes through the same means as many other decisions of project managers, by reference to the organisational strategy. If time performance is the most important issue for the organisation, then audits and reviews of planning, control and time performance should be carried out. Other aspects of performance can be the subject of particular reviews and it is important that the subject of the review changes over time. This would reflect the changes in strategy and attempts to close performance gaps, as identified in Chapter 3.

Long-term review

The case where a project was identified as a success at its completion but where the poor quality of the product of the project only became recognised later was identified in Chapter 3. Ongoing measurement of project outcomes has been established in the construction and engineering sectors for some time by identification of *whole-life costs* – the initial project cost with the ongoing maintenance and eventual disposal costs of the product. Given the level of dissatisfaction of many firms with their IT suppliers, this would be a useful measure to apply. Other forms of long-term review include individuals reflecting on their own experiences of the project. This adds real validity to the concept of experience. It is a feature of many people who participate in regular training on this subject that the training time provides them with an opportunity for this reflection. Some professions require the compilation of a log-book. This type of diary could be highly beneficial to the project management professional as a means of facilitating review of personal experience. This can form a third element of the learning model – learning after doing.[1]

Some further issues concerning how to carry out reviews are included in the following section.

14.5 Carrying Out Reviews

It was noted above that many firms do not bother to carry out reviews for a variety of reasons. During recent research it became clear that a major reason why this is so is that people resent the fact that reviews frequently have become major finger-pointing exercises, simply concerned with allocating blame for shortcomings in the project. Given that this often points at managers, it is perfectly understandable why they are so reluctant to have reviews! However, under some different guidelines it is possible for medium- to high-complexity projects to have very constructive formal reviews. These guidelines include:

- Focus on processes, not individuals – Dr Deming suggested, as has been stated before, that the majority of defects in our workplaces are the fault of the systems that people work in rather than the individuals. Given that this is the case, and that the systems and their design and redesign are under the control of managers, it is reasonable that changes could be expected to the systems rather than simply the individuals;
- Use factual data wherever possible – it is amazing after even a short period of time how people forget salient points relative to the project. This is a vital role for project documentation to help relieve the problems associated with short-term memory loss or resolve difference of opinion as to what happened and when;
- Allow rehearsal of alternatives, e.g. what would have happened if . . . ? This rehearsal actually can be very useful if allowed for a short part of the review, not to dominate it but to allow some exploration as to how the project system would have responded under different conditions. Given that the objective is the future improvement of the system, this is a legitimate part of the review;
- Use tools and techniques of problem-solving – in particular for ordering data and presenting the findings. This will further help to avoid jumping to conclusions and does help the process of review to be more objective;
- Discourage glib classification – this frequently arises, particularly in the absence of structured reviews and problem-solving activities. People participate in reviews often with very definite ideas of where the problems lie. As discussed in Chapter 13, using a structured cause–effect–cause analysis will yield the root cause, rather than simply discussing one of the intermediary effects. (For a more detailed discussion of there issues see Busby, 1999.)

Hewlett-Packard – Carrying out a review by following the project

In new product development it is traditional for the product to be designed, then engineered, then passed to manufacturing for making. The designers would be having battles with the engineers over the need for design features to be preserved, and the engineers with the manufacturing staff over what could, and could not be made (these were described in Chapter 5). Hewlett-Packard, as part of the linking process between the different functions, ensures that key staff who do the design work carry the project through. Not just to the end of the project, and its handover to manufacturing but to three months into mass production of the designed items. This provides ample opportunity for problems to emerge, and for the designer to witness the effects of their decisions on the end product. It is a case of knowledge management of the highest order – people gain great insight from this process, and retain this for subsequent projects. As a by-product of this, the networks of people who they have worked alongside during these extended handovers means that there is far better communications in the organisation.

As has been shown, reviews can be an immensely powerful tool for starting process improvement. In themselves, though, they do nothing. As with other decisions, it is how these improvements are followed up with changes in processes and improvements in the individuals and parties to the project that will make the difference in future. Part of the process of convincing firms and individuals to follow through and make these changes is to provide the business case for them. This is discussed in the following section through the tool of quality costing.

14.6 Justifying It All – Evaluate the Cost of Quality

The financial implications of many sorts of failure in performance can be calculated for the purpose of providing the business case for performance improvement activities. The costs are generally enormous and can be expressed as a percentage of turnover.

For the purposes of calculation, quality costs are broken down into three categories – prevention, appraisal and failure. The inclusions in each category are shown in Table 14.2. Failure can be broken down into internal failure (that which is detected by the organisation before the customer does, thus allowing a rapid remedy) and external failure (one that the customer detects after delivery of the product or consumption of the service). Generally, it can be stated that the failure costs are orders of magnitude higher than those of prevention and appraisal.

Crosby (1979) researched how the performance of the quality system related to the profitability of the organisation. The findings of this work were that:

> For a well developed quality system, the costs of quality can make up as little as 2 per cent of turnover. For an organisation with a poor or neglected quality system, they can make up in excess of 20 per cent.

Table 14.2 Elements of quality cost

Category	Activities included
Prevention	Quality planning, training and auditing, supplier development, costs of maintaining a quality improvement programme or system, maintenance of all testing equipment
Appraisal	Any checking activities (and materials consumed during these), analysis and reporting of quality data, auditing suppliers' quality systems, storing records of quality results
Failure	*Internal* – any wasted activities, be they in the production of an artefact that is scrap or the generation of a document that is not read, changing or rectifying work already done because it was not right first time, downgrading goods or services, problem-solving time *External* – replacement of faulty goods, having to return to a site to redo tasks, complaints and consequent loss of goodwill and repeat business, product and professional liability claims

A recent audit of a project organisation within the aerospace industry showed quality costs to be 36 per cent of turnover. This was a surprise for them, given that external failure happened very rarely (as one might hope with aircraft components!). Another study with a construction firm showed quality costs of 38 per cent of turnover. While the aerospace firm could rightfully claim that the precautions that they had to take to prevent failures in service were very costly, whether it justified such a large part of their costs was doubtful. A more realistic benchmark for them was 15–20 per cent in the medium term. For the construction firm there was no such excuse, and the opportunity for them very large (given that profit margins at the time were of the order of 3–8 per cent of turnover). A benchmark for this firm would be in the range 2–5 per cent.[2]

This is a major driver and source of cost savings if recognised and a system implemented properly. Savings are generally made through the increase of prevention and appraisal activities, which in the medium term will result in reduced failure costs. The project organisation has to accept that in the short term, overall costs are likely to increase as the improvements take their time to work through the system.

Help in identifying quality cost elements is available in BS 6143: Part 1: 1992. Part 2 gives the prevention, appraisal and failure model and includes some sample proformas for completing quality cost reports. Both have high practical value in a project management environment. Further discussion of quality costing is in the Further Information at the end of this chapter.

14.7 Relevant Areas of the Bodies of Knowledge

Both bodies of knowledge focus on the contractual and practical aspects of the completion process. Neither consider the potential for learning and the different types of audit and review that can be undertaken.

Table 14.3 Relevant area of the APM body of knowledge

Relevant section	Title	Summary
64	Hand-over	This is defined as a managed process where the outcome of the project along with all the associated project documentation is delivered to the project sponsor. It is an opportunity to reflect on the original business case for the project.
65	(Post-) project evaluation review [O&M/ILS]	This assumes that there is a definable product or system that is put into operation as a result of the project – hence the O&M (operation and maintenance) and ILS (integrated logistic support). It is stated that the review should be an integral part of the project, not just at the end, but also during the process, and the knowledge shared with other projects.

Table 14.4 Relevant areas of the PMI body of knowledge

Relevant section	Title	Summary
5.4	Project scope management – scope verification	This is a process of obtaining agreement between the stakeholder groups of which parts of the project scope have or have not been achieved. The latter is particularly applicable in projects that are terminated early.
10.4	Administrative closure	Document project processes and results to obtain acceptance by the project customer, provide the basis for review and determining lessons learned from the project. Archives should be established to contain the documentation for the project.
12.6	Contract close-out	Ensure that the contract is completed as required, and when this is achieved, close down the administration system, providing necessary documentation for audit and review. Issue close-out notices.

14.8 Summary

At the start of Chapter 2 the question was asked – where do we start? There were structures that would facilitate the thinking for that part of the process. A certainty of the definition of a project is that it will end in one way or another. The question could similarly be asked – how do we end the project? Again there are structures and ideas to help here. Two basic principles guide this. The first is that there must a positive statement of closure, rather than simply allowing the project to fizzle out. The second is that the knowledge gained by doing the project must be captured. This is achieved through the review and audit process, feeding back into both project process knowledge and technical knowledge. The project may have cost the organisation and individuals dearly – and now is the opportunity to realise some payback from that 'investment'.

Closing out the project involves the shut-down of all project systems, ensuring all activities are completed, and preparing for the forthcoming reviews. Audits are there to check conformance to procedure. In short – did you do what you said that you would do, in the way that you said that you would do it? Reviews look for opportunities for process improvement, at particular aspects of how the project was managed. The aspects of importance are determined by the project strategy – it is not feasible to review every aspect of performance.

The learning process from projects was suggested to be at least twofold, through learning before doing (through identification of appropriate knowledge in advance of need), learning by doing (through review and integration of that knowledge into the organisation), and longer-term reflection.

The costs of failure were identified above as an 'investment', and these should be calculated as part of a quality costing exercise. This is frequently a good starting point, as the extent of the failures and their costs are usually surprising to most organisations. They also provide considerable insight into what is really going on in the organisation.

Project Management in Practice

IT all goes pear-shaped at VCS

Introduction

The department that later became VCS was founded in 1987 to provide computer support in a major firm. Over time, this role expanded, and in 1992, the function was bought out by three of its managers to begin life as a company in its own right. In 1997 the firm was sold to a PLC, which made VCS one of its operating divisions. In January 1999 VCS was sold again to a corporate holdings firm, with interests in a number of software and hardware companies.

VCS's range of products all required regular upgrades to keep them competitive and consistent with changes in the hardware and other software used by its clients. The Time-Track product was undergoing a major revision when a number of problems became apparent. These included areas of the product which were far too complex for the task that was required of them (incurring significant problems elsewhere) and little control over time or cost. As a result, the product arrived late in the market, to the embarrassment of the firm and particularly their new owners. This was given significant attention at board level, and technical specialists conducted a number of internal reviews. Realising that there were more fundamental issues at stake here, the firm's management team was debating their next move.

The product

Time-Track is used as a means of compiling time data from employees as to how they have spent their time, so that clients may be billed accordingly. The product has to work with a company's own accounting software and is viewed by many firms as 'mission-critical' – if the product fails they are unable to bill their clients and thereby earn revenue. Reliability is therefore essential from the customer's point of view. A major review of the product was required, as many of VCS's clients were moving from thick to thin client systems.[3] This accompanied other changes in the technology that Time-Track needed to work with, in addition to the firm's ever-present imperative to continuously improve the product. Moving from Version 2 (V.2) of the software to V.3 meant that, in addition to obtaining upgrade revenue from existing clients, new features could be added to bring new clients in. It was therefore a project of the highest strategic importance for the firm.

The project

Looking back, the V.3 project does not appear to have ever been officially launched. Documents relating to technical aspects of the product were generated during 1997 – including a 200-page proposal which was circulated to the technical staff, though notably not the sales or marketing people who would be responsible for the income the new product would generate. In early 1999, no-one on the development team was able to produce a copy of this document.

The project was intended to be a collaborative venture between two companies from the same group, based on potential synergies generated by combining two of their existing offerings. The firms became part of the same owning group during the 1997 buyout. They had fundamentally different products but some commonality in the technology being used. There was significant excitement caused by the potential for the new product – it provided a much-needed replacement for the product sold by one of the firms based in Blackburn (north-west England), by upgrading an established product which was being sold by VCS in Cardiff (South Wales). This opened the market from predominantly public-sector clients to a much wider range including large corporations. Additional sales personnel with corporate sales experience were recruited and began selling the product into the market early in 1998 in expectation that the new product would soon be available.

At the end of 1997, there was a meeting of the project participants from both sites on neutral territory. They considered what could go wrong with the project. A total of 152 potential problems were identified that could lead to project failure. These included the departure of key personnel as well as failures in the technical elements of the process. At the VCS board of directors' monthly meeting in February 1998, the project manager, Dave Grant, reported that work had started in earnest. He noted then that there were differences in the approaches of the two sites involved in the project, but felt that these could be overcome. He himself was based at the Blackburn site, and much of the early project work on adding functionality was being carried out there. At VCS, their main role was detailed coding (programming) of the product.

Problems start to become evident

As early as March 1998, problems between the two sites became evident. VCS technical director, Steve Timms, reported to the monthly board meeting that things were not going right, that it was hard to know what was going on in Blackburn, and that there was a complete lack of agreement on technical protocols between the sites. Without these protocols, development work lacked any solid foundations on which to build. Dave Grant reported that progress at the Cardiff site had been disappointing. Overruns of the construction of one of the databases necessary for the system were due to overoptimistic estimates and the use of less experienced developers. He further commented in a direct criticism of VCS management that 'Work to motivate the team by improving the local supervision of their work is needed to ensure that this slippage is made up'. During the following month, this problem continued leading to a further report of poor progress on the new product. This time, he identified the problem as '. . . too many projects for the Cardiff staff to work on. While the staff in Blackburn have one project to work on, Cardiff have a whole list of projects to deliver before the end of the year. The whole of the development department at Cardiff is grossly overcommitted.'

The developers at Cardiff were also starting to become frustrated. As the development coordinator at VCS, Bill Jones noted, 'When our customer service people have a problem with something they don't understand or with a customer, we just have to go and do it. It's always V.3 that gets dropped. Worse – V.3 work will be the first thing that we get stopped to do something else. It's really hard to keep the guys (the programmers) geed up and saying "this is it – everybody's depending on us". It does have an effect on the guys.' The disruption caused to the programmers by the constant changing of their roles was also noted. 'You can lose half a day easily if something takes you off the train of thought for as little as half an hour.'

The May report continued in a similar vein, with good reported progress at Blackburn and poor or non-existent progress at Cardiff. The addition of a new team member at Cardiff with significant relevant experience gave some hope that the situation would improve from then on. A prototype of the new system was produced and demonstrated to the company's user group (firms who were already using their products) during May. This provided the developers with a first opportunity to gain feedback on their ideas for the new product.

The first target date for completion of the project was announced for August 1998. At the end of May there was still some belief that this deadline could be met. Marketing and sales people were informed accordingly, creating an expectation for V.3 in the market – among existing clients who wished for the promised upgrades, and new customers who were interested in the potential functionality.[4] However, despite the addition of extra staff, there were underlying problems. Mark Small, a member of the development team, commented, 'When I came in in May 1998, programmers were doing things, but nobody could tell you why they were doing it and who had made the decision that it should be done this way. What they were trying to achieve did not seem to be defined anywhere.' Another of VCS's development coordinators noted the result of this to be that 'The development guys were making lots of decisions that they should never have been expected to make – they were getting little or no guidance.'

Following concerns about the speed of progress a review of the work outstanding identified a further 90 person-days of work required in one area alone, which had not previously been included in any plans or workload considerations.

Problems come to a head

June 1998 was a watershed for the companies and the project. At this time, it became apparent to the Blackburn firm that the product (VCS Time-Track V.2) which they had decided to build upon was nowhere near as sophisticated as first thought. This meant that in order for it to do half of what their existing product did (which it was intended to supersede), there would have to be a substantial rework of the Cardiff product. In addition, there were many problems with the programming quality which required significant rectification work before it could be developed further.

These two problems were a major blow for the project and soon led to the departure of the two members of the team from Blackburn. One of these had been promised a project management role in this project, but was given charge of only one programmer. To make matters worse, there was little management required in this role and he ended up doing much of the coding work – contrary to his expectations. When his management role did not materialise, he started looking for work elsewhere.

The pressure to complete a product (whatever that was) mounted on the Cardiff team. They still had neither design specification nor method of testing the product. Furthermore, their lack of experience of the business processes involved was starting to tell on the product. Steve Timms, technical director at Cardiff, probably sensing the mounting problems and the impending product disaster, decided to leave. He had been noted for his ability to have the whole vision for the product in his head. This led staff to comment that 'We all knew what we were doing, nobody knew why.' His departure caused a significant vacuum within the project team. Meanwhile, Dave Grant at Blackburn was taking active steps to dissociate himself from the project. Indeed, the Cardiff staff perceived that the only time that Dave Grant was interested was just before a board meeting.

By the June report, there was a real sense of growing frustration for the project manager. The newly appointed project coordinator at Cardiff, who now played a pivotal role in the development, was unexpectedly off work due to personal circumstances. Since it was a small firm, replacement cover was provided on a goodwill basis from other areas. With little coordination on the ground, slow progress was being made, and the project was increasingly seen as unbalanced. Work carried out at Blackburn was innovative and complete; that at Cardiff was outside any plans that had been laid down (though no-one could actually find any detailed plans for the Cardiff work at this stage). Dave Grant continued, in his words, 'to try to manage things from afar', though this was debatable from the Cardiff staff's perspective. Additional developers were added to the team at Cardiff, though at the same time, an updated version (V.2.1) of the previous release of the software was sent out. Andy Morgan was brought in as the new development manager and described some of the problems being faced in a report he prepared at the end of June:

Proposed work	Planned time	Actual time
General enhancements	15 days	20 days
Specific programming	29 days	6 days
Data structuring	8 days	5 days
Maintenance for V.2.1	15 days	27 days
General support for other products	5 days	5 days

As the table shows, little progress was being made on the specific programming– of the 29 days allocated to it, only six were actually used to carry out work on the main programming for the project. This resulted in a significant part of this work being carried forward for completion the following month, which only compounded the time shortage. Andy Morgan stated: 'We've allowed in the plans for a day a week per programmer for maintenance. But it's not working, we're constantly being knocked sideways, in terms of planning, because of the pull from maintenance.' This was indeed a significant issue – customers were demanding that problems in their existing products were resolved, but this resource could only come from the development team. Further complications arose when a programmer was removed from the already small team to work on a 'more critical project' – Y2K changes for another product.

In June, Andy Morgan was appointed as project manager for the V.3 project, and from then on, Dave Grant's role was unclear, as Blackburn were no longer very interested in the project – it would not provide them with the product they wanted. The work was completely transferred to the Cardiff site.

In July, Dave Grant noted that there had been some progress with the project and suggested that the software be released for Quality Assurance (QA – the people who will test that the product works before it is released to customers). A separate Cardiff report for July stated that they were on target for a controlled release of the software in late October, though no mention was made of the earlier agreed August deadline. In August, this became 'controlled release in November'. The problem for Andy Morgan in Cardiff was a lack of the resources to carry out the necessary QA of the product, and too much work left too late in the project.

In September, Andy Morgan reported that due to further requests for additional functionality from the user group the software would undergo controlled release in January 1999. In October, this was still 'the schedule'. To facilitate this, he commented that the QA had been set up next to the development office, and that a whiteboard had been installed to give the project higher visibility. At this point, concerns were raised about the quality of the final software. This appeared to be vital – that quality was rated 'above all else', to ensure that it is relatively 'bug-free' when put on general release. Not only would the software need to be checked, but any problems found would have to be solved. With such a complex piece of software this would inevitably mean further problems as when you change one area it inevitably affects another. He reiterated his point that 'Quality is the most important feature of Version 3 and it will go on general release when we are confident of its quality.' Controlled release was then scheduled for the third week of January.

During QA, it became apparent that the original programming, so highly praised by Dave Grant, was poorly constructed and regularly failed to perform simple tasks, let alone the complex ones it was designed to do. The problems with the coding (programming) were exacerbated by an attitude of 'QA is there to find the problems – that's their job'. When this was investigated further, it was found that while some of the programmers were excellent and always checked their own work before it went to QA, others were consistently not doing so. This lack of commitment to the project was further noted by one of the board members who stated that 'They [the programmers] just come in at 9:00 and leave by 5:15. Nobody would think we were having major problems with the product.'

Product release

Limited parts of the software were indeed released to a key client at the end of January, though the product was nowhere near ready. Here, the situation was described as 'lose–lose – if we deliver any later, we lose the client, if we deliver and it doesn't work, we lose the client.' The controlled release served one purpose – it showed that there were further problems with the software. On the positive side, the users liked the parts that they saw, and even said that they perceived the implementation to be managed well by VCS by not releasing the full version until it was ready.

Commenting on the controlled release, the sales director noted, 'The consultant went on-site at the client and started trying to make the product work. There was no documentation or other help available other than the members of the development team. Even then, there were many parts of the product that nobody knew how they were supposed to work. After three days of trial and error, we had to take the software out again. They are probably our largest client. They wanted V.3 because there were so many bugs in V.2.1 and they wanted fixes for them. We had to stop supporting V.2.1 and told them to go to V.3 to get these things fixed. They do not want a whole load of new features, just the ones they had bought initially to work. The testing was to see that nothing had got worse. This was a shock to me – I thought they wanted the enhancements.'

In addition, one key technical feature (which most users would not be in a position to evaluate anyway) was causing major problems for the developers. The implications of this feature were an increased level of technical complexity, which had been introduced by Steve Timms. As was commented, 'He was technically brilliant – he'll do everything to the nth degree, try to get everything perfect, but half of it won't relate to user requirements. The other problem we've got is that it is an enormous program, it is horribly complex, and every time we fix a bug somewhere, it causes a bug somewhere else. That is the problem for us – the wrong person given too much rope. He built on things we didn't need, but that he thought were a good idea technically.' During the period of uncertainty this one person was able to make all sorts of changes as and when he saw fit. Later comments include 'One of the things we desperately need to implement is change control throughout maintenance as well as new product development.'

The product was fully released in June 1999, ten months after the original deadline. It has cost the company dearly. As the sales director commented: 'We've lost £500k worth of business in the past 3 months alone because of these problems.' For a company with a £5 million annual turnover this was a significant amount of revenue. He further noted that the result of the problems with V.3 was that the firm had gone from being a leader in the field to being one that was now pushing obsolete technology and had been overtaken by their competitors. Moreover, they had gained a reputation for being unable to deliver products to the market as they had promised – either at the time or with the full list of promised features.

A final comment on the development process concerned the role of the departments that were concerned with the product and its roll-out to customers. The developers were responsible for the product until it left the firm while a separate function, the consultancy group within the firm, were the ones who would take the product to a customer's site, install it and then train staff in its usage. This placed a heavy burden on the consultants, often requiring them to 'fix' problems that became evident with the product during implementation.

After the launch, one of the development team concluded: 'The project was and still is a nightmare.'

The review

Following the project, the management team and the staff at VCS carried out a review. Issues raised during the review included the split-site working where 'The communications simply did not work. There were lots of tests made early on to define standards – ways of doing things, and then latterly to transfer the knowledge of the Blackburn work down to us. There were lots of attempts made, meetings etc. – it was a struggle all the way along. Towards the end the communications broke down quite badly.'

When they considered the project planning Andy Morgan commented that 'Another problem that we have faced is the constant underestimate made by the guys of the work remaining. What we've tried to do as part of a philosophy of getting the ownership down a couple of levels (development coordinator etc.), is to try to get the programmers to commit to their own estimates. They do, but they always get it wrong, and fundamentally wrong – particularly in the most complex parts. Part of this is inexperience, and part because they do not have any specification to work to. They do not have a technical breakdown – it's pure guesswork.' Related to this, the managing director commented that 'We didn't know until things were going wrong that there was a problem, which is vital for managing customer expectations.' Further planning issues were raised by staff, including the comment that 'We need hands-on project management – regular meetings, not just once a month the day before the board meetings. The team never worked as a team – too much them and us.'

Another member of staff commented, 'A key problem was that there were too few people involved at the start of the project. As a result, when the Cardiff technical director left in June 1998 so much of the product knowledge left with him. None of this was down in writing, so we lost it. The knowledge base in future must be spread a lot more.' In addition, he noted: 'There was never any business case for the features that were being built into the system. I cannot see how either the existing or future client base is going to benefit from many of the features. The amount of effort we have put into it is disproportionate to the benefit that will be gained.'

The need to start work on V.4 was pressing – many of their clients were demanding Web-based features that were not available on V.3. As the management team contemplated the review there were clearly a significant number of issues that required attention. 'Above all,' the financial director commented, 'this must never happen again.'

Case discussion

1 What are the root causes of the problems that VCS faced during the V.3 project? Carry out a review of the project to determine what went wrong.
2 How do you suggest that they ensure that these problems 'never happen again'? Use an appropriate framework to structure your arguments.
3 What are the barriers to progress likely to be?
4 How could these be overcome?
5 What additional suggestions do you have for the company?

Key Terms

close-out	completion
handover	termination
review	audit
documentation	sign-off
stakeholder satisfaction	product surround
management paralysis	learning before doing
learning by doing	training
education	critical mass
consultant	cost of quality
prevention	appraisal
failure	

Review Questions and Further Exercises

1 Why is there a tendency for personal projects in particular, to spend '90 per cent of their time 90 per cent complete'.

2 Show the activities that must be completed during the final phases of a project.

3 Why might compiling project documentation be considered such a burden to the team, yet be so essential?

4 What issues must be considered when deciding how far post-delivery service should extend (such as providing free consultancy with new IT systems)?

5 What are the likely benefits that will be realised from reviews at different times?

6 Construct an audit questionnaire of management performance, which could be given to members of a project team. Test this on someone who has managed you. What areas would you suggest for improvement?

7 Distinguish between audits and reviews.

8 What are the criteria that should be taken into consideration when selecting an auditor/reviewer?

9 Considering the very varied nature of the different audits and reviews that can be carried out, is it likely that these can be done at one time by one person?

10 Discuss the role of review in the process of continuous improvement and why this is vital for the survival of organisations.

References

Busby, J. (1999) 'An Assessment of Post Project Reviews,' *Project Management Journal*, Vol. 30 No. 3, pp. 23–29.

Crosby (1979) *Quality is Free*, McGaw-Hill, New York.

Pisano, G.P. (1997) *The Development Factory*, HBS Press, Boston, MA.

Further Information

BS 6143: A guide to assessment of quality-related costs.

Dale, B.G. and Plunkett, J. (2000) *Quality Costing*, 2nd edition, Chapman & Hall, London.

Pisano, G.P. (1994) 'Knowledge, Integration, and the Locus of Learning: An Empirical Analysis of Process Development', *Strategic Management Journal*, Vol. 15, pp. 85–100.

Notes

1 I am grateful to one of the reviewers for this addition.

2 These figures were arrived at following an analysis of the elements of quality cost. The majority of the failures in each case were preventable, and these are costs that would be incurred to carry out the necessary prevention and appraisal measures, with a given level of 'inevitable' failure.

3 This indicates the relative processing power of a central computing facility versus that which an individual has in the PC on their desk. Thin client systems require less powerful PCs as more of the processing is done by a central mainframe/server system.

4 Functionality is literally 'what the product will do'.

15 Improving project performance

Given the widespread poor performance of companies identified in Chapter 1, the potential here for financial benefit in the medium to long term is enormous. How organisations rise to the challenge of improving their processes will determine their success in the long term, and many of the aspects that require attention have been discussed in the preceding chapters. There are some further issues that practitioners are working with in the search for process improvement. As we shall see, however, this search for improvement is by no means universal, despite the potential.

Also – where to now for project management? With its level of economic importance there is clearly an opportunity for the development of both the practices and the academic knowledge of the area. Given the relatively topical nature of this chapter, it is no surprise that there are no relevant areas of the bodies of knowledge, but it is anticipated that the material will have considerable influence on these in the future.

Contents

By the time you have completed this chapter, you should be able to:
- Identify relevant features of project management performance that can be used to identify the current level of development of the organisation;
- Demonstrate the role of BPR, benchmarking and lean processes in the search for project process improvement;
- Design an effective implementation strategy for new processes in project management;
- Identify areas within project management that require further development.

15.1 Project Management Maturity

Why is it that some organisations have well-developed project processes and others have something that closely resembles chaos? Surely each has the same commercial imperative and desire to be successful? Why also do some organisations become totally bogged down in structures and intensive documentation, losing sight of the reasons for their processes? In an effort to start to provide answers to some of these questions we will first consider the effects of such characteristics, and how they change over time. Some of the process characteristics associated with these effects can be identified. Subsequent sections then consider the approaches that organisations have taken in an attempt to change. The final section in this chapter considers the drivers for change, all of which must be in place before meaningful process improvement can be undertaken.

There are many ways of characterising organisations, and for the purpose of this discussion we will consider their ability to meet basic objectives of time, cost and quality, and then to improve these over time. Four types of organisation become apparent. They are:

- Group 1 – *the flatliners*: despite good intentions to improve, these make little or no progress in project performance. Mistakes are repeated and performance stays flat over time.
- Group 2 – *the improvers*. Some improvement actions are put in place and performance shows some increase over time.
- Group 3 – *the wannabes*. This group generally follows every initiative in the book, in an attempt to catch up with the best.
- Group 4 – *the world-class performers*. This small number of organisations set an ever-increasing standard for performance.

These are shown in Fig. 15.1.

The figure shows a number of features of performance:

- The performance gap between the best and 'the rest' is large;
- The performance gap doesn't seem to be narrowed over time, indeed it appears that 'the best are better at getting better.'

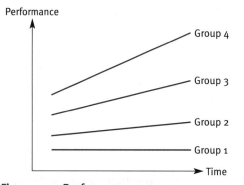

Figure 15.1 Performance groups

Table 15.1 Project management maturity stages

Type	Characteristics
Group 1	Little by way of processes or disciplines. Every project is novel and little learning takes place as a result of project activities. External ideas rejected as being 'not invented here'. Goal of projects poorly established, if at all.
Group 2	Some processes and systems in place, resulting in pockets of acceptable performance. Little learning from one project to another. Goal of projects sometimes established, and focused on conformance to objectives.
Group 3	Processes well documented and systems imposed as to how to run projects. Improvement based on trying to keep up with the best by imitating their processes, but limited by the constraints of system documentation. Goals of projects routinely established and focused on conformance to objectives.
Group 4	Processes mapped (see Project Management in Practice at the end of this chapter) and based around a core, which is forever being improved. Learning evident within and between projects. Goal of project is to exceed the objectives and deliver the best project possible (performance).

The second of these points shows that there are some fundamentally different mechanisms for improvement in place in the four groups of organisations.

Looking more closely, there are some characteristics of each of these types of organisations that can be discerned. This is their level of 'project management maturity'. The characteristics are shown in Table 15.1.

These characteristics enable some prediction of the likely performance of the organisation and also represent a path for improvement. While process changes (see following sections) are needed, a fundamental change in the approach that is taken will be required to move between the groups. Many organisations have moved from group 1 to group 2 – showing the application of some systems to their project management. Moving to group 3 requires considerable discipline, and this is usually imposed through rules and well-defined structures and documentation. While not a good vehicle for improvement, this does instil the necessary disciplines in the organisation. It is only when the procedures are eventually discarded and the organisation has the maturity to be able to take the standard systems and tailor them to each individual project and project team requirements that real improvement takes place. It is usual that a firm will need to move through the stages in sequence. Jumping stages is unlikely, as the disciplines learned at each stage are required later.

In moving between the groups, a number of the following topics have been used as the means of generating the necessary changes.

15.2 Major Influences on Process Change (1) – Business Process Re-engineering

Business process re-engineering or BPR was one of the main management 'fads' of the 1990s. It resulted in dramatic headlines (which seem to appear with every new 'good idea' – see section 10.8), including 'Ford cuts accounts payable headcount by 75 per cent' and similar stories from the great and the good. The fundamental principle is that companies redesigned their processes to remove unnecessary elements and consequently reduced the time, labour and resources required to perform those tasks. The early writers on the subject (see, for example, Hammer, 1990) provided the necessary credibility that the idea required to make it of general interest.

The main themes of BPR have been discussed in some detail already in this book though not under this particular banner. The focus is on improving processes, and rather than the kind of incremental change suggested by the learning cycles identified in the previous chapter, the goal is for step change. This is shown in Fig. 15.2.

There is always the tendency with such initiatives to make the whole thing sound considerably grander than it is. In reality, the excellent performers identified in the previous section were re-engineering their processes all the time. As one firm put it 'it is part of the way we work'. They did not draw the distinction between the grand processes of change suggested by BPR and the more incremental improvements that can be achieved every day in our organisations. There was some agreement in the steps to process change. These, predictably, should start with an examination of strategy, and be clear that the objective of the BPR is to create project processes that

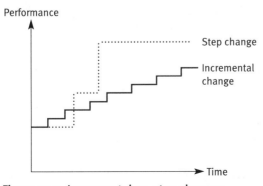

Figure 15.2 Incremental vs. step changes

more closely meet the needs of the organisation as set out in their strategy. For instance, if the objective is to be the cheapest deliverer of projects, then the focus of the re-engineering process should be on cost reduction. The next step is the mapping of processes. It was noted in the previous section that only the most advanced organisations had process maps available – enabling everyone involved to be able to understand the process and analyse how improvements could be made. BPR has the same approach. The process objectives are stated at the outset and a process is designed to meet those objectives. This can then be compared with the existing process and changes made where necessary.

Considering the impact on the organisation in which the BPR activities are being undertaken, the project manager has to consider the assumptions that underlie the existing processes and how these might be removed. Organisational rules and working practices are certain to be compromised by the changes. The objectives of activities will also be reassessed in line with a process rather than a function. The comfort of 'the way it has always been done' will disappear as processes are analysed. This may require that different people or organisations are used for tasks than has been the case in the past. The scope of such processes is not limited to the one organisation. Where projects affect many organisations, all these need to be involved as discussed in Chapter 12.

In short, the case for arguing for continuous improvement is proven, while the case for going with BPR as described here is not. Trying to find the substance to it is difficult, and the notion of step changes, while often favoured by Western companies at one time, is not necessarily superior to the incremental route. Many firms have used such initiatives to improve performance and it is not always necessary to badge it as BPR. Balfour Beatty, identified in the Project Management in Practice in Chapter 6, had implemented a Business Process Improvement Team. This provided the mechanism by which it was possible to attempt such changes in terms of both sourcing the necessary knowledge and some of the additional work that was required.

In setting the objectives of the re-engineering process, many organisations have chosen to try to become more 'lean'. This provides a set of principles that will guide the organisation in its re-engineering efforts and these are discussed following the section on benchmarking.

15.3　Major Influences on Process Change (2) – Benchmarking

This is another example of management jargon which has resulted in a large amount of business for the consultancy industry. Organisations are being told 'How can you be certain that you are as good as you say you are, unless you compare your performance with that of others?' This is a very persuasive logic, but before engaging in any benchmarking activities, a deeper understanding of the possibilities and protocols should be explored.

A benchmark is a reference point – some standard by which other phenomena are judged. It is a temporarily fixed point, with the location or magnitude decided by relevant metrics or measures. The original use of benchmarks was claimed by the early map-makers who needed certain reference points by which to judge others – in this case in spatial distance along three dimensions from the reference point. The distances having been assessed, the new point could also be considered to be a reference point, though the accuracy would be diluted the further one went from the original data.

The large-scale commercialisation of benchmarking activities was begun by Rank Xerox in 1979. Managers from its American operations were encouraged to go to view how its Japanese operations were being managed and compare their performance. Where there were performance differences, the methods used were noted to explore the possibilities for adapting the methods to their own plants. Initially fairly informal, the methodology has become more formalised and is viewed as one good way of obtaining ideas for improving both performance and processes.

In project management, the adoption of KPIs (Key Performance Indicators) has been tried across a range of sectors to allow some performance benchmarking to take place. In the construction sector, for instance, KPIs of per cent of projects delivered ontime, budget conformance and customer-satisfaction indices are becoming more widely used, though, as will be shown, this is a very limited approach and one that has not been without its problems.

Indeed, this follows a normal development where the initial approach to benchmarking involves consideration of very basic data, usually financial ratios, which provided a means of comparison of the overall effectiveness of management. Figures without explanation of their means of collection and the meanings of each, with clear bounds established as to what they include, are misleading. This understanding of what lay behind the numbers caused problems at a large UK specialist manufacturer when its German holding company carried out a benchmarking study to compare ratios of direct to non-direct staff. The UK operation appeared to be significantly overstaffed with non-directs compared to other companies in the group. On analysis, however, the comparison was not valid as the definitions of direct and non-direct employees were very different. The German company, for example, counted transport operatives as direct employees, while the UK operation counted them as support (non-direct) staff. The comparison was between unlike sets of statistics – termed 'apples and oranges'. The comparison therefore does not work well.

The numbers can therefore provide useful data, but with caveats. Of much greater interest and potential benefit to the project manager is to consider the processes behind the figures. Mapping processes provide far more useful information on how particular constraints are handled, obstacles overcome and problems solved. These can be collected through benchmarking clubs, established where a group of individuals have a particular interest, and meet to discuss this. This is being used to some effect where project management professionals meet to discuss particular issues. Such networking provides an informal method for benchmarking processes, and it is often found that problems being faced by managers were more easily solved by others than themselves (see www.bath.ac.uk/projectmanagement/networks).

The generation of benchmarking data does have clear benefits. The nature of the comparison can be with:

- functional projects – those conducted within the same functional part of the organisation;
- internal projects – others conducted by the same organisation;
- generic projects – process-related studies comparing projects with similar processes;
- competitor benchmarking – comparison with competitors.

The objective is to find how the best performers are doing and how these results are achieved. Thus a functional benchmarking exercise is clearly limited to the level of improvement, but it provides a good starting point and is likely to be highly cost-effective. The use of internal studies again develops benchmarking experience among staff and can be considered to be 'safe' as the information is developed and kept in-house. Generic processes are where the most benefit can often be gained, but where the comparisons are likely to be the most difficult.

Consider the project activities associated with publishing a book. If the publisher wished to decrease the time to market, they might consider benchmarking themselves against one of the newspapers, who regularly have to take copy from writers and turn it into printed material within a few hours. For most textbooks, the development process takes months (7 months from submission of manuscript to publication is normal). The methods or processes are similar, the end-product is considered to be very different.

Competitive benchmarking is possibly the most difficult to execute effectively, due to the defensive attitudes of organisations towards their performance. This most certainly should involve a 'code of conduct', including retaining confidentiality of data. The activities do not necessarily involve site visits as much of the information can be collected and exchanged by telephone or e-mail. Other data is often in the public domain and, while it is almost always out of date as soon as it is printed, provides useful indicators, particularly where a project organisation is at the start of its improvement activities.

Any criteria where data is gathered as part of the review process can be used to provide benchmarks. The minimum criteria are that an organisation consistently improves on its own benchmark data, and targets for improvement form an intrinsic part of organisational strategy.

One key measure that is often cited in large benchmarking studies[1] is that of productivity. Most simply stated, this is the output achieved per unit of input resources. In operations management, this may be associated with units per hour of output of production lines. In project management, while the measure can be applied to some of the execution phase of the project where repetitive tasks exist, applying it to one-off activities is unlikely to be useful. It was stated in Chapter 11 that it is difficult to control activities where there is a non-tangible output, such as in design. As the output and the output rate are very difficult to define (designs produced per month does not consider the quality of the design and can focus attention on the wrong priorities – speed over quality or completeness), productivity at this level is also likely to be meaningless. Overall productivity measures (such as engineering hours per major design activity) are more useful but again focus on speed rather than quality. The achievement of 'right first time' is a worthwhile goal, and so measures of numbers of engineering change requests or manufacturing problems that are accredited to design are more relevant.

In a discussion of this vital aspect of performance assessment, Kaplan and Norton (1992) show how providing a kind of scorecard which contains both process and performance measures can be beneficial (demonstrated in Chapter 11). For each of the following categories, both goals and measures are constructed:

- financial perspectives (how do we look to shareholders?);
- customer perspectives (how do customers see us?);
- internal business perspectives (what must we excel at?);
- innovation and learning perspectives (can we continue to improve and create value?).

This kind of balance to measures can now provide the basis for benchmarking activities as the organisation seeks to improve its scores, as was discussed in Chapter 11.[2] A measure of activity-centred progress would be the number of improvement programmes being carried out within an organisation or the number of staff who have been through the quality improvement training programme. Measures of performance include the percentage improvement in customer satisfaction as a result of improvement activities and reductions in quality costs, for example.

15.4 Major Influences on Process Change (3) – Lean Project Management

The output of a benchmarking activity can be the data that establishes which organisation is either 'best-in-class' or even 'world-class'. These two terms are widely used and not always consistently. Best-in-class (BIC) implies that in one or other aspects of performance measure the organisation is rated as being the best within a limited class of organisations, such as a competitive group. This is often confused with being truly world-class, where the performance of that attribute would rank alongside the best in the world *in that measure*. A world-class company is one that is considered to be world-class in a number of measures. In the recent benchmarking exercise cited above, world-class companies were those that had achieved considerably better performance in measures of quality and productivity than their counterparts. These may be considered now to be benchmarks for other manufacturing industries. This discrepancy between what constitutes world-class performance and managers' perceptions of it was highlighted recently when a survey showed that 78 per cent of companies questioned said that they were world-class. On further investigation, only 2 per cent of these were achieving world-class levels of quality or productivity.

From the above discussion, it can be seen that the definition of world-class performance is open to debate and that this is not always totally objective. More than one company can be world-class at any one time in any one sphere of activity, though the gap between the world-class performers and the others can be considerable. In general, the Japanese automotive assemblers are considered to be the epitome of such companies, though little research has been carried out in the project management environment. The way in which their operations have been improved has been summarised and can be adapted to the project environment.

The fundamental characteristics for being progressive can be compared to conventional organisations as follows (Suzaki, 1987):

- structures (organisational) are flexible rather than rigid to accommodate changes in customer requirements. This must be within the context that has been discussed of change/configuration management. As discussed in Chapter 3, flexibility is not free;
- the organisation focuses on optimisation of the entire flow of projects through it, rather than through a single area or department (see below);
- open communications from flat organisational structures as opposed to tall hierarchies leading to long chains of command (where messages are interpreted and changed at each link in the chain). This is a particular challenge for project managers, where they may not have direct authority over the individuals in their 'team' on whom they have to rely. The system for making important projects heavyweight matrix organisations is consistent with this objective;
- agreements between parties (including suppliers) are trust-based rather than contractual; this reiterates the principles discussed in Chapter 12. As stated, there are particular problems with this approach for certain project-based sectors;
- the skills base of the teams is wide to allow flexibility rather than narrow and specialist. The cross-training of individuals allows them to spend time outside their normal field of work (as described in the Hewlett-Packard example in Chapter 14, section 14.5). This also recognises the need for processes and process-thinking rather than functional thinking;
- education and training are significant parts of work activity rather than inconvenient distractions from the work in hand. This is an area where there is so much opportunity for improvement in project management. Training often involves little more than a guide to using Gantt charts, network techniques and some of the basics, and many firms undertake it just so that they can tick the box on the Human Resources Training Record marked 'project management'. Unless this is placed in an appropriate structure, it is unlikely to be beneficial.

As stated, there is little by way of rocket science here, except that it brings together all the themes covered in this book. Is lean project management the same as good project management? There is much to suggest that it is, but that the structures within which the project managers work are different. In addition, there is the treatment of the concept of waste not mentioned in either of the bodies of knowledge, and, given the costs of quality identified in the previous chapter, presenting a significant improvement opportunity.

A lean approach to management (developed by Womack *et al.*, 1990), continues the ideas of Henry Ford who is quoted as saying: 'if it doesn't add value, it's waste'. This principle may be applied to the project environment as shown in Table 15.2. The first of these points concerns the flow of information through a project organisation as a manufacturing engineer would plan the routing of a product through a process. The focus is on the simplification of flows so that it becomes visible where problems and hold-ups are occurring. In order not to be seen to be idle, people tend to build up inventories of tasks to be completed, regardless of the consequences of this hold-up in the flow of information being progressed. Consequently problems get hidden. The role of simplification is to move the type of information flow from

Table 15.2 Lean principles applied to project management

Line management	Project management
Integrated single-piece workflow produced just in time	Information treated as inventory and processed immediately rather than spending long periods of time waiting
Absolute elimination of waste	See section on seven wastes
Focus on global rather than local optima	Focus on achieving the goals of the organisation through this and other project activities and considering the project in this light rather than as a totally independent item (develops idea of the role of the stakeholders)
Defect prevention	Defect prevention
Multi-skilling in team-based operations	Multi-skilling in team-based projects
Few indirect staff	Few indirect staff

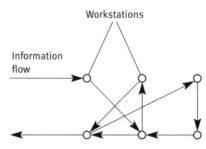

Figure 15.3 Complex information flow around systems

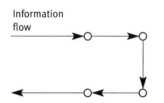

Figure 15.4 Simplified information flow through system

that shown in Fig. 15.3 to that shown in Fig. 15.4. In the latter case, there are no inventories. This means that periodically a person may complete their tasks with no further work to be done. In this case, rather than them creating inventory for downstream activities, they may engage in other work through being multi-skilled.

Apart from becoming faster at processing information, the above leads to improved responsiveness – customer requests and the inevitable changes can be implemented more quickly.

In lean thinking, the seven wastes are identified as follows:

- do not carry out activities above and beyond what is required by the customer in terms of either quality or quantity;
- eliminate waiting time either for people or project information;
- the movement of information, people or materials is generally a non-value-adding process;
- eliminate the need for processes that generate the need for further processing;
- eliminate the wastes associated with the building up of inventory (as above);
- avoid the waste of motion – not having materials or information on-hand when needed and having to go and find them;
- continuously strive to reduce the waste caused by defects or mistakes, as discussed in Chapter 14.

Wherever possible:

- tasks should be simplified – procedures are often needlessly complicated and open to too much interpretation;
- tasks should be combined – putting together tasks through multi-skilling can eliminate the transfer time and reduces the need for handover information;
- non-value-adding tasks should be eliminated, such as bureaucracy, constricting accounting systems and computer-planning systems, which absorb large proportions of managers' time, etc.

The above represents some very basic disciplines which can be applied throughout the project organisation. While it is often tempting to seek technological solutions, 90 per cent of all improvement comes from the application of what is termed 'common sense'.

Further improvement activities need to be focused on the entire value-chain or value-network. It is not unusual for 60 per cent or more of a project spend to be with external suppliers and, unless these are also engaged in improvement activities, the scope for performance improvement of your own organisation is distinctly limited. The concept of removing local optima is applicable here. For example, where a supplier provides you with materials that are required for the execution phase of a project and will be used at a steady rate during this phase, there is little point in their delivering the entire order at the start of work, even though their machines may be geared to produce in such quantities. This would provide a local optimum, namely at the suppliers. The purchaser now has a stock or inventory which will require storing, checking and possibly guarding – all activities that involve costs. The optimum can be redistributed to benefit all parties, with staged deliveries, for example. Helping suppliers to become more responsive is part of many initiatives currently being promoted. Better utilisation of their expertise is provided through the Toyota production system, where suppliers are given a rough specification for the needs of a product and are required to carry out design activities themselves. In this way they can achieve better designs, as their manufacturing processes can be accommodated in the component design.

15.5   Making It Happen – the Three Pillars of Change

The performance and rate of improvement differences described at the start of this chapter provide some interesting material for the management researcher. Why do such differences exist? The answer does not lie with individual project processes but with the fundamentally different approach to change that underlies it. Research showed that these differences were the result of a large number of factors, but that they could be reduced to three main themes. These are shown in Fig. 15.5.

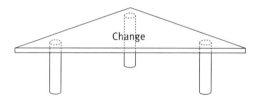

Figure 15.5   The three pillars of change

Figure 15.5 shows that all three of these need to be in place for change in processes to occur. For instance, referring back to the Balfour Beatty case from Chapter 6 again, the implementation of critical chain methods worked well initially, because all the pillars were in place. When one of these was removed, the changes were reversed over time, despite the gains achieved. The pillars and their constituent activities are summarised in Table 15.3.

Table 15.3   Key change issues

Strategy deployment	*Knowledge management*	*Implementation*
Strategy/policy deployment	Organisational learning	Measurement of impact of changes
Prioritisation of changes	Explicit structure for sources of change ideas	Implementation methodology
Drivers for change (internal/external)	Systematic evaluation of new ideas pre-implementation	
Coherence		

1   Strategy deployment

This has been discussed in Chapter 3, and throughout this text, with explicit strategy driving the decision-making processes of the organisation. The elements of this include how the organisation determines what to change and thereby avoid the problem of 'change paralysis' discussed previously where there are so many change possibilities that no-one knows where to start. Coherence is also vital – strategy ensuring that all changes are moving the processes in one particular direction. The nature of the drivers for change here is interesting. Many organisations cannot change until they are on the very edge of extinction. This is an extreme example of a driver. Other drivers for change are more usually internal initiatives or customers demanding improvements.

2 Knowledge management

In the previous chapter the role of *learning before doing* and *learning by doing* was discussed. The themes that need to be addressed are relevant to this. Specifically, how do we identify potential improvement targets and the means to achieve them? How do we evaluate the possibilities and identify the limited range of issues that can be addressed at one time?

3 Implementation

As a result of pressure from their customer, a large automotive supplier, a firm implemented a number of new tools and techniques. At least their procedure documents said that they had implemented those tools and techniques. People were trained in their use and pilot projects established, but it never went further than that. Why? Very simply, the measures by which people were assessed were not changed. Therefore, after the hype, the practices reverted to normal. In this case, the implementation failed also because there were problems, and there was no-one around with the necessary expertise to assist in finding solutions.

Organisations trying new ideas almost always adopt the 'poke-it-with-a-stick' method. If they don't get bitten, they may pursue it further. Or they may not. This is hardly the kind of systematic trial and evaluation that would lead to some conclusion as to whether the changes:

- were a success and should seek wider application;
- were a limited success and should be developed further;
- were a complete disaster and should be ditched forthwith.

Without relevant measures in place, practitioners are unable to be objective about the change.

The message from the implementation themes is that measures should be put in place to identify if the strategic objectives of the change are being met, and that implementation includes full training and support for changes. Such support may be required for a considerable period after the initial implementation.

The three pillars of change must all be in place for any change process to be successful. Indeed, any change is in itself a project, and one that is consistent with the approaches discussed in this text can show significant benefits from being managed in a way that shows people in the organisation what good project management looks like.

15.6 Future Challenges for Project Management

Chapter 2 used the 7-S structure to identify the main issues facing project managers. This structure is also ideal for the discussion of the requirements and likely changes in those issues in the future. The following is a summary.

- *Strategy* – the system for projects to become a means for the execution of strategy and a means to earn value has been discussed at length in this text. In future, the role of stategy will be more explicitly recognised by organisations, resulting in an increase in the use of devices such as the aggregate project plan. This will reduce conflict within and between organisations. Moreover, the ability to improve repetitive processes is being exhausted in many industries. They will have to look to their non-repetitive processes (i.e. their projects) for improvement in the future.
- *Structure* – at present it is common for organisations to fail to balance the importance of a project with the structure used for it. As project management asserts itself as of importance within organisations, more appropriate structures will be used. Furthermore, organisations will have to begin working outside the existing structures – using hybrids and new structures of their own to achieve their objectives.
- *Systems* – we will continue to see an increase in the visibility of project systems, with visual control being the driver. There is a challenge for IT providers to produce project management software that will help this process.
- *Staff* – the selection of staff for projects needs to be more objectively managed. The tools and techniques are available; it is vital that they find wider application.
- *Skills* – the skills of the project manager will increase in value as the changes noted in the section above on strategy start to take place. In many industries, people are given project responsibility because of their technical competence in one or more disciplines. In future, the skill-set of the project manager will become better recognised and valued by organisations.
- *Style/culture* – this has been used by many organisations as a reason for changes not being made to their way of working. It is vital that in future, managers take responsibility for the culture that they create around them and for their own style. Awareness of this should be routine, given the amount of research that has been carried out in this area. As for staff selection, there are well-developed tools and techniques for managers to use in this respect (e.g. through cultural audit). Their application will increase.
- *Stakeholders* – the marketing of achievements to stakeholders is in its relative infancy. The improved management of the information that stakeholders have is an important area in which project managers will need to work alongside their marketing colleagues.

One further issue concerns all the above, and that is *learning*. Organisations and individuals in many roles, not just project managers, are generally poor at learning from their own successes and failures, but particularly bad at learning from the successes and failures of others. It is a fact that those organisations that learn the fastest are also the best performers. The major challenge for project managers is how to bring in the necessary knowledge (both managerial and technical). All the issues from the 7-S given above provide potential areas for improvement. Part of the skill of the project manager is going to be identifying where the major benefits will be gained and the changes that will be needed to realise them. This will require a very wide knowledge of both theoretical and practical aspects of project management. It is noteworthy that this knowledge is rare in practitioners, but it is readily available in many publications on the subject.

One further aspect that I have noticed coming into the lives of the professionals that I have contact with is that their working lives must fit with their wider goals. The structures of regulating work by rational means are well understood in the context of providing aggregate project plans, and considering the scheduling of individuals as a non-elastic resource. The new application of this is to themselves. After all, why should individual project managers have to tolerate the notion that they would soak up any shortfalls in the resource requirements by compromising on their home lives? As stated in previous chapters, there is considerable personal application of this project management knowledge, and we are only just seeing its application beginning.

15.7 Summary

There have been many different improvement initiatives that have tried, and in most cases, failed to revolutionise the ways that we work. Project management is not one of these, whatever people may try to do with it. It is a business basic, a skill-set and will be required long after current business forms and firms have ceased to exist. Moreover, it is creative, requiring the greatest personal input.[3]

Some of the major changes that have affected project management in the recent past are BPR, benchmarking and the lean paradigm. BPR relies on step-changes, and many firms have pursued initiatives to try to achieve this. It is suggested that regular, incremental improvement is likely to be more successful, but that the process of redesigning core processes is valid. Benchmarking has only just begun to have repercussions for project management and has considerable real-world value still to offer the vast majority of practitioners and organisations. Comparison of processes will be the area that offers the greatest scope for benchmarking. Lean projects are still few and far between, though the principles are largely already imbedded in 'good project management.' The area that differs is in the treatment of *waste* and its pursuit. These ideas are fine, but are nothing more than 'of theoretical benefit' if they cannot be implemented. Research suggested that there are three pillars of change – those of strategy deployment, knowledge management and the actual practices of implementation. If any one is missing, the change process will fail. This is key to gaining change and improvement in project management processes.

There are many areas still requiring investigation in project management. A list of topic areas was suggested, but given the nature of the area, these should be viewed as fluid. As an academic discipline, the comment by Turner (1999) was that 'project management as a subject is not over-burdened with theory' suggests the potential for development of the area.

In conclusion, for the aspiring career project manager, there is a significant opportunity. With the increased recognition of the contribution of project managers will come greater rewards. Continuously improving our own processes should be the goal of every project manager. The knowledge exists: we need to find ways to apply it, mindful of strategic requirements and in a way that is open to evaluation. In future, we will need to be able to manage not only the improvement process but also its speed. Now there's a challenge that may also turn out to be great fun. Here's hoping.

Project Management in Practice

New product development at Toyota Forklift Truck – the X300 project

The whole design cycle is described by the system shown in Fig. 15.6 As can be seen, each step of the process is identified and quality assurance procedures assigned.

The terminology used in Fig. 15.6 is as follows:

- PPC – process plan chart: flowchart showing the steps involved
- FMEA – failure mode effect analysis: product or process review method, which assesses the likelihood of failure, the effect or severity of that failure and the probability of its being detected
- QCP – quality control plans
- QA – quality assurance

Assigning the procedures in this way at the outset enables quality to be 'built in' to the product. Processes are designed so that the right people have the right information at the right time and designs should be 'right first time'. The review of designs is an ongoing activity, rather than one that takes place at the end of the process. This ensures that checks are made very close to the time each part of the process is carried out, and amendments are incorporated before further cost is added.

Quality assurance starts with the information that the design process is being fed. The market research (note the departments involved from Fig. 15.6) provides an explicit statement of customer needs using a 'Quality Deployment Table', the output of a process known as 'Quality Function Deployment'. This method reduces the risk inherent in converting customer attributes into the language that the product developers understand, namely engineering characteristics. Further data on actual customer usage of products is obtained in this way, in this case from visits to dealers as well as customer and market research carried out by outside companies. Tools such as FMEA (see above) are applied to (a) designs at an early stage to ensure robustness and (b) the process by which the final products are to be made.

The review systems for product planning, product design and product preparation are shown in Figs 15.7, 15.8 and 15.9. A very high degree of systematisation exists, though the driver is not bureaucracy but customer satisfaction. Information flows are studied and, where work is becoming held up (engineering 'bottlenecks'), additional resources are provided to identify and solve the causes, preventing delay.

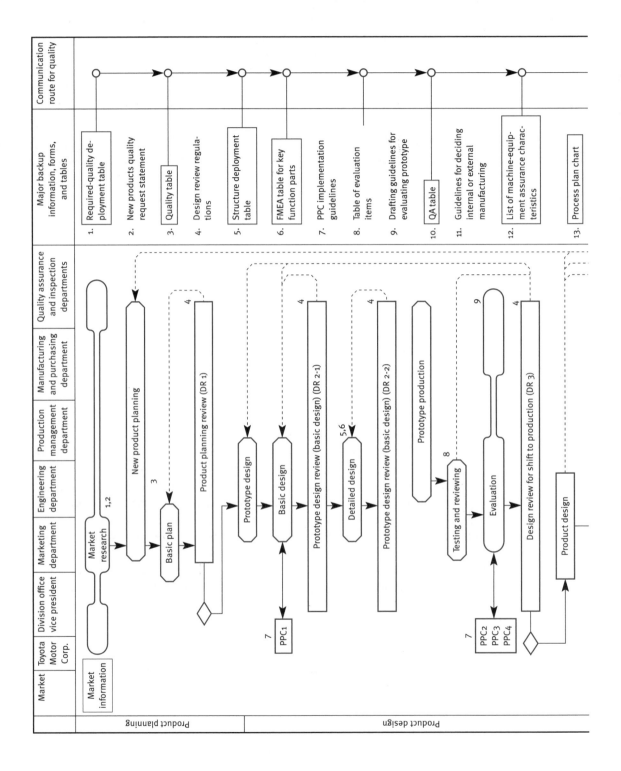

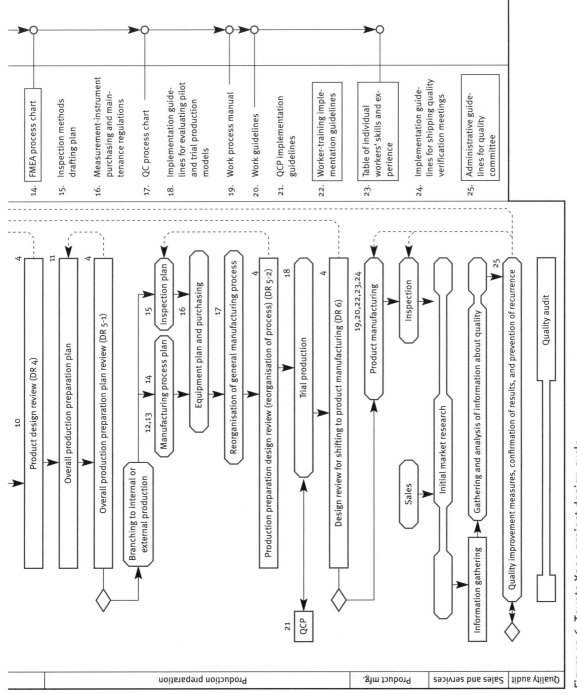

Figure 15.6 Toyota X300 project design cycle

(*Source*: Reprinted with permission of the Asian Productivity Organization from Kanemitsu Tsuzuki, in *Cross-Functional Management*, Kenji Kurogane (ed.). Copyright © 1993 by the Asian Productivity Organization)

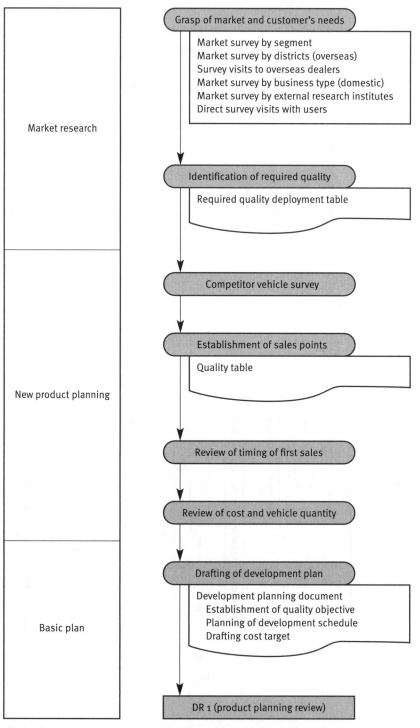

Figure 15.7 Product planning system
(*Source*: Reprinted with permission of the Asian Productivity Organization from Kanemitsu Tsuzuki, in *Cross-Functional Management*, Kenji Kurogane (ed.). Copyright © 1993 by the Asian Productivity Organization)

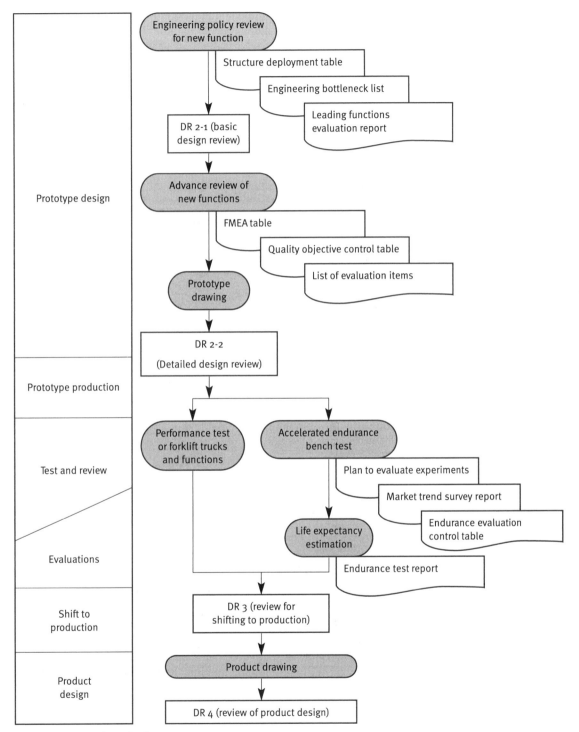

Figure 15.8 Product design system
(*Source*: Reprinted with permission of the Asian Productivity Organization from Kanemitsu Tsuzuki, in *Cross-Functional Management*, Kenji Kurogane (ed.). Copyright © 1993 by the Asian Productivity Organization)

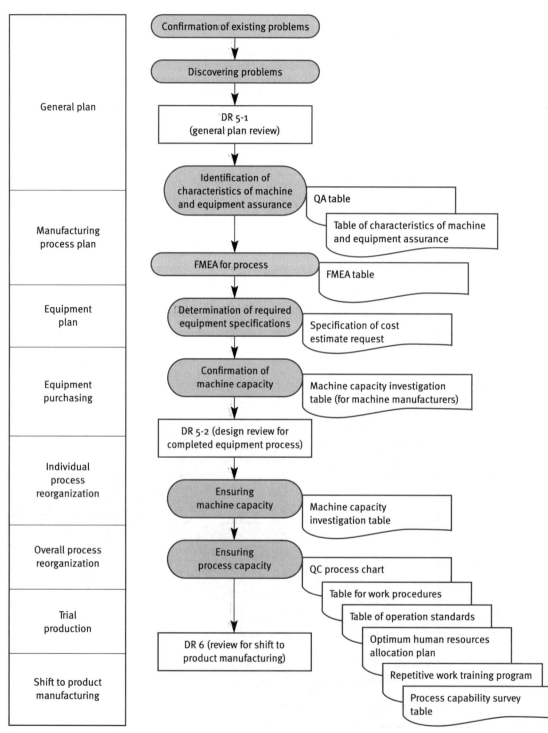

Figure 15.9 Production preparation system
(*Source*: Reprinted with permission of the Asian Productivity Organization from Kanemitsu Tsuzuki, in *Cross-Functional Management*, Kenji Kurogane (ed.). Copyright © 1993 by the Asian Productivity Organization)

The transfer to production was completed with a high degree of control. The product specifications were identified and transferred to the requirements of the machines on which the products were to be made (process capability). An objective of design was to work within the capability of the available production technology. Similarly, rather than wait for the product to arrive in production for workers to be trained on its manufacture, training was scheduled as the transfer process was ongoing.

1 Design review 1 (DR 1) is the process for ensuring that the unique selling points of a product are going to be achieved by the outline design. These should not have been removed or compromised by trade-offs in the process. At the same time, competitor analysis will reveal how long these features will provide competitive advantage, based on a knowledge of their products and design capability.
2 Design reviews 2, 3 and 4 (prototype design review, review for shifting to production, and product design review) ensure that the quality objectives are being met. This process used to be carried out by a user group, who would be asked to evaluate prototypes prior to production, but was abandoned due to cost and unreliability.
3 DR 5 (production preparation review) provided a check-point on the production preparation plan, particularly on elements of product quality, availability and cost. This is a feasibility check and does involve a corporate evaluation point. As production engineering had been involved from an early stage, however, the production preparation plan was very rapidly prepared, with minimal alterations or amendments to the product design.
4 DR 6 (review for shifting to product manufacturing) was the 'engineering sign-off' point, during which not only product quality was again reviewed but also the checks on process capability, staff training and the readiness of the manufacturing area to accept the new product.

All these processes ensured that the product was not 'thrown over the wall' between departments, and that there were no surprises when the plans landed in one department for further processing. All the time, the likely outcome was being reviewed against objectives and the theme of it being a superior product reiterated. The involvement of all departments in the development process ensured a very rapid development time and policy deployment through the participation of high-level staff ensured consistency with corporate objectives.

The above was a highly successful project with a highly competitive product being available on time, and within the development budget. Further improvements in the process are planned, based on the results of the review processes. Each provides a basis for future lessons to be learned and for refinement of the process and its control system.

Case discussion

1 Identify why the various design reviews should take place. How might they represent an improvement over and above a single design review process at the end of the product design stage?

2 Why is the 'voice of the customer' so important in this process?

3 Discuss the nature of the changes that can occur in passing information about customer requirements from a marketing department to the engineering department and to the manufacturing department.

4 Show how relating the customer attributes, in their own words, to 'engineering characteristics' may help the provision of a product that is more in line with their needs.

Key Terms

flatliners	improvers
wannabes	world-class
rate of improvement	core processes
BPR	incremental versus step-change
KPIs	benchmarking
lean	best-in-class
waste	information flow
strategy deployment	knowledge management
implementation	

Review Questions and Further Exercises

1 How might an organisation recognise their level of performance and plot a way forward?

2 Why are the best 'better at getting better?' Are there any limitations to this?

3 Identify the role that benchmarking and BPR can play in improving project performance in organisations. What are the potential drawbacks?

4 Are the principles of 'lean' truly applicable to project management? What are the limitations likely to be?

5 Carry out a review of the organisational change literature. Identify the overlaps with that on project management and, in particular, section 15.5.

6 What are the personal applications of the work that you have covered on project management? Draw up a list of five areas of personal change that you would want to make following on from this material.

7 Identify an overlap with another management discipline – such as marketing, finance, operations, HRM – and consider how this material has direct relevance to project management. What are the aspects of each of the subjects that overlap that could be developed?

References

Hammer, M. (1990) 'Reengineering Work: Don't Automate, Obliterate', *Harvard Business Review*, July–August, pp. 104–12.

Kaplan, R.S. and Norton, D.P. (1992) 'The Balanced Scorecard – Measures that Drive Performance', *Harvard Business Review*, January–February, pp. 71–79.

Schaffer, R.H. and Thomson, H.A. (1992) 'Successful Change Programs Begin With Results', *Harvard Business Review*, January–February, pp. 80–91.

Suzaki, K. (1987) *The New Manufacturing Challenge: Techniques for Continuous Improvement*, Free Press, New York.

Tsuzuki, K. (1993) in *Cross-Functional Management*, K. Kurogane (ed.), Tokyo, Asian Productivity Organization.

Turner, J.R. (1999) 'Editorial: Project Management: A Profession Based on Knowledge or Faith?' *International Journal of Project Management*, Vol. 17, No. 6, pp. 329–30.

Womack, J.P., Jones, D.T. and Roos, D. (1990) *The Machine That Changed The World*, Rawson Associates, New York.

Further Information

www.bprc.warwick.ac.uk – part of a network *of business process resource centres* in the UK.

Grover, V. and Malhotra, M.K. (1997) 'Business Process Reengineering', *Journal of Operations Management*, Vol. 15, pp. 193–212.

Kerzner, H. (1998) 'In Search of Excellence', in *Project Management: Successful Practices in High-Performing Organisations*, Van Nostrand Reinhold, New York.

Maylor, H. (2001) 'Beyond the Gantt Chart', *European Management Journal*, Vol. 19, No. 1, pp. 92–100.

Sobek, D.K. II, Liker, J.K. and Ward, A.C. (1998) 'Another Look at How Toyota Integrates Product Development', *Harvard Business Review*, July–August, pp. 36–49.

Winch, G. (1996) 'Thirty Years of Project Management: What Have We Learned?' www.bprc.warwick.ac.uk/repwinch.html

Notes

1 Such as the Worldwide Manufacturing Competitiveness Study, Andersen Consulting, 1995.

2 The focus on results and scores is echoed by Schaffer and Thomson (1992), who contrast the performance of results-oriented initiatives with those of activity-centred programmes.

3 Some may go as far as saying that it is 'art'.

Appendix Relevant Standards

Contents

A.1 ISO 9000

ISO 9000 evolution

Early quality systems were sets of procedures which developed with the emergence of international standards setting out how such systems should be constructed and operated. The first formalised specifications for quality systems were developed by military purchasers, who attempted to provide a generic standard for systems that would ensure that the specific needs laid down in procurement contracts would be met. These relied heavily on the requirement for checking or inspection actions – quality was simply 'conformance to specification'. Such systems would frequently cause conflict between the people who were carrying out the tasks and the inspectors, as the implicit assumption was that it is the people at the task level who are to blame for errors. (Deming argued for many years that it is the management system that is to blame for over 80 per cent of operational errors.)

These military standards, including AQAP 1 (Allied Quality Assurance Publication), have been used for 20 years by suppliers to NATO armed forces. These and other standards (DEF-STAN 05-21, 05-24, 05-29) provided the basis for the first UK commercial standard – BS 5750 (1979). This was amended and brought into line with the ISO 9000 series of standards in 1987 and subsequently renamed, along with the equivalent German and International standards, as the BS–EN–ISO 9000 series in 1994. Most of the major automotive manufacturers have their own standards in addition to this which they require their suppliers and contractors to work under (Ford's Q1, Rover's RG2000). Recently there have been moves to integrate their requirements, thereby simplifying the task for suppliers who service more than one manufacturer.

The standards provide details of the minimum specifications for systems, based on procedural adherence to ensure the quality of the process. They should never be taken as a guarantee of the absolute quality level of the outputs of the system. They set out the way in which the systems should be operated. The extent of the impact on the organisation depends on the particular standard chosen. BS–EN–ISO 9001 is the most extensive covering design, development, production, installation and servicing – the majority of the product life-cycle. BS–EN–ISO 9003 covers only final inspection and testing. The former will be discussed here as the commercial standards that are the most widely used.

From the language used in the specifications (see below) it is clear that the standards were developed for application in the manufacturing industry, particularly for contract manufacturers. However, the organisations that have applied the standard to date include banks, dentists, electricians, academic institutions(!), road recovery firms and distribution/logistics companies. There is clearly the need for interpretation of a generic set of rules to the specific situation. To enable this process, the BSI (British Standards Institution) has published a series of guides to accompany the standards, e.g.:

- BS–EN–ISO 9000–1 entitled 'Quality Management and Quality Assurance Standards; Part 1: Guidelines for selection and use'.
- BS–EN–ISO 9004–1 entitled 'Quality Management and Quality Systems Elements; Part 1: Guidelines'.
- BS 5750 Part 8: Guide to the Application of BS 5750 : Part 1 to services.
- BS 5750 Part 13: Guide to the Application of BS 5750 : Part 1 to the development, supply and maintenance of software.

ISO 9000 requirements

The twenty requirements of the standard BS–EN–ISO 9001 (2000) are paraphrased below.

1 Management responsibility – there must be a defined management representative to provide a single point of contact for customers.
2 Establish and maintain a documented quality system.
3 Establish and maintain a system for reviewing customer contracts to ensure that it brings together product offered and required.
4 The design process shall have a quality control system on inputs, outputs and the process itself.
5 Document control – all documents should be controlled to ensure that the current issue is the only one in use.
6 Ensure that the purchased product conforms to specified requirements, e.g. through auditing, and then supply under certificates of conformance or inspection of the incoming product.

7 Where a customer supplies a product for you to work on, it must be identified as belonging to the customer.

8 All products must be labelled during processing and must be traceable to records of component parts.

9 Processes should have the necessary degree of process control.

10 Need to keep receiving, in-process and final inspection and test records.

11 Any measurement equipment used must be labelled and calibrated as well as being suitable for the application (no mention, however, of measurement capability).

12 The product must be identified so that the inspection status (awaiting inspection, inspected and passed, failed or concessioned) is immediately obvious. This may be through the use of marked bins or appropriate tags.

13 Procedures must be identified so that when a non-conforming product is produced, there is a system for dealing with it.

14 Procedures must be identified for preventing recurrence of non-conformances through the analysis of defective data, procedural amendments, etc.

15 The product needs to be handled and stored so that there is no damage or deterioration in the product or accompanying documentation.

16 Procedures are required for the identification, filing, indexing, storage, maintenance and disposition of records.

17 'The supplier shall carry out a comprehensive system of planned and documented quality audits.'

18 Procedures need to be set up to identify needs for employee training and to ensure that records are kept accordingly.

19 Servicing must be carried out in accordance with the contract, if specified.

20 Statistical techniques must be used where appropriate.

The major requirements from the point of view of the project manager include:

• Point 2 – there is a need to provide a 'quality manual' to describe how the system works. This is a hierarchical series of documents which addresses each of the points within the standard and is structured as shown in Fig. A.1. At the top level is the statement of policy (the policy document) which outlines the aim of the

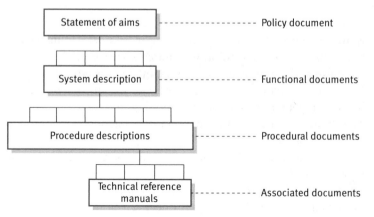

Figure A.1 Hierarchy of quality system documentation

system and the structure and names of the documents below it. At the next level is the functional documentation which provides statements as to how each of the functional areas is organised. Below this are the procedural documents, which state how each piece of work is to be carried out. At the lowest level are reference documents such as technical data manuals (e.g. for materials or machine specifications).

- Point 3 – the project manager must establish regular contact points and formalised review meetings so that the assent of the customer/sponsor to progress is gained and that the original requirements are regularly reviewed.
- Point 4 – treating one-off activities such as design as a process and requiring control of these requires much of the 'art' of such processes to be expressed as science.
- Point 17 – once the system is in place (documented and operational) the system needs to be audited in a similar way to financial auditing.
- Point 18 – people need to be appropriately trained to carry out their tasks. The project manager must be able to verify this through the production of training certificates, course records, etc. This process has been helped recently by the advent of National Vocational Qualifications (NVQs).

Obtaining ISO 9000 certification

The process of implementing a quality system to the requirements of a recognised specification should follow the route below.

1 Establish the reason for wanting the system – is it simply to obtain business through having certification or will it provide an advantage in a competitive bidding situation? Unless this reason is established at the start of the programme of implementation, it is unlikely to be effective. It is not unusual for an organisation to take two years to have implemented such a system fully, if the aim is to achieve recognition through having the quality system approved and certified.

2 Train people in working to the requirements of the system, including the preparation of documentation. This is a major task, and one that is particularly difficult for project organisations. The intention is to provide a set of procedures which describe in detail how each job will be performed. In project organisations, making these procedures generic enough to cover the variety of work that is carried out can be a real challenge. Similarly, convincing people that when they work outside the existing procedures their actions have to be documented is often fraught. People will need to be trained in the assessment of systems to provide for step 4.

3 Create the documentation including the necessary reference manuals.

4 Carry out an internal audit (check whether procedures are being adhered to) and review (consider the efficacy of the procedures). This should be done initially by someone within your own organisation, though it is normal for it to be someone outside your immediate function. Set a plan for the implementation of any changes identified by this process.

5 Have your systems audited by an external auditor from a registered assessment body. The progression from this audit is shown in Fig. A.2.

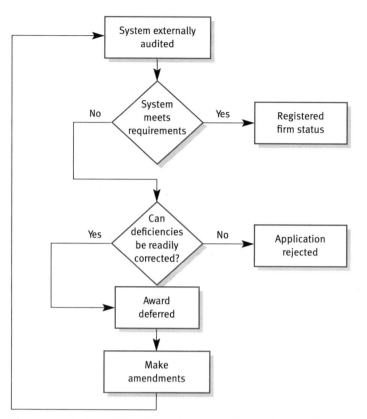

Figure A.2 Actions following external quality system audit

6 If you are granted 'registered firm' status, you may carry the BSI logo on your stationery and other publicity material. Your organisation will then be subject to periodic audits (usually annually) as well as 'flying visits' which are announced at 24 hours' notice.

The process of accreditation is not simple for an organisation going through it for the first time. Gaining accreditation can involve the use of consultants to provide services ranging from training of staff to providing you with a pre-written quality manual. This latter option is not to be recommended as much can be gained from compiling your own, through improved understanding of the processes and people then having ownership of that part of the quality manual.

For the project organisation, many of the structures necessary for compliance with such a standard will already be in place. However, where this is a requirement, the project manager should be aware that this provides an extra workload for team members – the approval process alone can absorb thousands of working hours. Where people are brought in on short-term contracts, the documentation services and control systems are likely to have to be provided centrally. The checks and administration, which affect every part of the organisation, will require an ongoing commitment of time. This *must* be built into the schedules. Expecting people to do it as an additional activity for which no time has been allowed is unreasonable and will certainly result in a system which frequently falls down.

Preparing quality manuals using flowcharts

One of the major challenges of attempting to gain certification to a recognised standard such as BS–EN–ISO 9001 is the volume of paperwork that has to be generated. For the project organisation particularly, the timescale in which this has to be completed will be short, and so it is often viewed as a burden. The BSI now recognises certain flowcharting methods as being valid replacements for large quantities of text. These have the added benefit of providing a method by which people can be helped to understand processes, which can in turn form the basis of improvement activities. Figure A.3 is a form of process map, which shows the means for meeting the criteria set out in section 5 of the standard (Document Control).

A.2 PRINCE2

PRINCE2 (**Pr**ojects **IN C**ontrolled **E**nvironments) is a structured method for managing projects, small and large. It is the accepted standard for the UK government's Central Computer and Telecommunications Agency (CCTA) and was revised in 1996. As a standard for project management, it is widely used in the IT industry and is finding application in other sectors.

PRINCE2 identified eight key processes, for which it lays down standards as to how they should be carried out. These are as follows:

1 *Directing the project* – carried out by the senior management team (previously called the project sponsors). These are the high-level decision-makers who define the need for the project, the resources to be allocated to it (if at all) and whether it should continue (if ongoing).

2 *Planning a project* – an ongoing activity which, using specified methods (many of which are identical or similar to those that are discussed in previous chapters), provides a model of the activities, their sequence, duration and resource requirements and associated risks.

3 *Starting up a project* – once the project has received approval, the project resources need to be organised. This starts with the appointment of the management team and assigning their individual objectives. A plan of work needs to be drawn up leading to the terms of the contract between the project organisation and its customer.

4 *Initiating a project* – this part of the process results in the overall project strategy and sets the criteria against which it will eventually be judged.

5 *Controlling a stage* – once the project activities have started in earnest, this activity includes those aspects of control and problem-solving required to ensure that the project meets the original objectives.

6 *Managing product delivery* – where there are multiple teams working on different aspects of the project, this process is vital to ensure that each knows their responsibilities and their interfaces with other parts of the project, and that activities are not omitted because they were not properly allocated.

7 *Managing the stage boundaries* – at the end of each stage, to report on the progress and problems encountered in that stage and their implications, and following this the plans for the next stage.

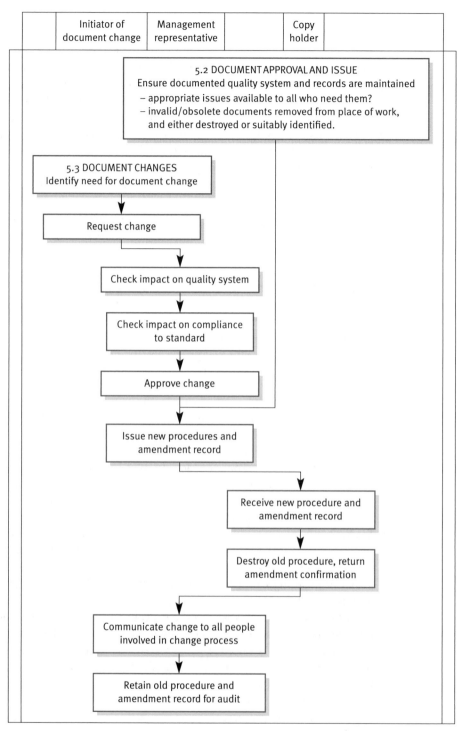

	Initiator of document change	Management representative		Copy holder	

5.2 DOCUMENT APPROVAL AND ISSUE
Ensure documented quality system and records are maintained
– appropriate issues available to all who need them?
– invalid/obsolete documents removed from place of work, and either destroyed or suitably identified.

5.3 DOCUMENT CHANGES
Identify need for document change

Request change

Check impact on quality system

Check impact on compliance to standard

Approve change

Issue new procedures and amendment record

Receive new procedure and amendment record

Destroy old procedure, return amendment confirmation

Communicate change to all people involved in change process

Retain old procedure and amendment record for audit

Figure A.3 Document approval and issue criteria
(*Source*: Excelsis consultants)

8 *Closing a project* – shut down the project systems, provide reports and feedback for future process improvement, establish the performance of the project relative to the original objectives.

All these aspects would normally be termed 'good project management'. The difference here is the level of structure and documentation that is required by the standard. Project structures – including the roles – are highly defined, for example the requirement of having a project board to oversee the project activities and its composition. This board has a number of specific roles which provide some differentiation from mainstream project management:

- *project assurance* – the ongoing tasks of ensuring that the outcome of the project conforms to the criteria specified at the outset and that business risks are managed (within certain preset tolerances);
- *project support* (optional) – providing a technical and managerial resource, where required, to the project team.

This organisational requirement has many similarities with the arrangement suggested in the previous chapter, where a senior management team was involved in the management of aggregate project plans. The role is similar, as it maintains an overview of the project in the context of all the organisation's activities. It differs in the element of project assurance that PRINCE2 specifies (this would normally be the responsibility of the project manager). The project board lacks the main strategic concerns of the senior management committee.

Subsequent to the organisational requirements, PRINCE2 specifies particular objectives and requirements of the planning process. These are helpful for the project manager in providing a detailed structure to their considerations. There are certain pieces of documentation that require completion. In addition to the conventional project documentation, these are:

- *quality log* – a record of any checks carried out on the product or on the process, including the nature of the checks and a signature of the person carrying them out;
- *issue log* – a record of any problems experienced and any changes made as a result of these;
- *risk log* – as a means of providing ongoing control to show that risks were actively managed, this document identifies the main risks associated with the project and the control actions (see Chapter 8) that were carried out.

PRINCE2 provides bureaucratic controls on the planning and execution of projects. In this way, it forces the identification of some of the potential problems that may arise in the project and does stress early conflict resolution – a feature of much of the recent literature on project management. It is limited, however, by its approach. It focuses on the 'product', usually a computer program or system, and does not provide any guarantees of success. Indeed, there have been a number of high-profile failures of projects, despite their being run in line with the standard. It is a standard for process – that is, it does not specify the *quality* of the outcome of a project, only the way in which it has to be carried out. There is little chance of specifying the precise processes that need to take place to ensure complete success, particularly where overoptimistic people are involved.

A.3   ISO 14000

Being and being seen to be environmentally responsible is an increasingly important issue for most firms in most countries. Companies have responded in different ways – e.g. the electricity generators' 'dash for gas' and insurance companies which started using paperless systems. More fundamentally, legislation has changed and the impact of breaches of legislative requirements is ever more severe. The majority of project managers should be aware of this issue, as if it is not already high on the management agenda, it will soon become that way. There are, however, a number of challenges associated with environmental issues. Many authors comment that the issue of 'environmental responsibility' has been the subject of much rhetoric, but less action due to the scarcity of practical guidance. Stakeholders who will have an interest in the environmental performance of the project organisation include:

- partner organisations in joint ventures;
- clients/customers;
- team members;
- sponsors;
- insurers – obtaining the necessary insurance to protect the organisation from the effects of claims is a serious issue in many construction projects, and will often involve demonstrating to the insurers that your organisation is going to carry out the project in a responsible manner (see systems below);
- legislators and law enforcers (see EU role below).

The role of pressure groups and the media as stakeholders (in the sense that they can cause much disruption to project activities) needs to be recognised. One of the effects of legislation is to make organisations' environmental performance open to scrutiny by the public and media. Publicity gained through poor performance is proving damaging to the public image of those companies and their products, directly affecting their financial performance.

The role of the EU in providing legislation on environmental matters is considerable. The Fifth European Community Environmental Action Programme sets out the aims of the Union for its environmental policy from 1993 to the year 2000. It is trying to create a worthwhile change in emphasis – to remove policies as a burden to industry and to make them self-sustaining. The requirement on industry is to become proactive rather than reactive, through the development of 'clean technologies' and the development of markets for products that are environmentally sound. This emphasis on making the process self-sustaining will occur after the enforcement of existing legislation through taxation (incentives and penalties) and legal liability.

'Eco-labelling' is well established (disposable food and household consumables containers being at the forefront of this), but the requirement for companies to treat their environmental performance as they have done their quality performance has been less successful. The parallel between the two is useful as:

- there is a requirement for policy to be made;
- documented systems are required;
- there is a standard for environmental systems – ISO 14000 (see below);
- it will be possible in the future for such systems to be accredited and for the organisation to obtain recognition in the same way as for BS–EN–ISO 9000.

The requirements of the environmental systems standard (ISO 14000) are as follows:

1 Commitment – required at the highest levels in the organisation to demonstrate that the intentions will be backed with authority.
2 Environmental policy – as for quality systems, there must be a documented policy which includes the steps that will be taken to ensure continuous improvement in this area.
3 Environmental review – carry out an initial review of the current state of environmentally relevant practices in order to provide a base for future action.
4 Organisation and personnel – ensures that all people involved in establishing and running the system have the appropriate authority.
5 Registers of environmental effects – the organisation must keep records of legislation as it affects their operation in addition to relevant permissions, e.g. discharge consents, planning permissions, etc.
6 Objectives and targets – in order that continuous improvement over and above legislative requirements can be demonstrated, the organisation must provide quantitative goals for itself.
7 Environmental management programme – a documented plan of action.
8 Environmental management documentation and manual – as for quality systems, the environmental management system must be described in the form of a written manual, which must be updated with changes in practice and legislation.
9 Operational control and records – where shortcomings are identified, procedures must exist for dealing with these and preventing recurrence.
10 Environmental audits – periodic reviews must be carried out in a planned and documented way to determine the level of procedural adherence.
11 Systems reviews must be carried out in accordance with a predetermined plan to consider the efficacy of the procedures laid down in the system.

The formulation of environmental policy should be focused on four main areas:

- the organisation and its products;
- the direct environmental impact of products and processes;
- the infrastructural implications of the activities of the organisation – impact on road usage, etc.;
- external relations with the community – through education, the role of a good 'corporate citizen'.

Implementing BS–EN–ISO 9000 in a health service environment

The international standard for quality systems BS–EN–ISO 9000 defines how an organisation should set its own standards and provide procedures for reaching those standards. It concerns the way that an organisation operates, rather than the standards of the output itself (products, services, etc.). The environment in which the unit was operating was that of intense financial pressure, coupled with the indication that the functions of the unit would be put out to commercial tender in the near future (through market-testing). It was also hoped that the discussion of quality and the formalisation of parts of the organisation would give accountability and help focus on customer needs.

The move to bring their method of operating within the requirements of the standard came as part of the measures to give them an advantage in any future competitive tendering situation for health services. The project was set a target of achieving the necessary certification within two years in some areas, and longer in others. Staff would need to be trained and the necessary documentation (detailing all working procedures) would have to be prepared.

The project was started and a new project manager (called the quality manager) recruited to provide both knowledge and a degree of independence from the other functions within the organisation. Across the organisation, there were pockets of enthusiasm, but otherwise annoyance from departmental managers who saw the changes as being bureaucratic and as interference from outsiders in the way they ran their departments. Above all, there was resistance to change which was both obstructive and destructive. The common feeling was that people had enough to do already, and this was an additional workload.

The result of this was that the areas which took the new standard on board, and made it work in their way, got through the process earliest and with greatest benefit. On reviewing the implementation, it was shown that one of the reasons that people had opposed the changes was a lack of comprehension as to what they would mean in practice. They could not see how the documentation of, adherence to and continuous improvement of working processes would improve their lives, or improve the organisation.

Case discussion

1 What was the need and how did the project go towards meeting this?
2 Describe the complexity of the project.
3 How might identifying all the people who could hold up progress earlier in the project have increased the speed of achieving the project goals?
4 Why might recruiting an external project manager be beneficial, and what risks would there be?

To PRINCE or not to PRINCE?

There are many opposing views as to whether the application of a standard such as PRINCE is useful. In searching for a way to improve their processes, a team was tasked with deciding appropriate standards, and reviewing their applicability to their environment. They interviewed two project managers – one from Big Computer Installation Company, and another from the Communications Hardware Design Company. The first was unashamedly up-beat about PRINCE:

> Our business is in the specification, installation and maintenance of networked computer systems. We supply predominantly large corporations, who have computers scattered over many sites. We use PRINCE2 for all our projects and all our staff and project managers have to work within the PRINCE2 methods. This provides us with a competitive advantage during the bidding process for contracts – several of our competitors do not have the level of approvals that we do, and it shows. Clients are demanding more and more that we assure our processes, and that is what we have done through PRINCE. I know that some people claim it is too bureaucratic, but just one instance this week showed its worth: a client was very vague about what they wanted in particular areas of the implementation. By convening a project board, we were able to provide a forum for discussion of what they really wanted. Other firms I have worked for, would simply have provided what they considered was best, rather than going back to the client. We also have a system for changes – the usual bug-bear of these projects. Clients can request changes at any time, but they are put through the process of calculation of the impact of those changes, including schedule and costing implications, before we seek approval to do the extra work. The systems provide us with the necessary traceability for our documents, and we simply see the procedures as the best way to deliver what our clients want. I don't know how other firms do without it.

This contrasted strongly with the communications hardware company:

> We design, develop and manufacture communications hardware – all the electronic parts of a modern communications system. We started using PRINCE2 four years ago, under our last managing director. He thought it would be a good thing for us to do – we always thought the idea came from one of his golfing mates. Since then, we have implemented all the changes that PRINCE required of us, and all our staff were trained. The problem was that all the extra cost was not offset by any improvement in performance – we still had problems delivering our projects on-time, and our client base is not demanding it. So when our new managing director was appointed, he removed the requirement to work this way and we had a ceremonial burning of the procedure manuals. We started again by looking at our processes – using the PRINCE2 documentation. With every project, we identified significant parts of the process that caused us work, but that did not

add any value to our customers. This removed something like 20 per cent of the effort required for each project. We still use some of the disciplines that the standard required – particularly with regard to how we handle clients and risk, but we have scaled the rest back. In retrospect, using the standard has imposed some discipline on the processes, but I'm very glad to be free of it now.

Further Information

Central Computer and Telecommunications Agency (1997) *PRINCE 2: An Outline*, Her Majesty's Stationery Office, London.

www.prince2.com
www.spoce.com
Project Manager Today – series of articles from February 2000 onwards covering various aspects of PRINCE2 application.

Index